Taste of Home's
Light&Tasty
Annual Recipes 2006

PICTURED ABOVE AND ON FRONT COVER: Chocolate Peanut Torte
(page 228), Rosemary Onion Focaccia (page 190)
and Tofu-Stuffed Pasta Shells (page 178).

Taste of Home's
Light&Tasty
Annual Recipes 2006

Editor: Michelle Bretl
Art Director: Kim Sumrall
Executive Editor/Books: Heidi Reuter Lloyd
Senior Editor/Books: Julie Schnittka
Proofreader: Julie Blume Benedict
Graphic Art Associates: Ellen Lloyd, Catherine Fletcher
Art Associate: Monica Bergwall
Editorial Assistant: Barb Czysz

Taste of Home's
Light&Tasty

Editor: Mark Hagen
Associate Editors: Julie Kastello, Mary Spencer, Mary Hanson
Food Editor: Janaan Cunningham
Associate Food Editor: Diane Werner RD
Creative Director: Ardyth Cope
Contributing Art Director: Kim Sumrall
Proofreader: Julie Blume Benedict
Recipe Editor: Janet Briggs
Senior Home Economist: Peggy Fleming RD
Home Economists: Wendy Stenman, Nancy Fridirici, Tina Johnson,
Ann Liebergen, Pat Schmeling, Amy Welk-Thieding RD
Test Kitchen Director: Mark Morgan RD
Assistant Food Editor: Karen Scales
Test Kitchen Assistants: Suzanne Kern, Kris Lehman, Rita Krajcir, Sue Megonigle
Editorial Assistants: Ursula Maurer, Mary Ann Koebernik
Photographers: Rob Hagen, Dan Roberts, Jim Wieland
Food Stylists: Sarah Thompson, Joylyn Trickel
Set Stylists: Sue Myers, Jennifer Bradley Vent
Associate Photographer: Lori Foy
Set Stylists' Assistant: Melissa Haberman
Contributing Set Stylists: Stephanie Marchese, Julie Ferron
Graphic Art Associates: Ellen Lloyd, Catherine Fletcher
Executive Editor Digital Media: Bob Ottum
President: Barbara Newton
Editor in Chief: Catherine Cassidy
Vice President/Advertising Sponsorship Director: J.P. Perkins
Founder: Roy Reiman

Taste of Home Books
© 2006 Reiman Media Group, Inc.
5400 S. 60th Street, Greendale WI 53129

International Standard Book Number: 0-89821-494-7
International Standard Serial Number: 1537-3134

Contents

504 Delicious Dishes That Fit Your Lifestyle

AS A registered dietician, I've found that most people resolve at one time or another to cut back on fat and calories in the foods they eat. Unfortunately, many folks fall victim to fad diets that don't help them reach their goals.

That's why I—and so many other health-conscious cooks from across the country—love *Light & Tasty* magazine.

You see, unlike most other food magazines, *Light & Tasty* takes a *commonsense* approach to calorie-wise eating. It's not a diet magazine, so it doesn't lecture or urge diet and exercise but instead suggests simple options with lighter ingredient choices.

The recipes in *Light & Tasty* are lean on fat and calories. But most importantly, they're full of flavor. So getting your family to eat healthy meals is easy. It's no wonder that folks who are lightening up their menus have come to rely on *Light & Tasty*, even when they're cooking for finicky eaters.

And now all 504 light-done-right recipes from the fifth year of *Light & Tasty* magazine are at your fingertips in this timeless cookbook, *2006 Light & Tasty Annual Recipes*.

Many of the dishes are family-favorites of our readers, so they're guaranteed to offer great, home-style flavor. The taste is still there…these recipes have just been lightened up a bit with less fat, calories, cholesterol, etc.

Yet, these dishes won't leave you hungry. You'll find plenty of great-tasting comfort foods, like Wintertime Beef Soup, Easy Chicken and Dumplings, Broccoli Mashed Potatoes, Caramel Apple Bread, Double Chocolate Pudding and much more. Each of these mouth-watering dishes is leaner on fat, calories or sodium but not leaner on flavor.

In addition, every recipe has been reviewed by a Registered Dietitian and includes Nutritional Analysis, plus Diabetic Exchanges where appropriate.

With *2006 Light & Tasty Annual Recipes*, healthy eating for the whole family has never been easier or more enjoyable!

Diane Werner, R.D.

Associate Food Editor, *Light & Tasty*

What's Inside These Recipe-Packed Pages?

AS IF the 504 great-tasting recipes isn't enough reason to love *2006 Light & Tasty Annual Recipes*, the following features will certainly make this book a valued reference in your kitchen for years to come.

At-a-Glance Information. If you are on a special diet—or someone you cook for is—finding suitable recipes is a breeze. That's because low-carb, low-fat, low-sodium and meatless dishes are clearly labeled right below the recipe title. (Turn the page for an explanation of these special diet indicators.) As an added bonus, preparation times are provided for *every* recipe in the book.

User-Friendly Chapters. To assist in your menu planning, we've compiled all 504 recipes into 15 convenient chapters, such as Light Bites & Beverages, Beefed-Up Main Dishes, Chicken & Turkey Entrees, Meatless Main Dishes, Side Dishes & Condiments and Dazzling Desserts. (For a complete listing of chapters, turn back to page 3.)

Mouth-Watering Meals. You'll find 13 complete meals (including pictures!), which are perfect for either weekend entertaining (page 261) or weekday family dining (page 237).

De-Light-Ful Dinner Planner. In addition to the meal chapters mentioned above, we've created 27 menu plans. (See the De-Light-Ful Dinner Planner on page 7.) Each meal features recipes found inside the book, as well as suggestions for "appealing partners" (side dishes, desserts or beverages) and meal-preparation pointers.

Hundreds of Color Photos. *More than half* of the 504 recipes in this timeless collection are shown in full color. So you can be sure these satisfying foods not only taste terrific but are eye-appealing as well.

Easy-to-Use Indexes. Finding all 504 recipes is a snap with two simple-to-use recipe indexes. The general index lists every recipe by food category, major ingredient and/or cooking technique. The alphabetical recipe listing is perfect for folks looking for a specific family favorite. There's also a reference index that directs you to the many helpful hints and tips throughout the book. The indexes begin on page 272.

Nutritional Analysis Nuggets

Our Nutritional Guidelines

EVERY RECIPE in *2006 Light & Tasty Annual Recipes* fits the lifestyle of health-conscious cooks. The recipe collection represents a variety of foods that will easily fit into a meal plan that is within the standards of the USDA's Daily Nutrition Guide (see box below). The target nutritional content of recipes, on a per serving basis, is:

- 400 calories (or less)
- 12 grams of fat (or less)
- 1,000 mg sodium (or less)
- 100 mg cholesterol (or less)

How we calculated the Nutritional Analysis

- Whenever a choice of ingredients is given in a recipe (such as 1/3 cup of sour cream or plain yogurt), the first ingredient listed is the one calculated in the Nutritional Analysis.
- When a range is given for an ingredient (such as 2 to 3 teaspoons), we calculate the first amount given.
- Only the amount of marinade absorbed during preparation is calculated.
- Garnishes listed in recipes are generally included in our calculations.

Diabetic Exchanges

ALL recipes in this book have been reviewed by a Registered Dietitian. Diabetic Exchanges are assigned to recipes in accordance with guidelines from the American Diabetic and American Dietetic Associations. The majority of recipes in *2006 Light & Tasty Annual Recipes* are suitable for diabetics.

Special Diet Indicators

TO HELP folks on restricted diets easily find dishes to suit their needs, we clearly indicate recipes that are low in carbohydrates, fat or sodium or that contain no meat. You'll find these colored, special diet indicators after the recipe title where appropriate:

Low-carb (One serving contains 15 grams or less of carbohydrates)
Low-fat (One serving contains 3 grams or less of fat)
Low-sodium (One serving contains 140 milligrams or less of sodium)
Meatless (Appetizers, salads, breads, side dishes and entrees that contain no meat)

Your Serving Size Guide

This list is a general guide for healthy eating for most adults.

Grains Group
1 bread slice, pancake or waffle
Half of an average bagel (the size of a hockey puck)
1 cup dry cereal
1/2 cup cooked cereal, rice or pasta

Vegetable Group
1 cup raw leafy greens
1/2 cup of any chopped vegetable, raw or cooked
6-ounce glass of vegetable juice
1 small potato

Fruit Group
1 medium piece of fruit
1/2 cup sliced fruit
6-ounce glass of orange juice or any 100% fruit juice

Milk Group
8-ounce container of yogurt
1/2 cup cottage cheese
1-1/2 ounces cheese (size of two dominoes)
8-ounce glass of milk

Meat and Beans Group
3 ounces cooked lean meat, poultry or fish (size of a deck of cards)
2 tablespoons peanut butter
1/2 cup beans

Daily Nutrition Guide

	Women 25-50	Women over 50	Men over 24
Calories	2,200	1,900 or less	2,900
Fat	73 g or less	63 g	96 g or less
Saturated Fat	24 g or less	21 g or less	32 g or less
Cholesterol	300 mg or less	300 mg or less	300 mg or less
Sodium	2,300 mg or less	2,300 mg or less	2,300 mg or less
Carbohydrates	335 g	283 g	446 g
Fiber	30-35 g	25-30 g	35-40 g
Protein	50 g	50 g or less	63 g

This chart is only a guide. Calorie requirements vary, depending on size, weight and amount of activity. Children's calorie and protein needs vary as they grow.

De-Light-ful Dinner Planner

To make meal planning easy,
turn to these 27 tasty menu suggestions
featuring recipes from this book, "appealing
partners" to round out the dinners and
meal-preparation pointers.

Satisfying Salad (page 9)

Skillet Pork Chops

Use your stovetop to prepare **Apples 'n' Onion Topped Chops** (p. 142). The tender pork chops are swiftly simmered with apple slices and caramelized onions in this recipe shared by Beverly McLain of Endicott, New York.

You'll need just five simple ingredients to fix **Garlic Green Beans** (p. 72) sent in by Howard Levine of Arleta, California. The tasty treatment for fresh green beans is especially appealing to garlic lovers.

Appealing Partners

◆ Bakery rolls
◆ Lemon Cream Pie (recipe on p. 198)

Practical Tips

🍎 The recipe for Apples 'n' Onion Topped Chops calls for sweet onion slices. When buying sweet onions, look for them in the produce section under the names Vidalia, Maui, Walla Walla, Rio Sweet or OSO Sweet.

🍎 To boost the flavor of the main dish, add 1/4 teaspoon of caraway seeds...or use two minced cloves of garlic instead of the garlic powder.

Mexican Mainstay

Christie Ladd of Rockville, Maryland relies on cumin and red pepper flakes to give her satisfying **Black Bean and Rice Enchiladas** (p. 172) a little zip.

For a refreshing accompaniment, serve **Chunky Cucumber Salsa** (p.18). The colorful medley from Sarah Lubner of Milwaukee, Wisconsin blends cucumber and mango for a refreshing change of pace.

Appealing Partners

◆ Baked tortilla chips
◆ Chicken soup

Practical Tips

🍎 The main dish recipe calls for 2 cups cooked brown rice. If you don't have leftover brown rice, consider preparing a big batch, then divide the extras into 1-cup portions and freeze for up to 3 months to use later in soups and casseroles. If you're in a hurry, cook instant brown rice instead.

🍎 The salsa recipe makes 4 cups, so Sarah says it's perfect when you need a crowd-pleaser for parties and buffets. "I serve it with lime-flavored tortilla chips," Sarah notes.

Hearty Barbecue

In San Antonio, Texas, Arlene Anderson uses leftover turkey to fix flavorful **Turkey Barbecue** (p.116).

For an appealing accompaniment, serve Judy Madsen's **Crunchy Peanut Coleslaw** (p. 46). The Ellis, Idaho cook tosses a crunchy combination of vegetables and chopped peanuts with a mild dressing for delicious results.

Appealing Partners

◆ Carrot sticks
◆ Canned pears

Practical Tips

🍎 Arlene likes to make the Turkey Barbecue filling ahead of time and keep it in the freezer for up to 3 months. "My husband and I get a lot of visitors from up north," she explains. "So having this in the freezer comes in handy."

🍎 If you don't have tarragon vinegar on hand to use for the coleslaw dressing, simply substitute the same amount of white wine vinegar and a dash of tarragon.

Home-Style Supper

You can have your main dish ready in 15 minutes when you fix **Spiced Tangerine Ham** (p. 143) from our Test Kitchen. Ginger, cloves and honey add flavor to the glossy citrus sauce that's served over ham slices.

Cap off the meal with **Granola Cereal Bars** (p. 19) from Helen Velichko of Kansas City, Missouri. The trimmed-down treats have a yummy peanut butter flavor and a touch of sweetness from mini chocolate chips.

Appealing Partners

- ◆ Steamed brussels sprouts
- ◆ Baked potatoes

Practical Tips

🍎 The fully cooked ham slices needed for Spiced Tangerine Ham are available in packages in the meat department near whole hams. Package weights vary, but pound packages are common.

🍎 When preparing a batch of Granola Cereal Bars, feel free to stir in 2 tablespoons of sunflower kernels or wheat germ to give the bars an extra nutritional boost.

Fare From The Grill

For a special meal, consider **Honey-Herb Pork** (p. 147). Shared by Kathy Kittell of Lenexa, Kansas, the entree marinates in a slightly sweet mustard sauce for an hour. Served with additional sauce, the pork is a fast fix for weeknight entertaining.

From Milnor, North Dakota, Darlene Gibbon offers an easy accompaniment in **Wild Rice Pepper Salad** (p. 55). The combination of colorful peppers and Italian salad dressing makes the chilled dish both eye-catching and full-flavored.

Appealing Partners

- ◆ Grilled mushrooms and sliced onions
- ◆ Berry Nectarine Salad (recipe on p. 59)

Practical Tips

🍎 To help streamline the tenderloins' preparation, substitute 1 cup of prepared honey-mustard from the grocery store for the honey and mustard called for.

🍎 When red and yellow peppers aren't in season, Darlene says she sometimes makes the side dish with chopped carrots and celery instead.

Satisfying Salad

Mix up your dinnertime routine with Janet Dingler's no-fuss **Spinach Beef Salad** (p. 70). The Cedartown, Georgia cook tosses fresh spinach leaves with stir-fried beef and a delightful sweet-and-sour dressing.

Edna Hoffman of Hebron, Indiana keeps meals big on flavor and low in cholesterol with **Raisin Rye Muffins** (p. 186). A tasty addition to supper, the down-home baked goods keep folks reaching for the breadbasket without feeling an ounce of guilt.

Appealing Partners

- ◆ Raspberry iced tea
- ◆ Frozen yogurt

Practical Tips

🍎 To shave a few minutes off the clock, replace the homemade salad dressing in the main course with a bottled sweet-sour or Asian-inspired variety. Check the nutrition label to make sure it's low-fat.

🍎 Instead of mixing raisins into the rye muffins, add an equal portion of dates, dried apricots or dried cranberries.

Sensational Sandwiches

With a little planning, you'll have no trouble finding the time to marinate the poultry for tangy **Turkey Tenderloin Sandwiches** (p. 118). Kathy Thompson likes to grill the juicy turkey breasts at her Clifton, Colorado home.

And from Midland, Texas, Grady Jones shares **Spicy Crunchy Veggies** (p. 56). The colorful vegetable salad is perfect for backyard barbecues and adds a bit of zip to any meal.

Appealing Partners

♦ Baked potato chips
♦ Grapes

Practical Tips

🍎 The tenderloins are so tasty that you can serve them without the buns. Or, try wrapping slices of the turkey in flour tortillas or stuffing them into pita bread for a fun change of pace.

🍎 If the veggie recipe sounds too spicy for your family, try eliminating the jalapeno pepper and decreasing the seasoning blend.

Pleasing Pasta Dinner

In Hemet, California, Margaret Wilson keeps taste buds watering with **Chicken Pasta Primavera** (p. 121). The classic entree is perfect when time is tight because it's ready in less than half an hour.

Cathy Yates of Cicero, New York has an ultra-fast finale to dinner. **Fruit-Filled Quesadillas** (p. 207) sandwich warm apricots and strawberries between crispy cinnamon-topped tortillas.

Appealing Partners

♦ Mixed greens salad
♦ Garden vegetable soup

Practical Tips

🍎 The main course calls for 4 cups cubed cooked chicken breasts. If you don't have cooked chicken on hand, you'll need to cook about 2 pounds of chicken in order to yield 4 cups.

🍎 If you happen to have some cooked turkey left over from a meal earlier in the week, feel free to cube it and use it in place of the cooked chicken in the pasta dish.

Catch of The Day

Unwind after a busy day with an impressive yet simple mainstay from Merrillville, Indiana's Karen Martis. **Catfish with Spiced Fruit Salsa** (p. 160) comes together quickly on the stovetop but gets its flavor from an abundance of seasonings.

Enjoy your supper with glasses of Ashley Braswell's **Pineapple Cooler** (p. 28). The Huntsville, Alabama subscriber relies on pineapple and lemon juices as well as coconut and vanilla extracts for the refreshing citrus beverage.

Appealing Partners

♦ Green beans
♦ Corn bread

Practical Tips

🍎 If catfish isn't a family favorite, fix the main course using orange roughy instead.

🍎 To cut dinnertime prep, Karen sometimes uses her microwave to prepare the salsa for the fish.

🍎 Keep the salsa in mind for future recipes. You'll find that it's a light yet lip-smacking way to jazz up grilled chicken, pork or even steak.

Scallop Stir-Fry

You'll liven up your week with **Stir-Fried Scallops and Asparagus** (p. 157). In her Napolean, Ohio kitchen, Barbara Schindler seasons the 25-minute entree with lime juice, sesame oil and hot pepper sauce.

Cap off your supper with a sweet specialty from Bonita Giesbrecht of Glenn, California. Her **Lemon Cake** (p. 205) makes for a delightful treat after any meal.

Appealing Partners

- Baked egg rolls
- Egg drop soup

Practical Tips

- If you do not have the ramen noodles called for in the stir-fry, Barbara suggests using spaghetti or angel hair pasta.

- You'll need to slice three green onions for the main course. While you're at it, finely chop the rest of the bunch, and store the onions in a resealable bag in your refrigerator. This will give you a head start when preparing a quick tossed salad later in the week.

Creamy Comfort Food

Your family is in for a comforting dinner when **Cheesy Broccoli Cauliflower Casserole** is on the menu (p. 146). Chock-full of vegetables and ham, the creamy dish was sent in by Nancy Whitford of Edwards, New York.

In Canaan, Maine, Tina Dierking has friends and family asking for the secret to hearty **Vegetable Bean Barley Soup** (p. 32). It's a flavorful way to get your gang to try grains without anyone suspecting that they're eating light.

Appealing Partners

- Herbed baked pita chips
- Strawberry shortcake

Practical Tips

- Instead of buying two bags of frozen vegetables for the casserole, consider purchasing a 24-ounce bag of frozen California blend, and you'll benefit from the addition of sliced carrots. Use 6-1/4 cups of the blend for the casserole.

- You can pick up cubed fully cooked ham for the hot dish at the supermarket. Look for it near the bacon or sliced lunchmeat area of your grocery store.

Easy Italian Feast

Bring a touch of Venice to the table with **Italian Turkey and Noodles** (p. 117). Sent by Racine, Wisconsin's Cindi Roshia, the delicious dish tops noodles with a combination of ground turkey, mushrooms, green pepper and your favorite jar of spaghetti sauce.

An Italian dinner just isn't complete without a loaf of garlic bread, and our Test Kitchen's **Herb Cheese Bread** (p. 184) fits that bill. With its blend of cumin, oregano and thyme, it's sure to be popular at your house.

Appealing Partners

- Blue Cheese 'n' Fruit Tossed Salad (recipe on p. 51)
- Lemon ice

Practical Tips

- The hot dish calls for 3 cups of cooked noodles. If you don't have any leftover noodles to use up, note that 2-3/4 cups uncooked noodles yields 3 cups cooked noodles.

- When seasoning the bread, substitute any of the dried herbs with rosemary, basil or even cayenne pepper.

Great Grilling

A Taste of The Tropics

Saucy Chicken

From Los Olivos, California, Susan Wilkins submits a carb-counter's dream with juicy **London Broil** (p. 114). An easy marinade and quick rub give the flank steak its flavor boost, and grilling it outside makes cleanup a breeze.

As long as you're cooking outdoors, consider trying Alice Nulle's **Grilled Broccoli** (p. 74). The Woodstock, Illinois cook uses a handful of ingredients to season the fresh spears before tossing them with Parmesan cheese.

Shonda Ford knows how to break up the weekday dinner doldrums. For **Lime Pork with Peppers** (p. 146), she sizzles onions, tomatoes, green peppers and lip-smacking pork on the stovetop of her DeRidder, Louisiana home.

Serve the eye-appealing supper with frosty glasses of **Pineapple Smoothies** (p. 20) from Darlene Brenden of Salem, Oregon. You'll be amazed at how quickly the refreshing five-ingredient beverage comes together.

A half hour is all you need to set Angela Schellenberg's **Chicken with Garlic-Tomato Sauce** on the table (p. 125). Angela, who is from Steinbach, Manitoba, boosts the flavor and nutrition of canned tomato sauce with plenty of rosemary and fresh vegetables.

With a little planning, you can easily dress up bowls of crispy greens with **Creamy Dill Salad Dressing** (p. 60). Randa Smaligo of Pryor, Oklahoma shared the four-ingredient recipe.

Appealing Partners

- New potatoes
- Makeover Rhubarb Shortcake Dessert (recipe on p. 209)

Appealing Partners

- Hawaiian bread
- Seasoned rice

Appealing Partners

- Italian bread
- Sauteed zucchini with Italian seasoning

Practical Tips

🍎 You can substitute the red wine vinegar that's called for in the steak's marinade with an equal portion of cider vinegar.

🍎 You'll need about 2 pounds of fresh broccoli for the side dish. When buying broccoli, look for firm but tender spears with compact florets that are dark green or have a slightly purple tint.

Practical Tips

🍎 If you don't have a grater for the lime peel, follow Shonda's lead and use a vegetable peeler instead. Finely dice the strips of peel and continue with the recipe.

🍎 There's no need to purchase buttermilk just for the smoothies. As an alternative, combine 2/3 cup of plain nonfat or low-fat yogurt with 1/2 cup 1% milk. Add this mixture to the blender instead of the buttermilk.

Practical Tips

🍎 If you're not a pasta-lover, Angela suggests serving the chicken alongside small red potatoes.

🍎 Using canned sauce in the entree saves time, but a homemade sauce could lower the dish's sodium. Substitute a cup of from-scratch sauce if you'd like.

🍎 If you don't have fresh dill on hand for the herb dressing, use 1/2 teaspoon dried dill weed instead.

Slow-Cooked Specialty

Get supper prep out of the way early with tender **Slow-Cooked Sirloin** from Vicki Tormaschy of Dickinson, North Dakota (p. 109). With chunks of onion and green pepper, the main course is both satisfying and low in carbohydrates.

The steak's tangy gravy is ideal over **Horseradish Mashed Potatoes** (p. 79). Sent by Melissa Merkle of Elizabeth, Illinois, the change-of-pace potatoes are a tasty addition to any meal.

Appealing Partners

♦ Steamed brussels sprouts
♦ Coconut-Cherry Cream Squares (recipe on p. 215)

Practical Tips

🍎 For a complete meal, Vicki sometimes adds potatoes, carrots or mushrooms to the onions and peppers in her sirloin recipe.

🍎 Melissa saves time by mashing the potatoes a day early and storing them in the fridge. Before dinner, she simply tops them with the creamy spread and pops them in the oven to bake.

Gumbo with A Kick

Break up the dinnertime routine with **Southern Seafood Gumbo** (p. 42). Susan Wright from Champaign, Illinois adds a little spice to the steamy mainstay with a hint of cayenne pepper.

Serve hearty bowlfuls alongside slices of **Four-Grain Bread** (p. 188). Sent by John Reed of Lees Summit, Missouri, the recipe calls for a handful of ingredients and bakes up easily in a bread machine.

Appealing Partners

♦ Whipped reduced-fat butter with herbs
♦ Apple crisp

Practical Tips

🍎 Susan suggests preparing the gumbo with your family's favorite seafood, such as crab or cod.

🍎 Clear out the fridge by stirring extra veggies into the gumbo. If you have carrots or tomatoes left over from a meal earlier in the week, finish them up here.

🍎 To give the bread extra flair, add a couple of tablespoons of sunflower kernels just before the final kneading.

Exceptional Pork Entree

Time is on your side with this main course from Clara Coulston of Washington Court House, Ohio. Her **Pork Medallions with Sauteed Apples** (p. 149) turns a classic combo of ingredients into a meal that's ideal for weeknight entertaining.

From Somerset, Pennsylvania, Lucinda Walker offers an easy accompaniment with buttery **Herbed Green Beans** (p. 78). Using the microwave for this dish streamlines mealtime preparation.

Appealing Partners

♦ Sauerkraut
♦ Mulled cider

Practical Tips

🍎 The pork calls for a little unsweetened apple juice. If you don't want to purchase a large bottle of juice, consider buying small juice boxes instead. The unopened boxes are easy to store.

🍎 When preparing the green onions for the entree, chop more than you need. Use 1/4 cup for the medallions and store the rest in the fridge or freezer for future use.

Casual Main Course

Before leaving for work, marinate the meat for **Flavorful Turkey Wraps** (on p. 126), and you're guaranteed an easy lip-smacking dinner that night. Josephine Piro of Easton, Pennsylvania grills the turkey before pairing juicy slices with a well-dressed slaw and wrapping it all in flour tortillas.

In her Golconda, Illinois kitchen, Helen Suter combines peas, broccoli and cauliflower with a creamy dressing for **Green Pea Salad** (p. 65). Bacon and cashews add a crunchy burst of flavor to the refreshing warm-weather dish.

Appealing Partners

◆ Fruit salad
◆ Chocolate pudding

Practical Tips

👌 You'll need to shred three medium carrots for the wraps. Save a little time by purchasing an 8-ounce bag of shredded carrots. Stir some of the leftover carrots into soups or use them to top off green salads.

👌 Josephine likes using spinach-flavored tortillas, but you may use whatever flour tortillas you prefer.

Simple Shrimp Dish

Some days may feel like the longest day of the week, but tonight's supper couldn't be quicker. Ready in just 30 minutes, **Sassy Shrimp Stir-Fry** (p. 170) was created by the family cooks on our staff.

Dessert is a breeze when you assemble it the day before. From Jean Shourds of Sault Sainte Marie, Michigan, **Velvety Orange Gelatin Pie** (p. 223) brightens up even the darkest of nights.

Appealing Partners

◆ Green tea
◆ Vegetable egg rolls

Practical Tips

👌 When stir-frying carrots for the entree, feel free to toss in water chestnuts or diced green pepper.

👌 Substitute Asian rice noodles for hot cooked rice with the stir-fry to make a fun change of pace.

👌 For extra flair, garnish the top of the pie with curls of orange peel.

New Life for Leftovers

For a comforting main course, count on Alice Slagter's **Leftover-Turkey Bake** (p. 136). She combines seasonal flavors into a mouth-watering specialty in her Wyoming, Michigan kitchen.

Couple the hot dish with a green salad featuring **Celery Seed Salad Dressing** (p. 69). Tammie Lee Carter of Wheatfield, New York shares the five-item recipe.

Appealing Partners

◆ Cranberry sauce
◆ Apple cider

Practical Tips

👌 If your family enjoys the taste of whole grain bread, feel free to increase the amount in the hot bake, decreasing the amount of white bread accordingly.

👌 Spoon some sliced mushrooms or cooked green beans into the casserole before baking it.

👌 Consider Celery Seed Salad Dressing the next time you need a thick, creamy dip for a vegetable tray.

Family Favorites

A little planning helps Linda Austin marinate **Moist Herbed Pork Chops** a day early (p. 153). "They've been a mainstay of our low-salt diet for years," she writes from Fayetteville, Arkansas.

Round out the main course of pork with **Lemon-Garlic Green Beans** (p. 92). "The side dish perfectly complements chicken or fish, too," notes Gail Orsillo of Lynnwood, Washington.

Appealing Partners

◆ Sauteed apples
◆ Roasted Garlic Mashed Potatoes (recipe on p. 88)

Practical Tips

👌 If you'd rather season the pork with fresh rosemary instead of dried, use 1-1/2 teaspoons of the finely chopped herb.

👌 Not crazy about pineapple? Substitute orange juice for the pineapple juice in the main course's marinade.

👌 Dress up the beans for company by topping them with a sprinkling of sesame seeds.

Can't-Miss Chicken

Richmond, Indiana's Beth Ann Stein beats the clock whenever she serves up **Tasty Italian Chicken** (p. 138). The juicy chicken tenderloins and homemade tomato sauce come together in only half an hour on the stovetop.

And what's a mouth-watering Italian meal without garlic? You'll find plenty of it in Brenda Nolen's **Creamy Noodles** (p. 87). "My daughter relied on this delicious recipe to help her lose 35 pounds," she shares from Folsom, Louisiana.

Appealing Partners

◆ Steamed broccoli
◆ Fat-free chocolate pudding

Practical Tips

👌 When shopping for chicken tenderloins, remember that some brands label the product as chicken tenders.

👌 Beth Ann finishes up any leftover rice she may have by serving the saucy chicken over it.

👌 For extra flavor and color, Brenda sometimes stirs a little of her favorite salsa into the noodles.

Slow-Cooked Cuisine

Get a jump start on the week with Martha Nickerson's **Slow-Cooked Sweet 'n' Sour Pork** (p. 151). With a bit of planning, this Hancock, Maine cook comes home to the welcoming aromas of tender pork, pineapple and green pepper.

Complete the dinner with **Oatmeal Date Bars** (p. 230). Helen Cluts of Sioux Falls, South Dakota shares the sweet treats.

Appealing Partners

◆ Spinach salad
◆ Pineapple wedges

Practical Tips

👌 To trim time in the morning, slice the pork and chop the onion and green pepper the night before.

👌 While you're chopping the vegetables for the entree, cut up extra veggies to use for a salad or other dish later in the week.

👌 For a change of pace, replace half of the dates in the oat bars with an equal amount of dried apricots.

Memorable Meat Loaf

Super Steak And Rice

Winning Meal-in-One

What's in a name? Well, tonight's entree isn't named **Terrific Turkey Meat Loaf** for nothing (p. 130). "My daughter won't eat meat loaf prepared with ground beef, but she just loves this turkey loaf," writes Wanda Bannister of New Bern, North Carolina.

Ideal with a cozy dinner, **Herbed Twice-Baked Potatoes** (p. 82) have so much buttery goodness that no one will suspect they're light. Ruth Andrewson of Peck, Idaho sent the rave-winning recipe.

Ten minutes is all the preparation time required for Betty Richardson's **Swiss Steak** (p. 110). The Springfield, Illinois reader simmers the meat, veggies and tangy sauce on her stovetop to free up time for other activities.

Delicate **Rosemary Rice** (p. 84) makes a comforting contribution to most dinner menus. Connie Regalado from El Paso, Texas adds garlic, rosemary and Parmesan cheese for delightful flavor.

After a busy day, it's tough to resist bubbling comfort foods...and with **Easy Chicken and Dumplings** (p. 130), you can dig in without guilt. Nancy Tuck of Elk Falls, Kansas whips up the meal-in-one dish in 30 minutes with help from a convenient biscuit mix.

Enjoy the entree alongside crisp greens, featuring **Salad Dressing with a Kick** (p. 66). Sent by Joyce Courser of Greenacres, Washington, the delicious six-ingredient dressing is guaranteed to perk up any salad you toss together.

Appealing Partners

♦ Frozen mixed vegetables
♦ Banana Chocolate Cake (recipe on p. 229)

Appealing Partners

♦ Steamed sugar snap peas
♦ Canned minestrone soup

Appealing Partners

♦ Reduced-fat crackers
♦ Meringue cookies

Practical Tips

🍎 Freeze any leftover turkey loaf for fast dinners on future nights or use extra slices for lunch sandwiches the next day.

🍎 Pick up a package of chopped onions from the grocery store's freezer case or produce department. They'll speed up tonight's main course, and you can use the extras to hurry along future meals, too.

Practical Tips

🍎 Use kitchen shears to cut the stewed tomatoes for the Swiss Steak while they're still in the can and eliminate unnecessary cleanup.

🍎 To give the hearty main course a flavor boost, purchase seasoned tomato sauce.

🍎 When Connie wants to trim even more sodium from her rice dish, she replaces the broth with water.

Practical Tips

🍎 Streamline the main course with three boxes (6 ounces each) of cooked chicken cubes.

🍎 You'll need three medium carrots for the chicken dinner's 1 cup of sliced carrots.

🍎 Joyce uses the dressing to top salad greens tossed with shredded cabbage, sliced zucchini, water chestnuts and fat-free croutons.

Light Bites &
Beverages

The next time you're in the mood for a satisfying snack or a thirst-quenching beverage, try one of the tempting treats or refreshing drinks on the following pages. They're anything but lightweight in taste!

Gouda Bites (page 22)

Breaded Ravioli

(Pictured above)

Prep: 20 min. + standing **Bake:** 10 min.

These lightly toasted ravioli, baked instead of deep-fried, are much kinder to your waistline. The homemade tomato and green pepper salsa is the best I've ever tried.
—Michelle Smith, Sykesville, Maryland

   1 **package (16 ounces) frozen beef ravioli**
1/2 **cup dry bread crumbs**
1/2 **to 1-1/2 teaspoons salt-free Italian herb seasoning**
1/4 **cup reduced-fat Italian salad dressing**
ITALIAN SALSA:
   1 **can (14-1/2 ounces) diced tomatoes, undrained**
1/2 **medium green pepper, quartered**
1/2 **small red onion, quartered**
   1 **tablespoon minced fresh oregano *or* 1 teaspoon dried oregano**
   1 **tablespoon minced fresh basil *or* 1 teaspoon dried basil**
   1 **garlic clove, minced**
   1 **teaspoon balsamic vinegar**
1/2 **teaspoon salt**
1/4 **teaspoon sugar**

Cook ravioli according to package directions; drain and let stand for 10 minutes. In a shallow bowl, combine bread crumbs and seasoning. In another shallow bowl, pour dressing. Dip ravioli into dressing, then coat with crumb mixture. Place on baking sheets coated with nonstick cooking spray. Lightly coat ravioli with nonstick cooking spray. Bake at 400° for 8-9 minutes or until lightly browned.

Meanwhile, in a food processor or blender, combine salsa ingredients. Pulse for 15-20 seconds. Serve ravioli with salsa. **Yield:** 6 servings.

Nutritional Analysis: 5 ravioli with 1/3 cup salsa equals 262 calories, 7 g fat (2 g saturated fat), 26 mg cholesterol, 924 mg sodium, 40 g carbohydrate, 4 g fiber, 10 g protein.
Diabetic Exchanges: 2 starch, 1 lean meat, 1 vegetable, 1 fat.

Garlic Feta Spread

Low-carb   *Meatless*

Prep/Total Time: 10 min.

With lots of garlic and feta cheese, this creamy spread is packed with flavor. It's a big hit at parties.
—Theresa Conroy, Santa Rosa, California

   4 **ounces reduced-fat cream cheese**
1/3 **cup fat-free mayonnaise**
   1 **to 2 garlic cloves, minced**
1/4 **teaspoon dried basil, crushed**
1/4 **teaspoon dried oregano, crushed**
1/8 **teaspoon dill weed**
1/8 **teaspoon dried thyme, crushed**
   4 **ounces crumbled feta cheese**
Fresh vegetables *and/or* crackers

In a food processor or blender, combine the first seven ingredients; cover and process until smooth. Transfer to a small bowl; stir in feta cheese. Serve with vegetables and/or crackers. **Yield:** 1-1/4 cups.

Nutritional Analysis: 2 tablespoons spread equals 63 calories, 5 g fat (3 g saturated fat), 17 mg cholesterol, 224 mg sodium, 2 g carbohydrate, trace fiber, 3 g protein.
Diabetic Exchange: 1 fat.

Chunky Cucumber Salsa

(Pictured below)

Low-fat   *Low-carb*   *Meatless*

Prep: 20 min. + chilling

Although this may sound like an "interesting" grouping of flavors, it has never let me down. People always try to guess the secret ingredient…it's mango!
—Sarah Lubner, Milwaukee, Wisconsin

   3 **medium cucumbers, peeled and coarsely chopped**
   1 **medium mango, coarsely chopped**
   1 **cup frozen corn, thawed**
   1 **medium sweet red pepper, coarsely chopped**

vanilla; add oats and cereal. Fold in chocolate chips. Press into a 9-in. square pan coated with nonstick cooking spray. Cool and cut into bars. **Yield:** 1 dozen.

Editor's Note: This recipe was tested in a 1,100-watt microwave.

Nutritional Analysis: 1 bar equals 199 calories, 7 g fat (2 g saturated fat), 0 cholesterol, 88 mg sodium, 31 g carbohydrate, 2 g fiber, 5 g protein.

Diabetic Exchanges: 2 starch, 1 fat.

Fresh Herb Dip

(Pictured below)

Low-fat **Low-sodium** *Low-carb* *Meatless*

Prep: 10 min. + chilling

People won't guess that this delicious dip, which is great with fresh vegetables, is also low in fat.
—Mitzi Sentiff, Alexandria, Virginia

3/4 cup fat-free mayonnaise
3/4 cup reduced-fat sour cream
1/4 cup minced fresh parsley
1/4 cup minced fresh chives
2 tablespoons minced fresh tarragon
1 tablespoon lemon juice
2 teaspoons minced garlic
1/8 teaspoon salt
1/8 teaspoon pepper
Assorted fresh vegetables

In a bowl, combine the first nine ingredients; mix well. Cover and refrigerate for 1 hour. Serve with fresh vegetables. **Yield:** 1-3/4 cups.

Nutritional Analysis: 2 tablespoons dip (calculated without vegetables) equals 27 calories, trace fat (trace saturated fat), 4 mg cholesterol, 135 mg sodium, 5 g carbohydrate, trace fiber, 1 g protein.

Diabetic Exchange: 1/2 starch.

1 small red onion, coarsely chopped
1 jalapeno pepper, finely chopped
3 garlic cloves, minced
2 tablespoons white wine vinegar
1 tablespoon minced fresh cilantro
1 teaspoon salt
1/2 teaspoon sugar
1/4 to 1/2 teaspoon cayenne pepper

In a large bowl, combine all the ingredients. Cover and refrigerate for 2-3 hours before serving. **Yield:** 4 cups.

Editor's Note: When cutting or seeding hot peppers, use rubber or plastic gloves to protect your hands. Avoid touching your face.

Nutritional Analysis: 1/2 cup equals 57 calories, trace fat (trace saturated fat), 0 cholesterol, 297 mg sodium, 13 g carbohydrate, 2 g fiber, 2 g protein.

Diabetic Exchanges: 1 vegetable, 1/2 fruit.

Granola Cereal Bars

(Pictured above)

Low-sodium

Prep: 15 min. + cooling

These sweet peanut butter bars are perfect for breakfast, dessert or anytime as a quick snack.
—Helen Velichko, Kansas City, Missouri

1/2 cup packed brown sugar
1/2 cup creamy peanut butter
1/4 cup light corn syrup
1 teaspoon vanilla extract
2 cups old-fashioned oats
1-1/2 cups crisp rice cereal
1/4 cup miniature chocolate chips

In a microwave-safe bowl, combine the brown sugar, peanut butter and corn syrup; cover and microwave on high for 2 minutes or until mixture comes to a boil, stirring once. Stir in the

Tex-Mex Rice and Bean Snack

(Pictured below)

Prep/Total Time: 30 min.

This zesty Southwestern-style dip, served with tortilla wedges, is perfect for tailgating and after-game parties...or for any occasion. If you're adventurous, you might want to add green chilies or hot peppers.
—Pat Habiger, Spearville, Kansas

10 corn tortillas (6 inches)
1/2 pound lean ground turkey
  1 can (16 ounces) pinto beans, rinsed and drained
  1 can (14-1/2 ounces) diced tomatoes, undrained
  3 tablespoons tomato paste
  1 tablespoon chili powder
3/4 teaspoon ground cumin
1/4 teaspoon salt
  2 cups hot cooked rice
1/2 cup shredded reduced-fat Mexican cheese blend
1/4 cup sliced green onions

Cut each tortilla into six wedges; arrange in a single layer on a baking sheet coated with nonstick cooking spray. Spray tortillas with nonstick cooking spray. Bake at 400° for 8-10 minutes or until crisp; remove to a wire rack to cool.

Meanwhile, in a large nonstick skillet coated with nonstick cooking spray, cook turkey over medium heat until no longer pink. Add the beans, tomatoes, tomato paste, chili powder, cumin and salt; bring to a boil. Reduce heat; simmer, uncovered, for 5-10 minutes or until heated through.

Spoon rice onto a serving platter. Top with turkey mixture, cheese and green onions. Arrange tortilla wedges around edge of platter. **Yield:** 10 servings.

Nutritional Analysis: 1/2 cup dip with 6 tortilla wedges equals 202 calories, 4 g fat (1 g saturated fat), 20 mg cholesterol, 331 mg sodium, 31 g carbohydrate, 5 g fiber, 11 g protein.
Diabetic Exchanges: 2 starch, 1 lean meat.

Pineapple Smoothies

(Pictured above)

Low-fat Low-sodium

Prep/Total Time: 10 min.

This cool, quick beverage reminds me of our visits to the Hawaiian Islands. It's sure to refresh any time of day.
—Darlene Brenden, Salem, Oregon

1-1/2 cups unsweetened pineapple juice
  1 cup 1% buttermilk
  2 cups ice cubes
  2 cans (8 ounces *each*) unsweetened crushed pineapple
1/4 cup sugar

Combine all ingredients in a blender or food processor; cover and process until smooth. Pour into glasses; serve immediately. **Yield:** 6 servings.

Nutritional Analysis: 1 cup equals 133 calories, trace fat (trace saturated fat), 1 mg cholesterol, 50 mg sodium, 31 g carbohydrate, 1 g fiber, 2 g protein.
Diabetic Exchanges: 1-1/2 fruit, 1/2 starch.

Calico Corn Salsa

(Pictured at right)

Low-fat Meatless

Prep/Total Time: 25 min.

A friend gave me the recipe for this colorful salsa...and when I took it to a luncheon, everyone loved it. Double the ingredients for larger gatherings.
—Jennifer Gardner, Sandy, Utah

1-1/2 cups frozen corn, thawed
  1 cup frozen peas, thawed
1/2 teaspoon ground cumin

1/8 teaspoon dried oregano
1 tablespoon olive oil
1 can (15 ounces) black beans, rinsed and drained
1 medium tomato, chopped
1/3 cup chopped red onion
1/4 cup lime juice
1 tablespoon Dijon mustard
1 garlic clove, minced
1/2 teaspoon salt
2 tablespoons minced fresh cilantro
Baked tortilla chips

In a large bowl, combine the corn and peas. In a nonstick skillet, cook cumin and oregano in oil over medium heat for 2 minutes. Pour over corn mixture; stir to coat evenly. Stir in the beans, tomato and onion.

In a small bowl, whisk the lime juice, mustard, garlic and salt. Stir in cilantro. Pour over corn mixture and stir to coat. Serve with tortilla chips. Refrigerate leftovers. **Yield:** 4 cups.

Nutritional Analysis: 1/2 cup salsa (calculated without chips) equals 107 calories, 2 g fat (trace saturated fat), 0 cholesterol, 317 mg sodium, 18 g carbohydrate, 4 g fiber, 5 g protein.
Diabetic Exchanges: 1 starch, 1/2 fat.

Creamy Guacamole

Low-sodium Low-carb Meatless

Prep/Total Time: 5 min.

This irresistible dip uses only four ingredients. It's ideal for serving with tortilla chips when entertaining.
—Ethel Anderson, Hemlock, New York

1 medium ripe avocado, peeled and pitted
7 tablespoons fat-free sour cream
2 tablespoons chopped green chilies
1/8 teaspoon lemon-pepper seasoning

Cut the avocado into chunks and place in a blender; add the remaining ingredients. Cover and process until smooth. Refrigerate leftovers. **Yield:** 1 cup.

Nutritional Analysis: 2 tablespoons equals 54 calories, 4 g fat (1 g saturated fat), 2 mg cholesterol, 29 mg sodium, 4 g carbohydrate, 1 g fiber, 1 g protein.
Diabetic Exchange: 1 fat.

Stuffed Potato Skins

(Pictured above)

Low-fat Low-sodium Meatless

Prep: 10 min. **Bake:** 50 min.

Fabulous as party appetizers, snacks or even light meals, these potatoes make it fun to eat your vegetables.
—Hollie Powell, St. Louis, Missouri

6 medium baking potatoes (6 ounces *each*)
1 tablespoon butter, melted
1 teaspoon hot pepper sauce, *divided*
1 cup thinly sliced green onions
1 large sweet red pepper, finely chopped
1/2 cup fresh broccoli florets, finely chopped
1 cup (4 ounces) shredded reduced-fat cheddar cheese, *divided*

Scrub and pierce potatoes. Bake at 400° for 40-50 minutes or until tender. Cool slightly; cut each potato in half lengthwise. Scoop out the pulp, leaving a thin shell (save pulp for another use). Place potato shells on an ungreased baking sheet.

Combine butter and 1/2 teaspoon hot pepper sauce; brush over shells. Broil 4 in. from the heat for 5 minutes or until edges are crispy and butter is bubbly. Meanwhile, in a bowl, combine the onions, red pepper, broccoli, 3/4 cup cheese and remaining hot pepper sauce; spoon into potato skins. Sprinkle with remaining cheese. Broil 2-3 minutes longer or until cheese is melted. **Yield:** 12 servings.

Nutritional Analysis: 1 potato skin equals 158 calories, 3 g fat (2 g saturated fat), 9 mg cholesterol, 35 mg sodium, 29 g carbohydrate, 5 g fiber, 5 g protein.
Diabetic Exchange: 2 starch.

🍎 Easy Alternatives

CREATE your own version of Stuffed Potato Skins (recipe above). Consider the following ideas or use the fillings of your choice:

Instead of...	Try using...
Broccoli	Cauliflower
Sweet red pepper	Mushrooms
Cheddar cheese	Mozzarella cheese
Green onions	Jalapeno peppers

Spinach Calzones

(Pictured below)

Meatless

Prep: 25 min. **Bake:** 10 min.

Refrigerated dough, frozen spinach and prepared pizza sauce make these calzones easy. White wine really complements the sit-down appetizers.
—Juliet Lodge, Prospect, Kentucky

- 1 package (10 ounces) frozen chopped spinach
- 1-1/2 cups (6 ounces) shredded reduced-fat Swiss cheese
- 1/2 cup fat-free ricotta cheese
- 1 green onion, sliced
- 1/2 teaspoon dried basil
- 1/4 teaspoon salt
- 1/4 teaspoon garlic powder
- 1/4 teaspoon pepper
- 1 tube (10 ounces) refrigerated pizza crust
- 1 egg white
- 1 teaspoon water
- 1/4 cup shredded Parmesan cheese

Pizza sauce, warmed, optional

Cook spinach according to package directions; drain well. In a bowl, combine the spinach, Swiss cheese, ricotta cheese, onion, basil, salt, garlic powder and pepper.

Roll pizza dough into a 15-in. x 10-in. rectangle; cut into six 5-in. squares. Spoon 1/3 cup spinach mixture onto the center of each square; brush edges of dough with water. Fold one corner over filling to the opposite corner, forming a triangle. Using a fork, crimp edges to seal.

Place in a 15-in. x 10-in. x 1-in. baking pan coated with nonstick cooking spray. Prick tops with a fork. Lightly beat egg white and water; brush over dough. Sprinkle with Parmesan cheese. Bake at 425° for 10 minutes or until golden brown. Let stand for 5 minutes. Serve with pizza sauce if desired. **Yield:** 6 servings.

Nutritional Analysis: 1 calzone (calculated without pizza sauce) equals 268 calories, 11 g fat (6 g saturated fat), 27 mg cholesterol, 579 mg sodium, 25 g carbohydrate, 2 g fiber, 18 g protein. Diabetic Exchanges: 2 lean meat, 1-1/2 starch, 1 fat.

Mulled Pomegranate Sipper

(Pictured above)

Low-fat Low-sodium

Prep: 10 min. **Cook:** 1 hour

This warm comforting cider fills the entire house with a wonderful aroma.
—Lisa Renshaw, Kansas City, Missouri

- 1 bottle (64 ounces) cranberry-apple juice
- 2 cups unsweetened apple juice
- 1 cup pomegranate juice
- 2/3 cup honey
- 1/2 cup orange juice
- 3 cinnamon sticks (3 inches)
- 10 whole cloves
- 2 tablespoons grated orange peel

In a 5-qt. slow cooker, combine all ingredients. Cover and cook on low for 1-2 hours. Discard cinnamon sticks and cloves. **Yield:** 16 servings (about 3 quarts).

Nutritional Analysis: 3/4 cup equals 131 calories, trace fat (trace saturated fat), 0 cholesterol, 21 mg sodium, 33 g carbohydrate, trace fiber, trace protein. Diabetic Exchange: 2 fruit.

Gouda Bites

(Pictured at right and on page 17)

Low-carb Meatless

Prep/Total Time: 25 min.

I season refrigerated dough with garlic powder to create golden cheese-filled cups.
—Phylis Behringer, Defiance, Ohio

- 1 tube (8 ounces) refrigerated reduced-fat crescent rolls
- 1/2 teaspoon garlic powder
- 5 ounces Gouda cheese, cut into 24 pieces

Unroll crescent dough into one long rectangle; seal seams and perforations. Sprinkle with garlic powder. Cut into 24 pieces; lightly press onto the bottom and up the sides of un-greased miniature muffin cups.

Bake at 375° for 3 minutes. Place a piece of cheese in each cup. Bake 8-10 minutes longer or until golden brown and cheese is melted. Serve warm. **Yield:** 2 dozen.

Nutritional Analysis: 2 bites equals 110 calories, 6 g fat (3 g saturated fat), 13 mg cholesterol, 252 mg sodium, 8 g carbohydrate, trace fiber, 4 g protein.
Diabetic Exchanges: 1-1/2 fat, 1/2 starch.

Smoked Salmon Dip

Low-fat **Low-carb**

Prep: 10 min. + chilling

Smoked salmon lovers will definitely enjoy this snack. Served with crackers or vegetables, this snack makes a great addition to an hors d'oeuvre buffet.
—Cathryn Buist, Jenison, Michigan

1-1/2 cups (12 ounces) 1% cottage cheese
4 ounces cooked smoked salmon, flaked
2 tablespoons prepared horseradish
Assorted crackers

Place cottage cheese in a food processor or blender; cover and process until smooth. Transfer to a bowl. Stir in salmon and horseradish. Cover and refrigerate for at least 3 hours or until chilled. Serve with crackers. **Yield:** 2-1/4 cups.

Nutritional Analysis: 1/4 cup dip (calculated without crackers) equals 44 calories, 1 g fat (trace saturated fat), 4 mg cholesterol, 416 mg sodium, 1 g carbohydrate, trace fiber, 7 g protein.
Diabetic Exchange: 1 lean meat.

Mushroom-Stuffed Shrimp

(Pictured above right)

Low-fat **Low-carb**

Prep/Total Time: 25 min.

These fancy appetizers can also make a tasty main course served with rice or pasta.
—Karolee Plock, Burwell, Nebraska

12 uncooked shell-on jumbo shrimp (about 1 pound)
1/2 teaspoon chicken bouillon granules
1 tablespoon hot water
3/4 cup soft bread crumbs
2 tablespoons finely chopped fresh mushrooms
2 tablespoons finely chopped celery
1 teaspoon reduced-fat butter
1/4 teaspoon garlic powder
4 drops hot pepper sauce

Peel and devein shrimp, leaving the tails on. Butterfly each shrimp along the outside curve. Open shrimp flat and place with tails up in an 8-in. square baking dish coated with non-stick cooking spray.

In a small bowl, dissolve bouillon in hot water. Stir in the re-maining ingredients. Spoon about 1 teaspoon onto each shrimp. Bake at 375° for 5-8 minutes or until shrimp turn pink. Serve warm. **Yield:** 1 dozen.

Editor's Note: This recipe was tested with Land O' Lakes light stick butter.

Nutritional Analysis: 3 stuffed shrimp equals 115 calories, 2 g fat (1 g saturated fat), 170 mg cholesterol, 353 mg sodium, 5 g car-bohydrate, trace fiber, 19 g protein.
Diabetic Exchange: 3 very lean meat.

Blueberry Fruit Smoothie

Low-fat **Low-sodium**

Prep/Total Time: 5 min.

This low-fat but yummy smoothie just might take you back to soda-fountain days.
—Mary Walton, Woodland, Washington

1 cup reduced-fat vanilla ice cream
1 cup fresh *or* frozen blueberries
1/2 cup chopped fresh *or* frozen peaches, thawed
1/2 cup pineapple juice
1/4 cup reduced-fat vanilla yogurt

In a blender or food processor, combine all of the ingredients; cover and process until smooth. Pour into chilled glasses; serve immediately. **Yield:** 3 servings.

Nutritional Analysis: 3/4 cup equals 149 calories, 2 g fat (1 g saturated fat), 7 mg cholesterol, 57 mg sodium, 30 g carbohydrate, 2 g fiber, 3 g protein.
Diabetic Exchanges: 2 fruit, 1/2 fat.

Broccoli Cheddar Spread

(Pictured above)

Low-carb *Meatless*

Prep: 15 min. **Bake:** 20 min.

I was able to lighten up the original recipe for this thick, warm spread without losing any of the flavor.
—Beth Parker, Graysville, Alabama

4 cups chopped fresh broccoli
1 tablespoon water
2 cups (16 ounces) reduced-fat sour cream
1/2 cup plus 1 tablespoon shredded reduced-fat cheddar cheese, *divided*
1 envelope vegetable soup mix
Reduced-fat crackers *or* **pita chips**

Place broccoli and water in a 1-1/2-qt. microwave-safe dish. Cover and microwave on high for 4 minutes or until crisp-tender; drain. In a large bowl, combine the sour cream, 1/2 cup cheese and soup mix. Gently stir in broccoli.

Transfer to an ungreased shallow 1-qt. baking dish. Sprinkle with remaining cheese. Bake, uncovered, at 350° for 20-25 minutes or until heated through. Serve with crackers or pita chips. **Yield:** 3 cups.

Editor's Note: This recipe was tested in a 1,100-watt microwave.

Nutritional Analysis: 1/4 cup spread (calculated without pita chips) equals 80 calories, 4 g fat (3 g saturated fat), 16 mg cholesterol, 230 mg sodium, 6 g carbohydrate, 1 g fiber, 5 g protein.
Diabetic Exchanges: 1/2 fat-free milk, 1/2 fat.

Chili-Cheese Wonton Cups

(Pictured at right)

Meatless

Prep/Total Time: 30 min.

Baked in miniature muffin cups, wonton wrappers add crunchy flair to these cheesy Southwestern bites.
—Lyn Renwick, Charlotte, North Carolina

24 wonton wrappers
Refrigerated butter-flavored spray

1 cup (4 ounces) shredded reduced-fat cheddar cheese
1/2 cup reduced-fat ricotta cheese
1 can (4 ounces) chopped green chilies, well drained
1 tablespoon minced chives
1/4 teaspoon salt
1/4 teaspoon ground cumin
3 tablespoons sliced ripe olives

Press the wonton wrappers into miniature muffin cups coated with nonstick cooking spray, forming a cup. Spritz with butter-flavored spray. Bake at 350° for 8-9 minutes or until the edges are golden.

In a small bowl, combine the cheeses, chilies, chives, salt and cumin. Spoon into cups. Top with olives. Bake for 10 minutes or until golden brown and bubbly. Serve warm. **Yield:** 2 dozen.

Editor's Note: This recipe was tested with I Can't Believe It's Not Butter Spray.

Nutritional Analysis: 2 wonton cups equals 229 calories, 4 g fat (2 g saturated fat), 14 mg cholesterol, 542 mg sodium, 38 g carbohydrate, trace fiber, 10 g protein.
Diabetic Exchanges: 2 starch, 1 fat, 1/2 lean meat.

Mini Sausage Bundles

(Pictured above right)

Low-fat *Low-carb*

Prep/Total Time: 30 min.

These tasty hors d'oeuvres cut fat as well as cleanup by keeping the deep fryer at bay. Our Test Kitchen filled the savory bundles with turkey sausage, garlic and onion.

1/2 pound turkey Italian sausage links, casings removed
1 small onion, finely chopped
1/4 cup finely chopped sweet red pepper
1 garlic clove, minced
1/2 cup shredded cheddar cheese
8 sheets phyllo dough (14 inches x 9 inches)
12 whole chives, optional

Crumble the sausage into a large nonstick skillet; add onion, red pepper and garlic. Cook over medium heat until

meat is no longer pink; drain. Stir in cheese; cool slightly.

Place one sheet of phyllo dough on a work surface; coat with nonstick cooking spray. Cover with a second sheet of phyllo; coat with nonstick cooking spray. (Until ready to use, keep remaining phyllo covered with plastic wrap and a damp towel to prevent drying out.) Cut widthwise into three 4-in. strips, discarding trimmings. Top each with 2 rounded tablespoons of sausage mixture; fold bottom and side edges over filling and roll up. Repeat with remaining phyllo and filling.

Place seam side down on an ungreased baking sheet. Bake at 425° for 5-6 minutes or until lightly browned. Tie a chive around each bundle if desired. Serve warm. **Yield:** 1 dozen.

Nutritional Analysis: 1 bundle equals 67 calories, 3 g fat (2 g saturated fat), 15 mg cholesterol, 168 mg sodium, 5 g carbohydrate, trace fiber, 5 g protein.
Diabetic Exchanges: 1 lean meat, 1/2 fat.

Roasted Red Pepper Dip

Low-carb Meatless

Prep/Total Time: 15 min.

This fast, creamy dip is a nice addition to an appetizer buffet and has received many compliments.
—Priscilla Gilbert, Indian Harbour Beach, Florida

  1 cup (8 ounces) fat-free sour cream
  1/2 cup reduced-fat mayonnaise
  1/2 teaspoon prepared horseradish
  1/8 teaspoon cayenne pepper
  4 drops hot pepper sauce
  1 jar (7 ounces) roasted sweet red peppers, drained and chopped
  1 medium sweet red pepper
Assorted fresh vegetables

In a small bowl, combine the first five ingredients. Stir in the roasted red peppers. Cut a thin slice off one long side of sweet red pepper; remove seeds. Spoon dip into pepper cup. Serve with vegetables. **Yield:** 10 servings.

Nutritional Analysis: 1/4 cup dip (calculated without red pepper cup and vegetables) equals 90 calories, 5 g fat (1 g saturated fat), 10 mg cholesterol, 192 mg sodium, 9 g carbohydrate, trace fiber, 2 g protein.
Diabetic Exchanges: 1 fat, 1/2 starch.

White Bean Dip

Low-fat **Low-carb** Meatless

Prep/Total Time: 10 min.

This low-fat party starter is a wonderful way to use fresh basil. Increase the amount of herbs if you like.
—Katina Tanner, Benton Harbor, Michigan

  2 cans (15 ounces *each*) white kidney *or* cannellini beans, rinsed and drained
  2 tablespoons olive oil
  2 garlic cloves, minced
  1/2 cup minced fresh basil
  2 tablespoons lemon juice
  1/2 teaspoon salt
  1/4 teaspoon white pepper
Baked pita chips

In a food processor, combine the beans, oil and garlic; cover and process until smooth. Add the basil, lemon juice, salt and pepper; cover and process until blended. Serve with pita chips. Refrigerate leftovers. **Yield:** 2-1/4 cups.

Nutritional Analysis: 1/4 cup dip (calculated without pita chips) equals 102 calories, 3 g fat (trace saturated fat), 0 cholesterol, 326 mg sodium, 14 g carbohydrate, 4 g fiber, 4 g protein.
Diabetic Exchanges: 1 starch, 1/2 fat.

Tuna Pate

Low-fat **Low-carb**

Prep: 15 min. + chilling

Hot pepper and chili sauces liven up this seafood spread.
—Eileen Blazik, Levittown, Pennsylvania

  1 package (8 ounces) reduced-fat cream cheese
  2 tablespoons chili sauce
  1 teaspoon dried minced onion
  1/2 teaspoon garlic powder
  1/2 teaspoon hot pepper sauce
  2 cans (6 ounces *each*) light water-packed tuna, drained and flaked
  2 tablespoons minced fresh parsley
Assorted crackers

In a small mixing bowl, combine the cream cheese, chili sauce, onion, garlic powder and hot pepper sauce until blended. Add tuna and parsley; mix well. Shape into a ball; place on a serving plate. Cover and refrigerate for at least 3 hours. Serve with crackers. **Yield:** 2 cups.

Nutritional Analysis: 2 tablespoons equals 60 calories, 3 g fat (2 g saturated fat), 14 mg cholesterol, 143 mg sodium, 2 g carbohydrate, trace fiber, 7 g protein.
Diabetic Exchange: 1 lean meat.

🍎 Simple Chips

FOR HOMEMADE pita chips, try cutting pita bread into wedges and lightly spray them with nonstick cooking spray. Top them with Italian seasoning and garlic powder, then pop them in the oven.

Crimson Cranberry Punch

(Pictured at right)

Low-fat Low-sodium

Prep: 20 min. + freezing

You can stir up this punch quickly because it calls for only a few ingredients. The pretty ice ring keeps it refreshing.
—Judie White, Florien, Louisiana

1/2 cup frozen cranberries
3-1/2 cups cold water
1 bottle (48 ounces) white grape juice, chilled
2 cans (12 ounces *each*) frozen cranberry juice concentrate, thawed
4 cans (12 ounces *each*) diet lemon-lime soda, chilled
3 orange slices
3 lemon slices

Place the cranberries in a 4-1/2-cup ring mold coated with nonstick cooking spray. Slowly pour a small amount of cold water into the mold to barely cover berries; freeze until solid. Add remaining water; freeze until solid.

Just before serving, combine the grape juice and cranberry juice concentrate in a large punch bowl; stir in soda. Unmold ice ring; place fruit side up in punch bowl. Add orange and lemon slices. **Yield:** 5 quarts.

Nutritional Analysis: 1 cup equals 113 calories, trace fat (trace saturated fat), 0 cholesterol, 13 mg sodium, 28 g carbohydrate, trace fiber, trace protein.
Diabetic Exchanges: 1 starch, 1 fruit.

Eggplant Bruschetta

Low-fat Low-carb Meatless

Prep: 10 min. + standing **Cook:** 5 min.

I top eggplant slices with chopped tomatoes, fresh basil and cheese before broiling them.
—Maxine Petersohn, Cortez, Florida

1 medium eggplant, peeled and cut into 1/4-inch slices
1/2 teaspoon salt
3 medium tomatoes, seeded and chopped
2 tablespoons minced fresh basil
1 cup (4 ounces) shredded part-skim mozzarella cheese
2 tablespoons shredded Parmesan cheese

Place eggplant slices in a colander over a plate; sprinkle with salt and gently toss. Let stand for 30 minutes. Rinse and drain well. Coat both sides of each slice with nonstick cooking spray. Place on a broiler pan. Top eggplant with tomatoes, basil and cheeses. Broil 6 in. from the heat for 5-7 minutes or until eggplant is tender and cheese is melted. **Yield:** 8 servings.

Nutritional Analysis: 2 slices equals 68 calories, 3 g fat (2 g saturated fat), 9 mg cholesterol, 242 mg sodium, 7 g carbohydrate, 2 g fiber, 5 g protein.
Diabetic Exchanges: 1 vegetable, 1 fat.

Vegetable Quesadillas

Meatless

Prep/Total Time: 30 min.

Broccoli, sweet red peppers and garlic take center stage in this staple. Use the microwave to streamline preparation.
—Shannon Wade, Kansas City, Kansas

4 cups fresh broccoli florets
2 small sweet red peppers, julienned
1 jalapeno pepper, seeded and chopped
1 tablespoon minced fresh cilantro
2 garlic cloves, minced
1 teaspoon chili powder
1 teaspoon canola oil
1/2 teaspoon ground cumin
1/4 teaspoon salt
12 flour tortillas (6 inches)
1-1/2 cups (6 ounces) shredded reduced-fat Mexican cheese blend

In a 1-1/2-qt. microwave-safe dish, combine the first nine ingredients. Cover and cook on high for 5 minutes or until vegetables are tender.

Divide vegetable mixture evenly over 6 tortillas; sprinkle with cheese. Top each with remaining tortillas. Place a filled tortilla on a microwave-safe plate; cover with a piece of waxed paper. Microwave on high for 30-45 seconds or until cheese is melted. Repeat with remaining quesadillas. Cut each quesadilla into wedges. **Yield:** 6 servings.

Editor's Note: This recipe was tested in a 1,100-watt microwave. When cutting or seeding hot peppers, use rubber or plastic gloves to protect your hands. Avoid touching your face.

Nutritional Analysis: 1 quesadilla equals 287 calories, 12 g fat (3 g saturated fat), 10 mg cholesterol, 764 mg sodium, 33 g carbohydrate, 1 g fiber, 16 g protein.
Diabetic Exchanges: 2 lean meat, 2 vegetable, 1 starch, 1 fat.

 Icy Idea

ADD a little flair to the ice ring in Crimson Cranberry Punch (recipe at top left) with slices of oranges, lemons and limes.

Festive Stuffed Dates

Low-fat **Low-sodium** *Meatless*

Prep: 15 min. + chilling

Four ingredients are all you need for these citrus-flavored change-of-pace treats.
—Diana Debruyn, Cincinnati, Ohio

3 ounces reduced-fat cream cheese
1/4 cup confectioners' sugar
2 teaspoons grated orange peel
30 pitted dates

In a small mixing bowl, beat the cream cheese, confectioners' sugar and orange peel until blended. Carefully make a slit in the center of each date; fill with cream cheese mixture. Cover and refrigerate for at least 1 hour before serving. **Yield:** 10 servings.

Nutritional Analysis: *3 stuffed dates equals 102 calories, 2 g fat (1 g saturated fat), 6 mg cholesterol, 37 mg sodium, 22 g carbohydrate, 2 g fiber, 1 g protein.*
Diabetic Exchanges: *1 fruit, 1/2 fat.*

Four-Fruit Drink

Low-fat **Low-sodium**

Prep: 5 min. + chilling

This refreshing beverage has a tropical flavor that goes well at summer barbecues. Be sure to make plenty for your next get-together!
—Bonnie Bufford, Nicholson, Pennsylvania

2 cups unsweetened pineapple juice
2 cups cranberry juice
2 cans (5-1/2 ounces *each*) apricot nectar
1/2 cup lime juice
9 lime slices
2 cans (12 ounces *each*) ginger ale, chilled

In a large bowl or pitcher, combine the pineapple juice, cranberry juice, apricot nectar, lime juice and lime slices. Cover and refrigerate for at least 2 hours. Just before serving, stir in ginger ale. **Yield:** 9 servings.

Nutritional Analysis: *1 cup equals 114 calories, trace fat (trace saturated fat), 0 cholesterol, 12 mg sodium, 30 g carbohydrate, 1 g fiber, trace protein.*
Diabetic Exchange: *2 fruit.*

Honeydew Lime Cooler

(Pictured at right)

Low-fat **Low-sodium**

Prep/Total Time: 30 min.

Serve up a frosty glass of this citrusy blend of lime sherbet and honeydew melon for a real thirst quencher.
—Mitzi Sentiff, Alexandria, Virginia

4-1/2 cups cubed honeydew (about 1 small melon)
1-1/2 cups lime sherbet

2 tablespoons lime juice
5 fresh strawberries

Place melon cubes in a 15-in. x 10-in. x 1-in. baking pan; cover and freeze until firm, about 15 minutes. Set aside five melon cubes.

In a food processor or blender, combine the sherbet, lime juice and remaining frozen melon; cover and process until smooth. Pour into glasses; garnish with strawberries and reserved melon. **Yield:** 5 servings.

Nutritional Analysis: *3/4 cup equals 135 calories, 1 g fat (trace saturated fat), 3 mg cholesterol, 34 mg sodium, 32 g carbohydrate, 1 g fiber, 1 g protein.*
Diabetic Exchanges: *1 starch, 1 fruit.*

Turkey Tortilla Spirals

Prep: 25 min. + chilling

No one suspects that these addictive pinwheels are light. People are always surprised by how easy they are.
—Peggy Grieme, Pinehurst, North Carolina

3/4 pound thinly sliced deli turkey
6 flour tortillas (8 inches)
1 package (8 ounces) fat-free cream cheese
6 tablespoons finely chopped pecans
1 can (16 ounces) whole-berry cranberry sauce, *divided*
1/4 cup chopped celery
2 green onions, thinly sliced

Place turkey on tortillas to within 1/4 in. of edge. Spread cream cheese over turkey; sprinkle with pecans. Spread each with 2 tablespoons cranberry sauce. Roll up jelly-roll style; wrap tightly in plastic wrap. Refrigerate for 1 hour or until firm.

Just before serving, cut each roll into six pieces. In a small bowl, combine the celery, onions and remaining cranberry sauce. Serve with tortilla spirals. **Yield:** 3 dozen.

Nutritional Analysis: *3 spirals with 1-1/2 teaspoons sauce equals 204 calories, 5 g fat (1 g saturated fat), 12 mg cholesterol, 485 mg sodium, 31 g carbohydrate, 1 g fiber, 10 g protein.*
Diabetic Exchanges: *1 starch, 1 lean meat, 1 fruit, 1/2 fat.*

1-1/2 cups fat-free whipped topping
3 medium apples, sliced

In a small mixing bowl, beat the cream cheese and lemonade soft drink mix until smooth. Beat in 1/2 cup whipped topping. Fold in the remaining whipped topping. Cover and refrigerate the dip for at least 1 hour. Serve with sliced apples. **Yield:** 6 servings.

    Editor's Note: This recipe was tested with Pink Lemonade Crystal Light drink mix.

Nutritional Analysis: 1/2 apple with 3 tablespoons dip equals 90 calories, 1 g fat (trace saturated fat), 2 mg cholesterol, 113 mg sodium, 18 g carbohydrate, 2 g fiber, 3 g protein.
Diabetic Exchanges: 1 fruit, 1/2 starch.

Pineapple Cooler

(Pictured below)

Low-fat *Low-sodium*

Prep: 5 min. + chilling

Five ingredients are all it takes to mix up this refreshing citrus beverage. Sparkling water gives it a little fizz, making it ideal on a hot summer night.
—Ashley Braswell, Huntsville, Alabama

4 cups unsweetened pineapple juice
2 teaspoons lemon juice
1 teaspoon vanilla extract
1/2 teaspoon coconut extract
2 cups carbonated water

In a pitcher, combine the pineapple juice, lemon juice and extracts; chill. Just before serving, stir in carbonated water. Serve over ice. **Yield:** 3 servings.

Nutritional Analysis: 1 cup equals 120 calories, trace fat (trace saturated fat), 0 cholesterol, 5 mg sodium, 30 g carbohydrate, trace fiber, 1 g protein.
Diabetic Exchanges: 1-1/2 fruit, 1/2 starch.

Creamy Mocha Drink

(Pictured above)

Low-sodium

Prep: 15 min. + chilling

Our home economists love coffeehouse specialties but not the calories and sugar that accompany those beverages. These sippers allow them to indulge without regret.

Sugar substitute equivalent to 6 tablespoons sugar
2 tablespoons baking cocoa
2 tablespoons instant coffee granules
1 cup boiling water
1 cup 2% milk
1/4 teaspoon vanilla extract
1-1/2 cups no-sugar-added reduced-fat vanilla ice cream
4 tablespoons whipped topping
1/4 teaspoon ground cinnamon

In a small bowl, combine the sugar substitute, cocoa and coffee granules. Add boiling water; stir until coffee and cocoa are dissolved. Stir in milk and vanilla. Cover and refrigerate for at least 1 hour.

    Place coffee mixture in a blender; add ice cream. Cover and process until smooth. Pour into mugs or glasses; garnish with whipped topping and cinnamon. **Yield:** 4 servings.

    Editor's Note: This recipe was tested with Splenda No Calorie Sweetener.

Nutritional Analysis: 2/3 cup with 1 tablespoon whipped topping equals 138 calories, 5 g fat (3 g saturated fat), 13 mg cholesterol, 74 mg sodium, 18 g carbohydrate, 1 g fiber, 5 g protein.
Diabetic Exchanges: 1-1/2 starch, 1/2 fat.

Pink Lemonade Dip

Low-fat *Low-sodium*

Prep: 10 min. + chilling

This guilt-free dip is wonderful with fruit.
—Judi Laskovics, Harrisburg, Pennsylvania

4 ounces fat-free cream cheese
1 teaspoon sugar-free pink lemonade soft drink mix

Simmer Up a Souper Bowl!

Soups are naturally nutritious, oh-so flavorful
and sure to please in any season. Whether
it's a cool soup in summer or a steaming
pot of hearty chili on a winter's day,
soup is good for the body—and the spirit!

Makeover Cream of Tomato Soup (page 37)

Cannellini Comfort Soup

Prep: 15 min. **Cook:** 35 min.

Reduced-fat sausage, white beans and veggies make this nutritious soup plenty filling. Plus, it warms you from head to toe. If you are feeling creative, try adding some chopped fresh carrots along with onion and pepper...or more chicken broth for a "soupier" effect.
—Susan Coryell, Huddleston, Virginia

  1/2 **pound reduced-fat fully cooked smoked sausage, cut into bite-size pieces**
    1 **tablespoon olive oil**
  1/2 **cup chopped green pepper**
  1/3 **cup chopped onion**
    2 **garlic cloves, minced**
  1/3 **cup white wine *or* chicken broth**
    1 **can (14-1/2 ounces) reduced-sodium chicken broth**
  1/2 **teaspoon Italian seasoning**
  1/4 **teaspoon pepper**
    1 **can (19 ounces) cannellini *or* white kidney beans, rinsed and drained**
    3 **cups coleslaw mix**

In a large saucepan, cook sausage in oil for 2 minutes. Add the green pepper, onion and garlic. Cook and stir 2-3 minutes longer or until vegetables are tender. Stir in the 1/3 cup wine or broth; cook about 3 minutes longer. Stir in the broth, Italian seasoning and pepper. Bring to a boil. Reduce heat; cover and simmer for 15 minutes. Stir in beans and coleslaw mix. Return to a boil. Reduce heat; cover and simmer until beans are heated through and cabbage is tender. **Yield:** 4 servings.

    Nutritional Analysis: *1 cup equals 251 calories, 7 g fat (1 g saturated fat), 25 mg cholesterol, 939 mg sodium, 31 g carbohydrate, 7 g fiber, 14 g protein.*
    Diabetic Exchanges: *2 lean meat, 1-1/2 starch, 1 vegetable.*

Spinach Bean Soup

(Pictured above)

Meatless

Prep: 20 min. **Cook:** 35 min.

This easy soup is so good, I try to share the recipe with as many people as possible. Chock-full of pasta, beans and spinach, it makes a fresh-tasting and satisfying first course or a light meal in itself.
—Melissa Griffin, Lansing, Michigan

  1/2 **cup chopped onion**
    3 **garlic cloves, minced**
    1 **tablespoon olive oil**
    2 **cups water**
    1 **can (15 ounces) tomato puree**
    1 **can (14-1/2 ounces) reduced-sodium chicken broth *or* vegetable broth**
    1 **teaspoon dried oregano**
  1/2 **teaspoon sugar**
  1/2 **teaspoon salt**
  1/4 **teaspoon pepper**
    5 **cups packed torn fresh spinach**
    1 **can (16 ounces) navy beans, rinsed and drained**
1-1/2 **cups cooked small tube *or* other small pasta**
  1/2 **to 1 teaspoon hot pepper sauce**
    8 **teaspoons shredded Parmesan cheese**

In a large saucepan or Dutch oven, saute onion and garlic in oil until tender. Stir in the water, tomato puree, broth, oregano, sugar, salt and pepper. Bring to a boil. Reduce heat; cover and simmer for 20 minutes. Add the spinach, beans, cooked pasta and hot pepper sauce; heat through. Sprinkle with Parmesan cheese. **Yield:** 5 servings.

    Nutritional Analysis: *1-1/2 cups equals 243 calories, 4 g fat (1 g saturated fat), 2 mg cholesterol, 940 mg sodium, 39 g carbohydrate, 7 g fiber, 13 g protein.*
    Diabetic Exchanges: *2 starch, 2 vegetable, 1 lean meat.*

Ham and Bean Soup

Prep: 35 min. + soaking **Cook:** 3 hours 10 min. + cooling

This thick and hearty tomato-based soup is loaded with veggies and well-seasoned with herbs. Cayenne pepper gives it some zip. I always make up a soup recipe as I go along. My husband, who doesn't usually care much for soup, really likes this one.
—Erin Lembke, Bothell, Washington

  3/4 **cup dry navy beans**
1-1/2 **pounds smoked ham shank**
    6 **cups water**
    4 **celery ribs, sliced**
    4 **carrots, halved and sliced**
    1 **large onion, chopped**
    1 **cup fresh green beans, cut into 1-inch pieces**
    1 **can (14-1/2 ounces) diced tomatoes**
1-1/2 **teaspoons garlic powder**
1-1/2 **teaspoons dried basil**
    1 **teaspoon salt**
    1 **teaspoon paprika**
  1/2 **teaspoon dried oregano**
  1/4 **teaspoon *each* dried thyme, white pepper and Liquid Smoke**

1/8 teaspoon cayenne pepper
2 cups chopped cabbage

Place beans in a Dutch oven or soup kettle; add water to cover by 2 in. Bring to a boil; boil for 2 minutes. Remove from the heat; cover and let stand for 1 hour. Drain and rinse beans, discarding liquid.

In a Dutch oven or soup kettle, place ham shank and water. Cover and bring to a boil. Reduce heat; simmer for 1 hour. Add beans; simmer 1 hour longer or until meat and beans are tender. Remove from the heat. Cool slightly. Remove the ham shank. Cover and refrigerate the ham shank and soup.

Remove meat from ham bone; discard bone. Set meat aside. Remove fat from broth. Return broth with the beans and meat to pan. Add the celery, carrots, onion and green beans. Bring to a boil over medium heat. Reduce heat; simmer, uncovered, for 10 minutes. Add tomatoes and seasonings; cook for 10 minutes. Add cabbage; cook 35 minutes longer or until vegetables are tender. **Yield:** 7 servings.

Nutritional Analysis: 1-1/2 cups equals 269 calories, 10 g fat (3 g saturated fat), 34 mg cholesterol, 1,121 mg sodium, 27 g carbohydrate, 10 g fiber, 19 g protein.
Diabetic Exchanges: 2 lean meat, 2 vegetable, 1 starch, 1/2 fat.

Broccoli Cheese Soup

(Pictured below)

Meatless

Prep: 20 min. **Cook:** 35 min. + cooling

When my husband and I visit fresh-food stands, we often come home with more vegetables than we can eat. I lightened up this tarragon-flavored soup to use up the broccoli we buy. I like it with crusty bread, a salad or a sandwich.
—Marge Hill, Glenside, Pennsylvania

1/2 cup chopped sweet onion
3 garlic cloves, minced
2 tablespoons all-purpose flour
1 can (14-1/2 ounces) reduced-sodium chicken broth *or* vegetable broth

4 cups fresh broccoli florets
1/4 to 1/2 teaspoon dried tarragon
1/4 teaspoon dried thyme
1/8 teaspoon pepper
1-1/2 cups 1% milk
1-1/4 cups (5 ounces) shredded reduced-fat cheddar cheese, *divided*

In a large nonstick saucepan coated with nonstick cooking spray, saute onion and garlic until tender. Add flour; stir to coat evenly and cook for 1 minute. Gradually whisk in broth. Bring to a boil; cook and stir for 1-2 minutes or until slightly thickened.

Add the broccoli, tarragon, thyme and pepper; return to a boil. Reduce heat; cover and simmer for about 10 minutes or until broccoli is tender. Add milk; cook, uncovered, 5 minutes longer. Remove from heat; cool to room temperature.

In small batches, transfer soup to a blender; cover and process until smooth. Return soup to pan; heat through. Reduce heat. Add 1 cup cheese; stir just until melted. Serve immediately. Garnish with remaining cheese. **Yield:** 4 servings.

Nutritional Analysis: 1 cup equals 202 calories, 9 g fat (6 g saturated fat), 33 mg cholesterol, 340 mg sodium, 16 g carbohydrate, 3 g fiber, 17 g protein.
Diabetic Exchanges: 1 lean meat, 1 vegetable, 1/2 starch, 1/2 reduced-fat milk, 1/2 fat.

Ham and Lima Bean Soup

Low-fat

Prep: 20 min.+ soaking **Cook:** 1-1/4 hours

For a thicker version of this nourishing bean soup, add some instant potato flakes after it boils.
—Pam Feldstein, Owings Mills, Maryland

8 ounces dried baby lima beans
2 cups chopped onions
2 garlic cloves, minced
2 cans (14-1/2 ounces *each*) reduced-sodium chicken broth
1-1/2 cups cubed fully cooked lean ham
1 cup sliced fresh carrots (1/4-inch slices)
1/2 cup water
1 jalapeno pepper, seeded and chopped
2 tablespoons minced fresh parsley
1/2 teaspoon pepper

Place lima beans in a Dutch oven or soup kettle; add water to cover by 2 in. Bring to a boil; boil for 2 minutes. Remove from the heat; cover and let stand for 1 hour. Drain and rinse beans; discard liquid.

In a Dutch oven coated with nonstick cooking spray, cook onions and garlic until tender. Stir in the broth, ham, carrots, water, jalapeno, parsley, pepper and lima beans. Bring to a boil. Reduce heat; cover and simmer for 50 minutes or until beans are tender. **Yield:** 5 servings.

Editor's Note: When cutting or seeding hot peppers, use rubber or plastic gloves to protect your hands. Avoid touching your face.

Nutritional Analysis: 1-1/3 cups equals 263 calories, 3 g fat (1 g saturated fat), 13 mg cholesterol, 932 mg sodium, 39 g carbohydrate, 12 g fiber, 22 g protein.
Diabetic Exchanges: 3 very lean meat, 1 starch, 1 vegetable.

Vegetable Bean Barley Soup

(Pictured below)

Prep: 20 min. **Cook:** 1 hour

This hearty soup is as filling as it is comforting.
Full of zucchini, barley, tomatoes and carrots,
it's one recipe that people always ask for.
—Tina Dierking, Canaan, Maine

  1 medium onion, chopped
  1 garlic clove, minced
  1/2 teaspoon dried basil
  1/2 teaspoon dill weed
  2 tablespoons canola oil
  2 cans (14-1/2 ounces *each*) reduced-sodium
    chicken broth
1-3/4 cups water
  1 cup chopped carrots
  1/2 cup medium pearl barley
  1 can (16 ounces) pork and beans
  2 small zucchini, sliced
  1/2 teaspoon salt
  1/4 teaspoon pepper
  1 can (14-1/2 ounces) diced tomatoes, undrained
  1 teaspoon cider vinegar

In a large saucepan or Dutch oven, saute the onion, garlic, basil and dill in oil until onion is tender. Add the broth, water, carrots and barley. Bring to a boil. Reduce heat; cover and simmer for 30 minutes.

Add the pork and beans, zucchini, salt and pepper. Cover and simmer 10-15 minutes longer or until vegetables and barley are tender. Just before serving, stir in tomatoes and vinegar; heat through. **Yield:** 6 servings.

Nutritional Analysis: 1-1/2 cups equals 218 calories, 6 g fat (1 g saturated fat), 5 mg cholesterol, 1,003 mg sodium, 36 g carbohydrate, 9 g fiber, 9 g protein.
Diabetic Exchanges: *2 starch, 1 vegetable, 1 fat.*

Thrive-on-Five Soup

Low-carb   Low-fat

Prep: 25 min. **Cook:** 70 min.

My wife and I follow a low-carb diet. This hearty soup lets
us enjoy cubed turkey and eight different vegetables at the
same time. Try it with red cabbage if you like.
—Robert Hermann, Stockton, California

  1 cup chopped onion
  1/2 cup chopped celery
  1/2 cup chopped green pepper
  1/2 cup chopped peeled turnip
  1/3 cup sliced fresh carrot
  1 tablespoon olive oil
  3 cups reduced-sodium chicken broth
  1 can (14-1/2 ounces) stewed tomatoes, cut up
1-1/2 teaspoons dried thyme
  1 bay leaf
  1 cup coarsely chopped green cabbage
  1 cup cut fresh green beans (2-inch pieces)
1-1/2 cups cubed cooked turkey breast
  1 tablespoon cider vinegar
  1/2 teaspoon salt
  1/8 teaspoon pepper

In a large saucepan, saute the onion, celery, green pepper, turnip and carrot in oil for 7 minutes. Stir in the broth, tomatoes, thyme and bay leaf. Bring to a boil. Reduce heat; cover and simmer for 30 minutes.

Stir in cabbage and beans; return to a boil. Reduce heat; cover and simmer for 10 minutes. Stir in turkey; simmer 5 minutes longer. Stir in the vinegar, salt and pepper; heat through. Discard bay leaf. **Yield:** 7 servings.

Nutritional Analysis: 1 cup equals 112 calories, 3 g fat (1 g saturated fat), 26 mg cholesterol, 550 mg sodium, 9 g carbohydrate, 3 g fiber, 12 g protein.
Diabetic Exchanges: *2 vegetable, 1 very lean meat, 1/2 fat.*

Corn Seafood Chowder

Prep: 30 min. **Cook:** 40 min.

I lightened up this recipe by using less oil and reduced-fat
milk. The original called for crabmeat, but my family
prefers it with shrimp and imitation crab instead.
—Naomi Tarr, Salisbury, Maryland

1-1/2 cups cubed peeled potatoes
  3/4 cup chopped green pepper
  3/4 cup diced celery
  1 medium onion, chopped
  1 tablespoon canola oil
  1 tablespoon butter
  4 teaspoons seafood seasoning
  1 bay leaf
  5 tablespoons all-purpose flour
  1 can (14-1/2 ounces) reduced-sodium
    chicken broth
  4 cups 2% milk
  2 cans (14-3/4 ounces *each*) cream-style corn

**1/2 pound uncooked small shrimp, peeled and
  deveined
1 package (8 ounces) imitation crabmeat, flaked**

In a large Dutch oven, cook the potatoes, green pepper, celery and onion in oil and butter over medium heat for 10 minutes or until onion is tender. Stir in seafood seasoning and bay leaf. Cook and stir for 2 minutes.

Add flour; stir until vegetables are coated. Gradually stir in the broth. Add milk and corn. Bring to a boil. Reduce heat; simmer, uncovered, for 10 minutes or until potatoes are tender. Stir in shrimp and crab; cook for 3 minutes or until shrimp turn pink. **Yield:** 11 servings.

Nutritional Analysis: 1 cup equals 200 calories, 5 g fat (2 g saturated fat), 54 mg cholesterol, 836 mg sodium, 29 g carbohydrate, 2 g fiber, 13 g protein.
Diabetic Exchanges: 1-1/2 starch, 1 lean meat, 1/2 reduced-fat milk.

Summer Soup

(Pictured at right)

Low-fat   Meatless

Prep: 15 min. + chilling

*Unlike many chilled soups, this one isn't pureed,
so you'll find plenty of chunky vegetable bits
in each savory spoonful.*
—Liz Fick, Litchville, North Dakota

**1 bottle (46 ounces) reduced-sodium V8 juice
2 cans (14-1/2 ounces *each*) Italian diced
  tomatoes, undrained
2 cans (5-1/2 ounces *each*) spicy hot V8 juice
1 medium green pepper, chopped
1 cup shredded carrots
1/2 cup chopped green onions
1/2 cup reduced-fat zesty Italian salad dressing
2 tablespoons lemon juice
1 tablespoon sugar
2 teaspoons Worcestershire sauce
1 garlic clove, minced
3/4 teaspoon celery salt
1/2 teaspoon salt**

In a large bowl, combine all of the ingredients. Cover and refrigerate soup for at least 2 hours before serving. **Yield:** 12 servings.

Nutritional Analysis: 1 cup equals 95 calories, 2 g fat (trace saturated fat), 0 cholesterol, 695 mg sodium, 16 g carbohydrate, 2 g fiber, 2 g protein.
Diabetic Exchanges: 3 vegetable, 1/2 fat.

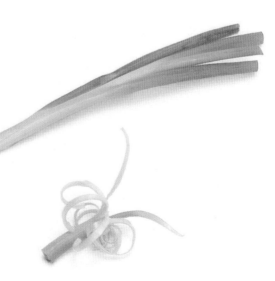

Turkey Pasta Soup

(Pictured below)

Prep/Total Time: 30 min.

*This quick soup has such great flavor that everyone
I've shared it with has added the recipe to her collection.*
—Marie Ewert, Richmond, Michigan

- 1 cup uncooked small pasta shells
- 1 pound lean ground turkey
- 2 medium onions, chopped
- 2 garlic cloves, minced
- 3 cans (14-1/2 ounces *each*) reduced-sodium chicken broth
- 2 cans (15 ounces *each*) white kidney *or* cannellini beans, rinsed and drained
- 2 cans (14-1/2 ounces *each*) Italian stewed tomatoes
- 2 teaspoons dried oregano
- 2 teaspoons dried basil
- 1 teaspoon fennel seed, crushed
- 1 teaspoon pepper
- 1/2 teaspoon salt
- 1/4 teaspoon crushed red pepper flakes

Cook pasta according to package directions. Meanwhile, in a Dutch oven or soup kettle, cook the turkey, onions and garlic over medium heat until meat is no longer pink; drain. Stir in the broth, beans, tomatoes and seasonings. Bring to a boil. Reduce heat; simmer, uncovered, for 10 minutes.

Drain pasta and add to the soup. Cook 5 minutes longer or until heated through. **Yield:** 10 servings.

Nutritional Analysis: 1-1/3 cups equals 211 calories, 4 g fat (1 g saturated fat), 36 mg cholesterol, 868 mg sodium, 28 g carbohydrate, 6 g fiber, 15 g protein.
Diabetic Exchanges: 2 very lean meat, 2 vegetable, 1 starch.

Italian Wedding Soup

Prep: 35 min. **Cook:** 20 min.

*I think this soup is absolutely delicious. Lean beef
and reduced-sodium broth help keep it light.*
—Paula Sullivan, Barker, New York

- 1 egg, lightly beaten
- 1 tablespoon dry bread crumbs
- 1 tablespoon dried parsley flakes
- 1 tablespoon plus 1/4 cup grated Parmesan cheese, *divided*
- 1/2 teaspoon onion powder
- 1/2 teaspoon salt, *divided*
- 1/8 teaspoon plus 1/4 teaspoon pepper, *divided*
- 1/2 pound lean ground beef
- 1/4 cup uncooked orzo *or* acini di pepe pasta
- 1 medium onion, finely chopped
- 3 celery ribs, chopped
- 2 garlic cloves, minced
- 1 tablespoon olive oil
- 4 cans (14-1/2 ounces *each*) reduced-sodium chicken broth
- 1 can (16 ounces) kidney beans, rinsed and drained
- 4 cups chopped fresh spinach

In a large bowl, combine the egg, bread crumbs, parsley, 1 tablespoon Parmesan cheese, onion powder, 1/4 teaspoon salt and 1/8 teaspoon pepper. Crumble beef over mixture and mix well. Shape into 42 meatballs. Place in a 15-in. x 10-in. x 1-in. baking pan coated with nonstick cooking spray. Bake at 350° for 8-10 minutes or until juices run clear; drain.

Cook pasta according to package directions; drain. In a large saucepan or soup kettle, saute the onion, celery and garlic in oil until tender. Stir in the chicken broth, beans and spinach. Stir in pasta, meatballs and remaining salt and

pepper. Cook until spinach is tender and meatballs are heated through. Garnish with remaining Parmesan cheese. **Yield:** 7 servings.

Nutritional Analysis: 1-1/3 cups equals 205 calories, 6 g fat (2 g saturated fat), 49 mg cholesterol, 1,024 mg sodium, 20 g carbohydrate, 4 g fiber, 17 g protein.
Diabetic Exchanges: 2 lean meat, 1 starch, 1 vegetable.

Chipotle Turkey Chili

(Pictured at right)

Prep: 25 min. **Cook:** 1-1/2 hours

I combined a few chili recipes I had and came up with this spicy, low-fat variety. It's great served with crusty rolls or baked tortilla chips.
—Christie Ladd, Mechanicsburg, Pennsylvania

  1 can (7 ounces) chipotle peppers in adobo sauce
1-1/4 pounds lean ground turkey
  3 medium carrots, chopped
  1 medium green pepper, chopped
1/2 cup chopped onion
  4 garlic cloves, minced
  1 can (28 ounces) crushed tomatoes
  1 can (14-1/2 ounces) reduced-sodium chicken broth
  1 can (8 ounces) tomato sauce
1-1/2 teaspoons dried oregano
1-1/2 teaspoons dried basil
  1 teaspoon chili powder
1/2 teaspoon ground cumin
  1 can (16 ounces) kidney beans, rinsed and drained
  1 can (15 ounces) garbanzo beans *or* chickpeas, rinsed and drained

Drain chipotle peppers; set aside 2 tablespoons adobo sauce. Seed and chop three peppers; set aside. (Save remaining peppers for another use.) In a large saucepan coated with nonstick cooking spray, cook the turkey, carrots, green pepper, onion, garlic and reserved peppers over medium heat until meat is no longer pink; drain. Stir in the next seven ingredients and reserved adobo sauce. Bring to a boil. Reduce heat; cover and simmer for 1 hour. Stir in the beans. Cover and simmer for 15-20 minutes or until heated through. **Yield:** 8 servings.

Editor's Note: When cutting or seeding hot peppers, use rubber or plastic gloves.

Nutritional Analysis: 1 cup equals 293 calories, 8 g fat (2 g saturated fat), 56 mg cholesterol, 844 mg sodium, 35 g carbohydrate, 9 g fiber, 22 g protein.
Diabetic Exchanges: 3 lean meat, 3 vegetable, 1 starch.

Spinach Vegetable Soup

Low-fat   Meatless

Prep: 15 min. **Cook:** 25 min.

Here's a thick soup that combines a bevy of fresh vegetables with fragrant herbs for unbeatable flavor.
—Jennifer Neilsen, Winterville, North Carolina

1/2 cup chopped onion
1/2 cup chopped celery
  1 tablespoon butter
  2 cans (14-1/2 ounces *each*) reduced-sodium chicken broth *or* vegetable broth
1-1/2 cups diced potatoes
  1 small turnip, peeled and chopped
  1 cup chopped carrot
1/2 cup chopped green pepper
  1 teaspoon *each* dried thyme, basil and rosemary, crushed
  1 teaspoon garlic powder
  1 teaspoon rubbed sage
1/2 teaspoon salt
1/4 teaspoon pepper
Dash to 1/8 teaspoon cayenne pepper
  2 packages (10 ounces *each*) frozen chopped spinach, thawed and well drained
  1 can (14-3/4 ounces) cream-style corn

In a Dutch oven, saute onion and celery in butter until tender. Add the broth, potatoes, turnip, carrot, green pepper and seasonings. Bring to a boil. Reduce heat; cover and simmer for 15-20 minutes or until vegetables are tender.

Stir in the spinach and corn; cool slightly. Puree half of the soup in a blender; return to the pan and heat through. **Yield:** 6 servings.

Nutritional Analysis: 1-1/3 cups equals 139 calories, 3 g fat (1 g saturated fat), 5 mg cholesterol, 788 mg sodium, 26 g carbohydrate, 6 g fiber, 7 g protein.
Diabetic Exchanges: 2 vegetable, 1 starch.

Harvest Corn Chicken Chowder

(Pictured above)

Prep: 20 min. **Cook:** 35 min.

With lots of chicken and ham, this lightened-up corn chowder has become a favorite at my house. I like to use sweet corn I grow myself.
—*Janet Boote, Hull, Iowa*

1/2 cup chopped onion
1/2 cup chopped sweet red pepper
2 garlic cloves, minced
1 tablespoon olive oil
1 cup cubed fully cooked ham
2 cups water
2 cups cubed red potatoes
1-1/2 cups fresh *or* frozen corn
1 teaspoon reduced-sodium chicken bouillon
   granules
3/4 teaspoon dried thyme
1/2 teaspoon poultry seasoning
1/2 teaspoon salt
1/4 teaspoon pepper
1 cup cubed cooked chicken breast
1 can (12 ounces) fat-free evaporated milk
3/4 cup 1% milk, *divided*
1/4 cup all-purpose flour

In a large saucepan, saute the onion, red pepper and garlic in oil until onion is tender. Add ham; cook and stir for 2 minutes. Stir in the water, potatoes, corn, bouillon, thyme, poultry seasoning, salt and pepper. Bring to a boil. Reduce heat; cover and simmer for 15 minutes or until potatoes are tender.

Add chicken; heat through. Stir in the evaporated milk and 1/2 cup milk; bring to a boil. Combine flour and remaining milk until smooth; gradually stir into soup. Cook and stir for 2 minutes or until thickened. **Yield:** 5 servings.

Nutritional Analysis: 1-1/3 cups equals 306 calories, 6 g fat (2 g saturated fat), 37 mg cholesterol, 763 mg sodium, 39 g carbohydrate, 3 g fiber, 25 g protein.
Diabetic Exchanges: 2 lean meat, 1-1/2 starch, 1 fat-free milk.

Spinach Lentil Soup

Low-fat Meatless

Prep: 15 min. **Cook:** 70 min.

You need just a few ingredients for this hearty soup. It's so easy and delicious. Add any other vegetables you'd like.
—*Sally Peters, Liverpool, New York*

1 cup shredded carrots
1 large onion, chopped
1 tablespoon olive oil
6 cups water
1 jar (16 ounces) salsa
1-1/4 cups dried lentils, rinsed
3/4 teaspoon salt
1 package (10 ounces) fresh spinach, torn

In a large saucepan or Dutch oven, saute carrots and onion in oil until tender. Add the water, salsa, lentils and salt. Bring to a boil. Reduce heat; cover and simmer for 50-60 minutes or until lentils are tender. Stir in spinach; simmer 5-10 minutes longer or until spinach is wilted. **Yield:** 6 servings.

Nutritional Analysis: 1-1/2 cups equals 208 calories, 3 g fat (trace saturated fat), 0 cholesterol, 696 mg sodium, 36 g carbohydrate, 20 g fiber, 18 g protein.
Diabetic Exchanges: 2 vegetable, 1 starch, 1 very lean meat, 1/2 fat.

Hidden Nutrition

HOMEMADE SOUPS are a great way to "disguise" new vegetables you'd like to introduce to your family. If a recipe is good to begin with, they usually won't even notice the healthy additions.
—*Cara Neth, Fort Collins, Colorado*

Favorite Recipe Made Lighter

CREAM OF TOMATO SOUP is a surefire chill chaser for Linda Parkhurst of Brooklyn, Michigan. She asked our Test Kitchen staff to lighten up her favorite recipe, and velvety Makeover Cream of Tomato Soup is the warm-you-up result.

Cream of Tomato Soup

Meatless

Prep/Total Time: 30 min.

1 can (14-1/2 ounces) stewed tomatoes
4 ounces cream cheese, cubed
1 medium onion, chopped
2 garlic cloves, minced
1/4 cup butter
3 cans (10-3/4 ounces *each*) condensed tomato soup, undiluted
2 cans (11-1/2 ounces *each*) V8 juice
1 cup half-and-half cream
1/2 teaspoon dried basil
SEASONED OYSTER CRACKERS:
3 cups oyster crackers
1/3 cup canola oil
1 tablespoon ranch salad dressing mix
1/2 teaspoon garlic powder
1/2 teaspoon dill weed
9 tablespoons shredded mozzarella cheese

In a food processor or blender, combine stewed tomatoes and cream cheese; cover and process until smooth. Set aside. In a large saucepan, saute onion and garlic in butter. Whisk in tomato soup and V8 until blended. Gradually stir in cream cheese mixture, cream and basil. Cook and stir until heated through (do not boil).

In a large bowl, combine the crackers, oil, dressing mix, garlic powder and dill; toss to coat. Ladle soup into bowls; sprinkle with crackers and mozzarella cheese. **Yield:** 9 servings (3 cups crackers).

Nutritional Analysis: 1 cup soup with 1/3 cup oyster crackers equals 387 calories, 24 g fat (10 g saturated fat), 46 mg cholesterol, 1,260 mg sodium, 36 g carbohydrate, 3 g fiber, 7 g protein.

Makeover Cream of Tomato Soup

Meatless

(Pictured at right and on page 29)

Prep/Total Time: 30 min.

1 can (14-1/2 ounces) stewed tomatoes
4 ounces reduced-fat cream cheese, cubed
1 medium onion, chopped
2 garlic cloves, minced
2 tablespoons butter
3 cans (10-3/4 ounces *each*) reduced-fat reduced-sodium condensed tomato soup, undiluted
4 cans (5-1/2 ounces *each*) reduced-sodium V8 juice
3 tablespoons tomato paste
1 cup fat-free half-and-half
1/2 teaspoon dried basil
SEASONED OYSTER CRACKERS:
3 cups oyster crackers
2 tablespoons canola oil
1 tablespoon ranch salad dressing mix
1/2 teaspoon garlic powder
1/2 teaspoon dill weed
9 tablespoons shredded part-skim mozzarella cheese

In a food processor or blender, combine stewed tomatoes and cream cheese; cover and process until smooth. Set aside. In a large saucepan, saute onion and garlic in butter. Whisk in tomato soup, V8 and tomato paste until blended. Gradually stir in cream cheese mixture, half-and-half and basil. Cook and stir until heated through (do not boil).

In a large bowl, combine the oyster crackers, oil, dressing mix, garlic powder and dill; toss to coat. Ladle soup into bowls; sprinkle with crackers and mozzarella cheese. **Yield:** 9 servings (3 cups crackers).

Nutritional Analysis: 1 cup soup with 1/3 cup oyster crackers equals 303 calories, 12 g fat (5 g saturated fat), 20 mg cholesterol, 893 mg sodium, 39 g carbohydrate, 3 g fiber, 8 g protein.
Diabetic Exchanges: 2-1/2 starch, 2 fat.

Carrot Soup

Low-fat Meatless

Prep: 20 min. **Cook:** 35 min.

Fat-free half-and-half gives velvety flair to this colorful recipe. The soup is especially satisfying on cold days.
—Barbara Richard, Houston, Ohio

- 3/4 cup finely chopped onion
- 3 garlic cloves, minced
- 2 teaspoons olive oil
- 3 cans (14-1/2 ounces *each*) reduced-sodium chicken broth *or* vegetable broth
- 6 cups sliced carrots (about 2-1/2 pounds)
- 3/4 cup cubed peeled potatoes
- 1 teaspoon salt
- 1 teaspoon dried thyme
- 1/4 teaspoon pepper
- 1 bay leaf
- 1 cup fat-free half-and-half

In a large saucepan, saute onion and garlic in oil until tender. Add the broth, carrots, potatoes, salt, thyme, pepper and bay leaf. Bring to a boil. Reduce heat; cover and simmer for 20-30 minutes or until vegetables are very tender.

Remove from the heat; cool slightly. Discard bay leaf. In a blender, puree carrot mixture in batches. Return to the pan. Stir in half-and-half; heat through (do not boil). **Yield:** 6 servings.

Nutritional Analysis: 1-1/3 cups equals 133 calories, 2 g fat (trace saturated fat), 0 cholesterol, 995 mg sodium, 24 g carbohydrate, 5 g fiber, 6 g protein.
Diabetic Exchanges: 3 vegetable, 1/2 starch, 1/2 fat.

Lentil-Barley Ham Soup

Prep: 15 min. **Cook:** 70 min.

This hearty veggie-and-herb soup is light and easy to prepare yet still has all the delicious taste of my grandmother's original recipe.
—Priscilla Gilbert, Indian Harbour Beach, Florida

- 1/2 cup chopped onion
- 1/2 cup chopped celery
- 1 garlic clove, minced
- 1 tablespoon butter
- 4 cups reduced-sodium chicken broth
- 1/2 cup dried lentils, rinsed
- 1/2 teaspoon *each* dried basil, oregano and rosemary, crushed
- 1/4 teaspoon pepper
- 1-1/2 cups cubed fully cooked lean ham
- 3/4 cup sliced fresh carrots
- 1/2 cup quick-cooking barley
- 1 can (14-1/2 ounces) diced tomatoes, undrained

In a large saucepan, saute the onion, celery and garlic in butter until tender. Stir in the broth, lentils, basil, oregano, rosemary and pepper. Bring to a boil. Reduce heat; cover and simmer for 20 minutes.

Add the ham and carrots. Cover and simmer 10 minutes longer. Return to a boil; stir in the barley. Reduce heat; cover and simmer for 15 minutes or until barley and lentils are tender. Stir in tomatoes; heat through. **Yield:** 5 servings.

Nutritional Analysis: 1-1/3 cups equals 247 calories, 5 g fat (2 g saturated fat), 22 mg cholesterol, 1,172 mg sodium, 33 g carbohydrate, 12 g fiber, 19 g protein.
Diabetic Exchanges: 2 lean meat, 1-1/2 starch, 1 vegetable.

Old-Fashioned Turkey Noodle Soup

(Pictured at right)

Prep: 3-1/2 hours + chilling **Cook:** 45 min.

Our Test Kitchen created this down-home soup to make the most of leftover turkey. Roasting the turkey bones, garlic and vegetables adds richness and depth to the flavor without additional fats.

BROTH:
- 1 leftover turkey carcass (from a 12- to 14-pound turkey)
- 2 cooked turkey wings, meat removed
- 2 cooked turkey drumsticks, meat removed
- 1 turkey neck bone
- 1 medium unpeeled onion, cut into wedges
- 2 small unpeeled carrots, cut into chunks
- 6 to 8 garlic cloves, peeled
- 4 quarts plus 1 cup cold water, *divided*

SOUP:
- 3 quarts water
- 5 cups uncooked egg noodles
- 2 cups diced carrots
- 2 cups diced celery
- 3 cups cubed cooked turkey
- 1/4 cup minced fresh parsley
- 2-1/2 teaspoons salt
- 2 teaspoons dried thyme
- 1 teaspoon pepper

🍎 Skim the Fat

TO COOL a large quantity of broth quickly, first place the pot in an ice-water bath in the sink. Moving the broth straight from the stovetop into the refrigerator without this cooling bath extends the cooling time and increases the temperature inside your refrigerator. Both situations can create food-safety problems.

After the broth has been refrigerated overnight, any fat rises to the top. Remove and discard the fat by skimming it from the top of the broth with a large spoon.

2 teaspoons Italian seasoning
3/4 teaspoon salt
1/2 cup uncooked elbow macaroni

In a Dutch oven, cook the beef, onion and garlic over medium heat until meat is no longer pink; drain. Add the water, tomatoes, zucchini, beans, corn, cabbage, celery, bouillon, Italian seasoning and salt; bring to a boil. Add macaroni. Reduce heat; cover and simmer for 15 minutes or until macaroni is tender. **Yield:** 9 servings (about 3 quarts).

Nutritional Analysis: 1-1/2 cups equals 194 calories, 4 g fat (2 g saturated fat), 25 mg cholesterol, 714 mg sodium, 25 g carbohydrate, 6 g fiber, 15 g protein.
Diabetic Exchanges: 2 vegetable, 1 starch, 1 lean meat.

Creamy Split Pea Soup

Low-fat   Meatless

Prep: 15 min. **Cook:** 1-1/2 hours

I love this simple soup. Because it's so creamy, people are surprised to learn that it has only 1 gram of fat per serving.
—*Tracy Fay, Redmond, Oregon*

    1 medium onion, chopped
    1 cup chopped celery
    9 cups water
    1 package (16 ounces) dried green split peas
    2 cups cubed peeled sweet potatoes
    1 bay leaf
1-1/2 teaspoons salt
    1 teaspoon dried thyme
    1/2 teaspoon pepper

In a large saucepan coated with nonstick cooking spray, cook onion and celery until tender. Stir in the water, peas, sweet potatoes, bay leaf, salt, thyme and pepper. Bring to a boil. Reduce heat; cover and simmer for 70-80 minutes or until peas are tender.

Remove from the heat; cool slightly. Discard bay leaf. In a blender, puree soup in batches. Return to the pan; heat through. **Yield:** 10 servings.

Nutritional Analysis: 1-1/3 cups equals 191 calories, 1 g fat (trace saturated fat), 0 cholesterol, 375 mg sodium, 36 g carbohydrate, 13 g fiber, 12 g protein.
Diabetic Exchanges: 2 starch, 1 very lean meat.

Place the turkey carcass, bones from wings and drumsticks, neck bone, onion, carrots and garlic in a 15-in. x 10-in. x 1-in. baking pan coated with nonstick cooking spray. Bake, uncovered, at 400° for 1 hour, turning once.

Transfer the carcass, bones and vegetables to an 8-qt. soup kettle. Add 4 qts. cold water; set aside. Pour remaining cold water into baking pan, stirring to loosen browned bits. Add to kettle. Bring to a boil. Reduce heat; cover and simmer for 3-4 hours.

Cool slightly. Strain broth; discard bones and vegetables. Set soup kettle in an ice-water bath until cooled, stirring occasionally. Cover and refrigerate overnight.

Skim fat from broth. Cover and bring to a boil. Reduce heat to a simmer. Meanwhile, in a Dutch oven, bring 3 qts. water to a boil. Add noodles and carrots; cook for 4 minutes. Add celery; cook 5-7 minutes longer or until noodles and vegetables are tender. Drain; add to simmering broth. Add cubed turkey; heat through. Stir in the parsley, salt, thyme and pepper. **Yield:** 10 servings (about 4 quarts).

Nutritional Analysis: 1-1/2 cups equals 188 calories, 4 g fat (1 g saturated fat), 69 mg cholesterol, 663 mg sodium, 17 g carbohydrate, 2 g fiber, 20 g protein.
Diabetic Exchanges: 2 lean meat, 1 starch.

Hamburger Minestrone

Prep/Total Time: 30 min.

This hearty soup is filled with Italian seasoning, vegetables, ground beef and macaroni.
—*Maudie Breen, Salt Lake City, Utah*

    1 pound lean ground beef
    1/2 cup chopped onion
    1 garlic clove, minced
    6 cups water
    1 can (28 ounces) diced tomatoes, undrained
1-1/2 cups sliced zucchini
    1 can (16 ounces) kidney beans, rinsed and drained
1-1/2 cups frozen whole kernel corn, thawed
    1 cup shredded cabbage
    1 celery rib with leaves, chopped
    2 teaspoons beef bouillon granules

🍎 Cooking with Split Peas

KEEP the following in mind when preparing recipes with split peas:

- Split peas don't need to be pre-soaked. Just rinse the peas and sort through them, discarding any pebbles or debris that may be in the package.
- For every 1 cup of plain, dried split peas, you need 2 cups of liquid for proper cooking. Bring the peas and liquid to a boil and cook for about 30 minutes or until the peas reach desired tenderness; drain.
- One cup of dried peas will yield 2 cups cooked.
- Just 1/4 cup of cooked peas contains 130 calories, less than 1 g fat, 10 g fiber and 8 g protein.

Try Something New: Fresh Kale

SHAKE UP your supper time routine with a leafy green guaranteed to grab everyone's attention—kale. With its earthy and sometimes peppery flavor, kale makes an exciting replacement for spinach in a variety of dishes.

A member of the cabbage family, kale has a rich assertive flavor. Some enjoy it mixed into a salad with other greens, but most prefer it sauteed as a side dish or simmered in soups, sauces and stews. Many cooks work the greens into their omelet, lasagna or meat loaf recipes, and some even top pizza with it.

A Keen Green

Kale is a powerhouse of nutrients. In fact, it's the most nutritious green of them all. Low-calorie kale is an excellent source of:

- vitamins A and C.
- manganese, fiber, calcium and copper.
- phytochemicals that can help protect against cancer.
- carotenoids that promote good vision.

In addition to a wide array of health benefits, kale is grown in several colors. Very ornamental kale is often called salad savoy. In general, bright green curly-leaved kale is the best for cooking and eating.

You can purchase kale year-round, but it is at its peak during cold-weather months. Select delicate kale leaves that are moist yet crisp. The smaller the leaves, the better. Stems should be plump but not withered.

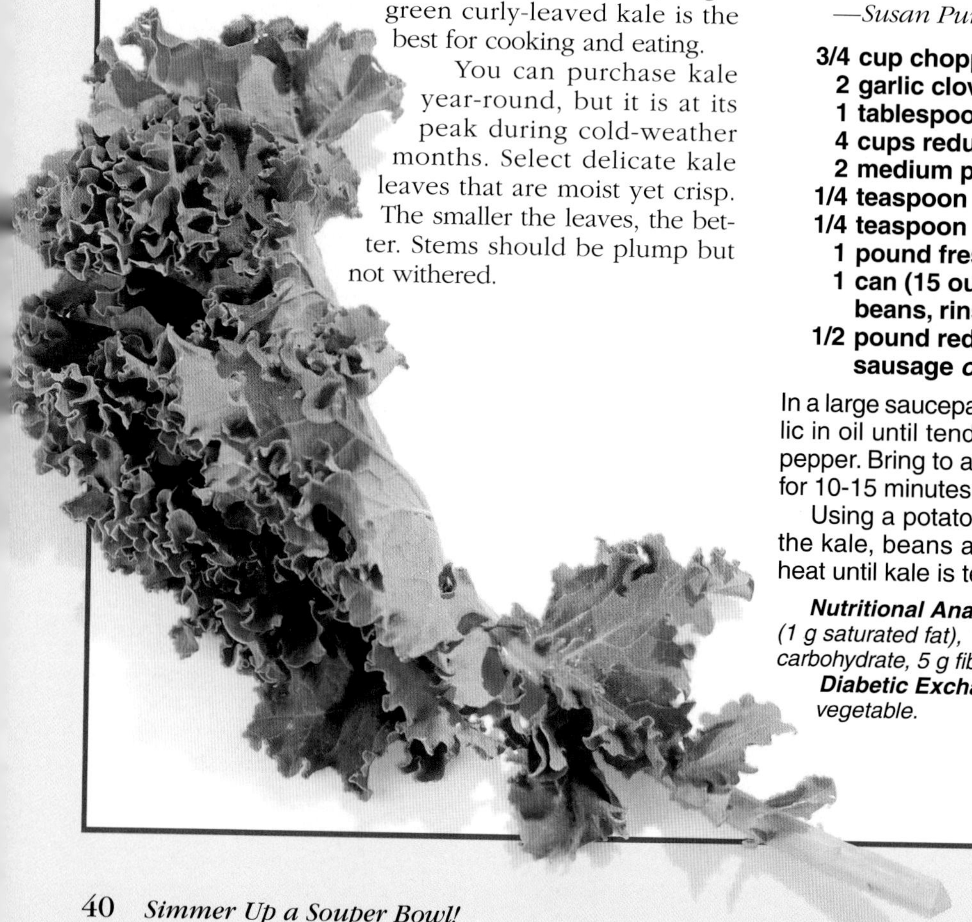

You've Got Kale

Like spinach, kale is simple to prepare as a side dish.
1. Wash the leaves by submerging them in cool water.
2. Trim away the stem.
3. Blanch or cook the leaves in water to mellow their flavor and soften their texture.
4. Saute the leaves, adding your choice of seasonings.

You'll be surprised at the variations you can create by adding other vegetables and herbs to sauteed kale. Or, use kale in place of the fresh spinach called for in a casserole or stir-fry. And for a surefire success, try the following heart-smart reader recipe.

Sausage Kale Soup

(Pictured at right)

Prep: 10 min. **Cook:** 25 min.

When autumn hits, I simmer up this quick comforting soup. Hearty sausage slices, beans and tasty kale are guaranteed to have your gang asking for second helpings.
—*Susan Pursell, Fountain Valley, California*

3/4 cup chopped onion
 2 garlic cloves, minced
 1 tablespoon olive oil
 4 cups reduced-sodium chicken broth
 2 medium potatoes, peeled and cubed
1/4 teaspoon salt
1/4 teaspoon pepper
 1 pound fresh kale, trimmed and chopped
 1 can (15 ounces) white kidney *or* cannellini beans, rinsed and drained
1/2 pound reduced-fat fully cooked Polish sausage *or* turkey kielbasa, sliced

In a large saucepan or Dutch oven, saute onion and garlic in oil until tender. Add the broth, potatoes, salt and pepper. Bring to a boil. Reduce heat; cover and simmer for 10-15 minutes or until potatoes are tender.

Using a potato masher, mash potatoes slightly. Add the kale, beans and sausage; cook over medium-low heat until kale is tender. **Yield:** 7 servings.

Nutritional Analysis: 1 cup equals 194 calories, 4 g fat (1 g saturated fat), 14 mg cholesterol, 823 mg sodium, 28 g carbohydrate, 5 g fiber, 11 g protein.
Diabetic Exchanges: 1-1/2 starch, 1 lean meat, 1 vegetable.

shrimp; cook about 7 minutes longer or until fish flakes easily with a fork and shrimp turn pink. Place rice in individual serving bowls; top with gumbo. **Yield:** 12 servings.

Nutritional Analysis: 1 cup gumbo with 1/4 cup rice equals 180 calories, 5 g fat (1 g saturated fat), 60 mg cholesterol, 512 mg sodium, 22 g carbohydrate, 3 g fiber, 14 g protein.
Diabetic Exchanges: 2 very lean meat, 2 vegetable, 1 starch.

French Sweet Onion Soup

Prep: 25 min. **Cook:** 1 hour

Though I prefer sweet Vidalia onions, I have used every kind of onion in this delicious soup and always achieved wonderful results. I've even added mushrooms, and it was still well-received by family and friends.
—*Marion Lowery, Medford, Oregon*

    1 tablespoon butter
    1 tablespoon olive oil
    5 large sweet onions, sliced
    2 cans (14-1/2 ounces *each*) reduced-sodium
       beef broth
1-2/3 cups water
1-1/4 cups apple cider *or* juice
    1 bay leaf
  1/2 teaspoon dried thyme
  1/4 teaspoon salt
  1/4 teaspoon pepper
    7 slices French bread (1/2 inch thick)
  3/4 cup grated reduced-fat Swiss cheese
  1/4 cup grated Parmesan cheese

In a Dutch oven or large kettle, melt butter. Add olive oil and onions. Cover and cook over low heat until onions are soft, about 30 minutes, stirring occasionally. Stir in the beef broth, water, cider or juice, bay leaf, thyme, salt and pepper. Bring to a boil; reduce heat. Cover and simmer for 20 minutes. Discard bay leaf.

Arrange bread on a broiler pan; broil and turn until each side is golden brown. Ladle soup into ovenproof soup bowls. Float a slice of bread in each bowl, sprinkle with Swiss cheese and top with Parmesan. Broil bowls 6 in. from heat until cheese is melted and bubbly. Serve immediately. **Yield:** 7 servings.

Nutritional Analysis: 1-1/4 cups soup with 1 slice of cheese-topped bread equals 256 calories, 9 g fat (4 g saturated fat), 16 mg cholesterol, 483 mg sodium, 35 g carbohydrate, 4 g fiber, 10 g protein.
Diabetic Exchanges: 3 vegetable, 1 starch, 1 lean meat, 1 fat, 1/2 fruit.

Southern Seafood Gumbo

(Pictured above)

Prep: 25 min. **Cook:** 25 min.

I enjoyed a similar gumbo at a local restaurant and duplicated it pretty closely. I lightened it up a bit, but no one in my family seemed to mind.
—*Susan Wright, Champaign, Illinois*

    1 medium onion, chopped
    2 celery ribs with leaves, chopped
    1 medium green pepper, chopped
    3 garlic cloves, minced
    1 tablespoon olive oil
    1 bottle (46 ounces) spicy hot V8 juice
    1 can (14-1/2 ounces) diced tomatoes, undrained
  1/4 teaspoon cayenne pepper
    1 package (16 ounces) frozen sliced okra, thawed
    1 pound catfish fillets, cut into 3/4-inch cubes
  3/4 pound uncooked medium shrimp, peeled and
       deveined
    3 cups cooked long grain rice

In a large saucepan, saute the onion, celery, green pepper and garlic in oil until tender. Stir in the V8 juice, tomatoes and cayenne; bring to a boil. Reduce heat; cover and simmer for 10 minutes.

Stir in okra and catfish; cook 8 minutes longer. Add the

Wintertime Beef Soup

(Pictured above)

Prep: 10 min. **Cook:** 55 min.

Kidney beans, ground beef, green pepper and chopped cabbage make this thick soup hearty and satisfying.
—*Carol Tupper, Joplin, Missouri*

- 1 pound lean ground beef
- 4 celery ribs, coarsely chopped
- 1 medium onion, coarsely chopped
- 1 medium green pepper, coarsely chopped
- 1 garlic clove, minced
- 2 cups water
- 2 cups reduced-sodium tomato juice
- 1 can (14-1/2 ounces) diced tomatoes, undrained
- 1 can (8 ounces) tomato sauce
- 2 teaspoons reduced-sodium beef bouillon granules
- 2 teaspoons chili powder
- 1/2 teaspoon salt
- 2 cans (16 ounces *each*) kidney beans, rinsed and drained
- 2 cups coarsely chopped cabbage

In a large saucepan or Dutch oven, cook the beef, celery, onion, green pepper and garlic over medium heat until meat is no longer pink; drain. Stir in the water, tomato juice, tomatoes, tomato sauce, bouillon, chili powder and salt. Bring to a boil. Reduce heat; cover and simmer for 30 minutes.

Stir in kidney beans; return to a boil. Stir in cabbage. Reduce heat; cover and cook 12 minutes longer or until cabbage is tender. **Yield:** 8 servings.

Nutritional Analysis: 1-2/3 cups equals 238 calories, 4 g fat (2 g saturated fat), 28 mg cholesterol, 703 mg sodium, 30 g carbohydrate, 8 g fiber, 20 g protein.
Diabetic Exchanges: 2 lean meat, 2 vegetable, 1 starch.

Cream of Butternut Soup

(Pictured above)

Prep: 35 min. **Cook:** 30 min.

Ginger, turmeric, cinnamon and a little sherry deliciously season this slightly sweet creation.
—*Shelly Snyder, Lafayette, Colorado*

1 cup chopped onion
2 celery ribs, chopped
2 tablespoons butter
2 cans (14-1/2 ounces *each*) reduced-sodium
   chicken broth
1 teaspoon sugar
1 bay leaf
1/2 teaspoon salt
1/2 teaspoon ground ginger
1/2 teaspoon ground turmeric
1/4 teaspoon ground cinnamon

1 butternut squash (2-1/2 pounds), peeled
   and cubed
3 medium potatoes, peeled and cubed
1-1/2 cups 1% milk
2 tablespoons sherry *or* additional
   reduced-sodium chicken broth

In a large saucepan coated with nonstick cooking spray, cook onion and celery in butter until tender. Stir in the broth, sugar, bay leaf, salt, ginger, turmeric and cinnamon. Add the squash and potatoes. Bring to a boil. Reduce heat; cover and simmer for 15-20 minutes or until vegetables are tender.

Remove from the heat; cool slightly. Discard bay leaf. In a blender, puree vegetable mixture in batches. Return to the pan. Stir in milk and sherry or broth; heat through (do not boil). **Yield:** 8 servings.

Nutritional Analysis: 1-1/4 cups equals 159 calories, 4 g fat (2 g saturated fat), 10 mg cholesterol, 487 mg sodium, 29 g carbohydrate, 6 g fiber, 5 g protein.
Diabetic Exchanges: 2 starch, 1/2 fat.

Step Up to The Salad Bar

Whether you're looking for a standout side dish to accompany a main course, a tangy take-along for the neighborhood barbecue or an appealing addition to your lunchtime lineup, nothing beats garden-fresh salads!

Walnut Green Bean Salad (page 67)

Spicy Pork Tenderloin Salad

(Pictured below)

Prep: 20 min. **Cook:** 35 min.

A friend served this curry-flavored salad at a luncheon, and I tweaked it to fit our tastes. Since it's a meal in one, it's perfect for weeknights and entertaining.
—Pat Sellon, Monticello, Wisconsin

4-1/2 teaspoons lime juice
1-1/2 teaspoons orange juice
1-1/2 teaspoons Dijon mustard
  1/2 teaspoon curry powder
  1/4 teaspoon salt
  1/8 teaspoon pepper
    2 tablespoons olive oil
SPICE RUB:
  1/2 teaspoon salt
  1/2 teaspoon ground cumin
  1/2 teaspoon ground cinnamon
  1/2 teaspoon chili powder
  1/4 teaspoon pepper
    1 pork tenderloin (1 pound)
    2 teaspoons olive oil
  1/3 cup packed brown sugar
    1 tablespoon minced garlic
1-1/2 teaspoons hot pepper sauce
    1 package (6 ounces) fresh baby spinach

In a bowl, whisk the first six ingredients; gradually whisk in oil. Cover and refrigerate vinaigrette. Combine the salt, cumin, cinnamon, chili powder and pepper; rub over meat.
  In an ovenproof skillet, brown meat on all sides in oil,

Crunchy Peanut Coleslaw

(Pictured above)

Low-carb *Meatless*

Prep/Total Time: 20 min.

When entertaining my large family, I frequently serve this nutty and tangy salad.
—Judy Madsen, Ellis, Idaho

    1 cup (8 ounces) reduced-fat sour cream
  1/2 cup fat-free mayonnaise
    1 tablespoon sugar
    1 tablespoon tarragon vinegar
  1/2 teaspoon salt
  1/4 teaspoon white pepper
    4 cups finely chopped cabbage
    1 cup coarsely chopped cauliflower
    1 cup chopped celery
  1/4 cup finely chopped onion
  1/4 cup chopped green pepper
  1/4 cup finely chopped cucumber
  1/2 cup chopped peanuts

Combine the sour cream, mayonnaise, sugar, vinegar, salt and pepper; stir until blended. In a large bowl, combine the cabbage, cauliflower, celery, onion, green pepper and cucumber. Pour dressing over vegetables; toss to coat. Sprinkle with peanuts. **Yield:** 8 servings.

  Nutritional Analysis: 3/4 cup equals 121 calories, 7 g fat (2 g saturated fat), 12 mg cholesterol, 323 mg sodium, 14 g carbohydrate, 3 g fiber, 4 g protein.
  Diabetic Exchanges: 1 vegetable, 1 fat, 1/2 starch.

about 8 minutes. Combine the brown sugar, garlic and hot pepper sauce; spread over meat. Bake at 350° for 25-35 minutes or until a meat thermometer reads 160°. Let stand for 5 minutes before slicing.

Toss spinach with vinaigrette. Arrange spinach on four salad plates; top with sliced pork. Drizzle with pan juices. **Yield:** 4 servings.

Nutritional Analysis: 3 ounces cooked pork with 1-3/4 cups spinach equals 301 calories, 13 g fat (3 g saturated fat), 63 mg cholesterol, 591 mg sodium, 22 g carbohydrate, 2 g fiber, 24 g protein.

Diabetic Exchanges: 3 lean meat, 1 starch, 1 vegetable, 1/2 fat.

Tarragon Tuna Salad

(Pictured above)

Low-carb

Prep/Total Time: 10 min.

It's surprising how a few herbs can brighten up tuna salad. Made with reduced-fat mayonnaise, this version gets zip from mustard. It makes a great light lunch or Sunday brunch item.
—Billie Moss, El Sobrante, California

2 cans (6 ounces *each*) light water-packed tuna, drained and flaked
1 cup chopped celery
1/4 cup chopped sweet onion
1/3 cup reduced-fat mayonnaise
2 tablespoons minced fresh parsley
1 tablespoon lemon juice
1 teaspoon minced fresh tarragon *or* 1/4 teaspoon dried tarragon
1/2 teaspoon Dijon mustard
1/4 teaspoon white pepper
Lettuce leaves, optional

In a small bowl, combine the tuna, celery and onion. Combine the mayonnaise, parsley, lemon juice, tarragon, mustard and pepper. Stir into tuna mixture. Serve on lettuce leaves if desired. **Yield:** 4 servings.

Nutritional Analysis: 2/3 cup equals 169 calories, 7 g fat (1 g saturated fat), 31 mg cholesterol, 467 mg sodium, 4 g carbohydrate, 1 g fiber, 21 g protein.

Diabetic Exchanges: 3 very lean meat, 1 fat.

Carrot Bean Salad

Low-fat   Meatless

Prep: 20 min. + chilling

My husband and I spend most summer days working in our gardens, so I like dinner dishes that are healthy and easy. I created this salad when cilantro was taking over our herb garden.
—Virginia Arendt, Green Bay, Wisconsin

  2 cups thinly sliced carrots
  1 can (15 ounces) garbanzo beans *or* chickpeas, rinsed and drained
  1 cup thinly sliced celery
  2 tablespoons lemon juice
  2 teaspoons olive oil
  1/2 teaspoon lemon-pepper seasoning
  1/4 teaspoon salt
  1/2 cup minced fresh cilantro

Place carrots in a steamer basket; place in a saucepan over 1 in. of water. Bring to a boil; cover and steam for 5-6 minutes or until crisp-tender. Immediately place carrots in a bowl of ice water. In another bowl, combine the garbanzo beans and celery. Drain carrots and add to bean mixture.

In a small bowl, whisk the lemon juice, oil, lemon-pepper and salt. Pour over carrot mixture and toss to coat. Cover and refrigerate for at least 4 hours. Just before serving, stir in cilantro. **Yield:** 6 servings.

Nutritional Analysis: 3/4 cup equals 103 calories, 3 g fat (trace saturated fat), 0 cholesterol, 263 mg sodium, 17 g carbohydrate, 4 g fiber, 3 g protein.
Diabetic Exchanges: 1 starch, 1 vegetable.

Broccoli Tortellini Salad

(Pictured at right)

Prep: 25 min. + chilling

After tasting this wonderful side dish at a potluck, I had to have more, so I experimented with lightening it up. It ended up tasting as good as the original.
—Tiffany Anderson-Taylor, Gulfport, Florida

  4 cups broccoli florets
  2 packages (9 ounces *each*) refrigerated cheese tortellini
  1/2 cup finely chopped red onion
  1/4 cup raisins
  1/2 cup reduced-fat mayonnaise
Sugar substitute equivalent to 3 tablespoons sugar
  1 tablespoon cider vinegar
  5 slices bacon, cooked and crumbled
  1/4 cup unsalted sunflower kernels

In a large saucepan, cook broccoli in 6 cups boiling water for 2 minutes. Drain and immediately rinse in cold water. In the same saucepan, cook tortellini according to package directions. Drain and immediately rinse in cold water.

In a large bowl, combine the red onion, raisins, broccoli and tortellini. Combine the mayonnaise, sugar substitute and vinegar. Pour over tortellini mixture; toss to coat. Refriger-

ate for at least 1 hour. Just before serving, stir in bacon and sunflower kernels. **Yield:** 12 servings.

Editor's Note: This recipe was tested with Splenda No Calorie Sweetener.

Nutritional Analysis: 2/3 cup equals 217 calories, 10 g fat (3 g saturated fat), 24 mg cholesterol, 287 mg sodium, 25 g carbohydrate, 2 g fiber, 8 g protein.
Diabetic Exchanges: 1-1/2 starch, 1 lean meat, 1 fat.

Chicken and Pineapple Salad

(Pictured at right)

Prep: 25 min. **Cook:** 15 min. + chilling

This salad takes a little time, but it is truly worth the few extra steps. It has been a family favorite for years and makes a nice summer lunch...or a fun first course for an oriental vegetable stir-fry.
—Diane Sparrow, Osage, Iowa

  2 tablespoons sugar
  1 tablespoon cornstarch
  1/2 teaspoon salt
  1/4 cup unsweetened pineapple juice
  1/4 cup chicken broth
  2 tablespoons plus 1-1/2 teaspoons white vinegar
  1 tablespoon reduced-sodium soy sauce
  1 teaspoon canola oil
SALAD:
  1 pound boneless skinless chicken breasts, cut into 1/2-inch strips
  2 teaspoons reduced-sodium soy sauce
  1/2 teaspoon finely chopped fresh gingerroot *or* 1/8 teaspoon ground ginger
  2 teaspoons canola oil
  1 medium cucumber, quartered, seeded and thinly sliced
  1 large red onion, quartered and thinly sliced
  1 celery rib, thinly sliced
Lettuce leaves, optional
  5 pineapple slices, halved
  2 tablespoons sesame seeds, toasted

In a saucepan, combine the sugar, cornstarch and salt. Gradually add the pineapple juice, broth, vinegar, soy sauce and oil until smooth. Bring to a boil; cook and stir for 2 minutes or until thickened. Cover and refrigerate.

In a large bowl, toss chicken with soy sauce and ginger. In a large nonstick skillet, saute chicken in oil until no longer pink. Remove from the heat and allow to cool. Combine the cucumber, onion, celery and chicken. Pour chilled sauce over chicken; toss to coat.

Just before serving, line salad plates with lettuce if desired. Arrange chicken salad and pineapple over lettuce. Sprinkle with sesame seeds. **Yield:** 5 servings.

Nutritional Analysis: 1 cup equals 220 calories, 6 g fat (1 g saturated fat), 53 mg cholesterol, 552 mg sodium, 19 g carbohydrate, 2 g fiber, 23 g protein.
Diabetic Exchanges: 3 lean meat, 1 fruit, 1 vegetable.

Spicy Citrus Gelatin Mold

Low-fat

Prep: 30 min. + chilling

This dish is delicious served with ham. The creamy orange dressing makes this gelatin extra special.
—*Joan Hallford, North Richland Hills, Texas*

  2 cans (11 ounces *each*) reduced-sugar mandarin oranges
  1 cinnamon stick (3 inches)
  8 whole cloves
  1/8 teaspoon salt
  1 package (.3 ounce) sugar-free lemon gelatin
  1 package (.3 ounce) sugar-free orange gelatin
  1 cup cranberry juice
  1/8 cup lemon juice
DRESSING:
  1 cup (8 ounces) fat-free sour cream
  1 tablespoon orange juice
  1 tablespoon honey
  2 teaspoons grated orange peel
  1/8 teaspoon salt

Drain oranges, reserving juice; set oranges aside. Add enough water to juice to measure 2-1/2 cups; pour into a large saucepan. Add the cinnamon stick, cloves and salt. Bring to a boil. Reduce heat; cover and simmer for 10 minutes. Cool slightly. Strain liquid; discard spices.

Return the liquid to the pan and return to a boil. In a large bowl, combine the lemon and orange gelatins; add boiling liquid and stir until dissolved. Stir in the cranberry and lemon juices. Cover and refrigerate until syrupy, about 45 minutes. Fold in the mandarin oranges. Transfer to a 1-1/2-qt. mold coated with nonstick cooking spray. Cover and refrigerate until firm.

In a small bowl, combine dressing ingredients. Unmold gelatin onto a serving platter; serve with dressing. **Yield:** 8 servings.

Nutritional Analysis: 1 serving with 2 tablespoons dressing equals 117 calories, trace fat (trace saturated fat), 4 mg cholesterol, 154 mg sodium, 26 g carbohydrate, 1 g fiber, 3 g protein.
Diabetic Exchanges: 1 fruit, 1/2 starch.

Asparagus 'n' Vinaigrette

(Pictured above)

Low-carb *Meatless*

Prep: 20 min. + chilling

Living in the Midwest, we anticipate spring treats like fresh asparagus all winter long. Our three small children can't help but snitch a taste when this dish is chilling in the fridge. I use the vinaigrette dressing on salads, sliced tomatoes and other steamed vegetables as well.
—*Mickey Kelly, Burnsville, Minnesota*

  2 pounds fresh asparagus, trimmed and cut
    into 2-inch pieces
  2 green onions, thinly sliced
  2 tablespoons olive oil
  2 tablespoons red wine vinegar
1/2 teaspoon reduced-sodium teriyaki sauce
1/2 teaspoon sugar
1/2 teaspoon salt
1/8 teaspoon pepper

Place asparagus in a steamer basket. Place in a saucepan over 1 in. of water; bring to a boil. Cover; steam for 4-6 minutes or until crisp-tender. Immediately rinse in cold water. Place asparagus and green onions in a bowl.

Whisk together the oil, vinegar, teriyaki sauce, sugar, salt and pepper. Pour over asparagus mixture; toss to coat. Cover and refrigerate for at least 2 hours. Stir before serving. **Yield:** 6 servings.

Nutritional Analysis: 2/3 cup equals 74 calories, 5 g fat (1 g saturated fat), 0 cholesterol, 206 mg sodium, 6 g carbohydrate, 3 g fiber, 3 g protein.
Diabetic Exchanges: 1 vegetable, 1 fat.

Blue Cheese 'n' Fruit Tossed Salad

(Pictured below)

Low-carb *Meatless*

Prep/Total Time: 20 min.

I found this recipe in the newspaper but reduced the calories. I serve the dressing on the side so family members can add as much or as little as they wish.
—Michel Larson, Chandler, Arizona

1/4 cup canola oil
2 tablespoons water
2 tablespoons plus 1-1/2 teaspoons cider vinegar
Sugar substitute equivalent to 1 tablespoon sugar
1-1/4 teaspoons poppy seeds
3/4 teaspoon grated onion
1/2 teaspoon ground mustard
1/4 teaspoon salt
4 cups torn romaine
2 medium unpeeled Granny Smith apples, chopped
1 can (11 ounces) mandarin oranges, drained
1/3 cup pecan halves, toasted
1/2 cup crumbled blue cheese

In blender or food processor, combine the first eight ingredients; cover and process until blended. In a large bowl, combine the romaine, apples, mandarin oranges and pecans. Add dressing and toss to coat; sprinkle with blue cheese. **Yield:** 8 servings.

Editor's Note: This recipe was tested with Splenda No Calorie Sweetener.

Nutritional Analysis: 3/4 cup equals 170 calories, 13 g fat (2 g saturated fat), 6 mg cholesterol, 194 mg sodium, 11 g carbohydrate, 2 g fiber, 3 g protein.
Diabetic Exchanges: 2 fat, 1/2 starch, 1/2 fruit.

Grilled Chicken and Pear Salad

(Pictured above)

Prep/Total Time: 25 min.

I served this fabulous salad at a shower, and it received many compliments. The vinaigrette pairs wonderfully with the grilled chicken and Brie.
—Janet Duran, Des Moines, Washington

5 boneless skinless chicken breasts (4 ounces each)
7 cups torn mixed salad greens
2 ounces Brie *or* Camembert cheese, cubed
2 medium pears, chopped
1/4 cup chopped pecans, toasted
1/4 cup apple juice concentrate, thawed
2 tablespoons canola oil
4-1/2 teaspoons cider vinegar
2 teaspoons Dijon mustard
1/4 teaspoon salt
1/8 teaspoon pepper

Coat grill rack with nonstick cooking spray before starting the grill. Grill chicken, covered, over medium heat for 6-8 minutes on each side or until juices run clear.

Arrange the salad greens, cheese, pears and pecans on individual plates. Slice chicken; arrange over salad. In a jar with a tight-fitting lid, combine the apple juice concentrate, oil, vinegar, mustard, salt and pepper; shake well. Drizzle over salad and serve immediately. **Yield:** 5 servings.

Nutritional Analysis: 1 serving equals 329 calories, 16 g fat (4 g saturated fat), 74 mg cholesterol, 317 mg sodium, 19 g carbohydrate, 4 g fiber, 27 g protein.
Diabetic Exchanges: 3 very lean meat, 2-1/2 fat, 1 fruit, 1/2 starch.

Vegetarian Taco Salad

(Pictured above)

Low-fat   Meatless

Prep/Total Time: 25 min.

The cute tortilla bowls that hold this Southwestern salad are a snap to bake in the oven. We use canned beans that include hot spices to punch up the flavor.
—Susan LeBrun, Sulphur, Louisiana

  4 whole wheat tortillas (8 inches)
  6 cups shredded romaine
1/2 cup pinto beans, rinsed and drained
  1 small tomato, chopped
1/4 cup shredded reduced-fat cheddar cheese
1/4 cup chopped green onions
  2 tablespoons sliced ripe olives, drained
Sliced jalapeno pepper, optional
DRESSING:
1/2 cup fat-free sour cream
  2 tablespoons fat-free ranch salad dressing
  1 teaspoon taco seasoning
1/4 teaspoon hot pepper sauce, optional

Place four 10-oz. custard cups upside down in a shallow baking pan; set aside. Place tortillas in a single layer on ungreased baking sheets. Bake, uncovered, at 425° for 1 minute. Place a tortilla over each custard cup, pinching sides to form a bowl shape. Bake for 7-8 minutes or until crisp. Remove tortillas from cups to cool on wire racks.

In a large bowl, combine the romaine, beans, tomato, cheese, green onions, olives and jalapeno pepper if desired. Whisk together the sour cream, ranch dressing, taco seasoning and hot pepper sauce if desired; pour over lettuce mixture. Toss to coat. Serve salad in tortilla bowls. **Yield:** 4 servings.

Nutritional Analysis: 1 tortilla bowl with 1-1/4 cups dressed salad equals 194 calories, 3 g fat (1 g saturated fat), 10 mg cholesterol, 489 mg sodium, 38 g carbohydrate, 5 g fiber, 10 g protein.
Diabetic Exchange: 2-1/2 starch.

Greek Veggie Salad

(Pictured below)

Low-carb

Prep: 25 min. + chilling

Cucumbers, feta cheese and anchovies make this colorful vegetable salad popular. The homemade vinegar-and-oil dressing offers a touch of garlic and herbs that helps pull all of the flavors together.
—Sue Dannahower, Parker, Colorado

  3 medium tomatoes, cut into wedges
  3 medium green peppers, julienned
  2 medium cucumbers, peeled and sliced
  2 medium onions, coarsely chopped
1/4 cup olive oil
  2 tablespoons plus 2 teaspoons red wine vinegar
  1 tablespoon minced fresh dill
  1 garlic clove, minced
1/2 teaspoon minced fresh oregano
1/8 teaspoon salt
Dash pepper
  1 cup (4 ounces) crumbled feta cheese
  12 pitted Greek olives
  6 anchovy fillets, halved

In a large bowl, combine the tomatoes, green peppers, cucumbers and onions. Whisk together the oil, vinegar, dill, garlic, oregano, salt and pepper. Pour over tomato mixture; toss to coat. Cover and refrigerate for at least 2 hours. Top with the cheese, olives and anchovies. **Yield:** 12 servings.

Nutritional Analysis: 1 cup equals 105 calories, 7 g fat (2 g saturated fat), 7 mg cholesterol, 254 mg sodium, 7 g carbohydrate, 2 g fiber, 4 g protein.
Diabetic Exchanges: 1-1/2 fat, 1 vegetable.

Flavorful Cranberry Gelatin Mold

(Pictured below)

Low-sodium

Prep: 10 min. + chilling

A little port or Merlot wine offers a tasty twist to this traditional gelatin that also features pineapple and walnuts. I make it for holiday dinners.
—Jenice Gibson, Oregon City, Oregon

> 2 packages (.3 ounce *each*) sugar-free raspberry gelatin
> 1-1/2 cups boiling water
> 1 can (20 ounces) unsweetened crushed pineapple, drained
> 1 can (16 ounces) whole-berry cranberry sauce
> 1/2 cup chopped walnuts
> 1/3 cup port wine *or* red grape juice
> Mint leaves for garnish, optional

In a large bowl, dissolve raspberry gelatin in boiling water. Stir in pineapple, cranberry sauce, walnuts and wine or juice. Pour into a 5-cup mold coated with nonstick cooking spray. Run a knife through gelatin mixture to evenly distribute fruit. Refrigerate 2-1/2 hours or until firm. Unmold onto a serving plate and garnish with mint leaves if desired. **Yield:** 8 servings.

Nutritional Analysis: 1/2 cup equals 193 calories, 4 g fat (trace saturated fat), 0 cholesterol, 66 mg sodium, 33 g carbohydrate, 2 g fiber, 3 g protein.
Diabetic Exchanges: 1 starch, 1 fruit, 1 fat.

Cucumber Couscous Salad

(Pictured above)

Low-fat   Meatless

Prep: 25 min. + chilling

Chicken or grilled salmon are perfect alongside this refreshing salad. Its combination of cucumber and dill tastes great, and couscous makes it a hearty side dish.
—Evelyn Lewis, Independence, Missouri

> 1-1/4 cups water
> 1 cup uncooked couscous
> 2 medium cucumbers, peeled, quartered lengthwise and sliced
> 1 cup chopped sweet red pepper
> 1/4 cup thinly sliced green onions
> 1/2 cup 1% buttermilk
> 1/4 cup reduced-fat plain yogurt
> 2 tablespoons minced fresh dill
> 2 tablespoons white vinegar
> 1 tablespoon olive oil
> 1/2 teaspoon salt
> 1/4 teaspoon pepper

In a saucepan, bring water to a boil. Stir in couscous. Remove from the heat; cover and let stand for 5 minutes. Fluff with a fork. Cool to room temperature.

In a large bowl, combine the couscous, cucumbers, red pepper and onions. Whisk together the buttermilk, yogurt, dill, vinegar, oil, salt and pepper. Pour over couscous mixture. Cover and refrigerate salad for at least 1 hour. **Yield:** 8 servings.

Nutritional Analysis: 2/3 cup equals 126 calories, 2 g fat (trace saturated fat), 1 mg cholesterol, 172 mg sodium, 22 g carbohydrate, 2 g fiber, 5 g protein.
Diabetic Exchanges: 1 starch, 1 vegetable, 1/2 fat.

maine, chicken, peppers and tomatoes. Just before serving, drizzle with dressing and toss to coat. Top with wonton strips. **Yield:** 10 servings.

Nutritional Analysis: 1 cup equals 149 calories, 6 g fat (1 g saturated fat), 33 mg cholesterol, 253 mg sodium, 10 g carbohydrate, 1 g fiber, 14 g protein.
Diabetic Exchanges: 2 very lean meat, 1 fat, 1/2 starch.

Minty Cucumber Salad

Low-carb   Low-sodium   Meatless

Prep: 10 min. + chilling

This refreshing sensation of crunchy cucumbers offers a mild hint of orange and mint flavors that are perfect for spring.
—Katherine Hee, Colchester, Vermont

2 medium cucumbers, peeled, halved, seeded and sliced
1/4 cup red wine vinegar
2 tablespoons olive oil
1/4 cup minced fresh mint
2 tablespoons minced fresh parsley
1 tablespoon sugar
1 teaspoon grated orange peel

Place cucumbers in a bowl. In a small bowl, whisk together the vinegar and oil. Add the mint, parsley, sugar and orange peel; pour over cucumbers. Cover and refrigerate for at least 3 hours, stirring several times. **Yield:** 3 servings.

Nutritional Analysis: 3/4 cup equals 90 calories, 7 g fat (1 g saturated fat), 0 cholesterol, 4 mg sodium, 8 g carbohydrate, 1 g fiber, 1 g protein.
Diabetic Exchanges: 1 fat, 1/2 starch.

Chicken Salad with Crispy Wontons

(Pictured above)

Low-carb

Prep/Total Time: 30 min.

My mom made this when I was growing up, but I added veggies and lightened the sweet-and-sour dressing. I also bake the wontons instead of frying them.
—Kylea Rorabaugh, Kansas City, Missouri

10 wonton wrappers, cut into 1/4-inch strips
1/4 cup cider vinegar
3 tablespoons canola oil
3/4 teaspoon sesame oil
2 tablespoons sugar
3/4 teaspoon salt
1/4 teaspoon pepper
5 cups torn romaine
3 cups cubed cooked chicken breast
1 medium sweet red pepper, cut into 1/4-inch strips
1 medium sweet yellow pepper, cut into 1/4-inch strips
1/2 cup halved grape tomatoes

Lightly spray both sides of wonton strips with nonstick cooking spray; place strips on a baking sheet. Broil 4-6 in. from the heat for 2-3 minutes or until golden brown. Turn and broil 2-3 minutes longer or until golden brown. Remove to wire racks to cool.

In a small bowl, whisk together the vinegar, oils, sugar, salt and pepper; set aside. In a large bowl, combine the ro-

Marvelous Mint

CHOCK-FULL of invigorating flavor, mint is a sweet herb that jazzes up suppertime staples in a snap.

If you are using fresh mint, wrap the sprigs in paper towels and keep them in a resealable storage bag in your refrigerator. Dried mint should be stored away from light, heat and moisture. Crush dried mint in your hand to release its full flavor before adding it to recipes.

To bring some mint flavor to your menu, try:
- Mixing chopped fresh mint into prepared salsa for a fun fiesta.
- Adding mint to sauces and jellies for a refreshing flavor.
- Stirring a few sprigs into lemonade, iced coffee or even hot cocoa.
- Sprinkling some fresh mint into low-fat vanilla or chocolate frozen yogurt.

Tangy Four-Bean Salad

(Pictured below)

Meatless

Prep: 20 min. + chilling

This colorful salad is easy to fix, and a no-fuss dressing lends sweet-sour flair. Green pepper and mushrooms help it stand out from other bean medleys.
—Sharon Cain, Revelstoke, British Columbia

  1 can (19 ounces) garbanzo beans *or* chickpeas, rinsed and drained
  1 can (16 ounces) kidney beans, rinsed and drained
  1 can (14-1/2 ounces) cut green beans, drained
  1 can (14-1/2 ounces) cut wax beans, drained
  1 cup sliced fresh mushrooms
  1 cup chopped green pepper
  1 cup chopped onion
DRESSING:
  1/2 cup cider vinegar
  1/3 cup sugar
  1/4 cup canola oil
  1 teaspoon celery seed
  1/2 teaspoon pepper
  1/4 teaspoon salt
  1/8 teaspoon dried basil
  1/8 teaspoon dried oregano

In a large bowl, combine the first seven ingredients. In a jar with a tight-fitting lid, combine the dressing ingredients; shake well. Pour over bean mixture and stir to coat. Cover and refrigerate for at least 4 hours. Serve with a slotted spoon. **Yield:** 12 servings.

Nutritional Analysis: *3/4 cup equals 162 calories, 6 g fat (trace saturated fat), 0 cholesterol, 366 mg sodium, 24 g carbohydrate, 5 g fiber, 5 g protein.*
Diabetic Exchanges: *1 starch, 1 vegetable, 1 fat.*

Wild Rice Pepper Salad

(Pictured above)

Meatless

Prep: 10 min. **Cook:** 1 hour + chilling

Over the years, I've made this chilled salad countless times. Using leftover wild rice really cuts down kitchen work and helps clean out the refrigerator, too.
—Darlene Gibbon, Milnor, North Dakota

  2/3 cup uncooked wild rice
  3 cups water
  1 cup chopped green pepper
  1 cup chopped sweet red pepper
  1 cup chopped sweet yellow pepper
1/2 cup sunflower kernels
1/3 cup chopped onion
1/3 cup raisins
1/2 cup fat-free Italian salad dressing

In a small saucepan, bring the rice and water to a boil. Reduce heat; cover and simmer for 1 hour or until rice is tender. Drain and place in a bowl. Refrigerate until chilled. Add the remaining ingredients; toss to coat. **Yield:** 6 servings.

Nutritional Analysis: *3/4 cup equals 206 calories, 7 g fat (1 g saturated fat), 1 mg cholesterol, 357 mg sodium, 32 g carbohydrate, 3 g fiber, 6 g protein.*
Diabetic Exchanges: *1 starch, 1 vegetable, 1 fat, 1/2 fruit.*

Colorful Coleslaw

(Pictured above)

Low-carb *Meatless*

Prep: 25 min. + chilling

*Every time I prepare this salad, I adjust the
ingredients a bit. This version tastes the best
and has the fewest calories.*
—*Jeanette Jones, Muncie, Indiana*

  5 **cups shredded cabbage**
  1 *each* **medium green, sweet red and yellow
    pepper, julienned**
  2 **cups julienned carrots**
  6 **green onions, thinly sliced**
DRESSING:
  2/3 **cup rice wine vinegar**
  1/4 **cup olive oil**
Sugar substitute equivalent to 1/3 cup sugar
  1/4 **cup reduced-fat creamy peanut butter**
  1 **teaspoon salt**
  1 **teaspoon minced fresh gingerroot**
  1/2 **teaspoon pepper**

In a large bowl, combine the cabbage, peppers, carrots
and onions. In a blender, combine the dressing ingredients;
cover and process until smooth. Drizzle over vegetables and
toss to coat. Cover and refrigerate for at least 1 hour. Toss;
serve with a slotted spoon. **Yield:** 8 servings.

  Editor's Note: This recipe was tested with Splenda No
Calorie Sweetener.

  Nutritional Analysis: 2/3 cup equals 153 calories, 10 g fat
(1 g saturated fat), 0 cholesterol, 362 mg sodium, 15 g carbohydrate, 3 g fiber, 4 g protein.
  Diabetic Exchanges: 2 vegetable, 2 fat.

Spicy Crunchy Veggies

(Pictured below)

Low-carb *Meatless*

Prep: 15 min. + chilling

*This simple salad offers a lot of crunch and plenty of
spice. I like topping it off with ranch-flavored almonds
instead of toasting them myself.*
—*Grady Jones, Midland, Texas*

  2 **cups fresh broccoli florets**
  2 **ounces reduced-fat Monterey Jack cheese, cut
    into small cubes**
  1/3 **cup finely chopped red onion**
  1/4 **cup fresh cauliflowerets**
  1/4 **cup julienned carrot**
  2 **tablespoons finely chopped sweet red pepper**
  1 **small jalapeno pepper, seeded and chopped**
  2 **tablespoons fat-free plain yogurt**
  2 **tablespoons reduced-fat mayonnaise**
  1/2 **teaspoon salt-free spicy seasoning blend**
  1/8 **teaspoon salt**
  1 **tablespoon slivered almonds, toasted**

In a large bowl, combine the first seven ingredients. In a
small bowl, combine the yogurt, mayonnaise, seasoning
blend and salt. Stir into vegetable mixture. Cover and refrigerate for at least 1 hour. Just before serving, sprinkle with
almonds. **Yield:** 4 servings.

  Editor's Note: When cutting or seeding hot peppers, use
rubber or plastic gloves to protect your hands. Avoid touching your face.

  Nutritional Analysis: 3/4 cup equals 87 calories, 5 g fat (2 g
saturated fat), 12 mg cholesterol, 281 mg sodium, 7 g carbohydrate, 2 g fiber, 6 g protein.
  Diabetic Exchanges: 1 vegetable, 1 fat.

Red and Sweet Potato Salad

(Pictured above)

Meatless

Prep: 15 min. **Cook:** 20 min.

Two types of potatoes help this creamy side dish stand out at warm-weather get-togethers. People love the spicy mustard dressing.
—*Mary Relyea, Canastota, New York*

2 pounds red potatoes, cut into 1-inch chunks
1 pound sweet potatoes, peeled and cut into 1-inch chunks
1/4 cup red wine vinegar
1 tablespoon spicy brown mustard
1-1/4 teaspoons salt
1/2 teaspoon pepper
1/2 cup reduced-fat mayonnaise
1/4 cup 2% milk
2 celery ribs, chopped
1 small red onion, chopped
1/3 cup minced fresh parsley

Place the red potatoes in a large saucepan and cover with water; bring to a boil. Reduce heat; cover and cook for 2 minutes. Add sweet potatoes; return to a boil. Reduce heat; cover and cook 8-10 minutes longer or until potatoes are fork-tender.

In a large bowl, whisk the vinegar, mustard, salt and pepper. Drain potatoes; add to vinegar mixture and stir gently to coat. Cool.

In a small bowl, combine the mayonnaise and milk. Stir in the celery, onion and parsley. Gently stir into the cooled potato mixture. Serve immediately or cover and chill. **Yield:** 12 servings.

Nutritional Analysis: 2/3 cup equals 136 calories, 4 g fat (1 g saturated fat), 4 mg cholesterol, 360 mg sodium, 24 g carbohydrate, 3 g fiber, 2 g protein.
Diabetic Exchanges: 1-1/2 starch, 1/2 fat.

Beef Fajita Salad

(Pictured below)

Prep/Total Time: 30 min.

This easy salad features colorful peppers, beans, tomato and tender strips of beef. The beef marinates for only 10 minutes, but it gets great flavor from the lime juice, cilantro and chili powder.
—*Ardeena Harris, Roanoke, Alabama*

1/4 cup lime juice
2 tablespoons minced fresh cilantro
1 garlic clove, minced
1 teaspoon chili powder
3/4 pound boneless beef sirloin steak, cut into thin strips
1 medium green pepper, julienned
1 medium sweet red pepper, julienned
1 medium onion, sliced and halved
1 teaspoon olive oil
1 can (16 ounces) kidney beans, rinsed and drained
4 cups torn mixed salad greens
1 medium tomato, chopped
4 tablespoons fat-free sour cream
2 tablespoons salsa

In a large resealable plastic bag, combine the lime juice, cilantro, garlic and chili powder; add beef. Seal bag and turn to coat; refrigerate for 10 minutes, turning once.

Meanwhile, in a nonstick skillet, cook the peppers and onion in oil over medium-high heat for 5 minutes or until tender. Remove and keep warm. Add beef with marinade to the skillet; cook and stir for 4-5 minutes or until meat is tender and mixture comes to a boil. Add beans and pepper mixture; heat through.

Divide the salad greens and tomato among four bowls; top each with 1-1/4 cups beef mixture, 1 tablespoon sour cream and 1-1/2 teaspoons salsa. **Yield:** 4 servings.

Nutritional Analysis: 1 serving equals 291 calories, 6 g fat (2 g saturated fat), 50 mg cholesterol, 291 mg sodium, 34 g carbohydrate, 10 g fiber, 27 g protein.
Diabetic Exchanges: 2 lean meat, 2 vegetable, 1-1/2 starch.

Zippy Chicken Coleslaw

(Pictured at left)

Low-carb

Prep: 40 min. **Cook:** 10 min.

The ramen noodles give this hearty salad a little crunch, but it's still just as good the next day when they've softened up.
—Kathy Egan, Oceanside, California

1 tablespoon paprika
1/2 teaspoon dried thyme
1/4 teaspoon sugar
1/4 teaspoon salt
1/4 teaspoon onion powder
1/4 teaspoon garlic powder
1/4 teaspoon pepper
1/8 teaspoon cayenne pepper
1/2 pound boneless skinless chicken breast
1 package (3 ounces) hot and spicy ramen noodles
4 cups shredded cabbage
2 cups broccoli coleslaw mix
3 green onions, chopped
2 tablespoons sesame seeds, toasted
2 tablespoons sliced almonds, toasted
DRESSING:
3 tablespoons sugar
2 tablespoons reduced-sodium soy sauce
4-1/2 teaspoons cider vinegar
2-1/4 teaspoons water
2-1/4 teaspoons canola oil
1/8 teaspoon pepper

In a small bowl, combine the first eight ingredients; rub over both sides of chicken. Broil 3-4 in. from the heat for 5-6 minutes on each side or until juices run clear. When chicken is cool enough to handle, shred with two forks; cool completely.

Set aside the seasoning packet from the ramen noodles. Break the noodles into small pieces; place in a large bowl. Add the cabbage, broccoli coleslaw, onions, sesame seeds, almonds and chicken.

In a jar with a tight-fitting lid, combine the dressing ingredients. Add the contents of the noodle seasoning packet; shake well. Pour over the coleslaw and toss to coat. **Yield:** 9 servings.

Nutritional Analysis: *2/3 cup equals 132 calories, 5 g fat (1 g saturated fat), 14 mg cholesterol, 405 mg sodium, 15 g carbohydrate, 2 g fiber, 8 g protein.*
Diabetic Exchanges: *1 starch, 1 very lean meat, 1/2 fat.*

Berry Nectarine Salad

(Pictured at left)

Low-fat Low-sodium Meatless

Prep: 15 min. + chilling

I've been making this recipe for years. Whenever my family has a summer get-together, everyone requests it. The nectarines and berries look beautiful together, and the topping is the perfect accent.
—Mindee Myers, Lincoln, Nebraska

4 medium unpeeled nectarines, sliced
1/4 cup sugar
1/2 teaspoon ground ginger
1 teaspoon lemon juice
2 cups fresh raspberries
1 cup fresh blueberries
3 ounces reduced-fat cream cheese

Place the nectarines in a large bowl. Combine the sugar and ginger; sprinkle over nectarines and gently stir to evenly coat. Drizzle with lemon juice. Cover and refrigerate for 1 hour, stirring once.

Drain and reserve liquid. Gently stir raspberries and blueberries into nectarines. In a small mixing bowl, beat cream cheese until smooth. Gradually beat in reserved liquid. Spoon over fruit; serve immediately. **Yield:** 8 servings.

Nutritional Analysis: *3/4 cup fruit with 2 teaspoons dressing equals 117 calories, 2 g fat (1 g saturated fat), 6 mg cholesterol, 33 mg sodium, 23 g carbohydrate, 4 g fiber, 2 g protein.*
Diabetic Exchanges: *1-1/2 fruit, 1/2 fat.*

Fresh Ginger Carrot Salad

Low-sodium Meatless

Prep: 15 min. + chilling

I created this salad as a light alternative to the mayonnaise, raisin and carrot salad my mom used to make. I have a sweet tooth, and this salad satisfies it!
—Lauri Cherian, Scott Depot, West Virginia

2 cans (8 ounces *each*) crushed pineapple, undrained
3-1/2 cups shredded carrots
1 cup raisins
3/4 cup flaked coconut
1/2 cup chopped walnuts
1-1/2 cups fat-free plain yogurt
2 teaspoons minced fresh gingerroot

Drain crushed pineapple, reserving 3 tablespoons juice. In a bowl, combine the pineapple, carrots, raisins, coconut and walnuts. Combine the yogurt, ginger and reserved pineapple juice. Pour dressing over carrot mixture; toss gently to coat. Refrigerate for at least 1 hour. **Yield:** 6 servings.

Nutritional Analysis: *3/4 cup equals 286 calories, 11 g fat (4 g saturated fat), 1 mg cholesterol, 94 mg sodium, 46 g carbohydrate, 6 g fiber, 6 g protein.*
Diabetic Exchanges: *2 fruit, 2 fat, 1 vegetable, 1/2 fat-free milk.*

For dressing, combine the first 10 ingredients in a blender; cover and process until blended. Cook spaghetti according to package directions; drain and place in a large bowl. Add the broccoli, peas, red pepper, zucchini, celery and cooked beef. Add dressing and toss to coat. Cover and refrigerate for at least 2 hours. Just before serving, sprinkle with sesame seeds. **Yield:** 8 servings.

Nutritional Analysis: 1-1/4 cups equals 367 calories, 13 g fat (2 g saturated fat), 50 mg cholesterol, 880 mg sodium, 36 g carbohydrate, 3 g fiber, 25 g protein.
Diabetic Exchanges: 2 starch, 2 lean meat, 1-1/2 fat, 1 vegetable.

Thai Beef Noodle Salad

(Pictured above)

Prep: 30 min. + chilling

When I worked as a cook on the ferries that travel between Bellingham, Washington and southeastern Alaska, I served this salad to our passengers and crew, and it always received compliments. It's best chilled overnight.
—Patricia Morgan, Haines, Alaska

1/2 cup reduced-sodium soy sauce
1/2 cup rice wine vinegar
  3 tablespoons orange juice
  3 tablespoons canola oil
  1 tablespoon sesame oil
  2 garlic cloves, minced
  2 teaspoons ground ginger
  1 teaspoon peanut butter
3/4 teaspoon salt
1/2 teaspoon cayenne pepper
 12 ounces uncooked spaghetti
  1 cup fresh broccoli florets
  1 cup fresh *or* frozen snow peas, thawed
  1 cup julienned sweet red pepper
  1 cup julienned zucchini
1/2 cup thinly sliced celery
  1 pound boneless beef sirloin steak, cooked and cut into thin strips
  2 tablespoons sesame seeds, toasted

Creamy Dill Salad Dressing

(Pictured below)

Low-carb

Prep: 5 min. + chilling

I received this from-scratch salad dressing recipe from a restaurant. Even though I lightened it up a bit, it's still thick and delicious.
—Randa Smaligo, Pryor, Oklahoma

1/2 cup reduced-fat mayonnaise
1/3 cup fat-free evaporated milk
  1 teaspoon minced fresh dill
1/4 teaspoon seasoned salt

In a small bowl, whisk the mayonnaise, evaporated milk, dill and seasoned salt. Cover and refrigerate for at least 4 hours before serving. **Yield:** 3/4 cup.

Nutritional Analysis: 2 tablespoons equals 60 calories, 4 g fat (1 g saturated fat), 6 mg cholesterol, 255 mg sodium, 5 g carbohydrate, trace fiber, 1 g protein.
Diabetic Exchanges: 1/2 starch, 1/2 fat.

Melon 'n' Grape Medley

(Pictured at right)

Low-fat   Low-sodium   Meatless

Prep: 15 min. + chilling

This colorful fruit salad from our Test Kitchen has a zesty honey-orange dressing with a surprising twist—a hint of jalapeno!

1-1/2 cups cantaloupe balls
1-1/2 cups watermelon balls
1-1/2 cups green grapes
DRESSING:
   1/4 cup orange juice
    1 tablespoon honey
    1 tablespoon lime juice
    2 teaspoons chopped seeded jalapeno pepper
   1/2 teaspoon grated lime peel

In a resealable plastic bag, combine the cantaloupe, watermelon and grapes.

In a small bowl, whisk the orange juice, honey and lime juice. Stir in the jalapeno and lime peel. Pour over fruit. Seal bag, removing as much air as possible, and turn to coat; refrigerate for at least 1 hour. Serve with a slotted spoon. **Yield:** 6 servings.

Editor's Note: When cutting or seeding hot peppers, use rubber or plastic gloves to protect your hands. Avoid touching your face.

Nutritional Analysis: 3/4 cup equals 74 calories, 1 g fat (trace saturated fat), 0 cholesterol, 6 mg sodium, 18 g carbohydrate, 1 g fiber, 1 g protein.
Diabetic Exchange: 1 fruit.

Fruit-Packed Gelatin Salad

Low-sodium

Prep: 20 min. + chilling

A rich, creamy layer makes this fruity gelatin stand out from the rest. I always get compliments on it.
—Linda Kaufman, Columbus, Ohio

    2 packages (.3 ounce *each*) sugar-free strawberry gelatin
    2 cups boiling water
    2 packages (12 ounces *each*) frozen unsweetened strawberries, thawed and cut in half
    1 can (20 ounces) unsweetened crushed pineapple
    3 medium firm bananas, sliced
    1 package (8 ounces) reduced-fat cream cheese
    1 cup (8 ounces) fat-free sour cream
   1/2 cup chopped walnuts, toasted

In a large bowl, dissolve gelatin in boiling water. Stir in the strawberries, pineapple and bananas. Transfer to a 13-in. x 9-in. x 2-in. dish coated with nonstick cooking spray. Cover and refrigerate for about 1 hour or until partially set.

In a small mixing bowl, combine the cream cheese and sour cream until blended. Carefully spread over gelatin mixture. Cover and refrigerate until firm. Just before serving, sprinkle with walnuts. **Yield:** 15 servings.

Nutritional Analysis: 1 piece equals 142 calories, 6 g fat (2 g saturated fat), 13 mg cholesterol, 105 mg sodium, 19 g carbohydrate, 2 g fiber, 5 g protein.
Diabetic Exchanges: 1 fruit, 1 fat, 1/2 starch.

 Savvy Produce Shopping

EVER BOUGHT a cantaloupe, honeydew melon or watermelon only to discover later that it's spoiled? On your next trip to the supermarket, keep these tips in mind:

CANTALOUPE
* Look for smooth round cantaloupe with netting all the way around and a depressed area at the stem end. Then sniff it! If it has a good cantaloupe aroma, it's the one for you.
* Avoid soft or bruised cantaloupes.

HONEYDEW MELON
* If the melon has a velvety texture, a yellowish-white to creamy white color and a pleasing aroma, add it to your cart.
* Avoid hard, pure-white or green honeydews, as well as those that are cut or bruised.

WATERMELON
* A good watermelon is roughly 92% water. Look for heavy, smooth and symmetrical fruits with a dark-red flesh and a cream-colored area on the bottom.
* Avoid dented or bruised watermelon with white streaks or white seeds.

In a large nonstick skillet or wok coated with nonstick cooking spray, stir-fry carrots and red pepper in 3/4 teaspoon olive oil for 2 minutes. Add snow peas and garlic; stir-fry 2 minutes longer. Add to linguine.

Stir-fry the zucchini, bean sprouts and onion in remaining olive oil for 2 minutes; add to linguine mixture. Cover and refrigerate for at least 2 hours. Just before serving, add dressing and toss to coat. **Yield:** 8 servings.

Nutritional Analysis: *3/4 cup equals 141 calories, 2 g fat (trace saturated fat), 0 cholesterol, 415 mg sodium, 25 g carbohydrate, 2 g fiber, 5 g protein.*
Diabetic Exchanges: *1-1/2 starch, 1/2 fat.*

🍎 Freshen Up with Snow Peas

SNOW PEAS are a wonderful way to make everyday salads a little more exciting. Keep the following suggestions in mind if you're tossing together Asian Linguine Salad (recipe below) or simply adding snow peas to your green-leaf creation.

- Refrigerate fresh unwashed snow peas in a plastic bag for up to 3 days.
- To prepare snow peas, wash the pods, then snap off the stem ends and remove the strings if desired.
- In addition to salads, the veggies are excellent in stir-fries.
- Tasty substitutes include sugar snap peas, asparagus and canned bean sprouts.

Asian Linguine Salad

(Pictured at left)

Low-fat   Meatless

Prep: 35 min. **Cook:** 10 min. + chilling

With loads of vegetables and a delicious dressing, this chilled pasta toss offers guilt-free enjoyment.
—Pat Hilmer, Oshkosh, Wisconsin

        8 ounces uncooked linguine
    1/3 cup reduced-sodium soy sauce
    1/4 cup water
        2 tablespoons lemon juice
1-1/2 teaspoons sesame oil
        2 medium carrots, julienned
    1/2 medium sweet red pepper, julienned
1-1/2 teaspoons olive oil, *divided*
    1/2 cup fresh snow peas
        1 garlic clove, minced
        1 small zucchini, julienned
    1/2 cup canned bean sprouts
        1 green onion, julienned

Cook linguine according to package directions; drain and place in a large serving bowl. In a small bowl, whisk the soy sauce, water, lemon juice and sesame oil. Refrigerate 1/4 cup for dressing. Pour remaining mixture over the hot linguine; toss to coat evenly.

Southwestern Chicken Salad

(Pictured at left)

Prep/Total Time: 30 min.

I mix chicken, beans and corn with fresh jicama for a change-of-pace entree. Barbecue-ranch dressing and crunchy tortilla strips add a bit of fun.
—Virginia Stencel, North Richland Hills, Texas

        2 flour tortillas (6 inches), cut into 1/2-inch strips
Butter-flavored nonstick cooking spray
        1 pound boneless skinless chicken breasts, cut into 1-inch cubes
        1 teaspoon olive oil
        6 cups ready-to-serve salad greens
        1 can (15-1/4 ounces) whole kernel corn, drained
        1 can (15 ounces) black beans, rinsed and drained
        2 cups chopped tomatoes, *divided*
        1 medium green pepper, diced
    1/2 cup cubed peeled jicama *or* sliced water chestnuts
    1/3 cup chopped green onions
    1/2 cup shredded reduced-fat cheddar cheese
    2/3 cup fat-free ranch salad dressing
        4 teaspoons barbecue sauce

Place tortilla strips on a baking sheet; spritz both sides of strips with butter-flavored cooking spray. Bake at 350° for 4-5 minutes or until crisp. Meanwhile, in a large nonstick skillet, cook chicken in oil over medium heat until no longer pink; set aside.

Combine the salad greens, corn, beans, 1 cup tomatoes, green pepper, jicama and onions; arrange on a serving platter. Place chicken in center of salad; sprinkle with cheese and remaining tomatoes. Arrange tortilla strips around chicken. In a small bowl, combine the ranch dressing and barbecue sauce; serve with salad. **Yield:** 6 servings.

Nutritional Analysis: *1 serving equals 331 calories, 7 g fat (2 g saturated fat), 49 mg cholesterol, 865 mg sodium, 40 g carbohydrate, 7 g fiber, 25 g protein.*
Diabetic Exchanges: *2-1/2 starch, 2 very lean meat, 1 vegetable, 1 fat.*

Calico Cranberry Couscous Salad

(Pictured above)

Meatless

Prep/Total Time: 20 min.

It's easy to jazz up couscous with a Dijon dressing, dried cranberries and green onions.
—*Rosemarie Matheus, Germantown, Wisconsin*

   1 cup water
   3/4 cup uncooked couscous
   1/2 cup dried cranberries
   1/2 cup chopped celery
   1/2 cup shredded carrot
   1/4 cup chopped green onions
   1/4 cup slivered almonds, toasted
DRESSING:
   3 tablespoons red wine vinegar
   1 tablespoon olive oil
   1 tablespoon Dijon mustard
   1/4 teaspoon salt
   1/4 teaspoon pepper

In a small saucepan, bring water to a boil. Stir in couscous; cover and remove from the heat. Let stand for 5 minutes. Fluff with a fork; cool.

In a serving bowl, combine the couscous, cranberries, celery, carrot, onions and almonds. In a jar with a tight-fitting lid, combine the dressing ingredients; shake well. Pour over salad and toss to coat. Serve at room temperature or chilled. **Yield:** 6 servings.

Nutritional Analysis: 1/2 cup equals 171 calories, 5 g fat (1 g saturated fat), 0 cholesterol, 176 mg sodium, 29 g carbohydrate, 3 g fiber, 5 g protein.
Diabetic Exchanges: 1-1/2 starch, 1 fat, 1/2 fruit.

Lentil Bulgur Salad

Meatless

Prep: 20 min. + standing **Cook:** 15 min. + chilling

Give any meal an exotic flair with this zesty twist on Middle Eastern tabbouleh—a traditional bulgur salad with tomatoes, onions and parsley. I toss this version with lentils and feta cheese.
—*Laura Bryant German, West Warren, Massachusetts*

1-1/2 cups boiling water
1-1/2 cups bulgur
   5 cups water
1-1/2 cups dried lentils, rinsed
   1 cup diced green pepper
   1 cup diced sweet red pepper
   1/2 cup chopped green onions
   1/2 cup minced fresh parsley
DRESSING:
   1/3 cup cider vinegar
   1/3 cup olive oil
   1 tablespoon dried basil
   1 tablespoon dill seed
   1 teaspoon salt
   1/4 teaspoon pepper
   3/4 cup feta cheese

In a large bowl, pour boiling water over the bulgur; let stand until the liquid is absorbed, about 30 minutes. Meanwhile, in a saucepan, bring water to a boil. Add the lentils. Reduce heat; cover and simmer until tender, about 15 minutes. Drain. In another large bowl, combine the bulgur and lentils; cool completely. Add the green pepper, sweet red pepper, green onions and parsley.

In a jar with a tight-fitting lid, combine the vinegar, oil, basil, dill, salt and pepper. Pour over salad; toss to coat. Crumble feta cheese over top; toss again. Cover and refrigerate for 4 hours or until serving. **Yield:** 10 servings.

Editor's Note: Look for bulgur in the cereal, rice or organic food aisle of your grocery store.

Nutritional Analysis: 1 cup equals 271 calories, 10 g fat (3 g saturated fat), 10 mg cholesterol, 370 mg sodium, 35 g carbohydrate, 13 g fiber, 13 g protein.
Diabetic Exchanges: *2 lean meat, 1-1/2 starch, 1 fat.*

Green Pea Salad

(Pictured below)

Low-carb

Prep: 25 min. + chilling

Fat-free sour cream and bottled ranch salad dressing keep this salad easy to prepare. Bacon and cashews punch up the flavor, and broccoli, cauliflower and peas make it nutritious.
—Helen Suter, Golconda, Illinois

1 cup fresh broccoli florets
1 cup fresh cauliflowerets
1 package (10 ounces) frozen peas, thawed
1 large celery rib, halved lengthwise and thinly sliced
1/4 cup thinly sliced green onions
5 tablespoons reduced-fat ranch salad dressing
3 tablespoons fat-free sour cream
1/4 cup salted cashew pieces
2 bacon strips, cooked and crumbled

Place broccoli and cauliflower in a steamer basket; place in a saucepan over 1 in. of water. Bring to a boil; cover and steam for 2-3 minutes. Rinse in cold water. In a large bowl, combine the broccoli, cauliflower, peas, celery and onions.

In a small bowl, combine the ranch dressing and sour cream. Stir into vegetable mixture. Cover and refrigerate for at least 1 hour. Just before serving, stir in cashews and bacon. **Yield:** 6 servings.

Nutritional Analysis: 3/4 cup equals 156 calories, 8 g fat (2 g saturated fat), 4 mg cholesterol, 294 mg sodium, 15 g carbohydrate, 4 g fiber, 6 g protein.
Diabetic Exchanges: *1-1/2 fat, 1 starch.*

Tomato Feta Salad

(Pictured above)

Low-carb   *Meatless*

Prep/Total Time: 20 min.

One summer I combined onions with a bumper crop of tomatoes and a homemade balsamic dressing. The result was this salad that receives thumbs-up approval whenever it's served.
—Robert Golus, Greer, South Carolina

2 tablespoons balsamic vinegar
1-1/2 teaspoons minced fresh basil *or* 1/2 teaspoon dried basil
1/2 teaspoon salt
1/2 cup coarsely chopped sweet onion
1 pound grape *or* cherry tomatoes, halved
2 tablespoons olive oil
1/4 cup crumbled feta cheese

In a bowl, combine the vinegar, basil and salt. Add onion; toss to coat. Let stand for 5 minutes. Add the tomatoes, oil and feta cheese; toss to coat. Serve with a slotted spoon. **Yield:** 4 servings.

Nutritional Analysis: 3/4 cup equals 121 calories, 9 g fat (2 g saturated fat), 8 mg cholesterol, 412 mg sodium, 9 g carbohydrate, 2 g fiber, 3 g protein.
Diabetic Exchanges: *2 fat, 1 vegetable.*

🍎 Calorie-Conscious Croutons

WE ARE on a point-based weight-loss system and enjoy eating lots of salads. When my husband said he missed croutons, I grabbed some light sandwich rolls that I knew were low in points. We cubed the rolls, spritzed them with cooking spray and topped them with seasonings.

After baking them to a golden brown, the crunchy bites made perfect croutons without using too many of our points.   *—Barbara Wassler*
Williamsport, Pennsylvania

Salad Dressing with a Kick

Low-carb Low-fat

Prep: 10 min. + chilling

After trying nearly every bottled fat-free salad dressing on the market, my husband created his own. We think this zesty blend is just fantastic.
—Joyce Courser, Greenacres, Washington

1/2 cup fat-free plain yogurt
1/4 cup chili sauce
1 teaspoon prepared horseradish
1 teaspoon steak sauce
1/2 teaspoon Worcestershire sauce
1/8 teaspoon garlic powder

In a small bowl, whisk all of the ingredients. Chill for at least 30 minutes before serving. **Yield:** 3/4 cup.
   Editor's Note: This recipe was tested with Heinz 57 steak sauce.

   Nutritional Analysis: 2 tablespoons equals 20 calories, trace fat (0 saturated fat), trace cholesterol, 187 mg sodium, 5 g carbohydrate, trace fiber, 1 g protein.
   Diabetic Exchange: Free food.

Pasta Fruit Salad

Prep: 20 min. + chilling

There's lots of texture in this salad, thanks to the fresh vegetables and water chestnuts, plus tender chicken and juicy mandarin oranges.
—Crystal Ralph-Haughn, Bartlesville, Oklahoma

1-1/3 cups uncooked spiral pasta
1-1/2 cups cubed cooked chicken breast
1-1/2 cups chopped celery
1 cup green grapes, halved
1 can (11 ounces) mandarin oranges, drained
1 can (8 ounces) sliced water chestnuts, drained
1/4 cup chopped green pepper
1/4 cup chopped red onion
1/4 cup fat-free mayonnaise
1/4 cup reduced-fat ranch salad dressing
1/2 teaspoon salt
1/8 teaspoon pepper
1/2 cup slivered almonds, toasted

Cook pasta according to package directions; drain and rinse with cold water. In a large bowl, combine the pasta, chicken, celery, grapes, oranges, water chestnuts, green pepper and onion.
   In a small bowl, combine the mayonnaise, ranch dressing, salt and pepper. Pour over the pasta mixture and toss to coat. Cover and refrigerate for 2 hours or until chilled. Sprinkle with toasted slivered almonds just before serving. **Yield:** 6 servings.

   Nutritional Analysis: 1-1/3 cups equals 236 calories, 9 g fat (1 g saturated fat), 34 mg cholesterol, 438 mg sodium, 25 g carbohydrate, 4 g fiber, 16 g protein.
   Diabetic Exchanges: 2 lean meat, 1 starch, 1/2 fruit, 1/2 fat.

Cranberry Spinach Salad

(Pictured below)

Low-sodium Meatless

Prep/Total Time: 20 min.

A few moments are all you need to create this pretty salad and classic dressing. It's a perfect addition to holiday dinners.
—Anne Smithson, Cary, North Carolina

8 cups fresh baby spinach
1 cup dried cranberries
2 medium pears, cored and chopped
1/4 cup cider vinegar
5 tablespoons sugar
1 teaspoon dried minced onion
1/2 teaspoon Worcestershire sauce
1/2 teaspoon ground mustard
1/4 teaspoon paprika
1/4 cup olive oil
1 tablespoon sesame seeds
1 teaspoon poppy seeds
2 tablespoons chopped pecans, toasted

In a large bowl, combine the spinach, cranberries and pears. In a blender, combine the vinegar, sugar, onion, Worcestershire sauce, mustard and paprika; cover and process until blended. While processing, gradually add oil in a steady stream.
   Add the sesame seeds and poppy seeds. Pour dressing over salad and toss to coat. Sprinkle with chopped pecans. **Yield:** 8 servings.

   Nutritional Analysis: 1 cup equals 189 calories, 9 g fat (1 g saturated fat), 0 cholesterol, 28 mg sodium, 29 g carbohydrate, 3 g fiber, 2 g protein.
   Diabetic Exchanges: 2 fat, 1 vegetable, 1 fruit, 1/2 starch.

Harvest Green Salad

(Pictured above)

Meatless

Prep: 25 min. **Bake:** 1 hour + cooling

This salad always gets rave reviews. Guests say that it fills them up without weighing them down.
—Beth Royals, Richmond, Virginia

3 whole medium fresh beets
1 large sweet potato, peeled and cubed
2 tablespoons water
1/2 cup reduced-fat balsamic vinaigrette
2 tablespoons jellied cranberry sauce
1 package (5 ounces) spring mix salad greens
1/2 cup dried cranberries
4 ounces crumbled Gorgonzola cheese

Wash beets; trim stem and leave root intact. Wrap beets in aluminum foil. Place on a baking sheet. Bake at 400° for 1 hour or until tender. Remove foil and cool.

In a microwave-safe bowl, combine the sweet potato and water. Cover and microwave on high for 4-5 minutes or until tender. Cool. In a blender, combine the vinaigrette and cranberry sauce; cover and process until smooth.

Peel beets and cut into slices. On six salad plates, arrange greens, beets and sweet potatoes. Sprinkle with berries and cheese. Drizzle with dressing. **Yield:** 6 servings.

Editor's Note: Use plastic gloves when peeling beets to avoid stains. This recipe was tested in a 1,100-watt microwave.

Nutritional Analysis: 1 serving equals 187 calories, 9 g fat (4 g saturated fat), 17 mg cholesterol, 438 mg sodium, 23 g carbohydrate, 3 g fiber, 6 g protein.
Diabetic Exchanges: 1 starch, 1 vegetable, 1 fat, 1/2 fruit.

Walnut Green Bean Salad

(Pictured below and on page 45)

Low-carb Low-sodium Meatless

Prep/Total Time: 20 min.

Sauteed green beans, blue cheese and toasted nuts make this an exquisite salad. I lightened up two recipes and combined them into this elegant specialty.
—Sarah Bartel, Kewaunee, Wisconsin

2 cups cut fresh green beans
2 tablespoons olive oil, *divided*
8 cups torn mixed salad greens
2 tablespoons plus 2 teaspoons balsamic vinegar
1/4 cup chopped walnuts, toasted
2 tablespoons plus 2 teaspoons crumbled blue cheese

In a large nonstick skillet, saute the green beans in 1 tablespoon oil until crisp-tender. In a large bowl, combine the salad greens and beans. In a small bowl, whisk the vinegar and remaining oil; drizzle over salad and toss to coat. Sprinkle with walnuts and blue cheese. Serve immediately. **Yield:** 10 servings.

Nutritional Analysis: 3/4 cup equals 68 calories, 5 g fat (1 g saturated fat), 2 mg cholesterol, 45 mg sodium, 4 g carbohydrate, 2 g fiber, 2 g protein.
Diabetic Exchanges: 1 vegetable, 1 fat.

Try Something New: Pomegranates

TO BRIGHTEN UP your table, consider ruby-red pomegranates. The rind of the pomegranate is inedible, but slice the fruit open and you'll find up to 800 translucent seeds filled with sweet-tart juice. Remove the seeds from the pith to lend exotic flavor to salads and stuffings, and use the juice as a tangy addition to sauces and glazes.

Powerful Pomegranates

Preliminary studies show that pomegranates have more antioxidants than red wine or green tea. And since antioxidants are believed to decrease the risk of cancer and heart disease, pomegranates make a great addition to any diet. The colorful fruit can also decrease high blood pressure, help keep arteries clean, and provide vitamin C, fiber and potassium.

Crimson Cuisine

Fresh pomegranates are available September through December in the produce section of most supermarkets. Look for orange-sized pomegranates that are bright or deep red with smooth, leather-like skin.

Available year-round, pomegranate juice is usually found in the produce department as well, but it's easy to make at home. For 1/2 cup of juice, simply process 3/4 cup of pomegranate seeds in a blender or food processor. Next, strain the juice through a fine sieve or cheesecloth-lined strainer and serve.

Pomegranate Spinach Salad

(Pictured at left)

Low-carb *Meatless*

Prep/Total Time: 25 min.

Whenever I take this salad to an event, people always ask for the recipe. It's perfect for the holidays.
—Sheila Saunders, Pleasant Grove, Utah

> 1 package (6 ounces) fresh baby spinach
> 1/2 cup reduced-fat shredded Swiss cheese
> 1/3 cup slivered almonds, toasted
> 1/2 cup pomegranate seeds
> DRESSING:
>   3 tablespoons canola oil
>   2 tablespoons sugar
>   2 tablespoons white vinegar
> 3/4 teaspoon poppy seeds
> 1/4 teaspoon salt
> 1/8 teaspoon ground mustard

In a salad bowl, combine the spinach, cheese, almonds and pomegranate seeds. In a blender, combine the oil, sugar, vinegar, poppy seeds, salt and mustard; cover and process until blended. Just before serving, drizzle dressing over spinach mixture; toss to coat evenly. **Yield:** 6 servings.

Nutritional Analysis: 1 cup dressed salad equals 149 calories, 11 g fat (1 g saturated fat), 4 mg cholesterol, 150 mg sodium, 9 g carbohydrate, 2 g fiber, 5 g protein.
Diabetic Exchanges: 2 fat, 1 vegetable, 1/2 starch.

🍎 Seeding a Pomegranate

TRY this method to simplify cleanup when removing the seeds from a pomegranate:

1. Cut off the crown end of the fruit, removing some of the white pith. Score into quarters and soak the fruit in a large bowl of cool water for 5 minutes.

2. Holding the fruit underwater, break each scored section apart, separating the seeds from the skin and membranes. Discard the skin and membranes and dry the seeds on paper towels.

Celery Seed Salad Dressing

(Pictured at right)

Low-carb Low-sodium

Prep/Total Time: 10 min.

This salad dressing is delicious over dark, leafy greens and tomatoes. When I have time, I prepare it the night before so the flavors really blend together.
—*Tammie Lee Carter, Wheatfield, New York*

1 cup reduced-fat mayonnaise
1/2 cup sugar
1/3 cup finely chopped onion
1/3 cup red wine vinegar
1 tablespoon celery seed

In a small bowl, whisk the mayonnaise, sugar, onion, vinegar and celery seed. Cover and refrigerate until serving. **Yield:** 1-3/4 cups.

Nutritional Analysis: *2 tablespoons equals 90 calories, 6 g fat (1 g saturated fat), 6 mg cholesterol, 138 mg sodium, 9 g carbohydrate, trace fiber, trace protein.*
Diabetic Exchanges: *1 fat, 1/2 starch.*

Sunshine Gelatin Salad

Low-sodium

Prep: 30 min. + chilling

This festive gelatin has a delightful, creamy topping.
—*Sharon Kriesel, Hatley, Wisconsin*

1 package (.3 ounce) sugar-free lemon gelatin
1 package (.3 ounce) sugar-free orange gelatin
2 cups boiling water
1-1/2 cups cold water
1 can (20 ounces) unsweetened crushed pineapple
3 medium firm bananas, chopped
1/3 cup miniature marshmallows
Sugar substitute equivalent to 1/4 cup sugar
2 tablespoons all-purpose flour
1 egg, lightly beaten
2 tablespoons butter, cubed
2-1/2 cups whipped topping

In a large bowl, dissolve lemon and orange gelatin in boiling water. Stir in cold water. Cover and refrigerate until partially set, about 1-1/2 hours.

Drain pineapple, reserving juice. Add enough water to juice to measure 1 cup.

Fold the bananas, marshmallows and pineapple into gelatin mixture. Transfer to a 13-in. x 9-in. x 2-in. dish. Cover and refrigerate until firm.

In a small saucepan, combine sugar substitute and flour. Gradually stir in pineapple juice mixture. Cook and stir over medium-high heat until thickened and bubbly. Reduce heat; cook and stir 2 minutes longer. Remove from the heat. Stir a small amount of hot filling into egg; return all to the pan, stirring constantly. Bring to a gentle boil; cook and stir for 2 minutes.

Remove from the heat; stir in butter until melted. Cool to room temperature without stirring. Fold in whipped topping. Spread over gelatin. Cover and refrigerate for at least 1 hour

before cutting. **Yield:** 12 servings.

Editor's Note: This recipe was tested with Splenda No Calorie Sweetener.

Nutritional Analysis: *1 piece equals 109 calories, 4 g fat (3 g saturated fat), 18 mg cholesterol, 49 mg sodium, 16 g carbohydrate, 1 g fiber, 2 g protein.*
Diabetic Exchanges: *1 fruit, 1/2 starch.*

Blue Cheese Waldorf Salad

Meatless

Prep/Total Time: 15 min.

A dash of cayenne adds zip to this crispy classic. Blue cheese gives it extra richness.
—*Renee Aupperle, Lititz, Pennsylvania*

1/4 cup fat-free mayonnaise
1/4 cup 1% buttermilk
2 teaspoons sugar
1-1/2 teaspoons cider vinegar
1/8 teaspoon salt
1/8 teaspoon cayenne pepper
1/8 teaspoon pepper
1/4 cup crumbled blue cheese
2 tablespoons grated onion
3 medium apples, chopped
3 celery ribs, chopped
1/2 cup raisins
1/4 cup chopped walnuts, toasted

In a small bowl, whisk the mayonnaise, buttermilk, sugar, vinegar, salt, cayenne and pepper. Stir in blue cheese and onion. In a large bowl, combine the apples, celery and raisins. Drizzle with dressing; toss to coat. Sprinkle with walnuts. **Yield:** 6 servings.

Nutritional Analysis: *1 cup equals 150 calories, 5 g fat (1 g saturated fat), 6 mg cholesterol, 237 mg sodium, 25 g carbohydrate, 3 g fiber, 4 g protein.*
Diabetic Exchanges: *2 fruit, 1 fat.*

Festive Fruit Salad

Low-fat   Low-sodium   Meatless

Prep: 20 min. + chilling

I dress up fruit with yogurt cheese—the solids that remain after the whey has been drained from yogurt.
—Ashley Braswell, Huntsville, Alabama

- 2 cups reduced-fat vanilla yogurt
- 4 large firm bananas, sliced
- 2 cans (11 ounces *each*) mandarin oranges, drained
- 1 can (20 ounces) pineapple chunks, drained
- 1 cup miniature marshmallows
- 1/4 cup flaked coconut, toasted

Line a strainer with 4 layers of cheesecloth and place over a bowl. Place yogurt in prepared strainer; cover yogurt with edges of cheesecloth. Refrigerate for 8 hours or overnight. Remove yogurt from cheesecloth; discard liquid from bowl.

Combine the bananas, oranges, pineapple, marshmallows and coconut. Add yogurt; stir gently to combine. Cover and refrigerate for at least 1 hour before serving. **Yield:** 8 servings.

Nutritional Analysis: 3/4 cup equals 192 calories, 2 g fat (1 g saturated fat), 5 mg cholesterol, 44 mg sodium, 42 g carbohydrate, 4 g fiber, 4 g protein.
Diabetic Exchanges: 2-1/2 fruit, 1/2 low-fat milk.

Spinach Beef Salad

(Pictured above)

Low-carb   Low-fat

Prep/Total Time: 30 min.

Refreshing cucumber, garlic and jalapeno pepper give this entree salad its flair. I like to heat up the tangy dressing a bit before tossing it with the greens.
—Janet Dingler, Cedartown, Georgia

- 1/2 pound boneless beef sirloin steak, cut into thin strips
- 1 jalapeno pepper, seeded and chopped
- 1 garlic clove, minced
- 1 large sweet red pepper, julienned
- 1/2 medium cucumber, peeled and julienned
- 1/4 cup lime juice
- 2 tablespoons brown sugar
- 2 tablespoons reduced-sodium soy sauce
- 1 teaspoon minced fresh mint *or* 1/2 teaspoon dried mint
- 1 teaspoon dried basil
- 1 teaspoon minced fresh gingerroot
- 6 cups torn fresh spinach

In a large nonstick skillet coated with nonstick cooking spray, saute the beef, jalapeno and garlic until the beef reaches desired doneness. Remove from the heat. Stir in the red pepper and cucumber.

In a small bowl, combine the lime juice, brown sugar, soy sauce, mint, basil and ginger. Place the spinach in a large bowl; add beef mixture and dressing. Toss to coat. **Yield:** 4 servings.

Editor's Note: When cutting or seeding hot peppers, use rubber or plastic gloves to protect your hands. Avoid touching your face.

Nutritional Analysis: 2 cups equals 136 calories, 3 g fat (1 g saturated fat), 31 mg cholesterol, 367 mg sodium, 15 g carbohydrate, 2 g fiber, 13 g protein.
Diabetic Exchanges: 2 lean meat, 1 vegetable, 1/2 fruit.

🍎 Spinach Stars at the Salad Bar

POPEYE'S PASSION for spinach is legendary…and it's easy to see why. It's a tasty addition to any salad calling for greens, plus it's a super source of good nutrition.

Spinach is rich in vitamins and minerals, particularly vitamins K, A and C, plus iron and folic acid. It has no cholesterol or fat…and only 23 calories per 1-cup serving.

The leafy green veggie is closely related to Swiss chard and beets. Three main types of spinach are popular in the United States:

- Savoy has crisp, creased curly leaves with a springy texture and slightly nutty flavor.
- Semi-savoy is less crinkled.
- Smooth-leaf spinach has flat, unwrinkled spade-shaped leaves and a milder taste than savoy.

When you're shopping for spinach, look for fresh, tender leaves with bright green color. Avoid spinach with yellow, wilted, bruised or broken leaves or signs of slime or mold. Store fresh spinach packed loosely in a plastic bag in the refrigerator crisper for up to a week.

Spinach is great for throwing together a good-for-you salad at a moment's notice…particularly with bagged spinach found in the produce section. Simply toss it with some tomato wedges and your favorite light dressing, and you've got a colorful salad that's sure to satisfy.

Side Dishes & Condiments

In this chapter, you'll find just the right accompaniment for your meals...from fresh vegetables, pleasing pasta and hearty potatoes to satisfying rice, mouth-watering relishes and perfectly seasoned sauces.

Herbed Brussels Sprouts (page 91)

Triple Mashed Vegetables

Meatless

Prep: 20 min. **Cook:** 25 min.

When I had trouble getting my family to eat rutabaga, I knew I'd need a flavor-filled recipe to convince them to try it. This is a nice variation on plain mashed potatoes, and it's very colorful.
—Noël Heckler, Wolcott, New York

1 medium rutabaga, peeled and cubed (about 3 cups)
6 medium potatoes, peeled and cubed (3-1/2 cups)
6 medium carrots, peeled and sliced (3 cups)
2 tablespoons butter
3/4 teaspoon salt
1/4 teaspoon pepper

Place vegetables in a large saucepan and cover with water. Bring to a boil. Reduce heat; cover and cook for 15-20 minutes or until very tender.

Drain vegetables and transfer to a bowl. Mash vegetables and add the butter, salt and pepper; beat until smooth and fluffy. **Yield:** 6 servings.

Nutritional Analysis: 2/3 cup equals 162 calories, 4 g fat (2 g saturated fat), 10 mg cholesterol, 402 mg sodium, 30 g carbohydrate, 6 g fiber, 3 g protein.
Diabetic Exchanges: 2 vegetable, 1 starch, 1 fat.

Garlic Green Beans

(Pictured above)

Low-carb *Low-fat* *Meatless*

Prep/Total Time: 20 min.

Here's a quick-and-easy treatment for fresh green beans that calls for just a handful of ingredients. Everyone who eats them loves them.
—Howard Levine, Arleta, California

1 pound fresh green beans, trimmed
1 to 2 garlic cloves, minced
1/2 teaspoon salt
1/8 teaspoon white pepper
2 teaspoons olive oil

Place beans and enough water to cover in a saucepan; bring to a boil. Cook, uncovered, for 8-10 minutes or until crisp-tender; drain. Toss beans with garlic, salt and pepper. Drizzle with oil. Serve immediately. **Yield:** 4 servings.

Nutritional Analysis: 3/4 cup equals 61 calories, 3 g fat (trace saturated fat), 0 cholesterol, 298 mg sodium, 9 g carbohydrate, 4 g fiber, 2 g protein.
Diabetic Exchanges: 1 vegetable, 1/2 fat.

Garlic Cauliflower

Low-carb *Low-fat* *Low-sodium*

Prep/Total Time: 20 min.

This is a no-fuss way to jazz up cauliflower…or most any vegetable. A friend used this recipe with broccoli. Now our sons enjoy both cauliflower and broccoli served this way.
—Teri Anne Finnerty, Marshalltown, Iowa

8 cups cauliflowerets
5 garlic cloves, minced
1 tablespoon butter
2 tablespoons reduced-sodium chicken broth
1/8 teaspoon salt
1/8 teaspoon pepper

Place cauliflower in a steamer basket. Place in a saucepan over 1 in. of water; bring to a boil. Cover and steam for 9-11 minutes or until crisp-tender.

Meanwhile, in a small nonstick skillet, saute garlic in butter for about 2 minutes or until tender. Stir in broth. Drain cauliflower and transfer to a serving bowl. Pour butter mixture over cauliflower. Sprinkle with salt and pepper; toss to coat evenly. Serve immediately. **Yield:** 8 servings.

Nutritional Analysis: 3/4 cup equals 38 calories, 2 g fat (1 g saturated fat), 4 mg cholesterol, 76 mg sodium, 5 g carbohydrate, 3 g fiber, 2 g protein.
Diabetic Exchanges: 1 vegetable, 1/2 fat.

Sweet Mustard

Low-carb   Low-fat   Low-sodium

Prep: 25 min. + chilling

I think this versatile spread is perfect paired with fat-free pretzels or spooned on a sandwich. Ham just doesn't taste the same without it.
—*Patricia Doetzel, Rosetown, Saskatchewan*

1/2 cup sugar
2 tablespoons ground mustard
1/3 cup white vinegar
1 egg

In a small saucepan, combine the sugar and mustard. Whisk in vinegar and egg. Cook and stir over low heat for 20 minutes or until thickened and a thermometer reads 160°. Pour into a storage container. Cool; cover and refrigerate for up to 3 weeks. **Yield:** 2/3 cup.

Nutritional Analysis: 2 teaspoons equals 54 calories, 1 g fat (trace saturated fat), 14 mg cholesterol, 9 mg sodium, 11 g carbohydrate, trace fiber, 1 g protein.
Diabetic Exchange: 1 starch.

Green Bean Corn Casserole

Meatless

Prep: 10 min. **Bake:** 35 min.

This is a classic church-social casserole, which has become a family favorite, even with my extended family. I reduced fat in many of the ingredients and find that it still has a very satisfying flavor that everyone loves.
—*Dawn Harvey, Danville, Pennsylvania*

1 can (10-3/4 ounces) reduced-fat condensed cream of celery soup, undiluted
1 cup (8 ounces) reduced-fat sour cream
1 cup (4 ounces) shredded reduced-fat cheddar cheese
1/2 cup finely chopped onions
1 package (16 ounces) frozen French-style green beans, thawed
2 cups frozen corn, thawed
1/4 cup crushed reduced-fat cheese crackers
Refrigerated butter-flavored spray

In a large bowl, combine the soup, sour cream, cheese and onions. Stir in beans and corn. Transfer to a 2-qt. baking dish coated with nonstick cooking spray. Cover and bake at 350° for 25 minutes.

Uncover; sprinkle edges with cracker crumbs. Spritz several times with butter spray. Bake, uncovered, 10-15 minutes longer or until edges are lightly browned and mixture is heated through. **Yield:** 7 servings.

Editor's Note: This recipe was tested with I Can't Believe It's Not Butter Spray.

Nutritional Analysis: 3/4 cup equals 178 calories, 7 g fat (4 g saturated fat), 18 mg cholesterol, 454 mg sodium, 22 g carbohydrate, 3 g fiber, 8 g protein.
Diabetic Exchanges: 1 starch, 1 vegetable, 1 lean meat, 1/2 fat.

Mint Sauce for Lamb

(Pictured below)

Low-carb   Low-fat   Low-sodium

Prep: 10 min. + standing

This recipe has been in our family for many years. Our backyard mint patch provided the main ingredient.
—*Ruth Bogdanski, Grants Pass, Oregon*

1/4 cup loosely packed mint leaves, finely chopped
1/4 cup boiling water
2 tablespoons cider vinegar
1 teaspoon sugar
1/4 teaspoon salt
1/8 teaspoon pepper

Place mint leaves in a small bowl. Stir in water, vinegar, sugar, salt and pepper until sugar is dissolved. Cover and let steep for 20 minutes, then serve immediately with lamb. **Yield:** 6 servings.

Nutritional Analysis: 1 tablespoon equals 4 calories, 0 fat (0 saturated fat), 0 cholesterol, 98 mg sodium, 1 g carbohydrate, trace fiber, trace protein.
Diabetic Exchange: Free food.

Grilled Broccoli

(Pictured below)

Low-carb *Meatless*

Prep: 5 min. + standing **Grill:** 10 min.

I started using this recipe in 1987, when I began cooking light, and it's been a favorite side dish ever since. With its lemon and Parmesan flavors, it once took second-place in a cooking contest.
—Alice Nulle, Woodstock, Illinois

6 cups fresh broccoli spears
2 tablespoons plus 1-1/2 teaspoons lemon juice
2 tablespoons olive oil
1/4 teaspoon salt
1/4 teaspoon pepper
3/4 cup grated Parmesan cheese

Place broccoli in a large bowl. Combine the lemon juice, oil, salt and pepper; drizzle over broccoli and toss to coat. Let stand for 30 minutes.

Coat grill rack with nonstick cooking spray before starting the grill. Prepare grill for indirect heat. Toss broccoli, then drain marinade. Place Parmesan cheese in a large resealable plastic bag. Add broccoli, a few pieces at a time; shake to coat. Grill broccoli, covered, over indirect medium heat for 8-10 minutes on each side or until crisp-tender. **Yield:** 6 servings.

Nutritional Analysis: 1 cup equals 107 calories, 8 g fat (3 g saturated fat), 8 mg cholesterol, 304 mg sodium, 5 g carbohydrate, 2 g fiber, 6 g protein.
Diabetic Exchanges: *1-1/2 fat, 1 vegetable.*

Sage Polenta

(Pictured above)

Meatless

Prep: 20 min. + chilling **Cook:** 25 min.

Bits of sweet red pepper peek through these pretty polenta squares which have a slightly sweet corn flavor and are nicely seasoned with sage. Serve this traditional ethnic dish with Italian entrees...or even Southwestern fare, suggests our Test Kitchen staff.

1/2 cup chopped onion
1/2 cup chopped sweet red pepper
1 garlic clove, minced
1 teaspoon butter
3 cups water
1 cup fat-free milk
1 cup cornmeal
1/4 cup grated Parmesan cheese
2 tablespoons minced fresh sage
3/4 teaspoon salt
1/4 teaspoon pepper
2 teaspoons canola oil

In a large nonstick saucepan, saute the onion, red pepper and garlic in butter until tender. Stir in water and milk; bring to a boil over medium heat. Gradually whisk in cornmeal, whisking constantly to prevent lumping. Reduce heat; cover and simmer for 8-10 minutes or until cornmeal is tender.

Stir in the Parmesan cheese, sage, salt and pepper. Spread into a 13-in. x 9-in. x 2-in. pan coated with nonstick cooking spray. Cover and refrigerate for 30-45 minutes or until firm.

Cut into 12 squares. In a large nonstick skillet, cook polenta in batches in oil over medium-high heat for 3-4 minutes on each side or until lightly browned. Serve warm. **Yield:** 6 servings.

Nutritional Analysis: 2 squares equals 143 calories, 4 g fat (1 g saturated fat), 5 mg cholesterol, 386 mg sodium, 22 g carbohydrate, 2 g fiber, 5 g protein.
Diabetic Exchanges: *1-1/2 starch, 1/2 fat.*

Spinach and Garbanzo Skillet

(Pictured below)

Meatless

Prep/Total Time: 30 min.

From our Test Kitchen, this colorful combination of beans, summer squash, tomatoes and spinach makes a bright addition to any meal. Topped with almonds, this tasty dish is sure to be requested often!

1 garlic clove, minced
1 tablespoon minced fresh basil *or* 1 teaspoon dried basil
1/8 teaspoon pepper
1 tablespoon olive oil
1 can (15 ounces) garbanzo beans *or* chickpeas, rinsed and drained
1 medium yellow summer squash, cut in half lengthwise, then into 1/4-inch slices
1/2 teaspoon cornstarch
2 tablespoons water
1 tablespoon rice vinegar
1 teaspoon honey
3 cups chopped fresh baby spinach
2 plum tomatoes, chopped
1/4 cup sliced almonds, toasted

In a large nonstick skillet or wok, saute the garlic, basil and pepper in hot oil for 30 seconds. Stir in beans and squash until evenly coated with seasonings. Cover and cook for 4 minutes, stirring three times.

In a small bowl, combine the cornstarch, water, vinegar and honey until smooth. Stir into bean mixture. Cook and stir for 1-2 minutes or until slightly thickened. Stir in spinach and tomatoes; heat through. Sprinkle with almonds. Serve immediately. **Yield:** 4 servings.

Nutritional Analysis: 3/4 cup equals 193 calories, 9 g fat (1 g saturated fat), 0 cholesterol, 158 mg sodium, 24 g carbohydrate, 7 g fiber, 7 g protein.
Diabetic Exchanges: 1 starch, 1 lean meat, 1 vegetable, 1 fat.

Greek Orzo and Broccoli

(Pictured above)

Meatless

Prep/Total Time: 30 min.

This recipe is certain to be a welcome treat at dinnertime. The warm side dish delivers strong feta and olive flavors while red pepper flakes add a little spice.
—Lillian Justis, Belleplain, New Jersey

3/4 cup uncooked orzo pasta
2 cups fresh broccoli florets
1/3 cup pitted Greek olives
1/4 cup crumbled feta cheese
1/4 cup grated Parmesan cheese
2 tablespoons minced fresh basil
4-1/2 teaspoons slivered almonds, toasted
1 tablespoon olive oil
1/4 teaspoon crushed red pepper flakes
1/4 teaspoon pepper

In a large saucepan, cook pasta in boiling water for 7 minutes. Add broccoli and cook 2-3 minutes longer or until pasta is tender; drain. Meanwhile, in a small bowl, combine the olives, feta cheese, Parmesan cheese and basil.

In a small nonstick skillet, saute almonds in oil for about 1 minute. Stir in red pepper flakes and pepper; cook and stir 1 minute longer. Pour over pasta mixture; toss to coat. Stir in olive mixture; toss to coat. **Yield:** 6 servings.

Nutritional Analysis: 2/3 cup equals 169 calories, 7 g fat (2 g saturated fat), 8 mg cholesterol, 208 mg sodium, 21 g carbohydrate, 2 g fiber, 7 g protein.
Diabetic Exchanges: 1-1/2 starch, 1 fat.

Polynesian Vegetables

(Pictured above)

Low-fat

Prep: 15 min. **Cook:** 20 min.

I can quickly prepare this colorful vegetable medley on the stovetop. Coated with a pineapple sauce, the pretty dinner accompaniment offers a tasty change of pace.
—Evelyn DeLuca, Hobe Sound, Florida

1-1/2 cups sliced fresh carrots
  1/2 cup water
1-1/2 teaspoons reduced-sodium soy sauce
    1 teaspoon beef bouillon granules
    1 teaspoon lemon juice
  1/4 teaspoon salt
1-3/4 cups fresh *or* frozen sugar snap peas
    1 can (8 ounces) sliced water chestnuts, drained
    1 tablespoon cornstarch
    1 can (6 ounces) unsweetened pineapple juice

In a large saucepan, combine the first six ingredients. Bring to a boil. Reduce heat; cover and simmer for 6-8 minutes; add snap peas and water chestnuts. Simmer 2-3 minutes longer or until vegetables are crisp-tender.

Combine cornstarch and pineapple juice until smooth; gradually add to pan. Bring to a boil; cook and stir for 1-2 minutes or until thickened. **Yield:** 4 servings.

Nutritional Analysis: 3/4 cup equals 107 calories, trace fat (trace saturated fat), trace cholesterol, 463 mg sodium, 25 g carbohydrate, 5 g fiber, 2 g protein.
Diabetic Exchanges: 2 vegetable, 1/2 starch, 1/2 fruit.

Maple-Glazed Parsnips And Carrots

Low-fat *Meatless*

Prep/Total Time: 25 min.

There's a sweet hint of spring in this vegetable dish drizzled with reduced-calorie pancake syrup.
—Bill Richards, Ironwood, Michigan

    1 pound carrots, cut into 1/4-inch slices
    1 pound parsnips, cut into 1/4-inch slices
4-1/2 teaspoons butter
  1/4 cup plus 2 tablespoons reduced-calorie
      pancake syrup
  1/4 cup orange juice
    2 teaspoons grated orange peel
  1/2 teaspoon salt
    1 teaspoon minced fresh parsley

In a large nonstick skillet, cook and stir carrots and parsnips over medium heat in butter for 5 minutes. Combine the pancake syrup, orange juice, orange peel and salt; pour over carrot mixture. Cook over medium-high heat until mixture comes to a boil.

Cover and cook for 6-7 minutes or until vegetables are crisp-tender. Uncover; cook 1-2 minutes longer or until vegetables are tender and syrup mixture thickens and coats vegetables. Sprinkle with parsley. **Yield:** 6 servings.

Nutritional Analysis: 2/3 cup equals 144 calories, 3 g fat (2 g saturated fat), 8 mg cholesterol, 279 mg sodium, 29 g carbohydrate, 4 g fiber, 2 g protein.
Diabetic Exchanges: 2 vegetable, 1 starch, 1/2 fat.

Favorite Recipe Made Lighter

WHETHER it's served as a savory side dish at brunch or offered alongside ham at dinnertime, one helping of Monterey Jack Corn Bake is never enough. "My family loves this egg bake, but I haven't made it in years because I know it isn't good for us," Donna Nortman writes from Camillus, New York. "I'd love for you to make it over so we can enjoy it again."

Our home economists were happy to help. Their aim was to lower the fat and cholesterol, yet maintain the smooth custard-like texture and rich taste of Donna's cheesy casserole.

Our Test Kitchen staff began by eliminating one of the whole eggs from the recipe…and substituting two egg whites instead. They also substantially reduced the fat in the recipe by substituting low-fat sour cream and cheddar cheese. And they cut way back on the Monterey Jack cheese, then diced it finely to better spread the flavor throughout the casserole.

The result? Makeover Monterey Jack Corn Bake boasts less than half the fat and saturated fat of the original. The cholesterol count was slashed by more than half…and calories were cut by a third. But the revised casserole is just as flavorful and crowd-pleasing as Donna's original!

Monterey Jack Corn Bake

Meatless

Prep: 10 min. **Bake:** 40 min.

2 eggs
1-1/2 cups (12 ounces) sour cream
2 cups fresh *or* frozen corn, thawed
8 ounces Monterey Jack cheese, cubed
1/2 cup soft bread crumbs
1/4 teaspoon pepper
1/2 cup shredded cheddar cheese

In a large bowl, combine eggs and sour cream. Add the corn, Monterey Jack cheese, bread crumbs and pepper; mix well.

Pour into a greased shallow 1-1/2-qt. baking dish. Bake, uncovered, at 350° for 35 minutes. Sprinkle with cheddar cheese; bake 5-10 minutes longer or until a knife inserted near the center comes out clean. Let stand for 5 minutes before serving. **Yield:** 6 servings.

Nutritional Analysis: 2/3 cup equals 373 calories, 27 g fat (16 g saturated fat), 159 mg cholesterol, 361 mg sodium, 15 g carbohydrate, 1 g fiber, 17 g protein.

Makeover Monterey Jack Corn Bake

(Pictured below)

Meatless

Prep: 10 min. **Bake:** 30 min.

1 egg
2 egg whites
1-1/2 cups (12 ounces) reduced-fat sour cream
2-3/4 cups fresh *or* frozen corn, thawed
1/2 cup soft bread crumbs
2 ounces Monterey Jack cheese, diced
1/2 teaspoon salt
1/8 teaspoon pepper
1/2 cup shredded reduced-fat cheddar cheese

In a large bowl, combine the egg, egg whites and sour cream. Add the corn, bread crumbs, Monterey Jack cheese, salt and pepper; mix well.

Pour into a shallow 1-1/2-qt. baking dish coated with nonstick cooking spray. Bake, uncovered, at 350° for 30-40 minutes or until a knife inserted near the center comes out clean. Sprinkle with remaining cheese; cover and let stand 5 minutes before serving. **Yield:** 6 servings.

Nutritional Analysis: 2/3 cup equals 225 calories, 11 g fat (7 g saturated fat), 70 mg cholesterol, 409 mg sodium, 20 g carbohydrate, 2 g fiber, 13 g protein.
Diabetic Exchanges: 2 fat, 1 starch, 1 lean meat.

Herbed Green Beans

(Pictured above)

Low-carb *Meatless*

Prep/Total Time: 15 min.

These beans take just moments to prepare in the microwave, making them perfect after a busy day when you're low on energy and time.
—Lucinda Walker, Somerset, Pennsylvania

> 1 pound fresh green beans, trimmed
> 4-1/2 teaspoons butter, melted
> 1/4 teaspoon salt
> 1/4 teaspoon dried savory
> 1/8 teaspoon dried oregano
> 1/8 teaspoon pepper

Place green beans in a microwave-safe dish. Combine the remaining ingredients; pour over beans and toss to coat evenly.

Cover and microwave on high for 6-8 minutes or until beans are tender. **Yield:** 4 servings.

Editor's Note: This recipe was tested in a 1,100-watt microwave.

Nutritional Analysis: 3/4 cup equals 69 calories, 4 g fat (3 g saturated fat), 11 mg cholesterol, 197 mg sodium, 7 g carbohydrate, 3 g fiber, 2 g protein.
Diabetic Exchanges: 1 vegetable, 1 fat.

🍎 Jalapeno Hint

BEFORE I chop jalapeno peppers, I place them in a resealable plastic bag and put them in the freezer. I still wear rubber gloves to protect my hands while chopping the frozen peppers, but there's not much juice. And the eye-watering aroma that often accompanies jalapenos is virtually gone.
—Martha Pollock, Oregonia, Ohio

Three-Pepper Chutney

(Pictured below)

Low-fat

Prep: 30 min. **Cook:** 1-1/2 hours + chilling

This sweet chutney is as delicious on pork, beef and poultry as it is on grilled hot dogs and burgers.
—Lisa Louw, Alachua, Florida

> 1-1/2 cups packed brown sugar
> 1-1/2 cups cider vinegar
> 3 *each* medium green and sweet red peppers, chopped
> 3 jalapeno peppers, seeded and chopped
> 1 medium onion, chopped
> 1 teaspoon salt

In a large saucepan, combine all ingredients. Bring to a boil. Reduce heat; simmer, uncovered, for 1-1/2 to 2 hours or until thickened. Pour into a serving bowl. Cover and refrigerate for 1-2 hours or until chilled. **Yield:** 2 cups.

Editor's Note: When cutting or seeding hot peppers, use rubber or plastic gloves to protect your hands. Avoid touching your face.

Nutritional Analysis: 2 tablespoons equals 97 calories, trace fat (trace saturated fat), 0 cholesterol, 157 mg sodium, 25 g carbohydrate, 1 g fiber, 1 g protein.
Diabetic Exchange: 1 starch.

Cajun Seasoning

Low-carb   Low-fat   Low-sodium

Prep/Total Time: 5 min.

A sprinkling of this savory seasoning is sure to lend a Louisiana accent to everything from pasta to meat.
—Della Stamp, Long Beach, California

1 tablespoon onion powder
1 tablespoon white pepper
1 tablespoon garlic powder
1 tablespoon ground mustard
1 tablespoon paprika
1-1/2 teaspoons celery seed
1-1/2 teaspoons dried thyme

In a small bowl, combine all ingredients. Store seasoning in an airtight container in a cool dry place for up to 6 months. **Yield:** 1/3 cup.

Nutritional Analysis: 1 teaspoon equals 10 calories, trace fat (trace saturated fat), 0 cholesterol, 1 mg sodium, 1 g carbohydrate, trace fiber, trace protein.
Diabetic Exchange: Free food.

Onions and Spice, Parsley and Rice

Meatless

Prep: 15 min. **Cook:** 30 min.

For a succulent side dish, try this nicely herbed and spiced rice. Onions, mint, dill and lemon all accent the tender grain, while the flecks of green dress it up a bit.
—Marion Karlin, Waterloo, Iowa

1-3/4 cups thinly sliced green onions
1-1/2 cups coarsely chopped onions
2/3 cup uncooked long grain rice
1/2 cup minced fresh parsley
2 tablespoons butter
1 teaspoon salt
1 teaspoon dill weed
1/2 teaspoon dried mint
1/4 teaspoon white pepper
1-1/2 cups water
3 tablespoons lemon juice
1/2 teaspoon grated lemon peel

In a large nonstick skillet, cook green onions, onions, rice and parsley in butter for about 3 minutes or until coated evenly with butter. Stir in the salt, dill, mint and pepper. Stir in the water, lemon juice and lemon peel. Bring to a boil. Reduce heat; cover and simmer for 16-18 minutes or until rice is tender. Fluff with a fork. **Yield:** 6 servings.

Nutritional Analysis: 2/3 cup equals 144 calories, 4 g fat (2 g saturated fat), 10 mg cholesterol, 442 mg sodium, 24 g carbohydrate, 2 g fiber, 3 g protein.
Diabetic Exchanges: 1 starch, 1 vegetable, 1 fat.

Horseradish Mashed Potatoes

(Pictured below)

Low-fat   Meatless

Prep: 35 min. **Bake:** 20 min.

This potato dish gets its flavor from reduced-fat sour cream and mayonnaise, chives and a little horseradish.
—Melissa Merkle, Elizabeth, Illinois

1-1/2 pounds Yukon gold potatoes, peeled and cubed
6 tablespoons reduced-fat sour cream, *divided*
3 tablespoons fat-free milk
2-1/4 teaspoons snipped chives, *divided*
1/2 teaspoon salt
4-1/2 teaspoons reduced-fat mayonnaise
2-1/4 teaspoons prepared horseradish
1/8 teaspoon pepper

Place potatoes in a large saucepan and cover with water. Bring to a boil. Reduce heat; cover and cook for 15-20 minutes or until tender. Drain.

Place potatoes in a large bowl; mash with 5 tablespoons sour cream, milk, 1-1/2 teaspoons chives and salt. Spoon into a 1-qt. baking dish coated with nonstick cooking spray.

In a small bowl, combine the mayonnaise, horseradish, pepper and remaining sour cream. Spread over potato mixture. Sprinkle with remaining chives. Bake, uncovered, at 400° for 20-25 minutes or until heated through. **Yield:** 6 servings.

Nutritional Analysis: 1/2 cup equals 130 calories, 3 g fat (1 g saturated fat), 6 mg cholesterol, 204 mg sodium, 22 g carbohydrate, 1 g fiber, 4 g protein.
Diabetic Exchanges: 1-1/2 starch, 1/2 fat.

Gingered Mango Salsa

(Pictured above)

Low-carb Low-fat *Low-sodium*

Prep: 15 min. + standing

Zesty cilantro meets cool mint in this change-of-pace salsa. We love it with grilled chicken. You can substitute papaya for the mango, if you like.
—Barb Fore, Saline, Michigan

   1 cup chopped peeled mango
1/4 cup chopped red onion
1/4 cup minced fresh cilantro
1/4 cup lime juice
   2 tablespoons minced fresh mint
   1 tablespoon minced fresh gingerroot
1/2 teaspoon olive oil
1/4 teaspoon salt

In a bowl, combine all ingredients. Let stand for 30 minutes before serving. **Yield:** 1-1/4 cups.

   Nutritional Analysis: *1/4 cup equals 39 calories, 1 g fat (trace saturated fat), 0 cholesterol, 120 mg sodium, 9 g carbohydrate, 1 g fiber, trace protein.*
   Diabetic Exchange: *1/2 fruit.*

Curry Blend

Low-carb Low-fat *Low-sodium*

Prep/Total Time: 5 min.

Bring a little Middle Eastern flair to your dinner table with this seasoning blend. Our home economists created the tasty combination of seasonings to jazz up plain rice.

3 tablespoons ground coriander
2 teaspoons ground turmeric

🍎 Saucy Picnic Carrier

HERE'S a handy idea for packing a picnic. Rather than carry several bottles, jars and containers to a cookout, I serve all the condiments from a muffin tin. I just fill each muffin cup with a different condiment and serving spoons. Include diced onions, sliced pickles and whatever other add-ons your picnic requires.

   Covered with foil, a muffin tray makes transporting salsas, chutneys, mustards and more a breeze, and it takes up less room in the cooler, too.
—*Gusty Crum, Dover, Ohio*

and stir for 1-2 minutes or until slightly thickened. Drain corn; serve with seasoned butter. **Yield:** 8 servings.

Nutritional Analysis: 1 ear of corn with 1-1/2 teaspoons seasoned butter equals 105 calories, 4 g fat (2 g saturated fat), 8 mg cholesterol, 63 mg sodium, 18 g carbohydrate, 2 g fiber, 3 g protein.
Diabetic Exchanges: 1 starch, 1/2 fat.

Brussels Sprouts With Green Peppers

(Pictured below)

Low-carb   Low-fat   Meatless

Prep/Total Time: 25 min.

This simple side dish goes well with poultry, seafood or almost any main course. The green pepper, celery and onion add to its nutritional value.
—*Diane Hixon, Niceville, Florida*

 1 pound fresh brussels sprouts, halved
1/4 cup chopped green pepper
1/4 cup sliced celery
1/4 cup chopped onion
 1 tablespoon butter
1/4 teaspoon salt
1/8 teaspoon pepper

Place brussels sprouts in a saucepan with 1 in. of water. Bring to a boil. Reduce heat; cover and simmer for 7 minutes. Meanwhile, in a large nonstick skillet, saute the green pepper, celery and onion in butter for 2 minutes. Drain brussels sprouts and add to vegetable mixture. Sprinkle with salt and pepper. Cook and stir for 3-5 minutes or until sprouts are tender. **Yield:** 6 servings.

Nutritional Analysis: 3/4 cup equals 82 calories, 3 g fat (2 g saturated fat), 8 mg cholesterol, 212 mg sodium, 12 g carbohydrate, 5 g fiber, 4 g protein.
Diabetic Exchanges: 2 vegetable, 1/2 fat.

 2 teaspoons ground cumin
3/4 teaspoon ground cloves
3/4 teaspoon ground cardamom
Dash cayenne pepper

In a small bowl, combine all ingredients. Store in an airtight container in a cool dry place for up to 6 months. **Yield:** about 1/4 cup.

Nutritional Analysis: 3/4 teaspoon equals 7 calories, trace fat (trace saturated fat), 0 cholesterol, 1 mg sodium, 1 g carbohydrate, 1 g fiber, trace protein.
Diabetic Exchange: Free food.

Cajun Buttered Corn

(Pictured above)

Low-sodium   Meatless

Prep/Total Time: 20 min.

I like to spice up summer meals with this seasoned butter. Garlic and chili powders make the butter a perfect complement to fresh corn.
—*Anne-Lise Botting, Duluth, Georgia*

 8 medium ears sweet corn
 2 tablespoons butter
1/4 teaspoon chili powder
1/4 teaspoon coarsely ground pepper
1/8 teaspoon garlic powder
1/8 teaspoon cayenne pepper
 1 teaspoon cornstarch
1/4 cup reduced-sodium chicken *or* vegetable broth

In a large kettle, bring 3 qts. of water to a boil; add corn. Return to a boil; cook for 3-5 minutes or until tender.
    Meanwhile, in a small saucepan, melt butter. Stir in the chili powder, pepper, garlic powder and cayenne; cook and stir for 1 minute. Combine cornstarch and broth until smooth; gradually whisk into butter mixture. Bring to a boil; cook

Herbed Twice-Baked Potatoes

(Pictured above)

Meatless

Prep: 15 min. **Bake:** 1-1/4 hours + cooling

Light cream cheese, garlic powder and butter make these classic potatoes irresistible. Replace the basil with parsley if you'd like, or mix in your favorite seasoning blend.
—Ruth Andrewson, Peck, Idaho

2 medium baking potatoes
1-1/2 ounces reduced-fat cream cheese, cubed
1 tablespoon snipped chives
1/4 teaspoon salt
1/4 teaspoon dried basil
Dash cayenne pepper
3 tablespoons fat-free milk
3 teaspoons butter, melted, *divided*
Dash garlic powder
Dash paprika

Scrub and pierce potatoes. Bake at 375° for 1 hour or until tender. Cool for 10 minutes. Cut potatoes in half. Scoop out pulp, leaving a thin shell.

In a bowl, mash the pulp with cream cheese, chives, salt, basil and cayenne. Add milk and 1-1/2 teaspoons butter; mash. Spoon into potato shells. Drizzle with remaining butter; sprinkle with garlic powder and paprika. Place on an ungreased baking sheet. Bake for 15-20 minutes or until heated through. **Yield:** 4 servings.

Nutritional Analysis: 1 potato half equals 150 calories, 5 g fat (3 g saturated fat), 15 mg cholesterol, 234 mg sodium, 23 g carbohydrate, 2 g fiber, 4 g protein.
Diabetic Exchanges: 1-1/2 starch, 1 fat.

🍎 Cauliflower Clue

CAULIFLOWER is a great source of vitamin C and the B vitamin, folate. When cooking, it's best to steam it to get the most of those nutrients.

Rice with Lemon and Spinach

Meatless

Prep: 20 min. **Bake:** 30 min.

This savory side dish has a light lemon flavor. Baked with feta and spinach, it's a lovely accompaniment to most main courses...and pairs perfectly with fish.
—Billie Moss, El Sobrante, California

1 small onion, chopped
1 cup sliced fresh mushrooms
2 garlic cloves, minced
1 tablespoon olive oil
3 cups cooked long grain rice
1 package (10 ounces) frozen chopped spinach, thawed and squeezed dry
3 tablespoons lemon juice
1/2 teaspoon salt
1/4 teaspoon dill weed
1/8 teaspoon pepper
1/3 cup crumbled feta cheese, *divided*

In a skillet, saute the onion, mushrooms and garlic in oil until tender. Stir in the rice, spinach, lemon juice, salt, dill and pepper. Reserve 1 tablespoon cheese. Stir remaining cheese into skillet; mix well.

Transfer to an 8-in. square baking dish coated with non-stick cooking spray. Sprinkle with reserved cheese. Cover and bake at 350° for 25 minutes. Uncover; bake 5-10 minutes longer or until heated through and cheese is melted. **Yield:** 6 servings.

Nutritional Analysis: 2/3 cup equals 167 calories, 4 g fat (2 g saturated fat), 7 mg cholesterol, 324 mg sodium, 27 g carbohydrate, 2 g fiber, 5 g protein.
Diabetic Exchanges: 1-1/2 starch, 1 vegetable, 1 fat.

Whipped Cauliflower

Low-carb *Meatless*

Prep/Total Time: 20 min.

Need a low-carb substitute for mashed potatoes? This five-ingredient dish from our Test Kitchen has a mild cauliflower flavor with a smooth creamy texture.

1 medium head cauliflower, cut into florets
1/4 cup fat-free milk
2 tablespoons canola oil
1/4 teaspoon salt
1/8 teaspoon white pepper

Place cauliflower in a steamer basket; place in a saucepan over 1 in. of water. Bring to a boil; cover and steam for 8-10 minutes or until tender. Cool slightly. Place the milk and oil in a blender or food processor. Add the cauliflower, salt and pepper; cover and process until blended. Serve immediately. **Yield:** 4 servings.

Nutritional Analysis: 1/2 cup equals 105 calories, 7 g fat (1 g saturated fat), 1 mg cholesterol, 199 mg sodium, 8 g carbohydrate, 4 g fiber, 3 g protein.
Diabetic Exchanges: 1-1/2 fat, 1 vegetable.

Favorite Recipe Made Lighter

FOND of spinach? Then you're sure to like Spinach Casserole, a flavorful side dish that makes the most of convenient frozen spinach.

"This is my all-time favorite spinach recipe," writes Janet Hornsby from her home in Palmyra, Indiana. "Even my kids liked it when they were little. Unfortunately, it is full of fat and it's very high in cholesterol. I'd like to eat it without feeling guilty. Is there any way you can help?"

Our home economists were happy to do just that. The majority of the fat and cholesterol in Janet's recipe comes from the butter, eggs and heavy whipping cream. To lighten the recipe, our Test Kitchen staff decreased the amount of butter and replaced the four whole eggs called for with two whole eggs and four egg whites.

To further reduce the fat and cholesterol, they used fat-free half-and-half instead of the heavy whipping cream. Next, they added flour to help stabilize the mixture. The result was a hit with our tasting panel.

Makeover Spinach Casserole has the same firm texture and robust spinach flavor as the original. But the fat and saturated fat had been slashed by more than 80%. Both the calories and cholesterol were reduced by more than 60%.

Spinach Casserole

Low-carb   *Meatless*

Prep: 10 min. **Bake:** 55 min.

> 2 packages (10 ounces *each*) frozen chopped
>   spinach, thawed and squeezed dry
> 4 eggs
> 1 cup heavy whipping cream
> 1/2 cup butter, melted
> 1/2 teaspoon salt
> 1/4 teaspoon pepper
> 2 tablespoons grated Parmesan cheese

In a blender or food processor, combine spinach and eggs; cover and process until smooth. Add the cream, butter, salt and pepper; process until blended.

Grease the bottom and sides of a 1-qt. straight-sided baking dish. Dust bottom and sides with Parmesan cheese. Transfer spinach mixture to dish. Bake, uncovered, at 350° for 55-60 minutes or until a knife inserted near the center comes out clean. Serve immediately. **Yield:** 6 servings.

Nutritional Analysis: 2/3 cup equals 351 calories, 34 g fat (20 g saturated fat), 238 mg cholesterol, 509 mg sodium, 5 g carbohydrate, 3 g fiber, 9 g protein.

Makeover Spinach Casserole

(Pictured above)

Low-carb   *Meatless*

Prep: 10 min. **Bake:** 50 min.

> 2 packages (10 ounces *each*) frozen chopped
>   spinach, thawed and squeezed dry
> 4 egg whites
> 2 eggs
> 1 cup fat-free half-and-half
> 2 tablespoons butter, melted
> 1 tablespoon all-purpose flour
> 1/2 teaspoon salt
> 1/4 teaspoon pepper
> 2 tablespoons grated Parmesan cheese

In a blender or food processor, combine the spinach, egg whites and eggs; cover and process until smooth. Add the half-and-half, butter, flour, salt and pepper; process until blended.

Coat a 1-qt. straight-sided baking dish with nonstick cooking spray. Dust bottom and sides with Parmesan cheese. Transfer spinach mixture to dish. Bake, uncovered, at 350° for 50-60 minutes or until a knife inserted near the center comes out clean. Serve immediately. **Yield:** 6 servings.

Nutritional Analysis: 2/3 cup equals 131 calories, 6 g fat (3 g saturated fat), 82 mg cholesterol, 434 mg sodium, 9 g carbohydrate, 3 g fiber, 9 g protein.
Diabetic Exchanges: 1 lean meat, 1/2 starch, 1/2 fat.

Broccoli Mashed Potatoes

Low-fat   Meatless

Prep/Total Time: 30 min.

I make mashed potatoes with a twist—I add broccoli.
This low-fat dish always gets rave reviews.
—Jim Hadley, Charlotte, North Carolina

1-1/2 pounds small unpeeled red potatoes, cubed
2 fresh broccoli spears
1-2/3 cups chopped onions
1/3 cup reduced-fat sour cream
1 teaspoon salt
1/4 teaspoon pepper

Place potatoes in a saucepan and cover with water; bring to a boil. Reduce heat; cover and cook for 10 minutes. Remove broccoli florets from stems. Peel stems and cut into 1/4-in. slices; cut slices in half. Add florets and stems to potatoes; cook for 10-12 minutes or until vegetables are tender; drain.

In a nonstick skillet coated with nonstick cooking spray, cook onions until tender. Add potato mixture with sour cream, salt and pepper; mash. **Yield:** 6 servings.

Nutritional Analysis: 2/3 cup equals 119 calories, 1 g fat (1 g saturated fat), 4 mg cholesterol, 413 mg sodium, 23 g carbohydrate, 3 g fiber, 4 g protein.
Diabetic Exchange: 1-1/2 starch.

Rosemary Rice

(Pictured above)

Meatless

Prep/Total Time: 25 min.

This quick dish is a favorite with my family. It's low in fat because it gets flavor from herbs, not butter.
—Connie Regalado, El Paso, Texas

1/4 cup chopped onion
1 garlic clove, minced
1 tablespoon olive oil
1 can (14-1/2 ounces) reduced-sodium chicken broth *or* vegetable broth
1/4 cup water
1 cup uncooked long grain rice
1 tablespoon minced fresh rosemary *or* 1 teaspoon dried rosemary, crushed
1/4 teaspoon pepper
1/4 cup shredded Parmesan cheese

In a saucepan, saute onion and garlic in oil until tender. Add broth and water. Stir in the rice, rosemary and pepper. Bring to a boil. Reduce heat; cover and simmer for 15-18 minutes or until rice is tender. Remove from the heat; stir in Parmesan cheese. **Yield:** 4 servings.

Nutritional Analysis: 3/4 cup equals 250 calories, 5 g fat (1 g saturated fat), 4 mg cholesterol, 367 mg sodium, 42 g carbohydrate, 1 g fiber, 7 g protein.
Diabetic Exchange: 3 starch.

Scalloped Tomatoes

Low-carb   Low-fat   Meatless

Prep: 20 min. **Bake:** 35 min.

Warm and comforting, this old-fashioned side dish is a great way to use up garden bounty. I lightened the original recipe by using less butter and flour and only a bit of honey.
—Norma Piper, West Salem, Wisconsin

1/2 cup chopped onion
1/2 cup chopped celery
1 tablespoon butter
1 tablespoon all-purpose flour
1 tablespoon honey
2 teaspoons prepared mustard
1/2 teaspoon salt
1/4 teaspoon pepper
2 slices whole wheat bread, toasted and cubed
4 cups chopped fresh tomatoes

In a nonstick skillet, cook onion and celery in butter until tender. Stir in the flour until blended; cook 1 minute longer. Stir in the honey, mustard, salt and pepper until blended. Stir in bread cubes and tomatoes.

Transfer to an 8-in. square baking dish coated with nonstick cooking spray. Bake, uncovered, at 350° for 35-40 minutes or until bubbly. **Yield:** 6 servings.

Nutritional Analysis: 3/4 cup equals 88 calories, 3 g fat (1 g saturated fat), 5 mg cholesterol, 304 mg sodium, 15 g carbohydrate, 2 g fiber, 2 g protein.
Diabetic Exchanges: 1 vegetable, 1/2 starch, 1/2 fat.

Vegetable Barley Bake

(Pictured below)

Low-fat   Meatless

Prep: 25 min. **Bake:** 55 min.

I rely on wholesome barley for a heart-smart dish that complements most any main course.
—Shirley Doyle, Mt. Prospect, Illinois

3 medium sweet red *or* green peppers, chopped
4 cups sliced fresh mushrooms
2 medium onions, chopped
2 tablespoons butter
2 cups reduced-sodium chicken broth *or*
   vegetable broth
1-1/2 cups medium pearl barley
1/8 teaspoon pepper

In a large nonstick skillet, saute the peppers, mushrooms and onions in butter for 8-10 minutes or until tender. Transfer to a 13-in. x 9-in. x 2-in. baking dish coated with nonstick cooking spray. Stir in the broth, barley and pepper.

Cover and bake at 350° for 50 minutes. Uncover; bake 5-10 minutes longer or until barley is tender and liquid is absorbed. **Yield:** 10 servings.

Nutritional Analysis: 3/4 cup equals 157 calories, 3 g fat (2 g saturated fat), 6 mg cholesterol, 153 mg sodium, 30 g carbohydrate, 6 g fiber, 5 g protein.
Diabetic Exchanges: 1-1/2 starch, 1 vegetable, 1/2 fat.

Pecan Rice Stuffing

Meatless

Prep/Total Time: 30 min.

Curry and cumin lend wonderful flavor to this dish that gets sweetness from raisins and crunch from pecans. The delicious stuffing works well with Cornish hens.
—Daphne Blandford, Gander, Newfoundland

1 tablespoon butter
2 teaspoons ground cumin
1 teaspoon curry powder
1-1/2 cups uncooked long grain rice
   2 cans (14-1/2 ounces *each*) reduced-sodium
      chicken broth *or* vegetable broth
   3 green onions, thinly sliced
   1/2 cup golden raisins
   1/2 cup chopped pecans

In a saucepan, combine the butter, cumin and curry powder. Add the rice; cook and stir until evenly coated. Add broth; bring to a boil.

Reduce heat; cover and simmer for 15-18 minutes or until rice is tender and liquid is almost absorbed. Stir in the onions, raisins and pecans. **Yield:** 9 servings.

Nutritional Analysis: 2/3 cup equals 215 calories, 6 g fat (1 g saturated fat), 3 mg cholesterol, 258 mg sodium, 35 g carbohydrate, 2 g fiber, 5 g protein.
Diabetic Exchanges: 2 starch, 1/2 fruit, 1/2 fat.

Corn with Basil Mustard

Low-fat Low-sodium Meatless

Prep/Total Time: 15 min.

Everyone will think you're a pro when you spruce up corn in this flavorful way.
—*Sarah Reinhardt, Plymouth, Minnesota*

1 package (16 ounces) frozen gold and white corn
1 tablespoon butter, softened
4 teaspoons Dijon mustard
2 tablespoons minced fresh basil *or* 1 teaspoon dried basil

Prepare corn according to package directions; drain. In a small bowl, combine the butter, mustard and basil. Stir into corn until butter is melted. **Yield:** 5 servings.

Nutritional Analysis: 1/2 cup equals 104 calories, 3 g fat (2 g saturated fat), 6 mg cholesterol, 122 mg sodium, 19 g carbohydrate, 2 g fiber, 3 g protein.
Diabetic Exchanges: 1 starch, 1/2 fat.

Spiced Cranberry Ketchup

(Pictured above)

Low-fat Low-sodium

Prep: 10 min. **Cook:** 30 min. + chilling

Here's a condiment that makes poultry dishes sing! It takes just 10 minutes to prepare, too. We like it with turkey burgers or roasted chicken.
—*Gilda Lester, Wilmington, North Carolina*

2-1/4 cups fresh *or* frozen cranberries
1/2 cup water
1/4 cup chopped green onions
2 bay leaves
3/4 cup plus 2 tablespoons sugar
1/4 cup white wine vinegar
1/4 cup balsamic vinegar
1-1/2 teaspoons Dijon mustard
1/2 teaspoon ground cinnamon
1/4 teaspoon salt
1/4 teaspoon ground allspice
1/4 teaspoon ground cloves
1/8 teaspoon ground cumin

In a small saucepan, combine the cranberries, water, onions and bay leaves. Cook over medium heat until the berries pop, about 15 minutes. Cool slightly. Discard bay leaves. Press cranberry mixture through a fine mesh strainer; discard cranberry skins.

Return the cranberry mixture to the pan. Stir in the remaining ingredients. Bring to a boil. Reduce heat; simmer, uncovered, for 8-10 minutes or until thickened. Cool. Cover and refrigerate (mixture will thicken more upon refrigeration). **Yield:** 1 cup.

Nutritional Analysis: 2 tablespoons equals 109 calories, trace fat (trace saturated fat), 0 cholesterol, 101 mg sodium, 28 g carbohydrate, 1 g fiber, trace protein.
Diabetic Exchange: 2 starch.

Grilling Herb Mix

Low-carb Low-fat Low-sodium

Prep/Total Time: 5 min.

This is a no-fuss seasoning blend that's especially good for flame-broiled chicken or pork.
—*Karyn Fischer, Decatur, Michigan*

2 teaspoons *each* dried basil, oregano and rosemary, crushed
1 teaspoon rubbed sage
1 teaspoon dried mint
1 teaspoon dried thyme
1 teaspoon pepper

In a small bowl, combine all of the ingredients. Store in an airtight container for up to 6 months. **Yield:** 8 teaspoons.

Nutritional Analysis: 1/2 teaspoon equals 3 calories, trace fat (trace saturated fat), 0 cholesterol, trace sodium, 1 g carbohydrate, trace fiber, trace protein.
Diabetic Exchange: Free food.

Orange Cranberry Chutney

Low-fat Low-sodium Meatless

Prep/Total Time: 30 min.

After my mother reminisced about the chutney my grandmother used to make, I combined a few recipes I had and came up with this simple citrus version. We love it served with turkey and pork.
—*Charlotte Carlile, Daytona Beach, Florida*

1 package (12 ounces) fresh *or* frozen cranberries
1 cup dried cranberries
1 cup orange juice
2/3 cup sugar

1/4 teaspoon ground cinnamon
1/4 teaspoon ground ginger
1/8 teaspoon ground allspice
1/8 teaspoon ground cloves
   1 cup chopped peeled Golden Delicious apple

In a small saucepan, combine the first eight ingredients. Cook over medium heat for 10 minutes or just until the cranberries start to pop.

Stir in the apple. Cook 8-10 minutes longer or until thickened and all berries have popped. Serve warm or cold. Store in the refrigerator. **Yield:** 10 servings.

Nutritional Analysis: 1/4 cup equals 122 calories, trace fat (trace saturated fat), 0 cholesterol, 1 mg sodium, 32 g carbohydrate, 2 g fiber, trace protein.
Diabetic Exchanges: 1 starch, 1 fruit.

Sweet Potato Pear Bake

Low-fat   Low-sodium   Meatless

Prep: 10 min. **Cook:** 25 min.

I can always rely on this comforting side dish to please everyone at the table. The combination of mellow pears and sweet potatoes is wonderful.
—Miriam Lavella, Kersey, Pennsylvania

   3 medium sweet potatoes
1/4 cup packed brown sugar
1-1/2 teaspoons cornstarch
1/4 cup orange juice
   3 tablespoons pear juice
4-1/2 teaspoons butter, cubed
1/8 teaspoon salt
   2 tablespoons raisins
   2 tablespoons golden raisins
   3 medium firm pears, peeled and cut
      into 1/4-inch slices

Pierce the sweet potatoes and place on a microwave-safe plate. Microwave, uncovered, on high for 13-15 minutes or until tender. Cool. Peel and cut sweet potatoes into 1/4-in. slices; set aside.

In a large microwave-safe bowl, combine the brown sugar and cornstarch. Stir in the orange juice and pear juice until smooth. Stir in butter and salt. Microwave, uncovered, on high for 1-1/2 to 2 minutes, stirring every 30 seconds, or until mixture is thickened and bubbly. Stir in raisins.

In an 8-in. square microwave-safe dish coated with nonstick cooking spray, layer half of the sweet potatoes, pears and sauce. Repeat layers. Cover and microwave on high for 8-10 minutes or until pears are tender. Let stand for 5 minutes before serving. **Yield:** 8 servings.

Editor's Note: This recipe was tested in a 1,100-watt microwave.

Nutritional Analysis: 1 serving equals 148 calories, 2 g fat (1 g saturated fat), 6 mg cholesterol, 66 mg sodium, 32 g carbohydrate, 3 g fiber, 1 g protein.
Diabetic Exchanges: 1 starch, 1 fruit.

Creamy Noodles

(Pictured below)

Meatless

Prep/Total Time: 25 min.

There's lots of garlic flavor in this filling side dish. I like it with grilled chicken, but it works well with any menu.
—Brenda Nolen, Folsom, Louisiana

   8 ounces uncooked thin spaghetti
   3 garlic cloves, minced
   3 tablespoons butter, *divided*
   6 ounces fat-free cream cheese, cubed
   3 tablespoons reduced-fat sour cream
   3 tablespoons fat-free milk
3/4 teaspoon salt
1/2 teaspoon onion powder
1/4 teaspoon Cajun seasoning
1/4 teaspoon white pepper
4-1/2 teaspoons minced fresh parsley

Cook spaghetti according to package directions. Meanwhile, in a saucepan, saute garlic in 1 tablespoon butter until tender. Add the cream cheese, sour cream, milk, salt, onion powder, Cajun seasoning, pepper and remaining butter. Cook and stir over low heat just until smooth (do not boil). Remove from the heat.

Drain spaghetti; toss with cream sauce. Sprinkle with parsley. Serve immediately. **Yield:** 6 servings.

Nutritional Analysis: 1 cup equals 234 calories, 7 g fat (4 g saturated fat), 20 mg cholesterol, 547 mg sodium, 32 g carbohydrate, 1 g fiber, 10 g protein.
Diabetic Exchanges: 2 starch, 1 very lean meat, 1 fat.

Sweet Thyme-Mustard Spread

Low-carb   Low-fat   Low-sodium

Prep/Total Time: 5 min.

This slightly sweet mustard is excellent when brushed over baked fish. With just four ingredients, it's also quick to mix up for sandwiches.
—*Mitzi Sentiff, Alexandria, Virginia*

1/2 cup whole grain *or* spicy brown mustard
1/2 cup Dijon mustard
3 tablespoons honey, warmed
1 tablespoon minced fresh thyme *or* 1 teaspoon dried thyme

In a small bowl, combine all ingredients. Store in the refrigerator for up to 3 weeks. **Yield:** about 1 cup.

Nutritional Analysis: 2 teaspoons equals 8 calories, trace fat (0 saturated fat), 0 cholesterol, 95 mg sodium, 1 g carbohydrate, trace fiber, trace protein.
Diabetic Exchange: Free food.

Sesame Snow Peas

(Pictured above)

Low-carb   Meatless

Prep/Total Time: 10 min.

I created this dish because I like seasoning with soy sauce and sesame seeds.
—*Kathleen Valle, Philadelphia, Pennsylvania*

1 pound fresh snow peas
1/2 cup water
2 tablespoons sesame seeds
2 tablespoons reduced-sodium soy sauce
1 tablespoon sesame oil
1/8 teaspoon pepper

Place the snow peas and water in a microwave-safe bowl. Cover and microwave on high for 6 minutes or until peas are crisp-tender; drain well. Stir in the remaining ingredients. **Yield:** 4 servings.
Editor's Note: This recipe was tested in a 1,100-watt microwave.

Nutritional Analysis: 1 cup equals 111 calories, 6 g fat (1 g saturated fat), 0 cholesterol, 307 mg sodium, 9 g carbohydrate, 3 g fiber, 5 g protein.
Diabetic Exchanges: 2 vegetable, 1 fat.

Roasted Garlic Mashed Potatoes

Meatless

Prep: 15 min. **Bake:** 30 min. + cooling

For a crowd-pleasing dinner addition that's lighter than you might think, try these tasty mashed potatoes. I use reduced-fat cream cheese and plenty of fresh garlic to flavor the rich side dish.
—*Nikki Dolan, Largo, Florida*

1 whole garlic bulb
1 teaspoon canola oil
6 medium red potatoes (about 2-1/4 pounds), cubed
1 package (8 ounces) reduced-fat cream cheese, cubed
1/4 cup milk
1/2 teaspoon salt
1/4 teaspoon pepper

Remove the papery outer skin from the garlic (do not peel or separate the cloves). Cut the top off the garlic bulb; brush the bulb with canola oil. Wrap in heavy-duty foil. Bake at 425° for 30-35 minutes or until softened. Cool for 10-15 minutes.
Meanwhile, place the potatoes in a large saucepan and cover with water. Bring to a boil. Reduce heat; cover and cook for 15-20 minutes or until tender. Drain. Squeeze softened garlic into a large mixing bowl. Add the potatoes, cream cheese, milk, salt and pepper; beat until blended. **Yield:** 8 servings.

Nutritional Analysis: 2/3 cup equals 207 calories, 7 g fat (4 g saturated fat), 21 mg cholesterol, 281 mg sodium, 30 g carbohydrate, 3 g fiber, 7 g protein.
Diabetic Exchanges: 2 starch, 1-1/2 fat.

🍎 Sweet Potato Smarts

HERE are some tasty facts from the North Carolina Sweet Potato Commission:
• Sweet potatoes are fat-free, cholesterol-free and low in sodium.
• Store uncooked sweet potatoes in a dry, well-ventilated spot at 55-60°.

Favorite Recipe Made Lighter

THANKSGIVING wouldn't be the same for Scott Jones' family without Crunchy Sweet Potato Casserole. "The recipe is from my brother-in-law," says Scott, of Tulsa, Oklahoma. "Can you lighten it up?"

Butter was the high-fat culprit in this hot dish, so our staff deleted more than half of it from the sweet potato mixture. They also used fat-free milk and egg substitute to trim down the filling.

The butter in the topping was decreased only slightly because it gives the nutty topping its caramelized crunch. However, to save on fat, the amounts of the topping ingredients were reduced.

Makeover Crunchy Sweet Potato Casserole still has its comforting flavor and sweet topping, but it boasts half the fat of the original. It also has fewer calories and contains 46% less cholesterol.

Crunchy Sweet Potato Casserole

Meatless

Prep: 20 min. **Bake:** 35 min.

1-3/4 **pounds sweet potatoes (about 3 large),**
   peeled and cut into 2-inch pieces
   2 **eggs**
1/2 **cup butter, softened**
1/3 **cup milk**
   1 **teaspoon vanilla extract**
   1 **teaspoon lemon extract**
TOPPING:
   1 **cup packed brown sugar**
1/3 **cup all-purpose flour**
   2 **tablespoons plus 1-1/2 teaspoons cold butter**
1/3 **cup chopped pecans**

Place the sweet potatoes in a large saucepan and cover with water. Bring to a boil. Reduce heat; cover and cook for 15-20 minutes or until tender. Drain and place in a food processor. Add the eggs, butter, milk and extracts; cover and process until smooth. Pour into a greased 1-1/2-qt. baking dish.

In a small bowl, combine brown sugar and flour. Cut in butter until crumbly. Sprinkle over sweet potato mixture; sprinkle with pecans. Bake, uncovered, at 350° for 35-40 minutes or until set. **Yield:** 6 servings.

Nutritional Analysis: 1/2 cup equals 379 calories, 20 g fat (10 g saturated fat), 95 mg cholesterol, 189 mg sodium, 47 g carbohydrate, 2 g fiber, 4 g protein.

Makeover Crunchy Sweet Potato Casserole

(Pictured above left)

Low-sodium   Meatless

Prep: 20 min. **Bake:** 35 min.

1-3/4 **pounds sweet potatoes (about 3 large),**
   peeled and cut into 2-inch pieces
   1 **egg**
1/4 **cup egg substitute**
   2 **tablespoons butter, softened**
1/3 **cup fat-free milk**
   1 **teaspoon vanilla extract**
   1 **teaspoon lemon extract**
TOPPING:
2/3 **cup packed brown sugar**
1/4 **cup all-purpose flour**
   1 **tablespoon cold butter**
1/4 **cup chopped pecans**

Place the sweet potatoes in a large saucepan and cover with water. Bring to a boil. Reduce heat; cover and cook for 15-20 minutes or until tender. Drain and place in a food processor. Add the egg, egg substitute, butter, milk and extracts; cover and process until smooth. Pour into a 1-1/2-qt. baking dish coated with nonstick cooking spray.

In a small bowl, combine brown sugar and flour. Cut in butter until crumbly. Sprinkle over sweet potato mixture; sprinkle with pecans. Bake, uncovered, at 350° for 35-40 minutes or until set. **Yield:** 6 servings.

Nutritional Analysis: 1/2 cup equals 331 calories, 10 g fat (4 g saturated fat), 48 mg cholesterol, 113 mg sodium, 55 g carbohydrate, 3 g fiber, 6 g protein.

Kale with Bacon

Prep: 15 min. **Cook:** 25 min.

The satisfying bacon flavor in this side dish makes you forget that you're eating light. Seasoned with garlic, it's a great way to enjoy the health benefits of kale.
—*Margaret Wagner Allen, Abingdon, Virginia*

- **2 pounds fresh kale, trimmed and torn**
- **8 bacon strips, diced**
- **2 large onions, chopped**
- **4 garlic cloves, minced**
- **1 teaspoon salt**
- **1/2 teaspoon pepper**

In a large saucepan, bring 1 in. of water to a boil. Add kale; cook for 10 minutes or until tender. Meanwhile, in a large nonstick skillet coated with nonstick cooking spray, cook bacon over medium heat until crisp. Using a slotted spoon, remove to paper towels; drain, reserving 1 teaspoon drippings. In the drippings, saute onions and garlic until onion is tender.

Drain the kale; stir into onion mixture. Add salt, pepper and bacon; heat through. **Yield:** 6 servings.

Nutritional Analysis: 1/2 cup equals 161 calories, 7 g fat (2 g saturated fat), 9 mg cholesterol, 604 mg sodium, 20 g carbohydrate, 4 g fiber, 8 g protein.
Diabetic Exchanges: 4 vegetable, 1 fat.

🍎 Trimming Tip

IF THE stems from kale leaves are thin and tender, you can easily snip them. If they're thick, however, you'll want to remove them completely.

To do so, place each leaf on a cutting board. Then fold the leaf in half lengthwise and use a knife to carefully slice away the stem.

Mashed Winter Vegetables

Low-fat Meatless

Prep: 20 min. **Cook:** 45 min.

I first saw this recipe on a cooking show, and it's become one of my autumn staples.
—*Kathy Lynch, Aloha, Oregon*

- **1 large rutabaga, peeled and cut into 3/4-inch cubes**
- **3 medium turnips, peeled and cut into 3/4-inch cubes**
- **2 medium parsnips, peeled and cut into 1/2-inch slices**
- **2 medium carrots, cut into 1/2-inch slices**
- **1/4 cup fat-free milk**
- **2 tablespoons butter**
- **1-1/4 teaspoons salt**
- **1/2 teaspoon pepper**
- **1/2 teaspoon sugar**

Place the rutabaga, turnips, parsnips and carrots in a large saucepan; cover with water. Bring to a boil. Reduce heat; cover and simmer for 40 minutes or until tender.

Drain and place the vegetables in a large bowl; mash. Add the milk, butter, salt, pepper and sugar; stir until blended. **Yield:** 10 servings.

Nutritional Analysis: 2/3 cup equals 89 calories, 3 g fat (1 g saturated fat), 6 mg cholesterol, 362 mg sodium, 16 g carbohydrate, 4 g fiber, 2 g protein.
Diabetic Exchanges: 1 starch, 1/2 fat.

Tarragon Broccoli

Low-carb Meatless

Prep/Total Time: 15 min.

I always served vegetables with rich sauces. So when I started cooking healthy, I was glad to find this broccoli recipe. Prepared in the microwave, the dish is wonderful alongside most entrees.
—*Kathleen Law, Pullman, Washington*

- **4 cups fresh broccoli florets**
- **1/4 cup water**
- **1/4 cup chopped onion**
- **1/4 teaspoon salt**
- **1/4 teaspoon pepper**
- **1 tablespoon butter**
- **1/4 cup reduced-fat sour cream**
- **1/2 teaspoon dried tarragon**

In a microwave-safe bowl, combine the broccoli, water, onion, salt and pepper. Cover and microwave on high for 3 minutes; stir. Microwave 1 minute longer or until broccoli is almost tender. Drain; stir in butter until melted. Combine sour cream and tarragon; stir into broccoli. Cover and let stand for 5 minutes. **Yield:** 4 servings.

Editor's Note: This recipe was tested in a 1,100-watt microwave.

Nutritional Analysis: 3/4 cup equals 69 calories, 5 g fat (3 g saturated fat), 14 mg cholesterol, 201 mg sodium, 5 g carbohydrate, 2 g fiber, 3 g protein.
Diabetic Exchanges: 1 vegetable, 1 fat.

Herbed Brussels Sprouts

(Pictured above and on page 71)

Low-fat   Meatless

Prep: 20 min. **Bake:** 15 min.

*This is a delicious take on a seasonal standby.
The sprouts are so tasty that even children enjoy them.*
—Debbie Marrone, Warner Robins, Georgia

  8 cups fresh brussels sprouts (about 2-1/2
     pounds)
  1 cup sliced fresh mushrooms
1/4 cup packed brown sugar
1/4 cup cider vinegar
  2 tablespoons butter, melted
1/2 teaspoon salt
1/2 teaspoon dried tarragon
1/2 teaspoon dried marjoram
1/2 teaspoon pepper
1/4 cup chopped pimientos

Remove any loose leaves and trim stem ends of brussels
sprouts. Cut an "X" in the core end with a sharp knife. Place
sprouts in a steamer basket; place in a saucepan over 1 in.
of water. Bring to a boil; cover and steam for 9-11 minutes or
until crisp-tender.

Transfer to a 13-in. x 9-in. x 2-in. baking dish coated with
nonstick cooking spray. Top with mushrooms. In a small bowl,
combine the brown sugar, vinegar, butter, salt, tarragon, marjoram and pepper. Drizzle over mushrooms and sprouts.
Sprinkle with pimientos. Bake, uncovered, at 350° for 15-20
minutes or until vegetables are tender. **Yield:** 8 servings.

*Nutritional Analysis: 3/4 cup equals 94 calories, 3 g fat (2 g
saturated fat), 8 mg cholesterol, 203 mg sodium, 16 g carbohydrate, 4 g fiber, 3 g protein.*
Diabetic Exchanges: 2 vegetable, 1/2 starch, 1/2 fat.

Grilled Onion Bloom

Low-carb   Low-fat   Meatless

Prep: 10 min. **Grill:** 30 min.

I grill this herb-flavored vegetable dish right alongside the main course. It's good when served with almost any type of flame-broiled meat.
—Johnnie McLeod, Bastrop, Louisiana

- **1 large sweet onion (14 ounces)**
- **1 tablespoon minced fresh thyme *or* oregano**
- **2 teaspoons minced fresh rosemary**
- **1/2 teaspoon salt**
- **1/8 teaspoon pepper**
- **1 tablespoon butter, melted**

With a sharp knife, slice 1/2 in. off the top of the onion; peel onion. Cut into 12-16 wedges to within 1/2 in. of root end.

Place the onion on a double thickness of heavy-duty foil (about 12 in. square). Open the wedges of onion slightly; sprinkle with thyme, rosemary, salt and pepper. Drizzle with butter. Fold the foil around the onion and seal tightly. Grill, covered, over medium heat for 30-35 minutes or until tender. **Yield:** 4 servings.

Nutritional Analysis: 1 serving equals 65 calories, 3 g fat (2 g saturated fat), 8 mg cholesterol, 327 mg sodium, 9 g carbohydrate, 2 g fiber, 1 g protein.
Diabetic Exchanges: 2 vegetable, 1/2 fat.

Lemon-Garlic Green Beans

(Pictured above)

Low-carb   Low-fat   Low-sodium   Meatless

Prep/Total Time: 20 min.

My brother made this light stovetop dish as his contribution to Christmas dinner one year. We liked it so much that it became a mainstay in our house.
—Gail Orsillo, Lynnwood, Washington

- **2 garlic cloves, minced**
- **2 teaspoons olive oil**
- **1 pound fresh green beans, trimmed and cut into 2-inch pieces**
- **1 tablespoon lemon juice**
- **1/4 teaspoon coarsely ground pepper**
- **1/8 teaspoon salt**

In a large nonstick skillet coated with nonstick cooking spray, cook the garlic in olive oil over medium heat for 30 seconds. Add the green beans; cook and stir for 10-13 minutes or until crisp-tender. Stir in the lemon juice, pepper and salt. **Yield:** 4 servings.

Nutritional Analysis: 3/4 cup equals 54 calories, 2 g fat (trace saturated fat), 0 cholesterol, 80 mg sodium, 8 g carbohydrate, 3 g fiber, 2 g protein.
Diabetic Exchanges: 1 vegetable, 1/2 fat.

Baked Mushrooms

Low-carb   Low-fat   Low-sodium   Meatless

Prep: 15 min. **Bake:** 25 min.

Mushroom-lovers just can't seem to get enough of this flavorful baked dish. It's easy to prepare and always disappears quickly.
—Patty Kile, Plymouth Meeting, Pennsylvania

- **1 pound whole fresh mushrooms**
- **1 celery rib, chopped**
- **2 green onions, thinly sliced**
- **1 tablespoon butter**
- **1/2 cup white wine *or* chicken broth**
- **1/8 teaspoon salt**
- **1/8 teaspoon pepper**

Place the mushrooms in an 8-in. square baking dish coated with nonstick cooking spray. In a nonstick skillet, saute the celery and onions in butter until tender. Stir in the white wine or chicken broth, salt and pepper; heat through. Pour over the mushrooms.

Bake, uncovered, at 350° for 25-30 minutes or until the mushrooms are tender, stirring several times. **Yield:** 6 servings.

Nutritional Analysis: 1/2 cup equals 52 calories, 2 g fat (1 g saturated fat), 5 mg cholesterol, 79 mg sodium, 4 g carbohydrate, 1 g fiber, 2 g protein.
Diabetic Exchanges: 1 vegetable, 1/2 fat.

Favorite Recipe Made Lighter

WHEN she first tried Garlic Spinach Balls, Amy Hornbuckle knew she found a new favorite. "They're so tasty that you can't stop at one," shares the Prattville, Alabama reader.

A wonderful side dish as well as an appetizer, the buttery bites also proved popular with Amy's young daughter, Sarah. "She's a picky eater," says Amy, "but she loves the spinach balls.

"They'd be a good way to get Sarah to eat green vegetables, but they're too high in cholesterol. I'm looking for suggestions for how I can make them healthier without losing their great taste."

Our home economists knew that the recipe's eggs, butter and cheese meant lots of fat and cholesterol. They replaced three of the eggs with egg substitute and reduced the cheese and butter.

Because the butter originally added necessary moisture, reduced-sodium chicken broth was added to the makeover recipe to help hold the stuffing mixture together.

Now Amy can serve this favorite to family and friends—and can enjoy it herself—with a clear conscience. Makeover Garlic Spinach Balls have all the flavor of the original recipe but with 44% fewer calories. More than half the total fat (and 67% of the saturated fat) was removed, and the cholesterol was reduced by a whopping 72%.

Garlic Spinach Balls

Meatless

Prep: 25 min. **Bake:** 15 min.

- 2 cups crushed seasoned stuffing
- 1 cup finely chopped onion
- 4 eggs, lightly beaten
- 3/4 cup butter, melted
- 1/2 cup grated Parmesan cheese
- 1 garlic clove, minced
- 1-1/2 teaspoons dried thyme
- 1/4 teaspoon salt
- 1/4 teaspoon pepper
- 2 packages (10 ounces *each*) frozen chopped spinach, thawed and squeezed dry

In a large bowl, combine the first nine ingredients. Stir in chopped spinach until blended. Roll into 1-in. balls. Place in a greased 15-in. x 10-in. x 1-in. baking pan. Bake at 350° for 15-20 minutes or until golden brown. **Yield:** 8 servings.

Nutritional Analysis: 3 balls equals 294 calories, 22 g fat (12 g saturated fat), 156 mg cholesterol, 625 mg sodium, 16 g carbohydrate, 4 g fiber, 9 g protein.

Makeover Garlic Spinach Balls

(Pictured below)

Meatless

Prep: 25 min. **Bake:** 15 min.

- 2 cups crushed seasoned stuffing
- 1 cup finely chopped onion
- 3/4 cup egg substitute
- 1 egg, lightly beaten
- 1/4 cup grated Parmesan cheese
- 1/4 cup butter, melted
- 3 tablespoons reduced-sodium chicken broth *or* vegetable broth
- 1 garlic clove, minced
- 1-1/2 teaspoons dried thyme
- 1/4 teaspoon pepper
- 1/8 teaspoon salt
- 2 packages (10 ounces *each*) frozen chopped spinach, thawed and squeezed dry

In a large bowl, combine the first 11 ingredients. Stir in chopped spinach until blended. Roll into 1-in. balls. Place in a 15-in. x 10-in. x 1-in. baking pan coated with nonstick cooking spray. Bake at 350° for 15-20 minutes or until golden brown. **Yield:** 8 servings.

Nutritional Analysis: 3 balls equals 165 calories, 8 g fat (4 g saturated fat), 44 mg cholesterol, 464 mg sodium, 16 g carbohydrate, 4 g fiber, 8 g protein.
Diabetic Exchanges: 1 starch, 1 vegetable, 1 fat.

1 cup orange juice concentrate
3 tablespoons coarsely chopped fresh gingerroot
1/2 teaspoon pepper
4 teaspoons butter, melted

Line a 15-in. x 10-in. x 1-in. baking pan with foil and coat with nonstick cooking spray; set aside. In a large bowl, toss the squash, orange juice concentrate, ginger and pepper. Arrange in a single layer in prepared pan.

Bake at 375° for 50-55 minutes or until the squash is tender, stirring twice. Stir in the butter before serving. **Yield:** 10 servings.

Nutritional Analysis: 1/2 cup equals 129 calories, 2 g fat (1 g saturated fat), 4 mg cholesterol, 23 mg sodium, 29 g carbohydrate, 5 g fiber, 2 g protein.
Diabetic Exchanges: 1 starch, 1 fruit, 1/2 fat.

Corn Pudding

Meatless

Prep: 5 min. **Bake:** 40 min.

A package of corn bread mix and a few other convenience items make this moist side dish a breeze to toss together. It's perfect for potlucks or any time you want something warm and comforting. The recipe makes a big batch, so you'll have plenty to share with your family or friends.
—Maurine Roehm, Terre Haute, Indiana

2 cups frozen corn
1 can (14-3/4 ounces) cream-style corn
1 cup (8 ounces) reduced-fat sour cream
1 package (8-1/2 ounces) corn bread/muffin mix
1/2 cup egg substitute
2 tablespoons butter, melted

In a large bowl, combine all ingredients. Pour into a 13-in. x 9-in. x 2-in. baking dish coated with nonstick cooking spray.

Bake, uncovered, at 350° for 40-45 minutes or until the top and edges of the pudding are golden brown and a toothpick inserted in pudding comes out clean. Serve pudding warm. **Yield:** 12 servings.

Nutritional Analysis: 1 piece equals 183 calories, 7 g fat (3 g saturated fat), 12 mg cholesterol, 375 mg sodium, 27 g carbohydrate, 2 g fiber, 5 g protein.
Diabetic Exchanges: 2 starch, 1/2 fat.

Ginger Orange Squash

(Pictured above)

Low-fat **Low-sodium** *Meatless*

Prep: 15 min. **Bake:** 50 min.

Bursting with citrus flavor, this tender side dish complements autumn dinner parties and weeknight suppers alike. Our Test Kitchen home economists developed the five-ingredient recipe—which is low in fat and sodium—so you can spend less time in the kitchen and more time with family.

2 butternut squash (2 pounds *each*), peeled and cut into 1-1/2-inch cubes

Molasses Baked Beans

Low-fat   Meatless

Prep: 20 min. **Bake:** 1 hour

*These beans are ideal at a summertime barbecue
or served with ham in the winter.*
—Erin Anderson, Far Hills, New Jersey

  1 cup chopped onion
  1 medium jalapeno pepper, seeded and chopped
  2 teaspoons olive oil
1/2 cup water
1/2 cup ketchup
  3 tablespoons brown sugar
  3 tablespoons molasses
  2 tablespoons prepared mustard
  1 tablespoon chili powder
1/2 teaspoon Liquid Smoke, optional
  2 cans (15-1/2 ounces *each*) great northern
    beans, rinsed and drained
  1 can (15 ounces) pinto beans, rinsed and
    drained

In a nonstick skillet, saute onion and jalapeno in oil until the onion begins to brown, about 5 minutes. Remove from the heat. In a large bowl, combine the water, ketchup, brown sugar, molasses, mustard, chili powder and Liquid Smoke if desired. Stir in the beans and onion mixture.

Transfer to a 1-1/2-qt. baking dish coated with nonstick cooking spray. Bake, uncovered, at 350° for 1 hour or until beans are bubbly and as thick as desired. **Yield:** 9 servings.

Editor's Note: When cutting or seeding hot peppers, use rubber or plastic gloves to protect your hands. Avoid touching your face.

Nutritional Analysis: 1/2 cup equals 191 calories, 2 g fat (trace saturated fat), 0 cholesterol, 422 mg sodium, 37 g carbohydrate, 7 g fiber, 7 g protein.
Diabetic Exchanges: 2 starch, 1 very lean meat.

Italian Roasted Potatoes

Meatless

Prep: 10 min. **Bake:** 40 min.

*The herbs in this recipe turn potatoes from ordinary
to extraordinary. Try the side dish with burgers
or your favorite meat loaf recipe.*
—Stacey Diehl, Westcliffe, Colorado

  2 pounds small red potatoes, quartered
  2 tablespoons olive oil
  4 garlic cloves, minced
  2 tablespoons dried parsley flakes
  1 teaspoon dried basil
  1 teaspoon dried oregano
3/4 teaspoon salt
1/4 teaspoon pepper

Place the potatoes in a large bowl. Drizzle with olive oil; toss to coat evenly. Combine the garlic, parsley, basil, oregano, salt and pepper; sprinkle over the potatoes and toss to coat evenly.

Transfer to an ungreased 13-in. x 9-in. x 2-in. baking pan. Bake, uncovered, at 425° for 30 minutes. Stir; bake 10-15 minutes longer or until potatoes are tender and golden brown. **Yield:** 8 servings.

Nutritional Analysis: 3/4 cup equals 124 calories, 4 g fat (trace saturated fat), 0 cholesterol, 228 mg sodium, 21 g carbohydrate, 2 g fiber, 3 g protein.
Diabetic Exchanges: 1-1/2 starch, 1/2 fat.

🍎 Cooking Spray Secret

THE MORE I used my can of nonstick cooking spray, the slipperier it became. I hated having greasy hands, so I cut 5 inches from the top of a clean gym sock and slipped it over the spray can. It kept my hands clean, and I can remove and wash it as needed. —Susan Lubiens, Folsom, California

Summer Squash Casserole

Low-fat   Meatless

Prep: 30 min. **Bake:** 40 min.

*Whenever I'm invited to a potluck or party, I'm asked to
bring this golden, crumb-topped side dish.
I rarely come home with leftovers.*
—Vicki Wrona, Grand Prairie, Texas

  6 small yellow summer squash (3 pounds),
    cut into chunks
  2 eggs, beaten
1/2 cup plus 2 tablespoons dry bread crumbs,
    divided
  2 tablespoons sugar
1-1/2 teaspoons dried minced onion
1/2 teaspoon salt
1/8 teaspoon pepper
  2 teaspoons butter, melted

Place squash in a large saucepan and cover with water. Bring to a boil; boil, uncovered, for 15-20 minutes or until tender. Drain well, pressing squash to remove excess liquid. In a bowl, mash the squash. Stir in the eggs, 1/2 cup bread crumbs, sugar, onion, salt and pepper until blended.

Transfer to a 1-1/2-qt. baking dish coated with nonstick cooking spray. Bake, uncovered, at 350° for 20 minutes. Toss the remaining bread crumbs with butter; sprinkle over the top of casserole. Bake 20-30 minutes longer or until golden. **Yield:** 8 servings.

Nutritional Analysis: 1/2 cup equals 101 calories, 3 g fat (1 g saturated fat), 56 mg cholesterol, 246 mg sodium, 16 g carbohydrate, 2 g fiber, 4 g protein.
Diabetic Exchanges: 1 vegetable, 1/2 starch, 1/2 fat.

Italian Broccoli Cheese Bake

(Pictured above)

Meatless

Prep: 25 min. **Bake:** 25 min.

This makes a great side dish, but I like to serve it as a meatless entree with bread and a crisp salad.
—*Rachel Keller, Roanoke, Virginia*

1-1/2 pounds fresh broccoli spears, cut into 1/4-inch slices
1/4 teaspoon salt
2 cups (16 ounces) 1% small-curd cottage cheese
2 egg whites
1/4 cup grated Parmesan cheese
3 tablespoons all-purpose flour
1/2 teaspoon Italian seasoning
3/4 cup meatless spaghetti sauce
1 cup (4 ounces) shredded part-skim mozzarella cheese

In a large saucepan, bring 8 cups water to a boil. Add broccoli and salt; cover and boil for 5 minutes. Drain and pat dry. In a blender, combine the cottage cheese, egg whites, Parmesan cheese, flour and Italian seasoning; cover and process until smooth.

Place half of the broccoli in an 11-in. x 7-in. x 2-in. baking dish coated with nonstick cooking spray; top with half of the cottage cheese mixture. Repeat layers. Spoon spaghetti sauce over the top; sprinkle with mozzarella cheese. Bake, uncovered, at 375° for 25-30 minutes or until bubbly. Let stand for 5 minutes before serving. **Yield:** 4 servings.

Nutritional Analysis: 1 serving equals 266 calories, 9 g fat (5 g saturated fat), 32 mg cholesterol, 977 mg sodium, 22 g carbohydrate, 4 g fiber, 27 g protein.
Diabetic Exchanges: 3 lean meat, 2 vegetable, 1/2 starch.

Creole Butter Beans

Low-fat   Meatless

Prep/Total Time: 30 min.

Here's a fantastic way to prepare butter beans, which are full of nutrition and low in fat. It's a warm and tangy side dish but filling enough to be the main course.
—*Grace Malone, Lafayette, Colorado*

1/2 cup chopped onion
1/4 cup chopped celery
1/4 cup chopped green pepper
2 garlic cloves, minced
1 tablespoon olive oil
1 tablespoon all-purpose flour
1/2 teaspoon salt
1/2 teaspoon pepper
1 cup water
2 cans (15 ounces *each*) butter beans, rinsed and drained
1 can (14-1/2 ounces) diced tomatoes, undrained
2 tablespoons brown sugar
4-1/2 teaspoons chili sauce
1/4 teaspoon prepared mustard
1/8 teaspoon hot pepper sauce

In a large saucepan, saute the onion, celery, green pepper and garlic in oil until onion is tender. Combine the flour, salt and pepper; sprinkle over onion mixture and stir until well blended. Cook 1 minute longer.

Gradually whisk in water. Bring to a boil; cook and stir for 1-2 minutes or until thickened. Stir in the remaining ingredients. Return to a boil. Reduce heat; simmer, uncovered, for 15-20 minutes. **Yield:** 8 servings.

Nutritional Analysis: 1/2 cup equals 113 calories, 2 g fat (trace saturated fat), 0 cholesterol, 641 mg sodium, 25 g carbohydrate, 6 g fiber, 6 g protein.
Diabetic Exchanges: 1 starch, 1 very lean meat.

Cinnamon Apple Syrup

Low-carb   Low-fat   Low-sodium

Prep/Total Time: 15 min.

Cinnamon and vanilla take center stage in this easy syrup. People enjoy it over both pancakes and crepes.
—*Alberta McKay, Bartlesville, Oklahoma*

2 tablespoons cornstarch
1/2 teaspoon ground cinnamon
1/8 teaspoon salt
1 cup water
3/4 cup unsweetened apple juice concentrate
1/2 teaspoon vanilla extract

In a small saucepan, combine the cornstarch, cinnamon and salt. Gradually stir in water and apple juice concentrate until smooth. Bring to a boil; cook and stir for 2 minutes or until thickened. Remove from the heat; stir in vanilla. Serve warm. Refrigerate leftovers. **Yield:** 12 servings.

Nutritional Analysis: 2 tablespoons equals 35 calories, trace fat (trace saturated fat), 0 cholesterol, 29 mg sodium, 9 g carbohydrate, trace fiber, trace protein.
Diabetic Exchange: 1/2 fruit.

Breakfast & Brunch

Breakfast boosts your energy level, which is bound to give you a sunny outlook on the day and help you perform your best. So open your family's eyes to good eating with these day-brightening recipes.

Broccoli-Ham Cheese Pie (page 102) and Maple Sausage Patties (page 103)

Crustless Mushroom-Spinach Quiche

(Pictured above)

Low-carb   *Meatless*

Prep: 20 min. **Bake:** 45 min. + standing

My aunt gave me this wonderful recipe, and I adapted it a bit. It's a tasty vegetarian dish that's easy to fix and full of nutritious vegetables. Because it doesn't have a crust, it's just right for low-carb diets.
—*Mary Ann Dell, Phoenixville, Pennsylvania*

1-1/2 cups sliced fresh mushrooms
1-1/2 cups thinly sliced zucchini
　1 cup chopped green pepper
1/2 cup chopped onion
　1 garlic clove, minced
　2 teaspoons canola oil
　1 carton (15 ounces) part-skim ricotta cheese
1-1/4 cups egg substitute
　1 package (10 ounces) frozen chopped spinach,
　　thawed and squeezed dry
3/4 cup crumbled feta cheese
　1 tablespoon minced fresh parsley
1-1/2 teaspoons minced fresh thyme
1/2 teaspoon salt
1/4 teaspoon pepper
　2 medium tomatoes, seeded and chopped

Line the bottom of a 9-in. springform pan coated with nonstick cooking spray with heavy-duty foil; set aside. In a large nonstick skillet, saute the mushrooms, zucchini, green pepper, onion and garlic in oil until tender; drain.

In a large bowl, combine ricotta cheese and egg substitute. Stir in the spinach, feta, parsley, thyme, salt and pepper. Stir in mushroom mixture.

Transfer to prepared pan. Bake at 350° for 45-55 minutes or until edges are lightly browned and a knife inserted near the center comes out clean. Let stand for 10 minutes. Carefully remove sides of pan. Top each serving with tomatoes. **Yield:** 6 servings.

Nutritional Analysis: 1 slice equals 244 calories, 13 g fat (7 g saturated fat), 39 mg cholesterol, 625 mg sodium, 13 g carbohydrate, 3 g fiber, 20 g protein.
Diabetic Exchanges: 3 lean meat, 1 vegetable, 1 fat.

Berries with Sour Cream Sauce

(Pictured at right)

Low-sodium   *Meatless*

Prep/Total Time: 10 min.

Delightfully dressed-up sour cream makes a delicious topping for fruit in this simple dish.
—*Linda Franceschi, Eldred, New York*

　1 quart fresh strawberries, halved
　1 pint fresh raspberries
　1 pint fresh blueberries
　1 pint fresh blackberries
　2 cups (16 ounces) reduced-fat sour cream
1/4 cup honey

In a large bowl, combine the first four ingredients. In another bowl, combine the sour cream and honey. Serve with berries. **Yield:** 10 servings.

Nutritional Analysis: 3/4 cup fruit with 3 tablespoons sauce equals 147 calories, 4 g fat (3 g saturated fat), 15 mg cholesterol, 32 mg sodium, 25 g carbohydrate, 6 g fiber, 4 g protein.
Diabetic Exchanges: 1 fruit, 1/2 starch, 1/2 fat.

Honey Bagels

(Pictured at right)

Meatless

Prep: 1 hour + resting **Bake:** 20 min.

Who has time to make from-scratch bagels? You do with this easy recipe from our Test Kitchen staff.

　1 tablespoon active dry yeast
1-1/4 cups warm water (110° to 115°)
　3 tablespoons canola oil
　3 tablespoons sugar
　3 tablespoons plus 1/4 cup honey, *divided*
　1 teaspoon brown sugar
　2 teaspoons salt
　1 egg
　4 to 5 cups bread flour
　2 tablespoons dried minced onion
　2 tablespoons sesame seeds
　2 tablespoons poppy seeds

In a large mixing bowl, dissolve yeast in warm water. Add the oil, sugar, 3 tablespoons honey, brown sugar, salt and egg; mix well. Stir in enough flour to form a soft dough.

Turn onto a floured surface; knead until a smooth firm dough forms, about 8-10 minutes. Cover and let rest for 10 minutes.

Shape into 12 pieces; roll each piece into a 10-in. rope. Form bagels by overlapping the ends; pinch to seal. Place on a lightly floured surface. Cover and let rest for 20 minutes.

In a large saucepan or Dutch oven, bring 8 cups water and remaining honey to a boil. Drop bagels, one at a time, into boiling water. Cook bagels for 45 seconds; turn and cook 45 seconds longer. Remove bagels with a slotted spoon; drain and sprinkle with onion and sesame and poppy seeds.

Place bagels 2 in. apart on baking sheets lined with parchment paper. Bake at 425° for 12 minutes. Turn and bake 5 minutes longer or until golden brown. **Yield:** 1 dozen.

Nutritional Analysis: 1 bagel equals 243 calories, 4 g fat (trace saturated fat), 18 mg cholesterol, 398 mg sodium, 44 g carbohydrate, 1 g fiber, 7 g protein.
Diabetic Exchanges: 2-1/2 starch, 1 fat.

Cinnamon Apple Pancakes

Meatless

Prep/Total Time: 25 min.

My family loves the classic apple and cinnamon flavor in these light yet hearty pancakes.
—*Kim McConnell, Tulsa, Oklahoma*

2 cups whole wheat flour
4 teaspoons baking powder
1 teaspoon ground cinnamon
1/2 teaspoon salt
2 eggs, lightly beaten
2 cups fat-free milk
2 tablespoons honey
1 tablespoon canola oil
1 medium apple, peeled, cored and chopped

In a large bowl, combine the flour, baking powder, cinnamon and salt. Combine the eggs, milk, honey and oil; stir into dry ingredients just until moistened. Add apple. Pour batter by 1/3 cupfuls onto a hot nonstick skillet coated with nonstick cooking spray. Turn when bubbles form on top; cook until second side is golden brown. **Yield:** 6 servings.

Nutritional Analysis: 2 pancakes equals 246 calories, 5 g fat (1 g saturated fat), 73 mg cholesterol, 416 mg sodium, 43 g carbohydrate, 5 g fiber, 11 g protein.
Diabetic Exchanges: 2 starch, 1 lean meat, 1/2 fruit.

bowl, whisk the egg substitute, milk, 1/3 cup syrup, vanilla and cinnamon; pour over the bread. Cover and refrigerate overnight.

Remove from the refrigerator 30 minutes before baking. Bake, uncovered, at 350° for 45-50 minutes or until top is lightly browned and a thermometer reads at least 160°. Serve with strawberries and remaining syrup. **Yield:** 10 servings.

Nutritional Analysis: *1 serving equals 306 calories, 3 g fat (1 g saturated fat), 3 mg cholesterol, 805 mg sodium, 54 g carbohydrate, 3 g fiber, 19 g protein.*

Blueberry Waffles

Meatless

Prep/Total Time: 20 min.

Waffles are my husband's favorite Sunday brunch. We like them with fresh fruit on the side.
—*Lori Daniels, Beverly, West Virginia*

 1 cup all-purpose flour
 2 tablespoons sugar
 1 teaspoon baking powder
1/4 teaspoon salt
 1 egg yolk
1/4 cup fat-free milk
1/4 cup orange juice
 1 tablespoon butter, melted
 1 teaspoon grated orange peel
1/8 teaspoon orange extract
 4 egg whites
 1 cup fresh blueberries
 1 tablespoon confectioners' sugar

In a large bowl, combine the flour, sugar, baking powder and salt. In another bowl, whisk the egg yolk, milk, orange juice, butter, orange peel and extract; stir into dry ingredients just until combined. In a small mixing bowl, beat egg whites until stiff peaks form; fold into batter. Fold in blueberries.

Bake in a preheated waffle iron according to manufacturer's directions until golden brown. Sprinkle with confectioners' sugar. **Yield:** 4 servings.

Nutritional Analysis: *1 waffle equals 235 calories, 5 g fat (2 g saturated fat), 61 mg cholesterol, 301 mg sodium, 40 g carbohydrate, 1 g fiber, 8 g protein.*
Diabetic Exchanges: *1-1/2 starch, 1 lean meat, 1 fruit.*

Overnight Stuffed French Toast

(Pictured above)

Low-fat   Meatless

Prep: 20 min + chilling **Bake:** 45 min.

This brunch dish is so rich that no one will suspect each generous serving has just 3 grams of fat. I don't like to cook a lot in the morning, so this make-ahead dish is perfect for us.
—*Brenda Childress, Broken Arrow, Oklahoma*

 20 slices French bread (1 inch thick)
  1 package (8 ounces) fat-free cream cheese
  3 cups egg substitute
  2 cups fat-free milk
1/3 cup plus 1-3/4 cups sugar-free maple-flavored
      syrup, *divided*
  1 teaspoon vanilla extract
1/4 teaspoon ground cinnamon
2-1/2 cups sliced fresh strawberries

Arrange 10 slices of bread in a 13-in. x 9-in. x 2-in. baking dish coated with nonstick cooking spray. Spread each slice with cream cheese. Top with remaining bread. In a large

Try Something New: Buckwheat

Buttermilk Buckwheat Pancakes

(Pictured at left)

Meatless

Prep/Total Time: 25 min.

Created by our home economists, this recipe uses buckwheat flour instead of the wheat-based variety and produces light, tender pancakes.

> 1 cup buckwheat flour
> 2 tablespoons brown sugar
> 1 teaspoon baking powder
> 1/2 teaspoon baking soda
> 1/2 teaspoon salt
> 1/8 teaspoon *each* ground cinnamon, nutmeg and cloves
> 1 egg
> 1 cup 1% buttermilk
> 1 tablespoon butter, melted

In a large bowl, combine the flour, brown sugar, baking powder, baking soda, salt, cinnamon, nutmeg and cloves. Whisk the egg, buttermilk and butter; stir into dry ingredients just until moistened.

Pour batter by 1/4 cupfuls onto a hot nonstick griddle coated with nonstick cooking spray. Turn when bubbles form on top of pancakes; cook until second side is golden brown. **Yield:** 4 servings.

Nutritional Analysis: 2 pancakes equals 195 calories, 6 g fat (3 g saturated fat), 63 mg cholesterol, 667 mg sodium, 31 g carbohydrate, 3 g fiber, 7 g protein.
Diabetic Exchanges: 2 starch, 1 fat.

A LONGTIME STAPLE in other countries, buckwheat flour is just beginning to pop up in kitchens across America. Buckwheat has a nutty flavor and lends a hearty texture to baked goods such as muffins, corn bread, pancakes and waffles.

Despite its name, buckwheat is not a member of the wheat family. The wholesome flour that is ground from buckwheat is gluten-free…and that's good news for folks who suffer from wheat-related food allergies.

Baking with Buckwheat Flour

Buckwheat flour is usually found in the baking aisle or whole foods section of many supermarkets. It is available in light, medium and dark varieties. The types are interchangeable; however, the dark flour offers the greatest flavor and the most lysine.

For the best results, combine buckwheat flour with wheat-based flours.

In general, you can substitute buckwheat flour for up to half of the wheat-based flour in a recipe. When baking with yeast, try replacing no more than one-fifth of the wheat-based flour with buckwheat flour.

If you need to eliminate wheat flour from your diet entirely, experiment with buckwheat flour to get the texture and taste you desire in your baked goods. For foolproof baking, consider recipes that specifically call for and have been tested with 100% buckwheat flour—as is the case with the pancake recipe above right.

Benefits of Buckwheat

EVEN THOUGH buckwheat is not a grain, it offers a harvest of health benefits. Buckwheat flour contains:

- zinc, copper, magnesium, potassium, phosphorus, folate, riboflavin and niacin.
- healthy amounts of soluble and insoluble fiber.
- essential amino acids that the body cannot produce on its own. Buckwheat is particularly high in the amino acids lysine and arginine.

Some studies even suggest that buckwheat can lower cholesterol and blood pressure and help manage diabetes.

Turkey Breakfast Sausage

(Pictured above)

Low-carb

Prep/Total Time: 25 min.

*These hearty patties are loaded with savory flavor
but contain a fraction of the sodium and fat of
commercial breakfast sausages.*
—Judy Culbertson, Dansville, New York

  1 pound lean ground turkey
3/4 teaspoon salt
1/2 teaspoon rubbed sage
1/2 teaspoon pepper
1/4 teaspoon ground ginger

Crumble turkey into a large bowl. Add the salt, sage, pepper and ginger. Shape into eight 2-in. patties. In a nonstick skillet coated with nonstick cooking spray, cook patties over medium heat for 6-8 minutes on each side or until no longer pink and a meat thermometer reads 165°. **Yield:** 8 servings.

Nutritional Analysis: 1 patty equals 85 calories, 5 g fat (1 g saturated fat), 45 mg cholesterol, 275 mg sodium, trace carbohydrate, trace fiber, 10 g protein.
Diabetic Exchanges: 1 lean meat, 1/2 fat.

Veggie Egg Scramble

(Pictured above)

Low-carb   *Meatless*

Prep/Total Time: 20 min.

*A splash of white wine turns these scrambled eggs
into a sophisticated brunch entree. It's a recipe I
adjusted to cut down on the calories and fat.*
—Phylis Behringer, Defiance, Ohio

  2 eggs
  6 egg whites
1/4 cup white wine *or* chicken broth
1/4 teaspoon salt
1/8 teaspoon pepper
1/8 teaspoon garlic powder

1/2 cup chopped green pepper
1/2 cup chopped onion
1/2 cup sliced fresh mushrooms
  1 teaspoon butter
  1 teaspoon olive oil
1/2 cup shredded reduced-fat cheddar cheese
  2 teaspoons minced fresh basil

In a bowl, whisk the eggs, whites, wine or broth, salt, pepper and garlic powder; set aside. In a large nonstick skillet, saute the green pepper, onion and mushrooms in butter and oil for 3 minutes or until crisp-tender.

Reduce heat to medium. Stir in the egg mixture; cook and stir until eggs are completely set. Sprinkle with cheese and basil. Cover and remove from the heat; let stand for 5 minutes or until cheese is melted. **Yield:** 3 servings.

Nutritional Analysis: 1 cup equals 201 calories, 10 g fat (5 g saturated fat), 158 mg cholesterol, 365 mg sodium, 8 g carbohydrate, 1 g fiber, 18 g protein.
Diabetic Exchanges: 2 lean meat, 1-1/2 fat, 1 vegetable.

Broccoli-Ham Cheese Pie

(Pictured below right and on page 97)

Prep: 25 min. **Bake:** 70 min. + standing

*Sheets of easy-to-use phyllo dough create a crisp buttery
crust for this entree. The egg and vegetable pie always gets
thumbs-up approval from my sons and husband.*
—Nancy Granaman, Burlington, Iowa

 12 sheets phyllo dough (14 inches x 9 inches)
Refrigerated butter-flavored spray
  1 package (16 ounces) frozen broccoli cuts,
    thawed and patted dry
  1 cup cubed fully cooked lean ham
  1 cup (4 ounces) shredded reduced-fat cheddar
    cheese
  1 small onion, chopped
  2 tablespoons minced fresh parsley
  2 garlic cloves, minced
1/2 teaspoon dried thyme
1/2 teaspoon salt
1/2 teaspoon pepper
  1 cup egg substitute
  1 cup fat-free evaporated milk
  2 tablespoons grated Parmesan cheese

Spritz one sheet of phyllo dough with butter-flavored spray. Place in a 9-in. pie plate coated with nonstick cooking spray; allow one end of dough to overhang edge of plate by 3-4 in. (Until ready to use, keep phyllo dough covered with plastic wrap and a damp towel to prevent drying out.) Repeat with remaining phyllo, overlapping the sheets (staggering the points around the plate) and spritzing with butter-flavored spray between each layer.

In a bowl, combine the broccoli, ham, cheese, onion, parsley, garlic, thyme, salt and pepper; spoon into crust. Combine egg substitute and milk; pour over broccoli mixture. Fold edges of dough over filling toward center of pie plate. Spritz edges with butter-flavored spray.

Cover the edge of the crust with foil. Bake at 375° for 40 minutes. Remove the foil. Sprinkle with Parmesan cheese. Bake 30-35 minutes longer or until a knife inserted near the center comes out clean. Let stand for 10 minutes before cutting. **Yield:** 6 servings.

Editor's Note: This recipe was tested with I Can't Believe It's Not Butter Spray.

Nutritional Analysis: 1 piece equals 232 calories, 6 g fat (3 g saturated fat), 25 mg cholesterol, 882 mg sodium, 24 g carbohydrate, 3 g fiber, 21 g protein.
Diabetic Exchanges: 1-1/2 starch, 1 lean meat, 1 vegetable, 1 fat.

Maple Sausage Patties

(Pictured below and on page 97)

Low-carb

Prep: 15 min. + chilling **Cook:** 10 min.

Maple syrup, sage and thyme give great flavor to these hearty pork patties. I developed the recipe with help from my neighbors. To save time, make the patties the night before and reheat them in the microwave.
—Margaret Eid, Huron, South Dakota

   1 pound ground pork
   1 tablespoon maple syrup
 1/2 teaspoon salt
 1/2 teaspoon onion powder
 1/2 teaspoon rubbed sage
 1/2 teaspoon dried thyme
 1/2 teaspoon poultry seasoning
 1/2 teaspoon ground nutmeg
 1/4 teaspoon cayenne pepper
   1 to 2 teaspoons mesquite Liquid Smoke, optional

In a large bowl, combine all of the ingredients. Shape into eight 2-1/2-in. patties. Cover and refrigerate for at least 1 hour.

In a large nonstick skillet coated with nonstick cooking spray, cook patties over medium heat for 4-6 minutes on each side or until meat is no longer pink and a meat thermometer reads 160°. **Yield:** 8 servings.

Nutritional Analysis: 1 patty equals 128 calories, 8 g fat (3 g saturated fat), 38 mg cholesterol, 177 mg sodium, 2 g carbohydrate, trace fiber, 10 g protein.
Diabetic Exchanges: 2 lean meat, 1/2 fat.

Toasted Almond Granola

(Pictured above)

Low-sodium *Meatless*

Prep: 15 min. **Bake:** 20 min.

I combined several granola recipes to come up with this crunchy cranberry-and-apricot-flavored treat. For fun, vary the kinds of fruits and nuts. The possibilities are endless.
—Tracy Weakly, Aloha, Oregon

   3 cups old-fashioned oats
   2 cups crisp rice cereal
 1/2 cup toasted wheat germ
 1/2 cup nonfat dry milk powder
 1/3 cup slivered almonds
 1/4 cup packed brown sugar
   2 tablespoons sunflower kernels
 1/4 teaspoon salt
 1/2 cup orange juice
 1/4 cup honey
   2 teaspoons canola oil
   2 teaspoons vanilla extract
 1/2 teaspoon almond extract
   1 cup golden raisins
   1 cup chopped dried apricots
 1/2 cup dried cranberries
Fat-free plain yogurt, optional

In a large bowl, combine the first eight ingredients. In a saucepan, combine the orange juice, honey and oil. Heat for 3-4 minutes over medium heat until honey is dissolved. Remove from the heat; stir in the extracts. Pour over the oat mixture; stir to coat.

Place in a 15-in. x 10-in. x 1-in. baking pan coated with nonstick cooking spray. Bake at 350° for 20-25 minutes or until crisp, stirring every 10 minutes. Remove and cool completely on a wire rack. Stir in fruit. Store in an airtight container. Serve with yogurt if desired. **Yield:** 8 cups.

Nutritional Analysis: 1/2 cup granola (calculated without yogurt) equals 212 calories, 4 g fat (trace saturated fat), 0 cholesterol, 88 mg sodium, 41 g carbohydrate, 32 g fiber, 6 g protein.
Diabetic Exchanges: 2 starch, 1 fruit.

three-fourths full with batter.

Combine topping ingredients; sprinkle about 1 tablespoon over each muffin. Bake at 350° for 18-22 minutes or until a toothpick comes out clean. Cool for 5 minutes before removing from pan to a wire rack. Combine glaze ingredients; drizzle over warm muffins. **Yield:** 1 dozen.

Editor's Note: If using frozen raspberries, do not thaw before adding to batter.

Nutritional Analysis: 1 muffin equals 181 calories, 5 g fat (2 g saturated fat), 26 mg cholesterol, 133 mg sodium, 31 g carbohydrate, 2 g fiber, 3 g protein.
Diabetic Exchanges: 2 starch, 1 fat.

Raspberry Streusel Muffins

(Pictured above)

Low-sodium Meatless

Prep: 25 min. **Bake:** 20 min.

These muffins always receive rave reviews.
Pecans, brown sugar and a sweet, yummy glaze
make them seem anything but light.
—Kristin Stank, Indianapolis, Indiana

1-1/2 cups all-purpose flour
1/4 cup sugar
1/4 cup packed brown sugar
2 teaspoons baking powder
1 teaspoon ground cinnamon
1/4 teaspoon salt
1 egg, lightly beaten
1/2 cup plus 2 tablespoons fat-free milk
2 tablespoons butter, melted
1-1/4 cups fresh *or* frozen raspberries
1 teaspoon grated lemon peel
TOPPING:
1/4 cup chopped pecans
1/4 cup packed brown sugar
2 tablespoons all-purpose flour
1 teaspoon ground cinnamon
1 teaspoon grated lemon peel
1 tablespoon butter, melted
GLAZE:
1/4 cup confectioners' sugar
1-1/2 teaspoons lemon juice

In a large bowl, combine the first six ingredients. Combine egg, milk and butter; stir into dry ingredients until just moistened. Fold in raspberries and lemon peel. Coat muffin cups with nonstick cooking spray or use paper liners; fill

Cransational Breakfast Drink

(Pictured at left)

Low-fat Low-sodium

Prep/Total Time: 10 min.

I whip up this colorful beverage at breakfast time.
The refreshing smoothie is a fast morning treat.
—Amanda Schafer, Perryville, Missouri

4 cups orange juice
2 medium firm bananas, cut into chunks
1-1/2 cups frozen cranberries
1/4 cup 2% milk
1/4 cup sugar
4 ice cubes

In a blender, place half of the orange juice, bananas, cranberries, milk, sugar and ice cubes; cover and process until smooth. Pour into a pitcher or chilled glasses. Repeat with remaining ingredients. Serve immediately. **Yield:** 8 servings.

Nutritional Analysis: 1 cup equals 121 calories, trace fat (trace saturated fat), 1 mg cholesterol, 5 mg sodium, 29 g carbohydrate, 2 g fiber, 1 g protein.
Diabetic Exchange: 2 fruit.

Fruit with Honey-Ginger Dressing

(Pictured above right)

Low-fat Low-sodium Meatless

Prep/Total Time: 15 min.

Here's a refreshing addition to any meal. The spiced
yogurt dressing is delicious over the fruit medley.
—Cheryl Perry, Elizabeth City, North Carolina

1-1/2 cups plain yogurt
2 tablespoons honey
2 teaspoons lemon juice
1/2 teaspoon ground ginger
1/2 teaspoon vanilla extract
2 cups cantaloupe balls *or* cubes
2 cups seedless red grapes
2 cups sliced fresh strawberries
2 cups fresh blueberries

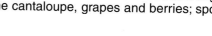

For dressing, in a small bowl, whisk the yogurt, honey, lemon juice, ginger and vanilla until smooth. In a large bowl, combine the cantaloupe, grapes and berries; spoon into serv-

ing bowls. Drizzle with dressing. **Yield:** 8 servings.

Nutritional Analysis: 3/4 cup fruit with 3 tablespoons dressing equals 121 calories, 2 g fat (1 g saturated fat), 6 mg cholesterol, 28 mg sodium, 25 g carbohydrate, 3 g fiber, 3 g protein.
Diabetic Exchanges: 1 fruit, 1/2 starch.

Dried Fruit Muesli

Low-sodium   *Meatless*

Prep: 10 min. + chilling

Your day will start just right when you prepare this comforting chilled cereal created by our Test Kitchen staff. Filled with wholesome ingredients, it sits in the fridge overnight for the perfect pick-me-up when the alarm clock rings.

    1 cup quick-cooking oats
    1 cup fat-free milk
1/4 cup orange juice
1/4 cup chopped dried apricots
1/4 cup dried cranberries
1/4 cup chopped dried apples
    2 tablespoons chopped almonds
    2 tablespoons honey
1/8 teaspoon salt
1/8 teaspoon ground cinnamon

In a large bowl, combine all ingredients; mix well. Cover and refrigerate for at least 8 hours or overnight. **Yield:** 4 servings.

Nutritional Analysis: 1/2 cup equals 228 calories, 4 g fat (trace saturated fat), 1 mg cholesterol, 112 mg sodium, 43 g carbohydrate, 4 g fiber, 7 g protein.
Diabetic Exchanges: 1-1/2 starch, 1 fruit, 1/2 fat-free milk, 1/2 fat.

Cinnamon Granola

(Pictured below)

Low-sodium   *Meatless*

Prep: 10 min. **Bake:** 35 min.

Cinnamon, nutmeg and honey lend comforting charm to this homemade granola. We like it over yogurt or with milk for breakfast, but it's also good as a snack.
—*Meg Potempa, Oshkosh, Wisconsin*

    4 cups old-fashioned oats
1/2 cup sliced almonds, toasted
1/4 cup oat bran
1/4 cup toasted wheat germ
1/4 cup unsalted sunflower kernels
    3 tablespoons flaxseed
1/2 teaspoon ground cinnamon
1/4 teaspoon ground nutmeg
1/2 cup honey
    2 tablespoons canola oil

In a large bowl, combine the first eight ingredients. Drizzle with honey and oil; toss to coat. Spread in a 15-in. x 10-in. x 1-in. baking pan coated with nonstick cooking spray. Bake at 300° for 35-40 minutes or until lightly browned, stirring twice. **Yield:** 11 servings.

Nutritional Analysis: 1/2 cup equals 250 calories, 10 g fat (1 g saturated fat), 0 cholesterol, 4 mg sodium, 38 g carbohydrate, 5 g fiber, 7 g protein.
Diabetic Exchanges: 2-1/2 starch, 1 fat.

Favorite Recipe Made Lighter

STARTING THE DAY with an appealing, hearty breakfast is certainly a step in the right direction when you're trying to follow a healthy eating plan. Unfortunately, some morning mainstays don't quite fit with those good-for-you goals, as subscriber Mary Balcomb discovered.

Her golden Overnight Yeast Waffles are crispy on the outside and tender on the inside. "These waffles are so good that I even freeze them for breakfast on busy mornings," she writes from Crooked River Ranch, Oregon. "I'm afraid that they're too high in fat, though. Is there any way to make them more nutritious?"

After sampling Mary's recipe, our home economists knew they didn't want to lose the waffles' delightful texture or buttery flavor…but they did want to significantly decrease the fat. They began by substituting fat-free milk for the whole milk. Canola oil replaced some of the butter, helping to reduce the saturated fat.

The two eggs called for in the original recipe were retained, but the whites were separated from the yolks. The yolks were added to the batter before it was refrigerated overnight. The egg whites were beaten and folded in the next day to help keep the fluffy interior and crispy exterior of Mary's waffles.

Our tasting panel was pleasantly surprised when they bit into Makeover Overnight Yeast Waffles. The revamped waffles have nearly 60% less fat and about 33% fewer calories, but our testers couldn't tell the difference between the two versions. Both were delicious!

Overnight Yeast Waffles

Meatless

Prep: 15 min. + chilling **Cook:** 5 min.

1 package (1/4 ounce) active dry yeast
1/2 cup warm water (110° to 115°)
1 teaspoon sugar
2 cups warm milk (110° to 115°)
1/2 cup butter, melted
2 eggs, lightly beaten
2 cups all-purpose flour
1 teaspoon salt

In a large mixing bowl, dissolve yeast in warm water. Add sugar; let stand for 5 minutes. Add the milk, butter and eggs; mix well. Combine flour and salt; stir into milk mixture. Cover and refrigerate overnight.

Stir batter. For each waffle, pour by 1/4 cupfuls into a preheated waffle iron; bake according to manufacturer's directions until golden brown. **Yield:** 10 servings.

Nutritional Analysis: *2 waffles equals 220 calories, 12 g fat (7 g saturated fat), 74 mg cholesterol, 366 mg sodium, 22 g carbohydrate, 1 g fiber, 6 g protein.*

Makeover Overnight Yeast Waffles

(Pictured below)

Meatless

Prep: 15 min. + chilling **Cook:** 5 min.

1 package (1/4 ounce) active dry yeast
1/2 cup warm water (110° to 115°)
1 teaspoon sugar
2 cups warm fat-free milk (110° to 115°)
2 eggs, *separated*
2 tablespoons butter, melted
1 tablespoon canola oil
1-3/4 cups all-purpose flour
1 teaspoon salt

In a large mixing bowl, dissolve yeast in warm water. Add sugar; let stand for 5 minutes. Add the milk, egg yolks, butter and oil (refrigerate egg whites). Combine flour and salt; stir into milk mixture. Cover and refrigerate overnight.

Let egg whites stand at room temperature for 30 minutes. In a small mixing bowl, beat egg whites until stiff peaks form. Stir batter; fold in egg whites.

For each waffle, pour batter by 1/4 cupfuls into a preheated waffle iron; bake according to manufacturer's directions until golden brown. **Yield:** 10 servings.

Nutritional Analysis: *2 waffles equals 148 calories, 5 g fat (2 g saturated fat), 50 mg cholesterol, 298 mg sodium, 20 g carbohydrate, 1 g fiber, 5 g protein.*
Diabetic Exchanges: *1 starch, 1 fat.*

Beefed-Up Main Dishes

Even folks watching their diets can indulge in a meaty entree. The secret is to select lean beef cuts and to trim down the accompanying sauces. No one will guess you cheated these dishes out of fat and calories!

London Broil (page 114)

Coat grill rack with nonstick cooking spray before starting the grill. Grill beef, covered, over medium heat for 5-6 minutes on each side or until meat reaches desired doneness. Let stand for 10 minutes before cutting into 4 slices.

Serve warm on bread with garlic mayonnaise, arugula and onion mixture. **Yield:** 4 servings.

Nutritional Analysis: *1 sandwich equals 418 calories, 15 g fat (4 g saturated fat), 75 mg cholesterol, 702 mg sodium, 40 g carbohydrate, 3 g fiber, 31 g protein.*
Diabetic Exchanges: *3 lean meat, 2 starch, 1 vegetable, 1 fat.*

Luau Beef Tenderloin Steaks

(Pictured below)

Low-carb

Prep: 10 min. + marinating **Grill:** 15 min.

Pineapple juice, soy sauce and cider vinegar give these juicy steaks their tangy taste. We found that the sweet and tropical marinade is also good on pork.
—Lorraine Darocha, Mountain City, Tennessee

 1/4 cup unsweetened pineapple juice
 1/4 cup reduced-sodium soy sauce
 1/4 cup olive oil
 2 tablespoons lemon juice
 2 tablespoons cider vinegar
 1 tablespoon minced garlic
 1 tablespoon chopped sweet onion
1-1/2 teaspoons ground mustard
 1/2 teaspoon minced fresh parsley
 4 beef tenderloin steaks (4 ounces *each*)

In a small bowl, combine the first nine ingredients. Pour 3/4 cup marinade into a large resealable plastic bag; add the steaks. Seal bag and turn to coat; refrigerate for several hours or overnight. Cover and refrigerate the remaining marinade.

Drain steaks and discard marinade. Coat grill rack with nonstick cooking spray before starting the grill. Grill the steaks, covered, over medium heat for 6-8 minutes on each side or until the meat reaches desired doneness (for medi-

Grilled Beef Tenderloin Sandwiches

(Pictured above)

Prep: 15 min. + marinating **Cook:** 70 min.

My daughter shared these hearty sandwiches with me, and I think they're a savory melt-in-your-mouth treat. The sweet-sour onions and mushrooms are perfect over the tender beef and lip-smacking garlic mayonnaise.
—Ruth Lee, Troy, Ontario

 1 tablespoon brown sugar
 2 garlic cloves, minced
 1/2 teaspoon coarsely ground pepper
 1/4 teaspoon salt
 1 beef tenderloin (1 pound)
 1 whole garlic bulb
 1/2 teaspoon canola oil
 1/4 cup *each* fat-free mayonnaise and plain yogurt
ONION TOPPING:
 1 tablespoon olive oil
 1 large sweet onion, thinly sliced
 1/2 pound sliced fresh mushrooms
 2 tablespoons balsamic vinegar
1-1/2 teaspoons sugar
 1/8 teaspoon salt
 1/8 teaspoon pepper
 4 slices French bread (3/4 inch thick)
 1 cup fresh arugula

Combine the first four ingredients; rub over meat. Refrigerate for 2 hours. Remove papery outer skin from garlic (do not peel or separate cloves). Cut top off of garlic. Brush with canola oil. Wrap bulb in heavy-duty foil. Bake at 425° for 30-35 minutes or until softened. Cool 10 minutes. Squeeze garlic into food processor; add mayonnaise and yogurt. Process until smooth; chill.

In a large nonstick skillet, heat olive oil and saute onion for 5 minutes. Reduce heat; cook and stir for 10-12 minutes or until onion is golden. Add mushrooms; cook and stir until tender. Add next four ingredients; cook until reduced slightly.

oil for 3-4 minutes or until crisp-tender. Stir cornstarch mixture and add to the pan. Bring to a boil; cook and stir for 2 minutes or until thickened. Reduce heat; add beef and heat through. Serve over rice. **Yield:** 4 servings.

Nutritional Analysis: 1/4 cup beef mixture with 1/2 cup rice equals 372 calories, 16 g fat (5 g saturated fat), 74 mg cholesterol, 540 mg sodium, 28 g carbohydrate, 1 g fiber, 28 g protein.
Diabetic Exchanges: 3 lean meat, 2 starch, 1 fat.

Slow-Cooked Sirloin

Low-carb

Prep: 20 min. **Cook:** 3-1/2 hours

My family of five likes to eat beef, so this recipe is a favorite. I usually serve it with homemade bread or rolls to soak up the tasty gravy.
—Vicki Tormaschy, Dickinson, North Dakota

 1 boneless beef sirloin steak (1-1/2 pounds)
 1 medium onion, cut into 1-inch chunks
 1 medium green pepper, cut into 1-inch chunks
 1 can (14-1/2 ounces) reduced-sodium beef broth
 1/4 cup Worcestershire sauce
 1/4 teaspoon dill weed
 1/4 teaspoon dried thyme
 1/4 teaspoon pepper
Dash crushed red pepper flakes
 2 tablespoons cornstarch
 2 tablespoons water

In a large nonstick skillet coated with nonstick cooking spray, brown beef on both sides. Place onion and green pepper in a 3-qt. slow cooker. Top with beef.

Combine the beef broth, Worcestershire sauce, dill, thyme, pepper and red pepper flakes; pour over the beef. Cover and cook on high for 3-4 hours or until the meat reaches desired doneness and the vegetables are crisp-tender. Remove the beef and keep warm.

Combine cornstarch and water until smooth; gradually stir into cooking juices. Cover and cook about 30 minutes longer or until slightly thickened. Return beef to the slow cooker; heat through. **Yield:** 6 servings.

Nutritional Analysis: 1 serving equals 199 calories, 6 g fat (2 g saturated fat), 68 mg cholesterol, 305 mg sodium, 8 g carbohydrate, 1 g fiber, 26 g protein.
Diabetic Exchanges: 3 lean meat, 1 vegetable.

um-rare, a meat thermometer should read 145°; medium, 160°; well-done, 170°). Baste with reserved marinade during the last 2 minutes of cooking. **Yield:** 4 servings.

Nutritional Analysis: 1 steak equals 249 calories, 15 g fat (4 g saturated fat), 71 mg cholesterol, 356 mg sodium, 3 g carbohydrate, trace fiber, 25 g protein.
Diabetic Exchanges: 3 lean meat, 2 fat.

Mongolian Beef

(Pictured above)

Prep/Total Time: 25 min.

My family just loves this meal-in-one, including my husband, who is truly a meat-and-potatoes guy. The dish uses inexpensive ingredients to offer big flavor in a small amount of time.
—Heather Blum, Coleman, Wisconsin

 1 tablespoon cornstarch
3/4 cup reduced-sodium chicken broth
 2 tablespoons reduced-sodium soy sauce
 1 tablespoon hoisin sauce
 2 teaspoons sesame oil
 1 pound boneless beef top sirloin steak, cut into thin strips
 1 tablespoon olive oil, *divided*
 5 green onions, cut into 1-inch pieces
 2 cups hot cooked rice

In a small bowl, combine the cornstarch and chicken broth until smooth. Stir in the soy sauce, hoisin sauce and sesame oil; set aside. In a large nonstick skillet or wok, stir-fry beef in 1-1/2 teaspoons hot olive oil until no longer pink. Remove and keep warm.

In the same skillet, stir-fry the onions in remaining olive

🍎 Savvy Substitution

IN RECIPES that call for 1-1/2 to 2 pounds of ground beef, I use a beef and bean mixture instead. I brown 3/4 pound of extra-lean ground beef with whatever vegetables the recipe calls for. Then I add 1 can of drained and rinsed pinto beans and combine it all with a potato masher. I continue with the recipe using this mixture where the beef is called for.
—Stephanie Land, Sudbury, Ontario

Home-Style Pot Roast

(Pictured above)

Prep: 15 min. **Cook:** 3-1/4 hours

Tender meat, lots of vegetables and a pleasant gravy make this meal-in-one satisfying and filling.
—Olga Montecorboli, Hartsdale, New York

- 1 beef eye round roast (2-1/2 pounds)
- 6 tablespoons all-purpose flour, *divided*
- 1 tablespoon canola oil
- 1-1/2 cups plus 1/3 cup water, *divided*
- 1-1/2 cups dry red wine *or* reduced-sodium beef broth
- 2 teaspoons beef bouillon granules
- 1/4 teaspoon pepper
- 16 small red potatoes (2 pounds), halved
- 4 medium carrots (3/4 pound), halved lengthwise and cut into 2-inch pieces
- 2 medium onions, quartered
- 1/2 teaspoon salt
- 1/2 teaspoon browning sauce, optional

Coat the roast with 2 tablespoons flour. In a large nonstick skillet, brown roast on all sides in oil over medium-high heat; drain. Add 1-1/2 cups water, wine or broth, bouillon and pepper. Bring to a boil. Reduce heat; cover and simmer for 2 hours.

Add the potatoes, carrots and onions; cover and simmer for 45 minutes or until meat and vegetables are tender. Remove meat and vegetables; keep warm.

Pour pan juices into a measuring cup; skim fat. In a saucepan, combine remaining flour and water until smooth. Stir in salt and browning sauce if desired. Gradually stir in 2 cups of pan juices. Bring to a boil; cook and stir for 2 minutes or until thickened. Serve with roast and vegetables. **Yield:** 8 servings.

Nutritional Analysis: *1 serving equals 341 calories, 9 g fat (3 g saturated fat), 82 mg cholesterol, 500 mg sodium, 32 g carbohydrate, 4 g fiber, 30 g protein.*
Diabetic Exchanges: *3 lean meat, 2 vegetable, 1-1/2 starch.*

Balsamic-Seasoned Steak

Low-carb   Low-sodium

Prep/Total Time: 25 min.

A tasty sauce jazzes up this hearty sirloin. Created by our Test Kitchen staff, the Swiss cheese topping is one you'll surely enjoy.

- 2 tablespoons balsamic vinegar
- 2 teaspoons steak sauce
- 1 boneless beef sirloin steak (1 pound)
- 1/4 teaspoon coarsely ground pepper
- 2 ounces reduced-fat Swiss cheese, cut into thin strips

Combine vinegar and steak sauce; set aside. Rub steak with pepper. Broil 4 in. from the heat for 7 minutes. Turn; spoon half of the steak sauce mixture over steak. Broil 5-7 minutes longer or until meat reaches desired doneness (for medium-rare, a meat thermometer should read 145°; medium, 160°; well-done, 170°).

Remove steak to a cutting board; cut across the grain into 1/4-in. slices. Place on a foil-lined baking sheet; drizzle with juices from cutting board and remaining steak sauce mixture. Top with cheese. Broil for 1 minute or until cheese is melted. **Yield:** 4 servings.

Nutritional Analysis: *3 ounces cooked beef with 1/2 ounce of cheese equals 188 calories, 8 g fat (3 g saturated fat), 70 mg cholesterol, 116 mg sodium, 2 g carbohydrate, trace fiber, 26 g protein.*
Diabetic Exchanges: *3 lean meat, 1/2 fat.*

Swiss Steak

(Pictured below)

Prep: 10 min. **Cook:** 1 hour 35 min.

Here's a dinner that takes up very little time. We like it with mashed potatoes, rice or noodles. Add a green salad and supper is set.
—Betty Richardson, Springfield, Illinois

- 4 beef cube steaks (4 ounces *each*)
- 1 tablespoon canola oil
- 1 medium onion, chopped

1 celery rib with leaves, chopped
1 garlic clove, minced
1 can (14-1/2 ounces) stewed tomatoes, cut up
1 can (8 ounces) tomato sauce
1 teaspoon beef bouillon granules
1 tablespoon cornstarch
2 tablespoons cold water

In a large nonstick skillet, brown cube steaks on both sides in oil over medium-high heat; remove and set aside. In the same skillet, saute the onion, celery and garlic for 3-4 minutes or until tender. Add the tomatoes, tomato sauce and bouillon. Return steaks to the pan. Bring to a boil. Reduce heat; cover and simmer for 1-1/4 to 1-3/4 hours or until meat is tender.

Combine cornstarch and water until smooth; stir into tomato mixture. Bring to a boil; cook and stir for 2 minutes or until thickened. **Yield:** 4 servings.

Nutritional Analysis: 1 steak with 3/4 cup sauce equals 255 calories, 8 g fat (2 g saturated fat), 65 mg cholesterol, 746 mg sodium, 18 g carbohydrate, 3 g fiber, 28 g protein.
Diabetic Exchanges: 3 lean meat, 3 vegetable, 1/2 fat.

One-Pot Stuffed Pepper Dinner

Prep/Total Time: 30 min.

With its chili-like consistency and stuffed-pepper flavor, this dish will warm you up on chilly days.
—Charlotte Smith, McDonald, Pennsylvania

1 pound lean ground beef
3 garlic cloves, minced
3 cups chopped green pepper
2 cans (14-1/2 ounces *each*) Italian diced
  tomatoes
2 cups water
1 can (6 ounces) tomato paste
8 tablespoons shredded Parmesan cheese,
  divided
1 teaspoon garlic salt
1/4 teaspoon pepper
1 cup uncooked instant rice

In a large nonstick saucepan coated with nonstick cooking spray, cook beef over medium heat until no longer pink; drain. Add garlic; cook and stir for 1 minute. Add green pepper; cook and stir 3 minutes longer. Stir in the diced tomatoes, water, tomato paste, 2 tablespoons Parmesan cheese, garlic salt and pepper. Bring to a boil. Stir in rice. Remove from the heat. Cover and let stand for 5 minutes. Sprinkle with remaining Parmesan cheese. **Yield:** 6 servings.

Nutritional Analysis: 1-1/3 cups equals 286 calories, 7 g fat (3 g saturated fat), 41 mg cholesterol, 1,002 mg sodium, 32 g carbohydrate, 3 g fiber, 21 g protein.
Diabetic Exchanges: 3 vegetable, 2 lean meat, 1 starch, 1/2 fat.

Hearty Spaghetti Sauce

(Pictured above)

Prep: 15 min. **Cook:** 2 hours

This easy sauce requires just minutes of preparation and simmers until dinnertime.
—Kimberly Rockwell, Charlotte, North Carolina

1-1/2 pounds lean ground beef
1 large onion, chopped
1 large green pepper, chopped
1/2 pound sliced fresh mushrooms
3 cans (15 ounces *each*) crushed tomatoes
1 can (6 ounces) tomato paste
1/2 cup ketchup
1 tablespoon sugar
1 tablespoon chili powder
1 teaspoon salt
1 teaspoon garlic powder
1 teaspoon dried basil
1 teaspoon dried oregano
1 teaspoon Italian seasoning
1 teaspoon Worcestershire sauce
1/2 teaspoon pepper

In a large saucepan coated with nonstick cooking spray, cook the beef, onion and green pepper over medium heat until meat is no longer pink; drain. Add the mushrooms; cook and stir for 2 minutes. Stir in the remaining ingredients. Bring to a boil. Reduce heat; cover and simmer for 1-1/2 hours. **Yield:** 12 servings.

Nutritional Analysis: 2/3 cup equals 163 calories, 5 g fat (2 g saturated fat), 28 mg cholesterol, 516 mg sodium, 18 g carbohydrate, 4 g fiber, 14 g protein.
Diabetic Exchanges: 2 vegetable, 1 lean meat, 1/2 starch.

Cover and bake at 350° for 30 minutes. Uncover; sprinkle with cheese. Bake 5-10 minutes longer or until bubbly and cheese is melted. **Yield:** 4 servings.

Nutritional Analysis: 2 cabbage rolls equals 281 calories, 9 g fat (4 g saturated fat), 50 mg cholesterol, 897 mg sodium, 24 g carbohydrate, 4 g fiber, 24 g protein.
Diabetic Exchanges: 3 lean meat, 3 vegetable, 1/2 starch.

Cabbage Rolls

(Pictured above)

Prep: 35 min. **Bake:** 35 min.

This is a delicious recipe for traditional cabbage rolls. In summer when tomatoes are plentiful, I use peeled fresh tomatoes instead of canned diced tomatoes to reduce the sodium.
—Dolly Mullen, Langley, Washington

   1 medium head cabbage
3/4 pound lean ground beef
1/2 cup chopped onion
   1 can (14-1/2 ounces) diced tomatoes, undrained
1/2 cup water
1/3 cup instant brown rice
   1 can (15 ounces) tomato sauce
   1 tablespoon Worcestershire sauce
1/2 teaspoon dried basil
1/2 teaspoon dried thyme
1/2 teaspoon sugar
1/2 cup shredded part-skim mozzarella cheese

Cook cabbage in boiling water just until leaves fall off head. Set aside 8 large leaves for rolls. (Refrigerate remaining cabbage for another use.) Cut out the thick vein from the bottom of each reserved leaf, making a V-shaped cut. Set aside.

In a large nonstick skillet, cook the ground beef and onion over medium heat until meat is no longer pink; drain. Stir in tomatoes and water; bring to a boil. Stir in rice; return to a boil. Reduce heat; cover and simmer for 5 minutes. Place about 1/3 cup beef mixture on each reserved cabbage leaf; overlap cut ends of leaf. Fold in sides, beginning from the cut end. Roll up completely to enclose filling.

In a bowl, combine the tomato sauce, Worcestershire sauce, basil, thyme and sugar. Spread half on the bottom of an 11-in. x 7-in. x 2-in. baking dish coated with nonstick cooking spray. Top with cabbage rolls and remaining tomato sauce mixture.

Bavarian Beef Roast

Low-carb

Prep: 20 min. **Cook:** 2 hours 50 min.

This well-seasoned beef roast is so tender and juicy, I never have leftovers when I serve it. My husband and our four boys clean their plates down to the last vegetable. Try this with sweet-and-sour cabbage.
—Cynthia Gessner, Radway, Alberta

   1 boneless beef bottom round roast (3 pounds)
   1 garlic clove, cut into thin slivers
   1 teaspoon canola oil
   1 cup chopped carrots
   1 cup thinly sliced celery
   1 cup chopped onion
   1 cup sherry *or* beef broth
1/2 cup minced fresh parsley
   1 tablespoon sugar
   2 teaspoons caraway seeds
   1 teaspoon salt
1/2 teaspoon ground cardamom

With a sharp knife, cut thin slits in meat; place a piece of garlic in each slit. In a large saucepan or Dutch oven, brown meat in oil on all sides; drain. Add the carrots, celery and onion. Combine the sherry or broth, parsley, sugar, caraway seeds, salt and cardamom; pour over meat.

Bring to a boil. Reduce heat; cover and simmer for about 2-3/4 hours or until meat is tender. Remove and slice meat. Skim fat from cooking liquid and serve vegetables with meat. **Yield:** 8 servings.

Nutritional Analysis: 3 ounces cooked beef with 3 tablespoons vegetables equals 228 calories, 9 g fat (3 g saturated fat), 82 mg cholesterol, 360 mg sodium, 6 g carbohydrate, 1 g fiber, 28 g protein.
Diabetic Exchanges: 3 lean meat, 1 vegetable, 1 fat.

Yellow Pepper Beef Stir-Fry

Low-carb

Prep: 15 min. + marinating **Cook:** 15 min.

A quick marinade lends a bit of sweetness to tender beef strips in this meal-in-one from our Test Kitchen. Each generous serving also features a bevy of vegetables lightly coated in a savory sauce.

   2 teaspoons cornstarch, *divided*
   2 teaspoons brown sugar, *divided*
   1 garlic clove, minced
1/4 teaspoon pepper
   2 tablespoons rice wine vinegar, *divided*

1 pound beef sirloin steak, cut into 1/4-inch strips
1/4 cup reduced-sodium chicken broth
2 tablespoons reduced-sodium soy sauce
1 tablespoon canola oil
1 medium sweet onion, cut into wedges
2 cups cut fresh asparagus (1-inch pieces)
1 cup julienned sweet yellow pepper

In a large resealable plastic bag, combine 1 teaspoon cornstarch, 1 teaspoon brown sugar, garlic, pepper and 1 tablespoon vinegar. Add beef; seal bag and turn to coat. Refrigerate for at least 1 hour.

In a bowl, combine the remaining cornstarch and brown sugar. Add the broth, soy sauce and remaining vinegar; stir until smooth. Set aside.

In a large nonstick skillet or wok, heat oil; stir-fry beef until no longer pink. Remove and keep warm. In the same pan, stir-fry onion for 2 minutes. Add asparagus and yellow pepper; stir-fry for 5-6 minutes or until crisp-tender.

Return beef to the pan. Stir broth mixture and add to the pan. Bring to a boil; cook and stir for 1-2 minutes or until thickened. **Yield:** 4 servings.

Nutritional Analysis: 1 cup equals 253 calories, 10 g fat (3 g saturated fat), 67 mg cholesterol, 418 mg sodium, 13 g carbohydrate, 2 g fiber, 28 g protein.
Diabetic Exchanges: 3 lean meat, 2 vegetable, 1/2 fat.

Beef Noodle Casserole

Prep: 15 min. **Bake:** 25 min.

This is truly an old standby that's been in my family for years. It can be assembled the night before and baked the next day.
—Karen Mathis, Penfield, New York

4-1/2 cups uncooked yolk-free noodles
1 pound lean ground beef
1 small onion, chopped
1/2 cup chopped green pepper
1 can (10-3/4 ounces) reduced-fat reduced-sodium condensed cream of mushroom soup, undiluted
1/4 cup grated Parmesan cheese
1 can (4 ounces) mushroom stems and pieces, drained
1 jar (2 ounces) diced pimientos, drained
1 tablespoon butter, melted
1 teaspoon dried thyme
1/4 teaspoon salt

Cook noodles according to package directions; drain. In a nonstick skillet, cook the beef, onion and green pepper over medium heat until meat is no longer pink; drain. In a large bowl, combine the soup, Parmesan cheese, mushrooms, pimientos, butter, thyme and salt; mix well. Stir in the noodles and beef mixture.

Transfer to a 2-qt. baking dish coated with nonstick cooking spray. Cover and bake at 350° for 25-30 minutes or until heated through. **Yield:** 6 servings.

Nutritional Analysis: 1 cup equals 295 calories, 11 g fat (5 g saturated fat), 46 mg cholesterol, 527 mg sodium, 27 g carbohydrate, 3 g fiber, 21 g protein.
Diabetic Exchanges: 2 lean meat, 1-1/2 starch, 1 vegetable, 1 fat.

Spinach-Stuffed Beef Tenderloin

(Pictured above)

Low-carb

Prep: 20 min. **Bake:** 30 min.

This makes a wonderfully easy entree for company. Filled with a combination of spinach, blue cheese and mushrooms, it gets rave reviews whenever I serve it.
—Deborah DeMers, DeRidder, Louisiana

1/2 pound sliced fresh mushrooms
4 garlic cloves, minced
1 package (6 ounces) fresh baby spinach, chopped
1 cup (4 ounces) crumbled blue cheese
1 beef tenderloin (2 pounds)
1/2 teaspoon salt, *divided*
1/2 teaspoon pepper, *divided*

In a small nonstick skillet coated with nonstick cooking spray, saute the mushrooms until tender. Add the garlic; cook and stir for 1 minute. In a bowl, combine the mushroom mixture, spinach and cheese; set aside.

Cut a lengthwise slit down the center of the tenderloin to within 1/2 in. of bottom. Open tenderloin so it lies flat; cover with plastic wrap. Flatten to 3/4-in. thickness. Remove plastic; sprinkle with 1/4 teaspoon salt and 1/4 teaspoon pepper. Spread stuffing over the meat to within 1 in. of edges. Close tenderloin; tie at 2-in. intervals with kitchen string. Place tenderloin on a rack in a shallow roasting pan. Sprinkle with remaining salt and pepper.

Bake, uncovered, at 425° for 30 minutes or until meat reaches desired doneness (for medium-rare, a meat thermometer should read 145°; medium, 160°; well-done, 170°). Let stand for 5-10 minutes before slicing. **Yield:** 8 servings.

Nutritional Analysis: 5 ounces stuffed cooked beef equals 238 calories, 12 g fat (6 g saturated fat), 82 mg cholesterol, 417 mg sodium, 3 g carbohydrate, 1 g fiber, 28 g protein.
Diabetic Exchanges: 3 lean meat, 1-1/2 fat.

Pizza Burgers

(Pictured above)

Prep/Total Time: 30 min.

This better-for-you version of an all-time lunch counter classic is loaded with popular pizza flavor. The cheese-topped burgers are also fast to fix.
—Lisa Truckenbrod, Beloit, Wisconsin

  1 can (6 ounces) tomato paste
1/2 teaspoon salt
1/2 teaspoon dried oregano
1/4 teaspoon garlic salt
1/4 teaspoon pepper
1/4 teaspoon aniseed
1-1/2 pounds lean ground beef
1/2 cup shredded part-skim mozzarella cheese
  6 hamburger buns, split
  6 lettuce leaves
  6 tomato slices

In a large bowl, combine the first six ingredients. Crumble beef over mixture; mix well. Shape into six patties. Place on broiler pan coated with nonstick cooking spray. Broil 6 in. from heat for 5-6 minutes on each side or until juices run clear. Sprinkle with cheese. Broil 1 minute longer or until cheese is melted. Serve on buns with lettuce and tomato. **Yield:** 6 servings.

Nutritional Analysis: 1 burger equals 346 calories, 13 g fat (5 g saturated fat), 75 mg cholesterol, 628 mg sodium, 28 g carbohydrate, 3 g fiber, 28 g protein.
Diabetic Exchanges: 3 lean meat, 2 starch, 1/2 fat.

London Broil

(Pictured on page 107)

Low-carb

Prep: 10 min. + marinating **Grill:** 15 min.

I received this delicious recipe from my mother-in-law. Prepared on the grill, it's a real treat during warm-weather months.
—Susan Wilkins, Los Olivos, California

1/2 cup water
1/4 cup red wine vinegar
  2 tablespoons canola oil
  1 tablespoon tomato paste
1-1/2 teaspoons garlic salt, *divided*
  1 teaspoon dried thyme, *divided*
1/2 teaspoon pepper, *divided*
  1 bay leaf
  1 beef flank steak (1-1/2 pounds)

In a small bowl, whisk the water, vinegar, oil, tomato paste, 1 teaspoon garlic salt, 1/2 teaspoon thyme, 1/4 teaspoon pepper and bay leaf. Pour into a resealable plastic bag. Score the surface of the steak, making diamond shapes 1/4 in. deep; add the steak to the marinade. Seal the bag and turn to coat; refrigerate for 3 hours or overnight, turning occasionally.

Coat grill rack with nonstick cooking spray before starting the grill. Discard marinade. Pat steak dry with paper towels. Combine the remaining garlic salt, thyme and pepper; rub over both sides of steak.

Grill steak, covered, over medium-hot heat for 6-8 minutes on each side or until a meat thermometer reaches desired doneness (for medium-rare, a meat thermometer should read 145°; medium, 160°; well-done, 170°). To serve, thinly slice across the grain. **Yield:** 6 servings.

Nutritional Analysis: 3 ounces cooked steak equals 175 calories, 9 g fat (4 g saturated fat), 54 mg cholesterol, 294 mg sodium, 1 g carbohydrate, trace fiber, 22 g protein.
Diabetic Exchange: 3 lean meat.

Stovetop Beef 'n' Shells

Prep/Total Time: 30 min.

I fix this supper when I'm pressed for time. It's as tasty as it is fast. Team it with salad, bread and fruit for a comforting meal.
—Donna Roberts, Shumway, Illinois

  4 ounces uncooked medium pasta shells
  1 pound lean ground beef
  1 medium onion, chopped
  1 garlic clove, minced
  1 can (15 ounces) crushed tomatoes, undrained
  1 can (8 ounces) tomato sauce
  1 teaspoon sugar
1/2 teaspoon salt
1/2 teaspoon pepper

Cook pasta according to package directions. Meanwhile, in a large saucepan, cook the beef, onion and garlic over medium heat until meat is no longer pink; drain. Stir in the tomatoes, tomato sauce, sugar, salt and pepper. Bring to a boil. Reduce heat; simmer, uncovered, for 10-15 minutes. Drain pasta; stir into beef mixture and heat through. **Yield:** 4 servings.

Nutritional Analysis: 1-1/4 cups equals 339 calories, 9 g fat (4 g saturated fat), 56 mg cholesterol, 772 mg sodium, 36 g carbohydrate, 4 g fiber, 29 g protein.
Diabetic Exchanges: 3 lean meat, 3 vegetable, 1-1/2 starch.

Chicken & Turkey Entrees

You don't have to eat like a bird—or forego great flavor—to trim down on fat and calories. A simple solution is to choose chicken and turkey. Your family will flock to the table for these enticing entrees.

Herbed Cranberry Chicken (page 131)

Chicken Lo Mein

(Pictured above)

Prep/Total Time: 30 min.

This lo mein recipe is a low-calorie, eye-appealing dish that is very quick to make. With soy sauce, sherry, ginger and sesame oil, as well as red pepper and snow peas, it's as flavorful as it is colorful.
—*Jennifer Suster, Chicago, Illinois*

   1 tablespoon cornstarch
   1 teaspoon ground ginger
  1/4 cup reduced-sodium soy sauce
   2 tablespoons sherry *or* chicken broth
1-1/2 pounds boneless skinless chicken breasts,
     thinly sliced
   1 teaspoon reduced-sodium chicken bouillon
     granules
  1/2 cup hot water
   6 ounces uncooked linguine
  1/2 pound fresh mushrooms, sliced
  1/4 pound fresh snow peas
   1 large sweet red pepper, julienned
   2 green onions, cut into 2-inch pieces
   2 tablespoons canola oil, *divided*
   2 teaspoons sesame oil

In a large bowl, combine the cornstarch, ginger, soy sauce and sherry or broth until smooth. Add chicken and stir to coat; set aside. In a small bowl, dissolve bouillon granules in hot water; set aside. Cook linguine according to package directions.

In a large nonstick skillet or wok, stir-fry mushrooms, snow peas, red pepper and green onions in 1 tablespoon canola oil for 3-5 minutes or until crisp-tender. Remove with a slotted spoon and set aside.

In the same skillet, stir-fry the chicken mixture in the remaining canola oil for 2-3 minutes or until chicken is no longer pink. Stir in dissolved bouillon. Bring to a boil; cook and stir for 1-2 minutes or until thickened. Return vegetables

to skillet. Drain linguine; add sesame oil and linguine to skillet. Toss to coat. Cook 1-2 minutes longer or until heated through. **Yield:** 6 servings.

   Nutritional Analysis: *1-1/3 cups equals 328 calories, 10 g fat (1 g saturated fat), 67 mg cholesterol, 515 mg sodium, 27 g carbohydrate, 3 g fiber, 31 g protein.*
   Diabetic Exchanges: *3 lean meat, 1-1/2 starch, 1 vegetable, 1/2 fat.*

Turkey Barbecue

(Pictured below)

Prep: 15 min. **Cook:** 25 min.

I originally got this recipe from my daughter-in-law, who likes to cook healthy meals. I just added my Texas touch to give the chunky turkey sandwiches some zip. I serve them with a cranberry salad.
—*Arlene Anderson, San Antonio, Texas*

   1 celery rib, chopped
   1 medium onion, chopped
  1/4 cup chopped green pepper
   1 tablespoon canola oil
  1/4 cup packed brown sugar
  1/4 cup ketchup
  1/4 cup picante sauce
   2 tablespoons Worcestershire sauce
1-1/2 teaspoons chili powder
   1 teaspoon salt
  1/8 teaspoon pepper
Dash hot pepper sauce
   4 cups cubed cooked turkey
   8 whole wheat hamburger buns, split

In a large nonstick skillet, saute the celery, onion and green pepper in oil for 3-4 minutes or until tender. Stir in the brown sugar, ketchup, picante sauce, Worcestershire sauce, chili powder, salt, pepper and pepper sauce; bring to a boil. Reduce heat; simmer, uncovered, for 3-4 minutes. Add turkey; simmer 10 minutes longer or until heated through. Serve on buns. **Yield:** 8 servings.

Nutritional Analysis: *1 sandwich equals 295 calories, 7 g fat (2 g saturated fat), 53 mg cholesterol, 758 mg sodium, 33 g carbohydrate, 4 g fiber, 25 g protein.*
Diabetic Exchanges: *3 lean meat, 2 starch.*

Italian Turkey and Noodles

(Pictured above)

Prep: 35 min. **Bake:** 30 min.

A jar of meatless spaghetti sauces makes this easy dish a perfect supper during the week...just add a green salad, and dinner is set. Best of all, my whole family loves it.
—Cindi Roshia, Racine, Wisconsin

1-1/4 pounds lean ground turkey
1-1/2 cups sliced fresh mushrooms
1/2 cup chopped onion
1/2 cup chopped green pepper
1 jar (26 ounces) meatless spaghetti sauce
1/2 teaspoon onion salt
3 cups cooked yolk-free wide noodles
1 cup (4 ounces) shredded part-skim mozzarella cheese

In a large nonstick skillet, cook the turkey, mushrooms, onion and green pepper until turkey is no longer pink. Add spaghetti sauce and onion salt; bring to a boil. Reduce heat; simmer, uncovered, for 15 minutes.

Place cooked noodles in the bottom of a 2-1/2-qt. baking dish coated with nonstick cooking spray. Pour meat mixture over noodles. Sprinkle with cheese. Cover and bake at 350° for 20 minutes. Uncover; bake 10-15 minutes longer or until heated through. **Yield:** 6 servings.

Nutritional Analysis: *1 serving equals 392 calories, 12 g fat (5 g saturated fat), 86 mg cholesterol, 798 mg sodium, 39 g carbohydrate, 5 g fiber, 28 g protein.*
Diabetic Exchanges: *3 lean meat, 3 vegetable, 1-1/2 starch, 1/2 fat.*

Honey Rosemary Chicken Kabobs

(Pictured below)

Low-fat Low-sodium

Prep: 15 min. + marinating **Grill:** 10 min.

These tender kabobs are full of savory rosemary flavor, yet they're low in fat and sodium. I found the original recipe in a magazine but adjusted it to better suit the tastes in my household.
—Elisabeth Corcimiglia, Byron, New York

1/3 cup honey
1/4 cup lemon juice
2 tablespoons minced fresh rosemary *or* 2 teaspoons dried rosemary, crushed
1/4 teaspoon crushed red pepper flakes
1 pound boneless skinless chicken breasts, cut into 1-inch cubes
1 pint cherry tomatoes
1 small zucchini, cut into 1-inch pieces
1 can (8 ounces) unsweetened pineapple chunks, drained

In a bowl, combine the first four ingredients. Pour 1/3 cup marinade into a large resealable plastic bag; add the chicken. Seal bag and turn to coat; refrigerate for at least 30 minutes. Cover and refrigerate remaining marinade.

Coat grill rack with nonstick cooking spray before starting the grill. Drain and discard marinade from chicken. On eight metal or soaked wooden skewers, alternately thread chicken, vegetables and pineapple. Grill kabobs, covered, over low heat for 9-11 minutes or until chicken juices run clear, turning and basting frequently with reserved marinade.
Yield: 4 servings.

Nutritional Analysis: *2 kabobs equals 206 calories, 3 g fat (1 g saturated fat), 63 mg cholesterol, 66 mg sodium, 21 g carbohydrate, 2 g fiber, 24 g protein.*
Diabetic Exchanges: *3 very lean meat, 1 starch, 1 vegetable.*

Turkey Tenderloin Sandwiches

(Pictured below)

Prep: 10 min. + marinating **Cook:** 10 min.

We loved these absolutely delicious tenderloins when we visited the Iowa State Fair. We had to wait in line for more than an hour to order them, but with this recipe, we can enjoy them regularly.
—Kathy Thompson, Clifton, Colorado

 4 turkey breast tenderloins (4 ounces *each*)
1/4 cup canola oil
1/4 cup sherry *or* chicken broth
1/4 cup reduced-sodium soy sauce
 2 tablespoons lemon juice
 2 tablespoons dried minced onion
1/4 teaspoon ground ginger
1/8 teaspoon pepper
 4 whole wheat hamburger buns, split
 1 red onion slice, separated into rings
 4 tomato slices
 4 lettuce leaves

Flatten tenderloins to 3/4-in. thickness. In a large resealable plastic bag, combine the oil, sherry or broth, soy sauce, lemon juice, onion, ginger and pepper; add the turkey. Seal bag and turn to coat; refrigerate for at least 3 hours, turning occasionally.

If grilling the turkey, coat grill rack with nonstick cooking spray before starting the grill. Drain and discard marinade. Grill turkey, uncovered, over medium heat or broil 4 in. from the heat for 4-5 minutes on each side or until juices run clear. Serve turkey on buns with onion, tomato and lettuce. **Yield:** 4 servings.

Nutritional Analysis: 1 sandwich equals 281 calories, 7 g fat (1 g saturated fat), 56 mg cholesterol, 421 mg sodium, 25 g carbohydrate, 4 g fiber, 31 g protein.
Diabetic Exchanges: 4 very lean meat, 1-1/2 starch, 1/2 fat.

Roasted Lemon Chicken

(Pictured above)

Low-carb

Prep: 10 min. **Bake:** 1 hour + standing

This gorgeous herb-rubbed chicken is so moist and tender that you'll want to serve it for special occasions as well as family suppers.
—Margaret Wilson, Hemet, California

 1 whole broiler/fryer chicken (3-1/2 pounds)
1-1/2 teaspoons salt-free lemon-pepper seasoning
1/2 teaspoon onion powder
1/2 teaspoon garlic powder
1/2 teaspoon seasoned salt
1/2 teaspoon dried thyme
 1 medium lemon, halved
 2 fresh rosemary sprigs

Loosen skin around chicken breast, leg and thigh. Combine the seasonings; rub half under skin. Cut half of the lemon into quarters and place in the cavity along with rosemary sprigs. Skewer openings; tie drumsticks together with kitchen string.

Place chicken breast side up on a rack in a roasting pan. Squeeze the remaining lemon over chicken; rub remaining seasoning mixture over chicken. Bake, uncovered, at 375° for 1 to 1-1/2 hours or until chicken juices run clear and a meat thermometer reads 180° (cover loosely with foil if browning too quickly). Cover and let stand for 15 minutes. Remove and discard skin and discard lemon and herbs from cavity before carving. **Yield:** 6 servings.

Nutritional Analysis: 3-1/2 ounces cooked chicken equals 197 calories, 8 g fat (2 g saturated fat), 90 mg cholesterol, 215 mg sodium, 2 g carbohydrate, trace fiber, 29 g protein.
Diabetic Exchange: 4 lean meat.

Favorite Recipe Made Lighter

CREAMY CASSEROLES offer comforting flavor, but sometimes they're not the best choice.

"My husband has to watch his diet due to high cholesterol, and I have to watch my salt intake," says Diane Hyatt of Oregonia, Ohio. "But I don't know how to make this Turkey Biscuit Bake any lighter."

Our home economists slimmed it down, dramatically cutting the fat and saturated fat by more than 80% and reducing the calorie count, cholesterol and sodium by about half.

Turkey Biscuit Bake

Prep: 25 min. **Bake:** 15 min.

3 cups all-purpose flour
3 teaspoons baking powder
1/2 teaspoon salt
1 egg, lightly beaten
3/4 cup butter, melted
3/4 cup water
1 tablespoon lemon juice
FILLING:
1 cup butter
1 cup all-purpose flour
1/2 teaspoon salt
4 cups milk
2 cups diced cooked turkey
1 jar (6 ounces) sliced mushrooms, drained

In a large bowl, combine the flour, baking powder and salt. Combine the egg, butter, water and lemon juice; stir into dry ingredients until a soft dough forms. Spread half of the dough into a greased 13-in. x 9-in. x 2-in. baking dish.

In a large saucepan, melt butter. Stir in flour and salt until smooth; gradually add the milk. Bring to a boil; cook and stir for 1-2 minutes or until thickened. Stir in turkey and mushrooms. Pour over biscuit dough. Drop remaining dough into nine biscuits onto turkey mixture. Bake at 425° for 15-20 minutes or until biscuits are golden brown. **Yield:** 9 servings.

Nutritional Analysis: 2/3 cup turkey mixture with 1 biscuit equals 642 calories, 40 g fat (25 g saturated fat), 163 mg cholesterol, 936 mg sodium, 49 g carbohydrate, 2 g fiber, 21 g protein.

Makeover Turkey Biscuit Bake

(Pictured at right)

Prep: 30 min. **Bake:** 15 min.

1 cup baby carrots, halved lengthwise
1 cup julienned parsnips
1 tablespoon water

2 cups sliced fresh mushrooms
2 tablespoons butter
1/2 cup all-purpose flour
1/2 teaspoon salt
1/8 teaspoon white pepper
4 cups fat-free milk
3 cups diced cooked turkey breast
1/2 cup frozen peas, thawed
BISCUITS:
1 cup all-purpose flour
1/2 cup cake flour
3/4 teaspoon baking powder
1/2 teaspoon salt
1/8 teaspoon baking soda
1 egg
1/2 cup 1% buttermilk
2 tablespoons butter, melted

In a microwave-safe bowl, combine carrots, parsnips and water; cover and microwave on high for 4-5 minutes or until tender. Drain and set aside. In a large nonstick skillet, saute mushrooms in butter until tender. Combine flour, salt, white pepper and milk until smooth; stir into mushrooms. Bring to a boil; cook and stir for 1-2 minutes or until thickened. Stir in the carrots, parsnips, turkey and peas. Transfer to a 13-in. x 9-in. x 2-in. baking dish coated with nonstick cooking spray.

In a bowl, combine the flours, baking powder, salt and baking soda. In another bowl, combine the egg, buttermilk and butter; stir into dry ingredients until a soft dough forms. Drop dough into nine biscuits onto turkey mixture. Bake at 425° for 15-18 minutes or until a toothpick inserted in biscuits comes out clean and biscuits are golden brown. **Yield:** 9 servings.

Nutritional Analysis: 2/3 cup turkey mixture with 1 biscuit equals 290 calories, 7 g fat (4 g saturated fat), 82 mg cholesterol, 494 mg sodium, 32 g carbohydrate, 2 g fiber, 24 g protein.
Diabetic Exchanges: 2 starch, 2 very lean meat, 1 vegetable, 1 fat.

Turkey Marsala

(Pictured above)

Low-carb

Prep: 10 min. **Cook:** 30 min.

This recipe originally called for beef, but I substituted turkey to make it healthier. It's easy to prepare, but the rich sauce makes it seem like you spent all day in the kitchen. I serve this elegant entree with a baked sweet potato and a green vegetable.
—Deborah Williams, Wildwood, Missouri

  1 package (20 ounces) turkey breast tenderloins
1/4 cup all-purpose flour
1/2 teaspoon salt, *divided*
1/2 teaspoon pepper, *divided*
  1 tablespoon olive oil
1/2 pound fresh mushrooms, sliced
  1 tablespoon butter
1/2 cup reduced-sodium chicken broth
1/2 cup Marsala wine *or* 1/3 cup reduced-sodium
    chicken broth, 3 tablespoons white grape
    juice and 2 teaspoons white wine vinegar
  1 teaspoon lemon juice

Cut tenderloins in half and flatten to 3/4-in. thickness. In a large resealable plastic bag, combine the flour, 1/4 teaspoon salt and 1/4 teaspoon pepper. Add turkey and shake to coat. In a large nonstick skillet, cook turkey in oil over medium heat for 7-8 minutes on each side or until juices run clear. Remove and keep warm.

In the same skillet, saute mushrooms in butter for 4 minutes or until tender. Stir in the broth and wine or broth mixture. Cook for 12-15 minutes over medium heat or until liquid is reduced by half. Stir in lemon juice and remaining salt and pepper. Serve over turkey. **Yield:** 4 servings.

Nutritional Analysis: 4 ounces cooked turkey with 1/4 cup mushroom mixture equals 295 calories, 8 g fat (3 g saturated fat), 77 mg cholesterol, 482 mg sodium, 12 g carbohydrate, 1 g fiber, 36 g protein.
Diabetic Exchanges: 4 very lean meat, 1-1/2 fat, 1 starch.

Turkey Noodle Supper

Prep/Total Time: 25 min.

This was one of my favorites made by my mom when I was growing up. I lightened it up by using lean ground turkey, fat-free cream cheese, reduced-fat soup and fat-free milk. And it still tastes as good as Mom's!
—Lori Tinkler, Richland, Washington

  8 ounces yolk-free extra-wide noodles
  1 pound lean ground turkey
  1 medium onion, chopped
  1 can (10-3/4 ounces) reduced-fat
    reduced-sodium condensed cream of
    mushroom soup, undiluted
  1 package (8 ounces) fat-free cream cheese,
    cubed
  1 cup fat-free milk
1-1/2 cups frozen whole kernel corn, thawed
  1 jar (4 ounces) chopped pimientos, drained
3/4 teaspoon salt
1/8 teaspoon pepper

Cook noodles according to package directions; drain. Meanwhile, in a large nonstick skillet, cook turkey and onion over medium heat until meat is no longer pink; drain. Return to pan. Add the soup, cream cheese and milk. Cook and stir until smooth. Stir in the noodles, corn, pimientos, salt and pepper; cook until heated through. **Yield:** 6 servings.

Nutritional Analysis: 1-1/3 cups equals 376 calories, 8 g fat (3 g saturated fat), 68 mg cholesterol, 811 mg sodium, 46 g carbohydrate, 3 g fiber, 27 g protein.
Diabetic Exchanges: 3 lean meat, 2-1/2 starch, 1/2 fat-free milk.

Chicken Dressing Casserole

Prep: 10 min. **Bake:** 50 min.

This hearty bake is perfect after picking pumpkins or watching a football game in the crisp autumn air. Topped with buttery bread crumbs, the piping-hot combination of chicken, mixed vegetables and stuffing makes it a great one-dish wonder.
—Angela Oelschlaeger, Tonganoxie, Kansas

  1 can (14-1/2 ounces) reduced-sodium chicken
    broth
  1 can (10-3/4 ounces) reduced-fat
    reduced-sodium condensed cream of
    chicken soup, undiluted
  1 can (10-3/4 ounces) reduced-fat
    reduced-sodium condensed cream of
    mushroom soup, undiluted
  1 package (6 ounces) reduced-sodium stuffing
    mix
  2 cups cubed cooked chicken breast
1-1/2 cups frozen mixed vegetables, thawed
1/2 cup soft whole wheat bread crumbs
  1 tablespoon butter, melted

In a bowl, combine the broth and soups; set aside. In a 2-qt. baking dish coated with nonstick cooking spray, layer half of the stuffing mix, 1 cup chicken, 3/4 cup mixed vegetables and half of the soup mixture. Repeat layers. (Dish will be full.)

Cover and bake at 350° for 30 minutes. Uncover; bake for 15 minutes. In a small bowl, combine the bread crumbs and butter. Sprinkle over casserole. Bake 5-10 minutes longer or until casserole is heated through and the topping is golden brown. Let stand for 5 minutes before serving. **Yield:** 6 servings.

Nutritional Analysis: 1-1/2 cups equals 303 calories, 6 g fat (2 g saturated fat), 49 mg cholesterol, 930 mg sodium, 39 g carbohydrate, 3 g fiber, 21 g protein.
Diabetic Exchanges: 2-1/2 starch, 2 very lean meat, 1/2 fat.

🍎 Measuring Spaghetti

DO YOU need to measure a small amount of spaghetti—such as the 6 ounces in Chicken Pasta Primavera (recipe below left)—but you don't have a scale? If you're starting with an 8-ounce box of spaghetti, try this technique.

Take the noodles out of the package, separate them into 4 groups of similar size by eyeing the pasta, then use 3 of those groups to equal 6 ounces. Without a scale, this is about as close as you can get—but it should be close enough.

Chicken Pasta Primavera

(Pictured below)

Prep/Total Time: 20 min.

Canned soup, frozen vegetables and other kitchen staples bring this popular family meal together in no time. Simply add a green salad and some garlic bread, and dinner is ready.
—Margaret Wilson, Hemet, California

> 6 ounces uncooked spaghetti
> 1 can (10-3/4 ounces) reduced-fat reduced-sodium condensed cream of chicken soup, undiluted
> 3/4 cup water
> 1 tablespoon lemon juice
> 1-1/2 teaspoons dried basil
> 3/4 teaspoon garlic powder
> 1/2 teaspoon salt
> 1/4 teaspoon pepper
> 1 package (16 ounces) frozen California-blend vegetables, thawed
> 4 cups cubed cooked chicken breast
> 3 tablespoons grated Parmesan cheese

Cook spaghetti according to package directions. Meanwhile, in a saucepan, combine the soup, water, lemon juice, basil, garlic powder, salt and pepper. Stir in vegetables; bring to a boil. Reduce heat; cover and simmer for 3-5 minutes or until vegetables are tender.

Stir in chicken; heat through. Drain spaghetti; add to chicken mixture and toss to coat. Sprinkle with Parmesan cheese.**Yield:** 6 servings.

Nutritional Analysis: 1-1/3 cups equals 342 calories, 5 g fat (2 g saturated fat), 78 mg cholesterol, 526 mg sodium, 36 g carbohydrate, 4 g fiber, 35 g protein.
Diabetic Exchanges: 4 very lean meat, 2 starch, 1 vegetable.

Turkey Reubens

Prep/Total Time: 25 min.

Family and friends will never guess that sandwiches this filling and flavorful could be low in fat! They're sure to satisfy any fan of a traditional reuben.
—Elizabeth Myers, Williamsport, Pennsylvania

> 8 slices rye bread
> 1/2 pound thinly sliced deli turkey
> 1/2 cup sauerkraut, rinsed and well drained
> 4 slices reduced-fat Swiss cheese
> 1/4 cup fat-free Thousand Island salad dressing

On four slices of bread, layer the turkey, sauerkraut, cheese and salad dressing. Top with the remaining bread. Spritz both sides of the sandwiches with butter-flavored nonstick cooking spray.

In a large nonstick skillet, brown the sandwiches on both sides over medium heat until the cheese is melted. **Yield:** 4 servings.

Nutritional Analysis: 1 sandwich equals 310 calories, 8 g fat (3 g saturated fat), 35 mg cholesterol, 1,398 mg sodium, 39 g carbohydrate, 5 g fiber, 22 g protein.
Diabetic Exchanges: 2-1/2 starch, 2 very lean meat, 1 fat.

Italian Chicken Wraps

(Pictured above)

Prep/Total Time: 25 min.

*After enjoying a chicken wrap at a restaurant,
I experimented at home to create something similar.
This delicious version is as fast as it is light.*
—Cathy Hofflander, Adrian, Michigan

**1 package (16 ounces) frozen stir-fry vegetable
  blend
2 packages (6 ounces *each*) ready-to-serve
  grilled chicken breast strips
1/2 cup fat-free Italian salad dressing
3 tablespoons shredded Parmesan cheese
6 flour tortillas (8 inches), warmed**

In a saucepan, cook vegetables according to package directions; drain. Stir in the chicken, salad dressing and cheese.
Simmer, uncovered, for 3-4 minutes or until heated through.
Spoon about 3/4 cup down the center of each tortilla; roll
up tightly. **Yield:** 6 servings.

*Nutritional Analysis: 1 wrap equals 290 calories, 6 g fat (2 g
saturated fat), 40 mg cholesterol, 1,129 mg sodium, 38 g carbohydrate, 3 g fiber, 20 g protein.*
Diabetic Exchanges: 2 lean meat, 2 vegetable, 1-1/2 starch.

Caribbean Chicken

Prep/Total Time: 25 min.

*Tropical breezes and an ocean sunset aren't necessary
to enjoy this Caribbean cuisine. The zippy chicken recipe
makes a quick, easy and delicious meal. Sometimes I
substitute lean pork for the poultry.*
—Mary Tallman, Arbor Vitae, Wisconsin

**1 teaspoon cornstarch
1 can (6 ounces) pineapple juice, *divided*
1 tablespoon prepared mustard
1/2 teaspoon dried thyme
1/4 to 1/2 teaspoon crushed red pepper flakes
3/4 pound boneless skinless chicken breast, cut
  into thin strips
1/2 teaspoon salt**

**2 teaspoons canola oil
1/2 cup thinly sliced green onions
1/2 cup golden raisins
2 medium firm bananas, cut into 1/4-inch slices
Hot cooked rice, optional**

In a small bowl, combine cornstarch and 1/2 cup pineapple
juice until smooth. Stir in mustard, thyme and red pepper
flakes; set aside. Sprinkle chicken with salt. In a large nonstick
skillet, saute chicken in oil for 3-4 minutes or until chicken
juices run clear. Remove from skillet and keep warm.

Pour remaining pineapple juice into skillet. Stir in green
onions and raisins; cook and stir for 1 minute. Stir reserved
pineapple juice mixture and add to skillet. Bring to a boil;
cook and stir for 1-2 minutes or until thickened. Return chick-
en to skillet; heat through. Stir in bananas. Serve over rice
if desired. **Yield:** 3 servings.

*Nutritional Analysis: 1-1/4 cups (calculated without rice)
equals 314 calories, 6 g fat (1 g saturated fat), 63 mg cholesterol,
515 mg sodium, 43 g carbohydrate, 3 g fiber, 25 g protein.*
Diabetic Exchanges: 3 very lean meat, 2-1/2 fruit, 1 fat.

Chicken with Creamy Apple-Mushroom Sauce

Prep: 15 min. **Cook:** 30 min.

*When I found this recipe, I knew I could lighten it up.
Everyone who tries it loves the smooth sauce, tender
chicken and mild apple flavor.*
—Katherine Major, Kingston, Ontario

**4 boneless skinless chicken breast halves
  (4 ounces *each*)
1 tablespoon olive oil
3 cups sliced fresh mushrooms
1 medium onion, sliced
2 garlic cloves, minced
1-1/2 cups reduced-sodium chicken broth
1 teaspoon dried tarragon
1/2 teaspoon pepper
1/8 teaspoon salt
2 cups sliced peeled McIntosh (about 2 medium)
2 tablespoons cornstarch
3/4 cup reduced-fat evaporated milk, *divided*
1 tablespoon minced fresh parsley**

In a nonstick skillet, brown chicken in oil on both sides. Remove and keep warm. In the same skillet, saute the mushrooms, onion and garlic until tender. Stir in the broth, tarragon, pepper and salt; bring to a boil.

Add apples and reserved chicken. Reduce heat; cover
and simmer until chicken juices run clear. Remove chicken
to a serving platter.

Combine cornstarch and 1/4 cup milk until smooth; stir
in remaining milk. Add to skillet. Bring to a boil; cook and
stir for 2 minutes or until thickened. Serve over chicken; sprinkle with parsley. **Yield:** 4 servings.

*Nutritional Analysis: 1 chicken breast half with 1 cup sauce
equals 283 calories, 5 g fat (1 g saturated fat), 68 mg cholesterol,
440 mg sodium, 26 g carbohydrate, 3 g fiber, 33 g protein.*
*Diabetic Exchanges: 3 lean meat, 1 fruit, 1 vegetable, 1/2
fat-free milk.*

Favorite Recipe Made Lighter

COMBINING two mealtime classics, Dorothy Leone of Meredith, New Hampshire came up with a new family favorite—Sloppy Joe Mac and Cheese. "My grandchildren love it," she says. "But I'd like to see a lighter version of the recipe."

To create one, our Test Kitchen staff replaced half of the cheese with a reduced-fat variety, and extra milk was added to recreate the original recipe's creamy sauce.

The ground beef was swapped out for a smaller portion of ground turkey. Next, finely chopped celery and shredded carrot were added to bulk up the meat mixture and provide more nutrients.

Decreasing the butter and replacing the half-and-half with milk helped to cut a whopping 78% of the fat and 658 calories. What's more, the cholesterol was reduced by 75% and the sodium by 40%.

Sloppy Joe Mac and Cheese

Prep: 45 min. **Bake:** 35 min.

1 package (16 ounces) elbow macaroni
1 pound lean ground beef
1 can (14-1/2 ounces) diced tomatoes, undrained
1 can (6 ounces) tomato paste
1 envelope sloppy joe mix
1 small onion, finely chopped
1/4 cup butter
1/4 cup all-purpose flour
1 teaspoon salt
1 teaspoon ground mustard
1/4 teaspoon pepper
3 cups half-and-half cream
1 tablespoon Worcestershire sauce
4 cups (16 ounces) shredded cheddar cheese, *divided*

Cook macaroni according to package directions. Meanwhile, in a large skillet, cook beef over medium heat until no longer pink; drain. Add the tomatoes, tomato paste and sloppy joe mix. Bring to a boil. Reduce heat; cover and simmer for 10 minutes, stirring occasionally.

Drain macaroni; set aside. In a large saucepan, saute onion in butter until tender. Stir in the flour, salt, mustard and pepper until smooth. Gradually add cream and Worcestershire sauce. Bring to a boil; cook and stir for 1-2 minutes or until thickened. Remove from the heat. Stir in 3 cups cheese until melted. Add macaroni; mix well.

Spread two-thirds of the macaroni mixture in a greased 13-in. x 9-in. x 2-in. baking dish. Spread beef mixture to within 2 in. of edges. Spoon remaining macaroni mixture around edges. Cover and bake at 375° for 30 minutes. Uncover; sprinkle with remaining cheese. Bake 5-6 minutes longer or until cheese is melted. **Yield:** 10 servings.

Nutritional Analysis: 1-1/3 cups equals 1,117 calories, 72 g fat (51 g saturated fat), 280 mg cholesterol, 1,901 mg sodium, 54 g carbohydrate, 4 g fiber, 60 g protein.

Makeover
Sloppy Joe Mac and Cheese

Prep: 1 hour **Bake:** 30 min.

1 package (16 ounces) elbow macaroni
3/4 pound lean ground turkey
1/2 cup finely chopped celery
1/2 cup shredded carrot
1 can (14-1/2 ounces) diced tomatoes, undrained
1 can (6 ounces) tomato paste
1/2 cup water
1 envelope sloppy joe mix
1 small onion, finely chopped
1 tablespoon butter
1/3 cup all-purpose flour
1 teaspoon ground mustard
3/4 teaspoon salt
1/4 teaspoon pepper
4 cups 2% milk
1 tablespoon Worcestershire sauce
8 ounces reduced-fat process cheese (Velveeta), cubed
2 cups (8 ounces) shredded cheddar cheese, *divided*

Cook macaroni according to package directions. Meanwhile, in a large nonstick skillet, cook the turkey, celery and carrot over medium heat until meat is no longer pink and vegetables are tender; drain. Add the tomatoes, tomato paste, water and sloppy joe mix. Bring to a boil. Reduce heat; cover and simmer for 10 minutes, stirring occasionally.

Drain macaroni; set aside. In a large saucepan, saute onion in butter until tender. Stir in the flour, mustard, salt and pepper until smooth. Gradually add milk and Worcestershire sauce. Bring to a boil; cook and stir for 1-2 minutes or until thickened. Remove from the heat. Stir in the process cheese until melted. Add macaroni and 1 cup cheddar cheese; mix well.

Spread two-thirds of the macaroni mixture in a 13-in. x 9-in. x 2-in. baking dish coated with nonstick cooking spray. Spread turkey mixture to within 2 in. of edges. Spoon the remaining macaroni mixture around the edges of the pan. Cover and bake at 375° for 30-35 minutes or until bubbly. Uncover; sprinkle with the remaining cheddar cheese. Cover and let stand until the cheese is melted. **Yield:** 10 servings.

Nutritional Analysis: 1-1/3 cups equals 459 calories, 16 g fat (9 g saturated fat), 71 mg cholesterol, 1,140 mg sodium, 54 g carbohydrate, 3 g fiber, 26 g protein.

Chicken Bulgur Skillet

(Pictured above)

Prep: 15 min. **Cook:** 30 min.

*This recipe was passed on to me by a friend, and I've
altered it slightly to suit our tastes. We like it with
a fresh green salad.*
—Leann Hillmer, Sylvan Grove, Kansas

  1 pound boneless skinless chicken breasts,
   cut into 1-inch cubes
  2 teaspoons olive oil
  2 medium carrots, chopped
2/3 cup chopped onion
  3 tablespoons chopped walnuts
1/2 teaspoon caraway seeds
1/4 teaspoon ground cumin
1-1/2 cups bulgur
  2 cups reduced-sodium chicken broth
  2 tablespoons raisins
1/4 teaspoon salt
1/8 teaspoon ground cinnamon

In a large nonstick skillet, cook chicken in oil over medium-
high heat until no longer pink. Remove and keep warm. In
the same skillet, cook and stir the carrots, onion, nuts, caraway seeds and cumin for 3-4 minutes or until onion starts
to brown.

 Stir in bulgur. Gradually add broth; bring to a boil over
medium heat. Reduce heat; add the raisins, salt, cinnamon
and chicken. Cover and simmer for 12-15 minutes or until
bulgur is tender. **Yield:** 4 servings.

 Editor's Note: Look for bulgur in the cereal, rice or organic food aisle of your grocery store.

 *Nutritional Analysis: 1-1/2 cups equals 412 calories, 8 g fat
(1 g saturated fat), 66 mg cholesterol, 561 mg sodium, 51 g carbohydrate, 12 g fiber, 36 g protein.*
 Diabetic Exchanges: 3 lean meat, 2-1/2 starch, 2 vegetable.

Summer Tea Sandwiches

(Pictured below)

Prep: 45 min. **Bake:** 20 min + cooling

*Our home economists prepared these dainty
finger sandwiches that are perfect for casual
picnics or ladies' luncheons. Tarragon-seasoned
chicken complements cucumber and cantaloupe slices.*

1/2 teaspoon dried tarragon
1/2 teaspoon salt, *divided*
1/4 teaspoon pepper
  1 pound boneless skinless chicken breasts
1/2 cup reduced-fat mayonnaise
  1 tablespoon finely chopped red onion
  1 teaspoon dill weed
1/2 teaspoon lemon juice
 24 slices soft multigrain bread, crusts removed
  1 medium cucumber, thinly sliced
1/4 medium cantaloupe, cut into 12 thin slices

Combine the tarragon, 1/4 teaspoon salt and pepper; rub
over chicken. Place on a baking sheet coated with nonstick
cooking spray. Bake at 350° for 20-25 minutes or until
juices run clear. Cool to room temperature; thinly slice.

 Combine the mayonnaise, onion, dill, lemon juice and remaining salt; spread over one side of 12 slices of bread. Top
with cucumber, chicken, cantaloupe and remaining bread.
Cut sandwiches in half diagonally. Serve immediately.
Yield: 12 servings.

 *Nutritional Analysis: 2 sandwich halves equals 212 calories,
6 g fat (1 g saturated fat), 24 mg cholesterol, 450 mg sodium,
27 g carbohydrate, 4 g fiber, 13 g protein.*
 Diabetic Exchanges: 2 starch, 1 very lean meat, 1/2 fat.

Ginger Mushroom Chicken

(Pictured above)

Prep/Total Time: 30 min.

If you love fresh ginger, you're sure to love this dish. The stir-fry is so quick and easy to prepare, it's perfect for a busy weeknight.
—Christina Shape, Swartz Creek, Michigan

    1 cup fresh snow peas
    2 teaspoons cornstarch
1/2 teaspoon salt
1/8 teaspoon pepper
3/4 cup milk
3/4 pound boneless skinless chicken breasts, cut
      into thin strips
    3 teaspoons canola oil, *divided*
1/2 pound sliced baby portobello mushrooms
    1 teaspoon minced fresh gingerroot
    2 cups hot cooked brown rice
1/4 cup minced fresh parsley

Place snow peas in a small saucepan; cover with water. Bring to a boil; boil for 1 minute. Drain and set aside. In a small bowl, combine the cornstarch, salt, pepper and milk until smooth; set aside.

In a large nonstick skillet or wok coated with nonstick cooking spray, stir-fry chicken in 1 teaspoon hot oil for 5 minutes or until juices run clear. Remove and keep warm.

In the same pan, stir-fry mushrooms and ginger in remaining oil for 2 minutes. Add peas; stir-fry 2 minutes longer. Stir cornstarch mixture and stir into mushroom mixture. Return chicken to pan. Bring to a boil; cook and stir for 2 minutes or until thickened. Serve over rice. Sprinkle with parsley. **Yield:** 4 servings.

Nutritional Analysis: 3/4 cup chicken mixture with 1/2 cup rice equals 297 calories, 8 g fat (2 g saturated fat), 53 mg cholesterol, 369 mg sodium, 31 g carbohydrate, 4 g fiber, 24 g protein.
Diabetic Exchanges: 2 starch, 2 very lean meat, 1 vegetable, 1 fat.

Chicken with Garlic-Tomato Sauce

(Pictured below)

Low-carb

Prep/Total Time: 30 min.

My husband and I came up with this recipe, and we love the way it turned out. It reminds us of an entree served at an Italian eatery.
—Angela Schellenberg, Steinbach, Manitoba

    4 boneless skinless chicken breast halves
      (4 ounces *each*)
1/4 teaspoon pepper
    2 teaspoons olive oil, *divided*
    2 plum tomatoes, seeded and chopped
    2 garlic cloves, minced
    2 medium carrots, halved and thinly sliced
    1 cup Italian tomato sauce
3/4 cup reduced-sodium chicken broth
1/4 cup tomato paste
    1 teaspoon dried rosemary, crushed
Hot cooked pasta

Sprinkle both sides of chicken with pepper. In a large non-stick skillet over medium-high heat, brown chicken on each side in 1 teaspoon oil. Remove and keep warm.

In the same skillet, saute tomatoes and garlic in remaining oil for 1 minute. Add carrots; saute 2-3 minutes longer. Combine the tomato sauce, broth, tomato paste and rosemary; stir into skillet. Bring to a boil.

Return chicken to the pan. Reduce heat; cover and simmer for 10-12 minutes or until chicken juices run clear and carrots are crisp-tender. Serve with pasta. **Yield:** 4 servings.

Nutritional Analysis: 1 chicken breast half with 3/4 cup sauce (calculated without pasta) equals 197 calories, 5 g fat (1 g saturated fat), 63 mg cholesterol, 510 mg sodium, 10 g carbohydrate, 3 g fiber, 26 g protein.
Diabetic Exchanges: 3 lean meat, 2 vegetable.

Flavorful Turkey Wraps

(Pictured above)

Prep: 15 min. + marinating **Grill:** 15 min.

These tangy wraps blend grilled turkey with hoisin sauce, gingerroot, sesame oil and other Asian ingredients. Everyone always asks for seconds.
—Josephine Piro, Easton, Pennsylvania

1/4 cup hoisin sauce
2 tablespoons orange juice
2 tablespoons reduced-sodium soy sauce
1 tablespoon honey
2 teaspoons grated fresh gingerroot
1 garlic clove, minced
4 turkey breast tenderloins (4 ounces *each*)
3 cups shredded lettuce
3/4 cup shredded carrots
3/4 cup chopped green onions
1 tablespoon rice wine vinegar
1 tablespoon sesame oil
2 tablespoons sesame seeds, toasted
6 flour tortillas (8 inches), warmed

In a large resealable plastic bag, combine the first six ingredients; add turkey. Seal bag and turn to coat; refrigerate for 6 hours or overnight. Coat grill rack with nonstick cooking spray before starting the grill. Drain and discard marinade. Grill turkey, uncovered, over medium heat for 12-16 minutes or until juices run clear.

In a bowl, combine lettuce, carrots and onions. In a small bowl, whisk the vinegar and sesame oil; stir in sesame seeds. Drizzle over lettuce mixture; toss to coat. Cut turkey into 1/2-in. strips; place down the center of each tortilla. Top with lettuce mixture and roll up; secure with toothpicks. **Yield:** 6 servings.

Nutritional Analysis: 1 wrap equals 290 calories, 8 g fat (1 g saturated fat), 37 mg cholesterol, 430 mg sodium, 32 g carbohydrate, 2 g fiber, 23 g protein.
Diabetic Exchanges: 3 very lean meat, 2 starch, 1/2 fat.

Chicken-Stuffed Cubanelle Peppers

(Pictured below)

Prep: 20 min. **Bake:** 55 min.

Here's a new take on traditional stuffed peppers. I substituted chicken for the beef and used Cubanelle peppers in place of the usual green peppers.
—Ron Burlingame, Canton, Ohio

6 Cubanelle peppers *or* mild banana peppers
2 eggs
1 cup salsa
3 cups shredded cooked chicken breast
3/4 cup soft bread crumbs
1/2 cup cooked long grain rice
2 cups meatless spaghetti sauce, *divided*

Cut tops off peppers and remove seeds. In a bowl, combine the eggs, salsa, chicken, bread crumbs and rice. Spoon into peppers.

Coat a 13-in. x 9-in. x 2-in. baking dish and an 8-in. square baking dish with nonstick cooking spray. Spread 1 cup spaghetti sauce in larger pan and 1/2 cup sauce in smaller pan. Place peppers over sauce. Spoon remaining spaghetti sauce over peppers. Cover and bake at 350° for 55-60 minutes or until peppers are tender. **Yield:** 6 servings.

Nutritional Analysis: 1 stuffed pepper equals 230 calories, 4 g fat (1 g saturated fat), 125 mg cholesterol, 661 mg sodium, 22 g carbohydrate, 7 g fiber, 28 g protein.
Diabetic Exchanges: 3 very lean meat, 2 vegetable, 1 starch.

Honey-Citrus Chicken Kabobs

(Pictured above)

Low-fat Low-sodium

Prep: 15 min. + marinating **Grill:** 10 min.

It only takes 30 minutes to marinate the chicken for these tangy lemon-lime skewers, and they're easy to assemble.
—Amanda Mills, Austin, Texas

1/2 cup *each* lime juice, lemon juice and honey
1 garlic clove, minced
1 pound boneless skinless chicken breasts, cut into 1-inch cubes
1 *each* medium green, sweet red and yellow pepper, cut into 1-inch pieces

In a small bowl, combine the lime juice, lemon juice, honey and garlic. Pour 1-1/4 cups into a large resealable plastic bag; add the chicken. Seal bag and turn to coat; refrigerate for at least 30 minutes. Cover and refrigerate remaining marinade for basting.

Coat grill rack with nonstick cooking spray before starting grill. Drain and discard marinade from chicken. On eight metal or soaked wood skewers, alternately thread chicken and peppers. Grill, covered, over medium-hot heat for 8-10 minutes or until chicken juices run clear, turning and basting frequently with reserved marinade. **Yield:** 4 servings.

Nutritional Analysis: 2 kabobs equals 194 calories, 3 g fat (1 g saturated fat), 63 mg cholesterol, 57 mg sodium, 19 g carbohydrate, 2 g fiber, 24 g protein.
Diabetic Exchanges: 3 very lean meat, 1 starch, 1 vegetable.

Barbecued Mushroom-Turkey Burgers

(Pictured below)

Prep: 25 min. + chilling **Grill:** 20 min.

With their hint of wine, these moist patties taste like they came from a fancy restaurant.
—Sharon Spethman, Lincoln, Nebraska

3/4 cup chopped sweet onion
2 teaspoons butter
1 cup sliced fresh mushrooms
1 medium carrot, grated
1/4 cup dry red wine *or* chicken broth
1/2 teaspoon salt
1/4 teaspoon pepper
1 pound lean ground turkey
1/2 cup barbecue sauce, *divided*
4 hamburger buns, split
4 Bibb lettuce leaves
4 slices tomato

In a large nonstick skillet, saute onion in butter for 3 minutes. Add mushrooms and carrot; cook and stir for 3 minutes. Add the wine or broth, salt and pepper; simmer for 2-3 minutes or until liquid has evaporated. Transfer to a large bowl; cool slightly. Crumble turkey over mixture and mix well. Shape into four patties. Cover and refrigerate for at least 1 hour.

Coat grill rack with nonstick cooking spray before starting the grill. Grill patties, uncovered, over medium heat for 8-10 minutes on each side or until juices run clear, brushing occasionally with 1/4 cup barbecue sauce. Serve on buns with lettuce, tomato and remaining barbecue sauce. **Yield:** 4 servings.

Nutritional Analysis: 1 burger equals 371 calories, 14 g fat (4 g saturated fat), 95 mg cholesterol, 926 mg sodium, 32 g carbohydrate, 3 g fiber, 25 g protein.
Diabetic Exchanges: 3 lean meat, 2 starch, 1 fat.

Family-Pleasing Sloppy Joes

(Pictured above)

Prep/Total Time: 30 min.

My grandma gave me this recipe years ago, and I made a few adjustments to give the sandwiches more pizzazz.
—*Jill Zosel, Seattle, Washington*

1 pound lean ground turkey
1/2 cup chopped onion
2 garlic cloves, minced
1 tablespoon sugar
1 tablespoon all-purpose flour
1/4 teaspoon pepper
1 cup ketchup
1 tablespoon prepared mustard
1 tablespoon barbecue sauce
1 tablespoon Worcestershire sauce
6 sandwich buns, split

In a large nonstick skillet, cook the turkey and onion over medium heat until turkey is no longer pink; drain if necessary. Add garlic; cook for 1-2 minutes or until tender.

Stir in the sugar, flour and pepper. Add the ketchup, mustard, barbecue sauce and Worcestershire sauce. Bring to a boil. Reduce heat; cover and simmer for 5-10 minutes or until heated through. Serve on buns. **Yield:** 6 servings.

Nutritional Analysis: 1 sandwich equals 388 calories, 11 g fat (4 g saturated fat), 60 mg cholesterol, 969 mg sodium, 52 g carbohydrate, 3 g fiber, 22 g protein.
Diabetic Exchanges: 3-1/2 starch, 2 lean meat.

Spicy Curried Chicken

Prep/Total Time: 25 min.

It's easy to bring a little heat to dinner with this speedy meal-in-one. Not all of my family members like to eat low-fat foods, but they regularly request this dish.
—*Daucia Brooks, Westmoreland, Tennessee*

2 medium green peppers, chopped
1 medium onion, chopped
2 teaspoons canola oil

1-1/2 teaspoons curry powder
1 garlic clove, minced
1/2 teaspoon ground cumin
1/2 teaspoon salt
1/4 teaspoon ground ginger
1/4 teaspoon paprika
1/8 teaspoon cayenne pepper
1 can (28 ounces) whole tomatoes, undrained and quartered
2 cups cubed cooked chicken breast
1-1/2 teaspoons lemon juice
Hot cooked pasta, optional

In a nonstick skillet, saute peppers and onion in oil until tender. Add the curry, garlic, cumin, salt, ginger, paprika and cayenne; saute 1 minute longer. Add tomatoes and chicken. Bring to a boil. Reduce heat; simmer, uncovered, for 8-10 minutes or until heated through. Stir in lemon juice. Serve chicken mixture over pasta if desired. **Yield:** 4 servings.

Nutritional Analysis: 1-1/4 cups chicken (calculated without pasta) equals 211 calories, 5 g fat (1 g saturated fat), 60 mg cholesterol, 642 mg sodium, 17 g carbohydrate, 4 g fiber, 25 g protein.
Diabetic Exchanges: 3 lean meat, 3 vegetable.

Teriyaki Turkey Burritos

Prep: 20 min. **Bake:** 20 min.

This recipe is one of my husband's all-time favorites. Crunchy and delicious, the burritos make a great meal and even a hearty appetizer.
—*Ellen De Munnik, Chesterfield, Michigan*

12 fat-free flour tortillas (8 inches)
1 pound lean ground turkey
1/2 cup chopped onion
4 garlic cloves, minced
1 package (16 ounces) broccoli coleslaw mix
1 tablespoon canola oil
1/3 cup reduced-sodium teriyaki sauce
1/2 teaspoon Chinese five-spice powder
1/4 teaspoon garlic powder
1/4 teaspoon pepper
1-1/2 cups (6 ounces) shredded reduced-fat Mexican cheese blend

Wrap tortillas tightly in foil. Warm in oven at 350° for 10 minutes. Meanwhile, in a large skillet, cook the turkey, onion and garlic over medium heat until turkey is no longer pink; drain. Pour into a bowl and set aside.

In the same skillet, stir-fry the coleslaw mix in oil for 2 minutes. Add the teriyaki sauce, five-spice powder, garlic powder and pepper; cook and stir for 1 minute. Stir in cheese and turkey mixture; heat through.

Spoon 1/2 cup filling off center on each tortilla. Fold sides and ends over filling and roll up. Place seam side down in an ungreased 13-in. x 9-in. x 2-in. baking dish. Cover and bake at 350° for 20 minutes or until heated through. **Yield:** 6 servings.

Nutritional Analysis: 2 burritos equals 493 calories, 14 g fat (5 g saturated fat), 80 mg cholesterol, 982 mg sodium, 60 g carbohydrate, 4 g fiber, 32 g protein.

Try Something New: Sun-Dried Tomatoes

FRESH TOMATOES are available year-round...but they definitely taste best when picked at summer's peak. So why not try using sun-dried tomatoes during the off season? They add richness and flavor to appetizers, main dishes, soups, stews, casseroles, salads and more.

Sun-dried tomatoes can be found dry-packed or oil-packed in the produce department. Sometimes, the oil-packed variety is near the canned tomatoes or jarred artichokes.

A quarter cup of dry-packed sun-dried tomatoes contains about 35 calories, 1/2 gram fat and 280 mg sodium. A quarter cup of oil-packed sun-dried tomatoes contains about 60 calories, 4 grams fat and 70 mg sodium. Both kinds are a good source of potassium and lycopene.

Simple to Use and Store

Sun-dried tomatoes are easy to use. To rehydrate dry-packed tomatoes, simply soak them in warm water for 30 minutes, then drain. The flavorful liquid can be saved and substituted for broth when making a sauce or mashed potatoes. Rehydrated tomatoes are great tossed with pasta, added to cooked vegetables or tossed in an antipasto salad.

Store unopened dry-packed tomatoes at room temperature for up to 6 months; refrigerate or freeze them after opening.

To use oil-packed sun-dried tomatoes, simply drain the tomatoes well and use them as the recipe directs. Commercially oil-packed tomatoes should be stored in the refrigerator after opening.

Chicken Breasts with Sun-Dried Tomatoes

(Pictured at left)

Low-carb

Prep: 15 min. + standing **Cook:** 30 min.

Sun-dried tomatoes provide intense flavor in this chicken entree that's special enough for company.
—Heather Nandell, Johnston, Iowa

1/2 cup plus 3 tablespoons reduced-sodium chicken broth, *divided*
1/4 cup chopped dry-packed sun-dried tomatoes
1/2 cup sliced fresh mushrooms
1 green onion, thinly sliced
2 teaspoons minced garlic, *divided*
4 boneless skinless chicken breast halves (4 ounces *each*)
1 tablespoon olive oil
2 teaspoons cornstarch
1/2 teaspoon dried basil
1/4 teaspoon salt
1/4 teaspoon pepper
1/2 cup fat-free milk
Hot cooked pasta, optional

Bring 1/2 cup broth to a boil. Remove from the heat; stir in sun-dried tomatoes and let stand for 10 minutes. In a large nonstick skillet coated with nonstick cooking spray, saute the mushrooms, green onion and 1 teaspoon garlic for 1 minute. Stir in the remaining broth; cook 2 minutes longer or until mushrooms are tender. Remove mushroom mixture and set aside.

Rub chicken with remaining garlic. In same skillet, cook chicken in oil for 3 minutes on each side or until browned. Stir in tomato mixture; bring to a boil. Reduce heat; cover and simmer for 10-12 minutes or until chicken juices run clear. Remove chicken from skillet; cut into slices and keep warm.

Combine the cornstarch, basil, salt and pepper. Stir in milk until smooth; add to tomato mixture. Bring to a boil; cook and stir for 1-2 minutes or until thickened. Stir in mushroom mixture. Serve over chicken and with pasta if desired. **Yield:** 4 servings.

Nutritional Analysis: 1 chicken breast half with 1/4 cup sauce (calculated without pasta) equals 190 calories, 5 g fat (1 g saturated fat), 66 mg cholesterol, 416 mg sodium, 7 g carbohydrate, 1 g fiber, 29 g protein.
Diabetic Exchanges: 4 very lean meat, 1 fat.

Terrific Turkey Meat Loaf

(Pictured above)

Low-carb

Prep: 15 min. **Bake:** 55 min.

*We love this moist, tender entree that's loaded with
flavor but low in carbohydrates and saturated fat.
It's a tasty way to eat right on busy weeknights.*
—*Wanda Bannister, New Bern, North Carolina*

　　1 egg white
　　3 tablespoons ketchup
　　1 tablespoon Worcestershire sauce
1/2 teaspoon Dijon mustard
1/2 cup oat bran
1/2 cup chopped green pepper
1/4 cup finely chopped onion
　　2 tablespoons chopped ripe olives
　　1 garlic clove, minced
1/4 teaspoon celery salt
1/4 teaspoon dried marjoram
1/4 teaspoon rubbed sage
1/4 teaspoon pepper
　　1 pound ground turkey

In a large bowl, combine the egg white, ketchup, Worcestershire sauce and mustard. Stir in the oat bran, green pepper, onion, olives, garlic, celery salt, marjoram, sage and
pepper. Crumble turkey over mixture and mix well.

Pat into a loaf in an 11-in. x 7-in. x 2-in. baking dish coated with nonstick cooking spray. Bake, uncovered, at 350° for
55-65 minutes or until a meat thermometer reads 165°.
Yield: 4 servings.

*Nutritional Analysis: 1 serving equals 253 calories, 12 g fat
(3 g saturated fat), 82 mg cholesterol, 421 mg sodium, 14 g carbohydrate, 3 g fiber, 26 g protein.*
Diabetic Exchanges: 3 lean meat, 1 starch.

Easy Chicken and Dumplings

(Pictured below)

Prep/Total Time: 30 min.

*Perfect for autumn nights, this main course is speedy, low
in fat and a delicious one-dish meal. Try it when you
have a craving for a chicken pot pie.*
—*Nancy Tuck, Elk Falls, Kansas*

　　3 celery ribs, chopped
　　1 cup sliced fresh carrots
　　3 cans (14-1/2 ounces *each*) reduced-sodium
　　　chicken broth
1/2 teaspoon poultry seasoning
1/8 teaspoon pepper
　　3 cups cubed cooked chicken breast
1-2/3 cups reduced-fat biscuit/baking mix
　2/3 cup fat-free milk

In a Dutch oven coated with nonstick cooking spray, saute
celery and carrots for 5 minutes. Stir in the broth, poultry seasoning and pepper. Bring to a boil. Reduce heat; simmer, uncovered. Add the chicken.

For dumplings, combine biscuit mix and milk. Drop by
tablespoonfuls onto simmering broth. Cover and simmer
for 10-15 minutes or until a toothpick inserted into a dumpling
comes out clean (do not lift cover while simmering). **Yield:**
6 servings.

*Nutritional Analysis: 1 cup chicken mixture with 3 dumplings
equals 282 calories, 5 g fat (1 g saturated fat), 60 mg cholesterol,
1,022 mg sodium, 29 g carbohydrate, 1 g fiber, 28 g protein.*
*Diabetic Exchanges: 3 very lean meat, 1-1/2 starch, 1 veg-
etable, 1/2 fat.*

Herbed Cranberry Chicken

(Pictured below and on page 115)

Low-sodium

Prep: 20 min. **Cook:** 15 min.

Even though it has no added salt, this dish is full of flavor. The cranberry sauce makes the quick entree special.
—Margee Berry, White Salmon, Washington

   6 **boneless skinless chicken breast halves**
      (4 ounces *each*)
   1 **tablespoon salt-free herb seasoning blend**
   2 **tablespoons olive oil, *divided***
2/3 **cup chopped green onions**
1/2 **cup dried cranberries**
1/2 **cup reduced-sodium chicken broth**
1/3 **cup cranberry juice**
4-1/2 **teaspoons maple syrup**
   1 **tablespoon balsamic vinegar**
1/3 **cup chopped pecans, toasted**

Rub chicken with seasoning blend. In a large nonstick skillet, cook chicken in 1 tablespoon oil over medium heat for 4-5 minutes on each side or until juices run clear. Remove and keep warm.

In the same skillet, saute onions in remaining oil. Stir in the cranberries, broth, cranberry juice, syrup and vinegar; bring to a boil. Reduce heat; cook and stir for 2 minutes. Return chicken to the pan; cook for 1 minute or until heated through. Sprinkle with pecans. **Yield:** 6 servings.

Nutritional Analysis: 1 chicken breast half with 2 tablespoons cranberry mixture equals 263 calories, 12 g fat (2 g saturated fat), 63 mg cholesterol, 109 mg sodium, 16 g carbohydrate, 1 g fiber, 24 g protein.
Diabetic Exchanges: 3 very lean meat, 2 fat, 1/2 starch, 1/2 fruit.

Horseradish-Crusted Turkey Tenderlions

(Pictured above)

Low-carb

Prep: 10 min. **Bake:** 25 min.

This delicious low-carb entree won a local recipe contest and was featured on a restaurant's menu.
—Ellen Cross, Hubbardsville, New York

   2 **tablespoons reduced-fat mayonnaise**
   2 **tablespoons prepared horseradish**
   1 **pound turkey tenderloins**
1/2 **cup soft bread crumbs**
   2 **tablespoons minced fresh parsley**
   2 **tablespoons chopped green onion**
SAUCE:
1/4 **cup reduced-fat mayonnaise**
1/4 **cup fat-free plain yogurt**
   2 **tablespoons fat-free milk**
   1 **tablespoon prepared horseradish**
   1 **tablespoon Dijon mustard**
1/4 **teaspoon paprika**

Combine mayonnaise and horseradish; spread over turkey. In a shallow dish, combine crumbs, parsley and onion. Roll turkey in crumb mixture to coat. Place in an 11-in. x 7-in. x 2-in. baking dish coated with nonstick cooking spray.

Bake, uncovered, at 425° for 25-30 minutes or until a meat thermometer reads 170°. In a small bowl, combine the sauce ingredients. Slice turkey; serve with sauce. **Yield:** 4 servings.

Nutritional Analysis: 3 ounces cooked turkey with 3 tablespoons sauce equals 237 calories, 9 g fat (2 g saturated fat), 85 mg cholesterol, 404 mg sodium, 8 g carbohydrate, 1 g fiber, 29 g protein.
Diabetic Exchanges: 3 very lean meat, 2 fat, 1/2 starch.

Turkey Tetrazzini

(Pictured above)

Prep: 25 min. **Bake:** 25 min.

Your family will flip over this turkey and mushroom casserole. The Parmesan-topped tetrazzini is so hearty that no one will suspect it's lower in fat.
—*Irene Banegas, Las Cruces, New Mexico*

1/2 pound uncooked spaghetti
1/4 cup finely chopped onion
1 garlic clove, minced
1 tablespoon butter
3 tablespoons cornstarch
1 can (14-1/2 ounces) reduced-sodium chicken broth
1 can (12 ounces) fat-free evaporated milk
2-1/2 cups cubed cooked turkey breast
1 can (4 ounces) mushroom stems and pieces, drained
1/2 teaspoon seasoned salt
Dash pepper
2 tablespoons grated Parmesan cheese
1/4 teaspoon paprika

Cook spaghetti according to package directions; drain. In a large saucepan, saute onion and garlic in butter until tender. Combine cornstarch and broth until smooth; stir into the onion mixture. Bring to a boil; cook and stir for 2 minutes or until thickened. Reduce heat to low. Add the milk; cook and stir for 2-3 minutes.

Stir in the spaghetti, turkey, mushrooms, seasoned salt and pepper. Transfer to an 8-in. square baking dish coated with nonstick cooking spray. Cover and bake at 350° for 20 minutes. Uncover; sprinkle with Parmesan cheese and paprika. Bake 5-10 minutes longer or until heated through. **Yield:** 6 servings.

Nutritional Analysis: 1-1/4 cups equals 331 calories, 5 g fat (2 g saturated fat), 51 mg cholesterol, 544 mg sodium, 41 g carbohydrate, 1 g fiber, 28 g protein.
Diabetic Exchanges: 3 very lean meat, 2 starch, 1 vegetable, 1/2 fat-free milk.

Spinach-Stuffed Chicken Breasts

Low-carb

Prep: 25 min. **Bake:** 55 min.

After retiring to Tennessee, we missed the tastes of Chicago. Here's my version of a Greek entree we enjoyed.
—*Beverly Hemmerich, Fairfield Glade, Tennessee*

1 medium onion, chopped
1 garlic clove, minced
1/4 teaspoon crushed red pepper flakes
4 teaspoons olive oil, *divided*
1 package (10 ounces) frozen chopped spinach, thawed and squeezed dry
2 ounces crumbled feta cheese
1/4 cup grated Parmesan cheese
6 bone-in chicken breast halves (9 ounces *each*)
1/4 cup lemon juice
1 teaspoon dried basil
1 teaspoon dried oregano
1/2 teaspoon salt
1/2 teaspoon garlic powder
1/4 teaspoon pepper

In a nonstick skillet, saute the onion, garlic and pepper flakes in 2 teaspoons oil until tender. Add spinach; cook and stir for 2 minutes or until heated through. Remove from the heat. Stir in cheeses.

Cut a pocket in each chicken breast by slicing horizontally almost to the bone. Fill each pocket with 1/4 cup spinach mixture. Place chicken in a 13-in. x 9-in. x 2-in. baking dish. In a small bowl, whisk the lemon juice, basil, oregano, salt, garlic powder, pepper and remaining oil; brush over chicken.

Cover and bake at 400° for 45 minutes. Uncover; bake 10-15 minutes longer or until a meat thermometer reads 170°. Remove skin before serving. **Yield:** 6 servings.

Nutritional Analysis: 1 serving equals 248 calories, 8 g fat (3 g saturated fat), 92 mg cholesterol, 490 mg sodium, 6 g carbohydrate, 2 g fiber, 37 g protein.
Diabetic Exchanges: 5 very lean meat, 1 vegetable, 1 fat.

🍎 Spice It Up!

HERBS perk up flavor without increasing fat or sodium. For maximum taste, store your dried herbs in a cool dry place in tightly closed containers. They begin to lose flavor after 1 year, so remember to replace them from time to time.

If you prefer fresh herbs, use three times the amount of the dried herb called for. For example, in Spinach-Stuffed Chicken Breasts (recipe above), you'll need 3 teaspoons (or 1 tablespoon) of minced fresh basil to replace 1 teaspoon dried.

Favorite Recipe Made Lighter

SMOTHERED in a thick sauce and topped with buttery cracker crumbs, Swiss Chicken Supreme is a hit whenever Stephanie Bell serves it.

"Everyone requests the recipe," she writes from Kaysville, Utah, "but it's high in fat and cholesterol. I've tried to lighten it up, but I can't replicate the flavor. Any help would be appreciated."

Our makeover team started by cutting back on the quantity of sauce in the original recipe and scaling back on the golden topping a bit. These changes lowered the calories and fat, but that wasn't enough to satisfy our home economists.

Replacing the canned soup with a homemade sauce didn't work well with this recipe, so the team used a lighter version of the canned soup instead. Stephanie usually mixes the soup with water, but combining it with fat-free milk created a richer sauce.

Makeover Swiss Chicken Supreme has all the flavor of the original, even though it has 560 fewer calories, 81% less fat and nearly 75% less sodium.

After trying the makeover recipe, Stephanie reports, "My family barely noticed that anything had been changed. Everyone loved it, and now I can serve it without worrying about fat and cholesterol. Thanks!"

Makeover
Swiss Chicken Supreme

(Pictured above)

Prep: 15 min. **Bake:** 30 min.

- 4 boneless skinless chicken breast halves (4 ounces *each*)
- 1 tablespoon dried minced onion
- 1/2 teaspoon garlic powder
- 1/4 teaspoon salt
- 1/8 teaspoon pepper
- 4 slices (3/4 ounce *each*) reduced-fat Swiss cheese
- 1 can (10-3/4 ounces) reduced-fat reduced-sodium condensed cream of chicken soup, undiluted
- 1/3 cup reduced-fat sour cream
- 1/2 cup fat-free milk
- 1/3 cup crushed reduced-fat butter-flavored crackers (about 8 crackers)
- 1 teaspoon butter, melted

Place the chicken in a 13-in. x 9-in. x 2-in. baking dish coated with nonstick cooking spray. Sprinkle with minced onion, garlic powder, salt and pepper. Top each with a slice of cheese.

In a small bowl, combine the soup, sour cream and milk; pour over chicken. Toss the cracker crumbs and butter; sprinkle over chicken. Bake, uncovered, at 350° for 30-40 minutes or until chicken juices run clear and crumbs are golden. **Yield:** 4 servings.

Nutritional Analysis: 1 serving equals 310 calories, 11 g fat (5 g saturated fat), 89 mg cholesterol, 567 mg sodium, 17 g carbohydrate, trace fiber, 34 g protein.
Diabetic Exchanges: 3 very lean meat, 2 fat, 1 starch.

Swiss Chicken Supreme

Prep: 15 min. **Bake:** 30 min.

- 4 boneless skinless chicken breast halves (4 ounces *each*)
- 1 tablespoon dried minced onion
- 1/2 teaspoon salt
- 1/2 teaspoon garlic powder
- 1/4 teaspoon pepper
- 4 slices (1 ounce *each*) Swiss cheese
- 2 cans (10-3/4 ounces *each*) condensed cream of chicken soup, undiluted
- 1/2 cup sour cream
- 1/4 cup water
- 2 cups crushed butter-flavored crackers (about 50 crackers)
- 1/2 cup butter, melted

Place the chicken in a greased 13-in. x 9-in. x 2-in. baking dish. Sprinkle with minced onion, salt, garlic powder and pepper. Top each with a slice of cheese.

In a large bowl, combine the soup, sour cream and water; pour over chicken. Toss the cracker crumbs and butter; sprinkle over chicken. Bake, uncovered, at 350° for 30-40 minutes or until chicken juices run clear and crumbs are golden. **Yield:** 4 servings.

Nutritional Analysis: 1 serving equals 870 calories, 59 g fat (29 g saturated fat), 187 mg cholesterol, 2,174 mg sodium, 43 g carbohydrate, 2 g fiber, 39 g protein.

Chicken with Mushroom Sauce

(Pictured above)

Low-carb

Prep/Total Time: 25 min.

It looks impressive, but this mouth-watering dish comes together in no time. I think its flavor rivals that of many full-fat entrees found in fancy restaurants.
—*Jennifer Pemberton, Muncie, Indiana*

2 teaspoons cornstarch
1/2 cup fat-free milk
4 boneless skinless chicken breast halves
   (4 ounces *each*)
1 tablespoon olive oil
1/2 pound fresh mushrooms, sliced
1/2 medium onion, sliced and separated into rings
1 tablespoon reduced-fat butter
1/4 cup sherry *or* chicken broth
1/2 teaspoon salt
1/8 teaspoon pepper

In a small bowl, combine the cornstarch and milk until smooth; set aside. Flatten the chicken to 1/4-in. thickness. In a large nonstick skillet, cook the chicken in oil over medium heat for 5-6 minutes on each side or until juices run clear. Remove and keep warm.

In the same skillet, saute the sliced mushrooms and onion in butter until tender. Stir in the sherry or broth, salt and pepper; bring to a boil. Stir the cornstarch mixture; add to the pan. Bring to a boil; cook and stir for 2 minutes or until thickened. Serve mushroom sauce with the chicken. **Yield:** 4 servings.

Editor's Note: This recipe was tested with Land O' Lakes light stick butter.

Nutritional Analysis: 1 chicken breast half with 1/3 cup sauce equals 212 calories, 8 g fat (2 g saturated fat), 68 mg cholesterol, 387 mg sodium, 7 g carbohydrate, 1 g fiber, 26 g protein.
Diabetic Exchanges: 3 very lean meat, 1 vegetable, 1 fat, 1/2 starch.

Stuffed Cornish Hens

Prep: 25 min. **Bake:** 50 min.

Stuffed with a succulent combination of wild rice, mushrooms and dried cranberries, these golden hens are sure to become a much-requested main course. They're a wonderful change of pace from turkey.
—*Nancy Horsburgh, Everett, Ontario*

1/2 cup chopped celery
1/4 cup sliced fresh mushrooms
2 tablespoons butter
1 package (6.2 ounces) fast-cooking long grain and wild rice mix
1 can (14-1/2 ounces) reduced-sodium chicken broth
1/4 cup water
2/3 cup sliced water chestnuts, chopped
1/2 cup dried cranberries
1/2 cup chopped green onions
2 tablespoons reduced-sodium soy sauce
5 Cornish game hens (20 ounces *each*)

In a large saucepan coated with nonstick cooking spray, cook celery and mushrooms in butter until tender. Stir in rice; cook 1 minute longer. Stir in the contents of the rice seasoning packet, broth and water. Bring to a boil. Reduce heat; cover and simmer for 5-6 minutes or until rice is tender.

Stir in the water chestnuts, cranberries, onions and soy sauce. Stuff into hens. Place on a rack in a shallow roasting pan. Bake at 375° for 50-60 minutes or until juices run clear and a meat thermometer inserted into stuffing reads 165°. Cut each hen in half lengthwise to serve. **Yield:** 10 servings.

Nutritional Analysis: 1 hen half with 1/3 cup stuffing (calculated without skin) equals 257 calories, 7 g fat (3 g saturated fat), 123 mg cholesterol, 564 mg sodium, 20 g carbohydrate, 1 g fiber, 29 g protein.
Diabetic Exchanges: 4 very lean meat, 1-1/2 starch, 1/2 fat.

Rosemary Turkey Breast

(Pictured above)

Low-carb *Low-fat*

Prep: 10 min. **Bake:** 1-1/2 hours + standing

I season turkey with a blend of rosemary, garlic and paprika. Because I rub that mixture directly on the meat under the skin, I can remove the skin before serving and not lose any of the flavor. The result is a lower-in-fat yet delicious entree that makes the perfect centerpiece for holiday meals.
—Dorothy Pritchett, Wills Point, Texas

8 to 10 garlic cloves
3 tablespoons chopped fresh rosemary *or* 3
   teaspoons dried rosemary, crushed
2 tablespoons olive oil
1 teaspoon salt
1 teaspoon paprika
1/2 teaspoon coarsely ground pepper
1 bone-in turkey breast (4 pounds)

In a food processor, combine the garlic, rosemary, oil, salt, paprika and pepper; cover and process until garlic is coarsely chopped.

With your fingers, carefully loosen the skin from both sides of turkey breast. Spread half of the garlic mixture over the meat under the skin.

Smooth skin over meat and secure to underside of breast with toothpicks. Spread remaining garlic mixture over turkey skin.

Place turkey breast on a rack in a shallow roasting pan. Bake, uncovered, at 325° for 1-1/2 to 2 hours or until a meat thermometer reads 170°. Let stand for 10-15 minutes. Discard toothpicks before carving. **Yield:** 11 servings.

Nutritional Analysis: *4 ounces cooked turkey breast (calculated without skin) equals 166 calories, 3 g fat (1 g saturated fat), 85 mg cholesterol, 269 mg sodium, 1 g carbohydrate, trace fiber, 31 g protein.*
Diabetic Exchange: *4 very lean meat.*

Turkey Meatballs With Lemon Sauce

Prep: 25 min. **Cook:** 30 min.

*This is a delightful way to prepare ground turkey.
Add a crisp green salad to round out the meal.*
—Sally Livingstone, Lancaster, New Hampshire

  1 **egg, beaten**
1/4 **cup All-Bran**
  1 **teaspoon Worcestershire sauce**
1/2 **teaspoon grated lemon peel**
  1 **pound lean ground turkey**
  2 **cups chicken broth**
  2 **tablespoons cornstarch**
1/2 **cup fat-free plain yogurt**
  2 **teaspoons lemon juice**
  1 **small carrot, shredded**
  1 **green onion, sliced**
  4 **cups hot cooked noodles**

In a large bowl, combine the egg, bran, Worcestershire sauce and lemon peel. Crumble turkey over mixture; mix well. Shape into 20 meatballs.

In a large nonstick skillet coated with nonstick cooking spray, brown meatballs. Add broth; bring to a boil. Reduce heat; cover and simmer for 5-8 minutes or until turkey is no longer pink. Remove meatballs and keep warm.

Combine the cornstarch, yogurt and lemon juice until smooth; gradually stir into cooking juices. Bring to a boil over medium heat; cook and stir for 2 minutes or until thickened. Stir in carrot and onion; heat through. Serve over meatballs and noodles. **Yield:** 4 servings.

Nutritional Analysis: 5 meatballs with 1/2 cup sauce and 1 cup noodles equals 458 calories, 12 g fat (3 g saturated fat), 143 mg cholesterol, 642 mg sodium, 55 g carbohydrate, 4 g fiber, 31 g protein.

Leftover-Turkey Bake

(Pictured above)

Prep: 20 min. **Bake:** 35 min.

*Dotted with pretty cranberries, this moist casserole
is a wonderful way to finish extra turkey.*
—Alice Slagter, Wyoming, Michigan

1-1/2 **cups finely chopped onion**
  1/2 **cup finely chopped celery**
    1 **can (14-1/2 ounces) reduced-sodium chicken broth, *divided***
    2 **eggs, lightly beaten**
    2 **teaspoons poultry seasoning**
  1/2 **teaspoon salt**
  1/4 **teaspoon pepper**
    3 **cups cubed whole grain bread**
    3 **cups cubed white bread**
    2 **cups cubed cooked turkey breast**
  1/2 **cup chopped fresh *or* frozen cranberries**

In a large saucepan, bring the onion, celery and 1/2 cup broth to a boil. Reduce heat; simmer, uncovered, for 5-8 minutes or until vegetables are tender. Remove from the heat. Stir in the remaining broth, then add the eggs, poultry seasoning, salt and pepper; stir until blended. Add the bread cubes, turkey and cranberries; mix well. Spoon into a 2-qt. baking dish coated with nonstick cooking spray.

Cover and bake at 350° for 15 minutes. Uncover; bake 20-25 minutes longer or until lightly browned and a knife inserted near center comes out clean. **Yield:** 4 servings.

Nutritional Analysis: 1 serving equals 290 calories, 5 g fat (1 g saturated fat), 154 mg cholesterol, 916 mg sodium, 34 g carbohydrate, 4 g fiber, 27 g protein.
Diabetic Exchanges: 3 lean meat, 1-1/2 starch, 1 vegetable.

🍎 Meat 'n' Veggies

THIS HINT might help you get children to eat their vegetables. When I make meatballs, meat loaf or any similar entree, I grate a few carrots and combine them with the meat mixture.

I have had adults compliment me on the flavors of these dishes, unaware of the extra ingredient. I always share the secret…out of earshot of the youngsters, of course.
*—Darlene Stadsvold
Rochester, Minnesota*

Try Something New: Asian Rice Noodles

IT'S TIME to make dinner exciting again...and you don't need to take cooking classes or hunt down expensive ingredients to do so! Simply pick up a package of Asian rice noodles.

Rice noodles are an age-old staple in Asian cuisine, but today's cooks are finding them a lively addition to other heart-healthy standbys.

Using the Old Noodle

Because they are made with rice flour, the noodles are ideal for anyone with wheat-related food allergies. Best of all, they are low in fat and cholesterol as well.

Use the noodles in stir-fries, soups, salads or just about anywhere you'd add pasta or rice. They also make fantastic beds for fish and meat because they absorb the flavors of the dishes with which they are served.

Found in the Asian food aisle of most supermarkets, the slightly transparent noodles are available in several shapes and sizes:

- Rice sticks are flat noodles. Some are thin and look like spaghetti; others are wide and resemble fettuccine. Try rice sticks in most any dish where pasta is called for.
- Rice vermicelli is similar in thickness to angel hair pasta and comes in bunches. Serve it covered with a thin sauce or in your favorite stir-fry.
- Rice flakes are large, flat and triangular. The noodles resemble tortilla chips and are perfect in soups.

Cooking methods vary depending on the rice noodles you choose. In general, package directions involve merely soaking or boiling the noodles in water. They're that simple!

So what are you waiting for? Chase away the supper time doldrums with Asian rice noodles tonight.

Stir-Fried Chicken And Rice Noodles

(Pictured at left)

Prep: 25 min. **Cook:** 20 min.

This list of ingredients looks long and intimidating, but the stir-fry is easy to prepare.
—Kim Pettipas, Oromocto, New Brunswick

2-1/2 teaspoons cornstarch
1/3 cup reduced-sodium soy sauce
1/4 cup white wine *or* reduced-sodium chicken broth
2 teaspoons sesame oil
1-1/2 pounds boneless skinless chicken breasts, cut into 1-inch cubes
1/2 cup reduced-sodium chicken broth
2 tablespoons sugar
1 tablespoon Worcestershire sauce
3/4 teaspoon chili powder
3 ounces uncooked Asian rice noodles
4 teaspoons canola oil, *divided*
3 cups fresh broccoli florets
2/3 cup chopped green onions
3 garlic cloves, minced
2 teaspoons minced fresh gingerroot
1/4 cup unsalted dry roasted peanuts

In a bowl, combine the cornstarch, soy sauce, wine or broth and sesame oil until smooth. Pour 1/4 cup marinade into a large resealable plastic bag; add the chicken. Seal bag and turn to coat; refrigerate for 20 minutes. Add the broth, sugar, Worcestershire sauce and chili powder to remaining marinade; set aside.

Cook rice noodles according to package directions. Meanwhile, drain and discard marinade from chicken. In a large nonstick skillet or wok, stir-fry chicken in 2 teaspoons canola oil until juices run clear; remove and keep warm.

Stir-fry broccoli in remaining canola oil for 5 minutes. Add the onions, garlic and ginger; stir-fry 3-5 minutes longer or until broccoli is tender. Return chicken to the pan. Stir reserved broth mixture and stir into pan. Bring to a boil; cook and stir for 2 minutes or until thickened. Drain noodles; toss with chicken mixture. Garnish with peanuts. **Yield:** 6 servings.

Nutritional Analysis: 1 cup equals 293 calories, 10 g fat (2 g saturated fat), 63 mg cholesterol, 498 mg sodium, 22 g carbohydrate, 2 g fiber, 27 g protein.
Diabetic Exchanges: 3 very lean meat, 1-1/2 starch, 1-1/2 fat.

warm; repeat with remaining chicken and oil. Discard bay leaf from sauce. Serve over chicken. **Yield:** 6 servings.

Nutritional Analysis: 4 ounces cooked chicken with 3 tablespoons sauce equals 163 calories, 3 g fat (trace saturated fat), 67 mg cholesterol, 287 mg sodium, 8 g carbohydrate, 1 g fiber, 27 g protein.
Diabetic Exchanges: 3 very lean meat, 1/2 starch, 1/2 fat.

Thai-Style Chicken

Low-carb Low-fat

Prep: 10 min. + marinating **Bake:** 20 min.

I'm always happy to serve this lip-smacking main dish that's flavored with a zesty marinade.
—Vicki Floden, Story City, Iowa

1/4 cup reduced-sodium soy sauce
3 tablespoons lemon juice
3 tablespoons minced fresh basil *or* 1 tablespoon dried basil
3 garlic cloves, minced
2 tablespoons fat-free plain yogurt
2 teaspoons grated lemon peel
1 teaspoon ground ginger
1/2 to 1 teaspoon crushed red pepper flakes
4 boneless skinless chicken breast halves (4 ounces *each*)

In a bowl, combine the first eight ingredients. Set aside 1/4 cup; cover and refrigerate. Pour the remaining marinade into a large resealable plastic bag; add chicken. Seal bag and turn to coat; refrigerate overnight.

Drain and discard marinade. Place chicken in a 13-in. x 9-in. x 2-in. baking dish coated with nonstick cooking spray. Spoon reserved marinade over chicken. Bake, uncovered, at 375° for 20 minutes or until a meat thermometer reads 170°. **Yield:** 4 servings.

Nutritional Analysis: 1 chicken breast half equals 134 calories, 3 g fat (1 g saturated fat), 63 mg cholesterol, 360 mg sodium, 2 g carbohydrate, trace fiber, 24 g protein.
Diabetic Exchange: 3 lean meat.

Tasty Italian Chicken

(Pictured above)

Low-carb Low-fat

Prep/Total Time: 30 min.

A friend delivered this meal to me and my husband after our first child was born, and I lightened it up.
—Beth Ann Stein, Richmond, Indiana

1/2 cup chopped onion
1-1/8 teaspoons paprika, *divided*
3 teaspoons olive oil, *divided*
1-1/4 cups water
1/4 cup tomato paste
1 bay leaf
1/2 teaspoon reduced-sodium chicken bouillon granules
1/2 teaspoon Italian seasoning
1/4 cup all-purpose flour
1-1/2 teaspoons grated Parmesan cheese
1/2 teaspoon salt
1/4 teaspoon garlic powder
1/4 teaspoon dried oregano
1-1/2 pounds chicken tenderloins

In a small saucepan, saute onion and 1/8 teaspoon paprika in 1 teaspoon oil until tender. Stir in the water, tomato paste, bay leaf, bouillon and Italian seasoning. Bring to a boil. Reduce heat; simmer, uncovered, for 10 minutes.

Meanwhile, in a large resealable plastic bag, combine the flour, Parmesan cheese, salt, garlic powder, oregano and remaining paprika. Add chicken; seal bag and shake to coat.

In a large nonstick skillet coated with nonstick cooking spray, cook half of the chicken in 1 teaspoon oil for 2-3 minutes on each side or until juices run clear. Remove and keep

Turkey Soft Tacos

Prep/Total Time: 25 min.

These easy tacos are my 5-year-old's favorite. With the ground turkey, corn and beans, they're healthy, too.
—Pattie McGlinchey, San Antonio, Texas

1-1/4 pounds lean ground turkey
1 medium red onion, finely chopped
5 plum tomatoes, chopped, *divided*
2 tablespoons water
4 teaspoons paprika
1 teaspoon ground cumin
1 teaspoon chili powder
1/2 teaspoon salt
1 can (15 ounces) black beans, rinsed and drained
1 cup frozen corn, thawed
8 flour tortillas (8 inches), warmed

1 cup (4 ounces) shredded reduced-fat Mexican cheese blend, *divided*
4 green onions, thinly sliced
1 tablespoon minced fresh cilantro

In a large skillet, cook turkey and onion over medium heat until meat is no longer pink; drain. Add half of the tomatoes. Stir in the water, paprika, cumin, chili powder and salt. Add beans and corn; cook and stir for 2 minutes or until heated through.

Place about 1/2 cup turkey mixture down the center of each tortilla; top with 1 tablespoon cheese. Fold sides of tortilla over filling. Serve with green onions, cilantro and remaining tomatoes and cheese. **Yield:** 8 servings.

Nutritional Analysis: 1 taco equals 378 calories, 12 g fat (4 g saturated fat), 64 mg cholesterol, 727 mg sodium, 41 g carbohydrate, 5 g fiber, 25 g protein.
Diabetic Exchanges: 3 lean meat, 2-1/2 starch, 1/2 fat.

Tarragon-Lemon Turkey Breast

Low-carb   Low-fat

Prep: 10 min. **Bake:** 1-1/2 hours + standing

If you like tarragon, you'll love this wet rub for turkey or chicken from our Test Kitchen.

1/4 cup minced fresh tarragon
2 tablespoons olive oil
1 teaspoon lemon-pepper seasoning
1/2 teaspoon seasoned salt
1 bone-in turkey breast (4 pounds)

In a small dish, combine the first four ingredients. With your fingers, carefully loosen the skin from both sides of turkey breast. Spread half of the tarragon mixture over the meat under the skin. Smooth skin over meat and secure to underside of breast with toothpicks. Spread remaining tarragon mixture over turkey skin.

Place turkey breast on a rack in a shallow roasting pan. Bake, uncovered, at 325° for 1-1/2 to 2 hours or until a meat thermometer reads 170°. Let stand for 10-15 minutes. Discard toothpicks before carving. **Yield:** 11 servings.

Nutritional Analysis: 4 ounces cooked turkey breast (calculated without skin) equals 162 calories, 3 g fat (1 g saturated fat), 85 mg cholesterol, 165 mg sodium, trace carbohydrate, trace fiber, 31 g protein.
Diabetic Exchange: 4 very lean meat.

🍎 Flavor Without Fat

THOUGH they add a lip-smacking essence to just about any meat, rubs are especially great for poultry because they can be applied underneath the skin.

For maximum moisture and taste, gently pull the skin away, rub the mix on and set the skin back in place before cooking the poultry.

Before serving, simply remove the skin. Not only will you cut calories and fat, but you'll find that the rub has done a mouth-watering job of seasoning your main course.

Blackened Chicken and Beans

(Pictured below)

Prep/Total Time: 15 min.

My husband is a big fan of spicy food. This is a quick-to-fix, low-fat dish that we can both enjoy.
—*Christine Zongker, Spring Hill, Kansas*

2 teaspoons chili powder
1/4 teaspoon salt
1/4 teaspoon pepper
4 boneless skinless chicken breast halves (4 ounces *each***)**
1 tablespoon canola oil
1 can (15 ounces) black beans, rinsed and drained
1 cup frozen corn, thawed
1 cup chunky salsa

Combine the chili powder, salt and pepper; rub over both sides of chicken. In a large nonstick skillet, cook chicken in oil over medium heat for 4-5 minutes on each side or until juices run clear. Remove and keep warm.

Add the beans, corn and salsa to skillet; bring to a boil. Reduce heat; cover and simmer for 2-3 minutes or until heated through. Transfer to a serving dish; top with chicken. **Yield:** 4 servings.

Nutritional Analysis: 1 chicken breast half with 3/4 cup bean mixture equals 297 calories, 7 g fat (1 g saturated fat), 63 mg cholesterol, 697 mg sodium, 30 g carbohydrate, 10 g fiber, 33 g protein.
Diabetic Exchanges: 3 very lean meat, 2 starch, 1 fat.

Spicy Chicken

Low-carb Low-sodium

Prep/Total Time: 20 min.

With the seasonings in this entree, you won't even think about reaching for the salt shaker. Our Test Kitchen combined dried minced garlic, cayenne pepper and paprika with a few other kitchen staples.

    2-1/2 teaspoons paprika
        1 teaspoon dried minced onion
        1 teaspoon dried minced garlic
    1/2 teaspoon cayenne pepper
    1/4 teaspoon dried oregano
    1/4 teaspoon dried basil
    1/4 teaspoon white pepper
        4 boneless skinless chicken breast halves
          (4 ounces *each*)
        2 teaspoons canola oil

In a small bowl, combine the first seven ingredients. Sprinkle over both sides of chicken. In a large nonstick skillet, cook chicken in oil over medium-high heat for 5-7 minutes on each side or until juices run clear. **Yield:** 4 servings.

Nutritional Analysis: 1 chicken breast half equals 151 calories, 5 g fat (1 g saturated fat), 63 mg cholesterol, 55 mg sodium, 2 g carbohydrate, trace fiber, 23 g protein.
Diabetic Exchanges: 3 very lean meat, 1/2 fat.

Chicken Fried Rice

Prep/Total Time: 25 min.

Who would imagine fried rice could be light? This version is! It's an easy meal that can be fixed from second-day rice, chicken and vegetables.
—*Deborah Knobel, Fort Collins, Colorado*

        2 egg whites
        1 egg
    1/2 teaspoon salt, *divided*
        1 small onion, chopped
        1 garlic clove, minced
        1 cup frozen mixed vegetables
        2 cups diced cooked chicken breast
        3 tablespoons reduced-sodium soy sauce
        3 cups cold cooked rice

In a small bowl, combine the egg whites, egg and 1/4 teaspoon salt. In a large nonstick skillet or wok coated with nonstick cooking spray, cook the egg mixture over medium heat. As eggs set, lift edges, letting uncooked portion flow underneath. When the eggs are set, remove and cut into 1-in. pieces; keep warm.

In the same pan, stir-fry the onion and garlic until tender. Add vegetables; cover and cook over medium-high heat for 3-4 minutes or until no longer frozen. Stir in the chicken, soy sauce and remaining salt; cook for 1 minute. Add rice; stir-fry for 4-5 minutes or until heated through. Add eggs; heat through. **Yield:** 4 servings.

Nutritional Analysis: 1-1/4 cups equals 325 calories, 4 g fat (1 g saturated fat), 107 mg cholesterol, 854 mg sodium, 41 g carbohydrate, 2 g fiber, 29 g protein.
Diabetic Exchanges: 3 very lean meat, 2 starch, 1 vegetable.

Muenster Mushroom Chicken

(Pictured above)

Prep/Total Time: 30 min.

Topped with cheese and Marsala-seasoned mushrooms, these breaded chicken breasts are rich-tasting. I often bake them in the oven, but the stovetop speeds things up.
—*Elaine Anderson, Aliquippa, Pennsylvania*

        2 cups sliced fresh mushrooms
        4 teaspoons butter, *divided*
    1/2 cup Marsala wine *or* 1/4 cup white grape juice
          plus 1/4 cup reduced-sodium chicken broth
        2 eggs, lightly beaten
        2 tablespoons fat-free milk
    3/4 cup dry bread crumbs
        4 boneless skinless chicken breast halves
          (4 ounces *each*)
        1 teaspoon minced fresh parsley
    1/2 teaspoon salt
    1/4 teaspoon garlic powder
    1/4 teaspoon dried thyme
    1/4 teaspoon pepper
        2 slices Muenster cheese, halved

In a nonstick skillet coated with nonstick cooking spray, cook mushrooms in 2 teaspoons butter until tender. Stir in the wine or grape juice and broth; cook 3-4 minutes longer. Set aside and keep warm.

In a shallow bowl, combine eggs and milk. Place bread crumbs in another shallow bowl. Dip chicken in egg mixture, then in crumbs. Combine the parsley, salt, garlic powder, thyme and pepper; sprinkle over chicken.

In a large nonstick skillet, cook chicken in remaining butter for 6-7 minutes on each side or until juices run clear. Place chicken on a broiler pan; top with cheese. Broil 3-4 in. from the heat for 1-2 minutes or until cheese is melted. Serve with mushroom mixture. **Yield:** 4 servings.

Nutritional Analysis: 1 chicken breast half with 1/4 cup mushrooms equals 344 calories, 12 g fat (6 g saturated fat), 147 mg cholesterol, 634 mg sodium, 19 g carbohydrate, 1 g fiber, 31 g protein.
Diabetic Exchanges: 3 very lean meat, 2 fat, 1-1/2 starch.

Pork Favorites

Lean cuts of succulent pork
are ideal for people who are
eating a little lighter. Plus, with
a quick cooking time, versatile pork
can easily become a mealtime mainstay.

Glazed Rosemary Pork (page 152)

Apples 'n' Onion Topped Chops

(Pictured below)

Prep/Total Time: 30 min.

Now that my husband and I are trying to lose weight, I find it a challenge to come up with healthy dishes that are flavorful, quick and appealing to our young daughter. This one fits the bill on all counts.
—Beverly McLain, Endicott, New York

4 boneless lean pork loin chops (5 ounces *each*)
3 cups sweet onion slices
1 teaspoon canola oil
2 medium Granny Smith apples, peeled and sliced
1/2 cup water
2 tablespoons brown sugar
1 tablespoon cider vinegar
1 teaspoon garlic powder
1/2 teaspoon salt
1/4 to 1/2 teaspoon pepper
1/4 teaspoon dried rosemary, crushed

In a large nonstick skillet coated with nonstick cooking spray, cook chops for about 3 minutes on each side or until browned. Remove meat; set aside and keep warm.

In same skillet, cook and stir onion in oil for 7 minutes or until golden brown. Add apple slices; cook and stir 3 minutes longer. Combine the water, brown sugar, vinegar, garlic powder, salt, pepper and rosemary. Stir into skillet. Bring to a boil. Return meat to pan. Reduce heat; cover and simmer for 8-10 minutes or until apples are crisp-tender and a meat thermometer reads 160°. **Yield:** 4 servings.

Nutritional Analysis: *1 pork chop with 1/2 cup apple-onion mixture equals 326 calories, 11 g fat (4 g saturated fat), 79 mg cholesterol, 344 mg sodium, 25 g carbohydrate, 2 g fiber, 33 g protein.* ***Diabetic Exchanges:*** *4 lean meat, 2 vegetable, 1 fruit.*

Pineapple Bacon Pizza

(Pictured above)

Prep/Total Time: 15 min.

Eating pizza is fun, but making it with your favorite ingredients is even better—especially when you can do it in 30 minutes or less! One weekend, when I was home from college, I made this for my family and they absolutely loved it.
—Amanda Hoffman, Worthington, Minnesota

1 prebaked Italian bread shell crust (10 ounces)
1/2 cup sweet and sour sauce
3/4 cup unsweetened pineapple tidbits, drained
1/2 cup mixed nuts, coarsely chopped
1 package (7 ounces) sliced Canadian bacon, chopped
1 cup (4 ounces) shredded reduced-fat Mexican cheese blend

Place the crust on an ungreased 14-in. pizza pan. Top with sauce, pineapple, nuts, bacon and cheese. Bake at 450° for 8-12 minutes or until cheese is melted. Cut into wedges. Serve immediately. **Yield:** 6 servings.

Nutritional Analysis: *1 slice equals 335 calories, 13 g fat (4 g saturated fat), 23 mg cholesterol, 950 mg sodium, 37 g carbohydrate, 2 g fiber, 18 g protein.* ***Diabetic Exchanges:*** *2 lean meat, 2 starch, 1 fat, 1/2 fruit.*

Apple-Stuffed Pork Tenderloin

(Pictured below)

Prep: 30 min. **Bake:** 25 min.

My mother used to make stuffed pork tenderloin, but I added apples and nuts to the stuffing to make it more nutritious. I also reduced the amount of croutons called for and used the fat-free variety.
—*Sandra Harrison, Viera, Florida*

  6 tablespoons reduced-sodium chicken broth,
    divided
  2 tablespoons raisins
1/2 cup chopped apple
  1 celery rib, chopped
  2 tablespoons chopped onion
  1 garlic clove, minced
1-1/2 cups fat-free Caesar croutons
  2 tablespoons sliced almonds, toasted
1/8 teaspoon pepper
  1 pork tenderloin (1 pound)

In a small saucepan, bring 4 tablespoons broth to a boil. Remove from the heat; add raisins. Let stand for 5 minutes. In a nonstick skillet coated with nonstick cooking spray, saute the apple, celery, onion and garlic for 3-4 minutes or until tender. Remove from the heat; stir in the raisins with broth, croutons, nuts, pepper and the remaining broth.

Make a lengthwise slit down the center of the roast to within 1/2 in. of bottom. Open roast so it lies flat; cover with plastic wrap. Flatten to 1/2-in. thickness. Remove plastic wrap; fill with stuffing mixture. Close roast; tie at 2-in. intervals with kitchen string and secure ends with toothpicks.

Place on a rack in a shallow baking pan coated with nonstick cooking spray. Bake at 425° for 25-30 minutes or until a meat thermometer reads 160°. Let stand for 5 minutes before slicing. **Yield:** 3 servings.

Nutritional Analysis: 6 ounces stuffed cooked pork equals 336 calories, 7 g fat (2 g saturated fat), 84 mg cholesterol, 417 mg sodium, 27 g carbohydrate, 2 g fiber, 35 g protein.
Diabetic Exchanges: 4 lean meat, 1-1/2 starch.

Spiced Tangerine Ham

(Pictured above)

Prep/Total Time: 15 min.

Our home economists glazed slices of fully cooked ham with a thick fruit sauce that's nicely seasoned with ginger and cloves. This entree is special enough for company, yet it's ready in just 15 minutes.

  8 medium tangerines
  2 teaspoons cornstarch
  1 tablespoon honey
1/4 teaspoon ground ginger
1/4 teaspoon ground cloves
  4 slices fully cooked ham (1 pound)

Squeeze juice from six tangerines; strain pulp. Segment remaining tangerines; set aside. In a small bowl, combine cornstarch and tangerine juice until smooth; stir in the honey, ginger and cloves.

In a large nonstick skillet coated with nonstick cooking spray, brown ham slices on both sides; remove and keep warm. Stir tangerine juice mixture and add to the skillet. Bring to a boil; cook and stir for 2 minutes or until thickened. Stir in the tangerine segments; heat through. Serve over the ham. **Yield:** 4 servings.

Nutritional Analysis: 4 ounces cooked ham with 3 tablespoons sauce equals 232 calories, 6 g fat (2 g saturated fat), 53 mg cholesterol, 1,623 mg sodium, 22 g carbohydrate, 3 g fiber, 23 g protein.
Diabetic Exchanges: 3 lean meat, 1 fruit.

mometer reads 160°. Let stand for 5 minutes before slicing. Serve with warm red onion topping. **Yield:** 6 servings.

Nutritional Analysis: 3-1/2 ounces cooked pork with 2/3 cup onion mixture equals 336 calories, 12 g fat (3 g saturated fat), 84 mg cholesterol, 461 mg sodium, 20 g carbohydrate, 2 g fiber, 32 g protein.

Diabetic Exchanges: 4 lean meat, 1 vegetable, 1 fat, 1/2 starch.

Italian Rubbed Pork Chops

(Pictured below)

Low-carb   Low-sodium

Prep: 5 min. **Bake:** 40 min.

A perky garlic and herb rub adds pizzazz to these juicy chops that will have everyone at the table licking their lips. They're special enough for company, too...and so easy to prepare.
—Kathleen Taugher, East Troy, Wisconsin

3 tablespoons minced fresh parsley
1 teaspoon dried oregano
1/2 teaspoon fennel seed, crushed
1/4 teaspoon garlic powder
1/2 teaspoon pepper
4 boneless pork loin chops (1/2 inch thick
 and 4 ounces *each*)

In a bowl, combine the first five ingredients; rub over pork chops. Place in a 11-in. x 7-in. x 2-in. baking dish coated with nonstick cooking spray. Bake, uncovered, at 350° for 38-42 minutes or until juices run clear. **Yield:** 4 servings.

Nutritional Analysis: 1 pork chop equals 149 calories, 6 g fat (2 g saturated fat), 57 mg cholesterol, 48 mg sodium, 1 g carbohydrate, trace fiber, 22 g protein.

Diabetic Exchange: 3 lean meat.

Pork Tenderloin with Glazed Red Onion

(Pictured above)

Prep: 25 min. + marinating **Cook:** 1-1/4 hours

This colorful entree has been a longtime family favorite. I pair it with rice pilaf or orzo to complement the thyme in the pork and the vinegar in the onions.
—Patricia Schmidt, Sterling Heights, Michigan

1 tablespoon minced fresh thyme
1 tablespoon olive oil
3/4 teaspoon salt
1/2 teaspoon pepper
2 pork tenderloins (1 pound *each*)
RED ONION TOPPING:
 4 large red onions, sliced
 2 tablespoons olive oil
 3/4 cup dry red wine *or* chicken broth
 1/4 cup raisins
 2 tablespoons sugar
 1/4 teaspoon salt
 1/4 cup balsamic vinegar
1-1/2 teaspoons minced fresh thyme

In a large resealable plastic bag, combine the thyme, oil, salt and pepper; add pork. Seal bag and turn to coat; marinate at room temperature for 30 minutes.

Meanwhile, saute onions in oil until tender; add the wine or broth, raisins, sugar and salt. Bring to a boil. Reduce heat; cook, uncovered, for 45 minutes or until liquid is evaporated. Stir in vinegar and thyme; cook and stir 10 minutes longer to blend flavors. Set aside.

Drain and discard the marinade. Place pork on a rack coated with nonstick cooking spray in a shallow roasting pan. Bake, uncovered, at 425° for 20-30 minutes or until a ther-

Polynesian Pork Loin

(Pictured above)

Prep: 20 min. **Bake:** 2-1/2 hours + standing

I jazz up this tender pork roast with a chunky tomato sauce. After reducing the tangy sauce on the stovetop, I use a portion of it to flavor the pork, serving the extra on the side at dinner.
—Karyn Joyner, Hendersonville, North Carolina

    1 teaspoon salt, *divided*
1/2 teaspoon pepper
    1 boneless whole pork loin roast (4 pounds)
    1 cup water
    1 cup unsweetened crushed pineapple, undrained
2/3 cup tomato paste
1/2 cup packed brown sugar
    2 tablespoons diced onion
    2 tablespoons diced green pepper
    2 tablespoons cider vinegar
    1 teaspoon ground ginger

Rub 1/2 teaspoon salt and pepper over roast. Place on a rack in a shallow roasting pan. Bake, uncovered, at 350° for 1 hour.

Meanwhile, in a small saucepan, combine the water, pineapple, tomato paste, brown sugar, onion, green pepper, vinegar, ginger and remaining salt; bring to a boil. Reduce heat; simmer, uncovered, for 20-25 minutes or until slightly thickened, stirring occasionally. Reserve 1-1/4 cups sauce; set aside.

Pour remaining sauce over roast; bake 1-1/2 to 2 hours longer or until a meat thermometer reads 160°, basting occasionally. Let stand for 10-15 minutes before slicing. Serve with remaining sauce. **Yield:** 10 servings.

Nutritional Analysis: 4 ounces cooked pork with 2 tablespoons sauce equals 301 calories, 8 g fat (3 g saturated fat), 90 mg cholesterol, 305 mg sodium, 19 g carbohydrate, 1 g fiber, 36 g protein.
Diabetic Exchanges: 4 lean meat, 1 vegetable, 1/2 starch, 1/2 fruit.

Pork Medallions With Dijon Sauce

(Pictured below)

Prep/Total Time: 25 min.

I lightened up this recipe years ago, and I've been using it ever since. I brown pork in a skillet before swiftly stirring up a succulent sauce.
—Lois Kinneberg, Phoenix, Arizona

    1 pork tenderloin (1 pound)
1/3 cup all-purpose flour
1/4 teaspoon salt
1/4 teaspoon pepper
    1 tablespoon butter
    3 green onions
1/3 cup white wine *or* chicken broth
1/2 cup fat-free evaporated milk
    4 teaspoons Dijon mustard

Cut pork widthwise into 6 pieces; flatten to 1/4-in. thickness. In a large resealable plastic bag, combine the flour, salt and pepper. Add pork, a few pieces at a time, and shake to coat. In a large nonstick skillet, brown pork in butter over medium-high heat. Remove and keep warm.

Slice green onions, separating the white and green portions; reserve green portion for garnish. In the same skillet, saute the white portion of green onions for 1 minute. Add wine or broth. Bring to a boil; cook until liquid is reduced to about 2 tablespoons. Add milk. Reduce heat; simmer, uncovered, for 1-2 minutes or until slightly thickened. Whisk in mustard. Serve pork with Dijon sauce. Garnish with reserved green onions. **Yield:** 3 servings.

Nutritional Analysis: 4 ounces cooked pork with 3 tablespoons sauce equals 323 calories, 10 g fat (4 g saturated fat), 96 mg cholesterol, 516 mg sodium, 18 g carbohydrate, 1 g fiber, 35 g protein.
Diabetic Exchanges: 4 lean meat, 1 starch, 1/2 fat.

Cheesy Broccoli Cauliflower Casserole

(Pictured above)

Prep: 35 min. **Bake:** 25 min.

*After I found this recipe in an old church cookbook,
I adjusted it to make it lower in calories and fat.
The creamy cheese sauce makes it a tasty way
to get children to eat their vegetables.*
—Nancy Whitford, Edwards, New York

      1 tablespoon butter
  4-1/2 teaspoons all-purpose flour
  1-1/4 cups 1% milk
    3/4 cup shredded reduced-fat cheddar cheese
    1/3 cup grated Parmesan cheese
      1 package (10 ounces) frozen broccoli florets,
        thawed
      1 package (10 ounces) frozen cauliflowerets,
        thawed
      1 cup cubed fully cooked lean ham
      1 cup soft bread crumbs
Butter-flavored nonstick cooking spray

In a saucepan, melt butter. Stir in flour until smooth; gradually add the milk. Bring to a boil; cook and stir for 1-2 minutes or until thickened. Remove from the heat. Add cheeses; stir until melted.

Place vegetables in a 2-qt. baking dish coated with nonstick cooking spray; sprinkle with ham. Pour sauce over ham. Place bread crumbs in a bowl; spray with butter-flavored spray. Sprinkle around the edge of casserole. Bake, uncovered, at 350° for 25-30 minutes or until heated through and bubbly. **Yield:** 5 servings.

Nutritional Analysis: 1 serving equals 227 calories, 10 g fat (6 g saturated fat), 34 mg cholesterol, 707 mg sodium, 16 g carbohydrate, 3 g fiber, 18 g protein.
Diabetic Exchanges: 2 lean meat, 1 vegetable, 1 fat, 1/2 starch.

Lime Pork with Peppers

(Pictured below)

Prep: 15 min. + marinating **Cook:** 20 min.

*A little planning the night before or early in the day is all
it takes to get this entree on the table in a hurry. Loaded
with vegetables, tender pork and lots of lime flavor, it's an
outstanding meal-in-one.*
—Shonda Ford, DeRidder, Louisiana

      2 medium limes
    1/4 cup reduced-sodium soy sauce
      4 garlic cloves, minced
      1 teaspoon dried oregano
    1/2 teaspoon dried thyme
    1/8 teaspoon cayenne pepper
      2 to 3 sprigs fresh parsley, stems removed
      1 pork tenderloin (1 pound), cut into 1-inch cubes
      1 bay leaf
      1 tablespoon olive oil
      1 teaspoon brown sugar
      2 medium onions, each cut into 8 wedges
      2 small green peppers, cut into 1-inch pieces
      2 medium tomatoes, each cut into 8 wedges

Finely grate lime peel, reserving 2 tablespoons peel. Juice the limes. In a bowl, combine the soy sauce, garlic, oregano, thyme, cayenne, parsley, lime juice and reserved lime peel. Pour 1/2 cup marinade into a large resealable plastic bag; add the pork and bay leaf. Seal bag and turn to coat; refrigerate for at least 2 hours. Cover and refrigerate remaining marinade.

Drain pork and discard marinade. Discard bay leaf. In a large nonstick skillet, heat oil over medium-high heat. Add sugar; stir until bubbly. Add the meat; cook and stir for 3-4 minutes or until browned. Reduce heat; add the onions, peppers and the reserved lime mixture. Cook, uncovered, for 10-15 minutes or until vegetables are tender. Add the tomatoes; cook 1 minute longer. **Yield:** 4 servings.

Nutritional Analysis: 1-1/2 cups equals 240 calories, 8 g fat (2 g saturated fat), 63 mg cholesterol, 540 mg sodium, 18 g carbohydrate, 3 g fiber, 26 g protein.
Diabetic Exchanges: 3 lean meat, 2 vegetable, 1/2 fat.

Sweet 'n' Sour Cashew Pork

(Pictured below)

Prep/Total Time: 30 min.

A simple homemade sauce blends the tangy flavors in this stir-fry. Ginger, garlic and pineapple give it a traditional taste, and snow peas, green onions and cashews add a little crunch.
—Janet Rodakowski, Wentzville, Missouri

2 tablespoons cornstarch, *divided*
1 tablespoon sherry *or* chicken broth
1 pork tenderloin (1 pound), cut into 1-inch pieces
1/4 cup sugar
1/3 cup water
1/4 cup cider vinegar
3 tablespoons reduced-sodium soy sauce
3 tablespoons ketchup
1 tablespoon canola oil
1/3 cup unsalted cashews
1/4 cup chopped green onions
2 garlic cloves, minced
2 teaspoons minced fresh gingerroot
1/2 pound fresh snow peas (3 cups)
1 can (8 ounces) unsweetened pineapple chunks, drained
Hot cooked rice, optional

In a large bowl, combine 1 tablespoon cornstarch and sherry or broth until smooth; add pork and toss to coat. In another bowl, combine sugar and remaining cornstarch. Stir in the water, vinegar, soy sauce and ketchup until smooth; set aside.

In a large nonstick skillet or wok, stir-fry pork in hot oil until no longer pink. Add the cashews, onions, garlic and ginger; stir-fry for 1 minute. Add peas and pineapple; stir-fry 3 minutes longer or until peas are crisp-tender.

Stir cornstarch mixture and add to the pan. Bring to a boil; cook and stir for 1-2 minutes or until sauce is thickened. Serve over rice if desired. **Yield:** 4 servings.

Nutritional Analysis: 1 cup pork mixture (calculated without rice) equals 371 calories, 13 g fat (3 g saturated fat), 63 mg cholesterol, 714 mg sodium, 36 g carbohydrate, 3 g fiber, 27 g protein.

Diabetic Exchanges: 3 lean meat, 1-1/2 starch, 1 vegetable, 1 fat, 1/2 fruit.

Honey-Herb Pork

(Pictured above)

Prep: 10 min. + marinating **Grill:** 25 min. + standing

Mustard, honey and rosemary make a sensational marinade and sauce for these moist pork tenderloins. Whether prepared on the grill or in the oven, the recipe doesn't require much hands-on work.
—Kathy Kittell, Lenexa, Kansas

1 cup beer *or* ginger ale
1/2 cup prepared mustard
1/2 cup honey
2 tablespoons canola oil
2 tablespoons onion powder
1-1/2 teaspoons dried rosemary, crushed
1 teaspoon salt
1 teaspoon garlic powder
1/4 teaspoon pepper
2 pork tenderloins (1 pound *each*)

In a small bowl, combine the first nine ingredients. Pour 1 cup marinade into a large resealable plastic bag; add the pork. Seal bag and turn to coat; refrigerate for at least 1 hour. Cover and refrigerate the remaining marinade for basting.

Coat grill rack with nonstick cooking spray before preparing the grill for indirect heat. Drain and discard marinade from pork. Grill, covered, over indirect medium heat for 25-30 minutes or until a meat thermometer reads 160°, basting occasionally with reserved marinade. Let stand for 10 minutes before slicing. Serve with any remaining marinade if desired. **Yield:** 6 servings.

Nutritional Analysis: 4 ounces cooked pork equals 274 calories, 8 g fat (2 g saturated fat), 84 mg cholesterol, 432 mg sodium, 17 g carbohydrate, 1 g fiber, 31 g protein.

Diabetic Exchanges: 4 lean meat, 1 starch.

Greek Pork Cutlets

(Pictured below)

Low-carb   Low-sodium

Prep: 15 min. + marinating **Cook:** 15 min.

Treat your family to a meal filled with Mediterranean flair when you serve up these succulent slices of pork. Our home economists created a garden-fresh cucumber sauce to go with the herb-seasoned entree.

    1 pork tenderloin (1 pound)
    1 small onion, chopped
    2 tablespoons lemon juice
    1 tablespoon minced fresh parsley
    2 garlic cloves, minced
    3/4 teaspoon dried thyme
    1/8 teaspoon pepper
CUCUMBER SAUCE:
    1 small tomato, seeded and chopped
    2/3 cup reduced-fat plain yogurt
    1/2 cup chopped seeded cucumber
    1 tablespoon finely chopped onion
    1/2 teaspoon lemon juice
    1/8 teaspoon garlic powder

Cut pork into eight slices; flatten to 1/2-in. thickness. In a large resealable plastic bag, combine the onion, lemon juice, parsley, garlic, thyme and pepper; add pork. Seal bag and turn to coat; refrigerate for 4 hours or overnight. In a small bowl, combine the cucumber sauce ingredients. Cover and refrigerate until serving.

Drain pork and discard marinade. Place on a broiler pan coated with nonstick cooking spray. Broil 4 in. from the heat for 6-8 minutes on each side or until juices run clear. Serve with cucumber sauce. **Yield:** 4 servings.

Nutritional Analysis: 3 ounces cooked pork with 1/4 cup sauce equals 177 calories, 5 g fat (2 g saturated fat), 66 mg cholesterol, 114 mg sodium, 8 g carbohydrate, 1 g fiber, 25 g protein.
Diabetic Exchanges: 3 lean meat, 1 vegetable.

Grilled Pork with Avocado Salsa

(Pictured above)

Prep: 25 min. + marinating **Grill:** 10 min.

I love the zesty taste of this moist tenderloin. The cumin, avocado and jalapeno give it Southwestern flair.
—Josephine Devereaux Piro, Easton, Pennsylvania

    1/2 cup chopped sweet onion
    1/2 cup lime juice
    1/4 cup chopped seeded jalapeno peppers
    2 tablespoons olive oil
    4 teaspoons ground cumin
    2 pork tenderloins (3/4 pound *each*), cut
      into 3/4-inch slices
SALSA:
    2 medium ripe avocados, peeled and chopped
    2 plum tomatoes, seeded and chopped
    1 small cucumber, seeded and chopped
    2 green onions, chopped
    2 tablespoons minced fresh cilantro
    1 tablespoon honey
    1/4 teaspoon salt
    1/4 teaspoon pepper
    3 tablespoons jalapeno pepper jelly

In a small bowl, combine the first five ingredients. Pour 1/2 cup marinade into a large resealable plastic bag; add the pork. Seal bag and turn to coat; refrigerate for up to 2 hours. Reserve 1/3 cup of the remaining marinade. Place the rest of the marinade in a large bowl; add the avocados, tomatoes, cucumber, green onions, cilantro, honey, salt and pepper. Cover and refrigerate until serving.

In a small saucepan, combine the jelly and reserved marinade. Bring to a boil; cook and stir for 2 minutes or until slightly thickened.

Coat grill rack with nonstick cooking spray before starting the grill. Drain and discard marinade from pork. Grill, uncovered, over medium heat for 4-6 minutes on each side or until juices run clear, brushing occasionally with jelly mixture. Serve with avocado salsa. **Yield:** 6 servings.

Editor's Note: When cutting or seeding hot peppers, use rubber or plastic gloves to protect your hands. Avoid touching your face.

Nutritional Analysis: 3 ounces cooked pork with 1/2 cup salsa equals 326 calories, 18 g fat (3 g saturated fat), 63 mg cholesterol, 159 mg sodium, 19 g carbohydrate, 4 g fiber, 25 g protein.
Diabetic Exchanges: 3 lean meat, 2 fat, 1 starch.

Pork with Tangy Cherry Sauce

Prep/Total Time: 30 min.

Draped in a sweet cherry sauce, these tender pork slices are ready in mere moments.
—Suzanne Veverka, White Cloud, Michigan

1 cup dried cherries *or* cranberries
1 cup apple cider *or* juice, *divided*
2 pounds pork tenderloin, cut into 1/4-inch slices
1 teaspoon butter
1 teaspoon olive oil
1/2 teaspoon salt
1/8 teaspoon pepper
1/4 cup balsamic vinegar

In a small saucepan, bring cherries and 1/3 cup cider to a boil. Remove from the heat; cover and let stand.

In a large nonstick skillet over medium heat, cook pork in butter and oil for 3-4 minutes on each side or until juices run clear. Sprinkle with salt and pepper. Remove and keep warm. In the same skillet, bring the vinegar and remaining cider to a boil; cook until liquid is reduced by half. Stir in cherry mixture; heat through. Return pork to the pan; turn to coat. **Yield:** 6 servings.

Nutritional Analysis: 1 serving equals 305 calories, 7 g fat (2 g saturated fat), 91 mg cholesterol, 276 mg sodium, 24 g carbohydrate, 2 g fiber, 33 g protein.
Diabetic Exchanges: 4 lean meat, 1-1/2 fruit.

Pork Medallions With Sauteed Apples

(Pictured above right)

Low-carb

Prep/Total Time: 30 min.

This down-home entree doesn't have much fat, and it's wonderful with the apple slices and sauce.
—Clara Coulston, Washington Court House, Ohio

1 pork tenderloin (1 pound), cut into 1-inch slices
3/4 teaspoon dried thyme

1/2 teaspoon paprika
1/4 teaspoon salt
1/4 teaspoon pepper
1/4 cup sliced green onions
1 garlic clove, minced
1 tablespoon butter
2 medium apples, cut into wedges
2 teaspoons cornstarch
2/3 cup reduced-sodium chicken broth
1/4 cup unsweetened apple juice

Flatten pork to 1/2-in. thickness. Combine the thyme, paprika, salt and pepper; sprinkle over both sides of pork. Broil 3-4 in. from the heat for 3-4 minutes on each side or until meat juices run clear; keep warm.

In a nonstick skillet, saute onions and garlic in butter until tender. Add apples; cook and stir for 2 minutes or until apples are crisp-tender. Combine the cornstarch, broth and apple juice until smooth; stir into apple mixture. Bring to a boil; cook and stir for 1-2 minutes or until thickened. Serve with pork. **Yield:** 4 servings.

Nutritional Analysis: 3 ounces cooked pork with 1/2 cup apples equals 251 calories, 10 g fat (4 g saturated fat), 85 mg cholesterol, 335 mg sodium, 15 g carbohydrate, 3 g fiber, 25 g protein.
Diabetic Exchanges: 3 lean meat, 1 fruit.

Slash the Salt

HERE ARE a few easy ways to cut back on salt:
- Remove the salt shaker from the table.
- Use pepper instead of salt to season your meal.
- Cut back on fast food and processed convenience foods (frozen or boxed dinners, packaged mixes, canned soups and purchased pizza). Cook from scratch instead.

Plum Chutney with Pork

(Pictured above)

Prep: 30 min. + marinating **Cook:** 20 min.

With a hint of cardamom and citrus, this chutney is wonderful over herb-rubbed pork.
—Jacqueline Deibert, Klingerstown, Pennsylvania

  1 **garlic clove, peeled**
3/4 **teaspoon grated lemon peel**
1/2 **teaspoon salt**
1/2 **teaspoon ground cardamom**
1/2 **teaspoon ground ginger**
  1 **teaspoon canola oil**
  2 **pork tenderloins (1 pound *each*)**
CHUTNEY:
  1 **cup coarsely chopped onion**
  1 **tablespoon butter**
1/4 **teaspoon salt**
1/4 **teaspoon ground ginger**
1/8 **teaspoon ground cardamom**
1/2 **cup water**
1/3 **cup raisins**
1/4 **cup orange juice**
  2 **tablespoons sugar**
  1 **tablespoon white vinegar**
  2 **cups coarsely chopped plums**
  1 **cup coarsely chopped peeled peaches**

With a mortar and pestle, combine the garlic, lemon peel, salt, cardamom and ginger. Add oil; mix to form a paste. Spread over pork. Cover and refrigerate for 1 hour.

For chutney, in a saucepan, saute onion in butter for 2 minutes. Stir in the salt, ginger and cardamom. Cook and stir for 1-2 minutes or until onion is tender. Stir in the water, raisins, orange juice, sugar and vinegar. Bring to a boil. Reduce heat; cover and simmer for 10 minutes. Stir in plums; cover and simmer for 5-7 minutes or until plums are tender. Add peaches; simmer, uncovered, for 5 minutes or until peaches are tender.

Place tenderloins on a broiler pan coated with nonstick

cooking spray. Broil for 9 minutes. Turn; broil 9 minutes longer or until a meat thermometer reads 160°. Let stand for 5 minutes before slicing. Serve with chutney. **Yield:** 6 servings.

Nutritional Analysis: 4 ounces cooked pork with 1/2 cup chutney equals 323 calories, 9 g fat (3 g saturated fat), 89 mg cholesterol, 381 mg sodium, 30 g carbohydrate, 2 g fiber, 31 g protein.
Diabetic Exchanges: 4 lean meat, 1 fruit, 1/2 starch.

Pork Chop Packets

Low-carb

Prep/Total Time: 30 min.

A handful of ingredients is all you need for this no-fuss meal. It gives sauerkraut lovers a real treat.
—Holly Becker, Egg Harbor, New Jersey

  4 **bone-in center-cut pork loin chops (6 ounces *each*)**
1/2 **teaspoon salt-free lemon-pepper seasoning**
  1 **can (14 ounces) sauerkraut, rinsed and well drained**
1/4 **teaspoon caraway seeds**
1/4 **teaspoon ground nutmeg**

Sprinkle pork chops with lemon-pepper. Coat grill rack with nonstick cooking spray before starting the grill for indirect medium-hot heat.

Grill chops, uncovered, over direct heat area for 2-1/2 minutes on each side.

Place each chop on a double thickness of heavy-duty foil (about 12 in. square). Top with sauerkraut; sprinkle with caraway seeds and nutmeg. Fold foil around pork and seal tightly. Grill, covered, over indirect heat for 15-20 minutes or until a meat thermometer reads 160°. **Yield:** 4 servings.

Nutritional Analysis: 1 packet equals 157 calories, 6 g fat (2 g saturated fat), 58 mg cholesterol, 638 mg sodium, 3 g carbohydrate, 3 g fiber, 21 g protein.
Diabetic Exchanges: 3 lean meat, 1 vegetable.

Maple-Glazed Pork Tenderloin

Low-carb   Low-sodium

Prep/Total Time: 30 min.

My husband and I think this delicious entree tastes like a fancy restaurant dish.
—Colleen Mercier, Salmon Arm, British Columbia

  2 **pork tenderloins (3/4 pound *each*)**
3/4 **teaspoon rubbed sage**
  1 **teaspoon butter**
1/4 **cup maple syrup**
  3 **tablespoons cider vinegar**
1-3/4 **teaspoons Dijon mustard**

Rub pork with sage. In a large nonstick skillet coated with nonstick cooking spray, brown pork in butter. Place in a foil-lined roasting pan. Bake, uncovered, at 425° for 10 minutes.

Meanwhile, in a small bowl, whisk the syrup, vinegar and mustard until smooth. Pour into the same skillet. Bring to a boil; cook and stir for 1-2 minutes or until slightly thickened. Brush pork with 1 tablespoon of glaze; bake for 5 minutes. Brush with another tablespoon of glaze; bake 3-5 minutes longer or until a meat thermometer reads 160°. Brush with remaining glaze. Let stand for 5 minutes before slicing. **Yield:** 4 servings.

Nutritional Analysis: 5 ounces cooked pork equals 262 calories, 7 g fat (3 g saturated fat), 97 mg cholesterol, 134 mg sodium, 14 g carbohydrate, trace fiber, 34 g protein.
Diabetic Exchanges: 5 lean meat, 1 starch.

Slow-Cooked Sweet 'n' Sour Pork

Prep: 20 min. **Cook:** 6-1/2 hours

A co-worker gave me this recipe more than 20 years ago, and my family still enjoys this satisfying entree.
—Martha Nickerson, Hancock, Maine

2 tablespoons plus 1-1/2 teaspoons paprika
1-1/2 pounds boneless pork loin roast, cut
into 1-inch strips
1 tablespoon canola oil
1 can (20 ounces) unsweetened pineapple chunks
1 medium onion, chopped
1 medium green pepper, chopped
1/4 cup cider vinegar
3 tablespoons brown sugar
3 tablespoons reduced-sodium soy sauce
1 tablespoon Worcestershire sauce
1/2 teaspoon salt
2 tablespoons cornstarch
1/4 cup cold water
Hot cooked rice, optional

Place paprika in a large resealable plastic bag. Add pork, a few pieces at a time, and shake to coat. In a nonstick skillet, brown pork in oil in batches over medium-high heat. Transfer to a 3-qt. slow cooker.

Drain pineapple, reserving juice; refrigerate the pineapple. Add the pineapple juice, onion, green pepper, vinegar, brown sugar, soy sauce, Worcestershire sauce and salt to slow cooker; mix well. Cover and cook on low for 6-8 hours or until meat is tender. Combine cornstarch and water until smooth; stir into pork mixture. Add pineapple. Cover and cook 30 minutes longer or until sauce is thickened. Serve over rice if desired. **Yield:** 6 servings.

Nutritional Analysis: 1 cup pork mixture (calculated without rice) equals 312 calories, 10 g fat (3 g saturated fat), 73 mg cholesterol, 592 mg sodium, 28 g carbohydrate, 2 g fiber, 27 g protein.
Diabetic Exchanges: 3 lean meat, 1 fruit, 1/2 starch, 1/2 fat.

Ham-Stuffed Tomatoes

(Pictured above right)

Prep: 30 min. **Bake:** 15 min.

With a hearty filling and creamy sauce, these baked tomatoes appeal to even picky eaters.
—Delia Kennedy, Deer Park, Washington

8 large tomatoes
1 teaspoon celery salt

1/8 teaspoon garlic salt
2-1/2 cups soft bread crumbs
1 cup (4 ounces) shredded reduced-fat cheddar cheese
2/3 cup chopped fully cooked lean ham
1/3 cup minced chives
2 tablespoons plus 1/3 cup water, *divided*
2 teaspoons cornstarch
1 cup (8 ounces) reduced-fat sour cream
1/4 cup lemon juice
4 teaspoons sugar
1/2 teaspoon Worcestershire sauce

Cut a thin slice off the top of each tomato; remove core. Scoop out pulp and discard, leaving a 1/2-in. shell. Sprinkle celery salt and garlic salt inside tomatoes; invert onto paper towels to drain for 20 minutes.

In a bowl, combine the bread crumbs, cheese, ham, chives and 2 tablespoons water. Spoon into tomatoes. Place in a 13-in. x 9-in. x 2-in. baking dish coated with nonstick cooking spray.

In a small saucepan, combine cornstarch and sour cream until smooth. Stir in the lemon juice, sugar, Worcestershire sauce and remaining water. Cook and stir over low heat until heated through; drizzle over tomatoes. Bake, uncovered, at 400° for 15-20 minutes or until heated through. **Yield:** 8 servings.

Nutritional Analysis: 1 tomato with 2 tablespoons sauce equals 245 calories, 9 g fat (5 g saturated fat), 28 mg cholesterol, 737 mg sodium, 30 g carbohydrate, 3 g fiber, 15 g protein.
Diabetic Exchanges: 2 vegetable, 1 starch, 1 lean meat, 1 fat.

Hawaiian Pork Chops

(Pictured above)

Prep/Total Time: 30 min.

For a great meal when friends drop in unexpectedly, I recommend one of my husband's sweet-and-sour favorites. This tastes just like Hawaiian pizza, and I usually have all ingredients on hand.
—*Michelle Cavalier, Hampton, Virginia*

  4 boneless pork loin chops (3/4 inch thick and 4 ounces *each*)
1/4 teaspoon salt
1/4 teaspoon pepper
1/3 cup chopped green pepper
1/3 cup thinly sliced onion rings
  1 can (14-1/2 ounces) reduced-sodium beef broth
  1 can (8 ounces) unsweetened pineapple chunks, undrained
1/4 cup ketchup
  2 tablespoons brown sugar
  1 tablespoon cider vinegar
  2 tablespoons cornstarch
  3 tablespoons cold water
Hot cooked rice, optional

Sprinkle pork chops with salt and pepper. In a large nonstick skillet coated with nonstick cooking spray, cook the chops for 4-5 minutes on each side or until lightly browned. Remove and keep warm.

In the same skillet, saute green pepper and onion for 2 minutes or until almost tender. Stir in the broth, pineapple, ketchup, brown sugar and vinegar. Bring to a boil. Return pork to the pan. Reduce heat; cover and simmer for 6-10 minutes or until meat juices run clear.

Combine the cornstarch and water until smooth; stir into skillet. Bring to a boil; cook for 1-2 minutes or until thickened. Serve over rice if desired. **Yield:** 4 servings.

Nutritional Analysis: 1 pork chop with 3/4 cup sauce (calculated without rice) equals 250 calories, 7 g fat (2 g saturated fat), 57 mg cholesterol, 554 mg sodium, 24 g carbohydrate, 1 g fiber, 23 g protein.
Diabetic Exchanges: 3 lean meat, 1/2 starch, 1/2 fruit, 1/2 fat.

Glazed Rosemary Pork

(Pictured on page 141)

Low-carb

Prep/Total Time: 20 min.

With a honey-rosemary glaze, this delicately seasoned pork is as elegant as it is easy.
—*Barbara Sistrunk, Fultondale, Alabama*

  3 tablespoons honey
  2 teaspoons plus 1 tablespoon olive oil, *divided*
  1 tablespoon Dijon mustard
  1 tablespoon minced fresh rosemary *or* 1 teaspoon dried rosemary, crushed
  1 teaspoon balsamic vinegar
  4 garlic cloves, minced
1/8 teaspoon salt
1/8 teaspoon pepper
  2 pork tenderloins (1 pound *each*), cut into 1-inch slices

In a small bowl, combine the honey, 2 teaspoons oil, mustard, rosemary, vinegar, garlic, salt and pepper; set aside. Flatten pork slices to 1/2-in. thickness. In a large nonstick skillet, saute pork in remaining oil for 1 minute on each side or until browned.

Transfer to a 13-in. x 9-in. x 2-in. baking dish coated with nonstick cooking spray. Spoon honey mixture over meat. Bake, uncovered, at 350° for 10-12 minutes or until a meat thermometer reads 160°. **Yield:** 6 servings.

Nutritional Analysis: 4 ounces cooked pork equals 259 calories, 9 g fat (2 g saturated fat), 91 mg cholesterol, 174 mg sodium, 10 g carbohydrate, trace fiber, 32 g protein.
Diabetic Exchanges: 4 lean meat, 1/2 starch.

Teriyaki Pork Tenderloin

Low-carb

Prep: 10 min. + marinating **Bake:** 25 min.

When I need only one tenderloin, I marinate the other one in the freezer for later use.
—*Kristen Croke, Hanover, Massachusetts*

  5 tablespoons reduced-sodium soy sauce
  2 tablespoons olive oil
  2 garlic cloves, minced
  2 teaspoons brown sugar
  1 teaspoon ground ginger
  1 teaspoon coarsely ground pepper
  2 pork tenderloins (about 1 pound *each*)

In a large resealable plastic bag, combine the first six ingredients; add pork. Seal bag and turn to coat; refrigerate 8 hours or overnight.

Drain and discard marinade. Place meat in an 11-in. x 7-in. x 2-in. baking pan coated with nonstick cooking spray. Bake, uncovered, at 425° for 25-35 minutes or until a meat thermometer reads 160°. Transfer to a serving platter. Let stand for 5 minutes before slicing. Serve with pan drippings. **Yield:** 6 servings.

Nutritional Analysis: 4 ounces cooked pork equals 217 calories, 8 g fat (2 g saturated fat), 91 mg cholesterol, 317 mg sodium, 2 g carbohydrate, trace fiber, 33 g protein.
Diabetic Exchange: 4 lean meat.

Moist Herbed Pork Chops

(Pictured below)

Low-carb Low-sodium

Prep: 5 min. + marinating **Grill:** 10 min.

I found a pork recipe in a newspaper many years ago, but I lightened it up. This version is so tasty that I even use it for dinner parties.
—Linda Austin, Fayetteville, Arkansas

    1 cup unsweetened pineapple juice
  2/3 cup dry white wine *or* chicken broth
    2 tablespoons brown sugar
    1 garlic clove, minced
  1/2 teaspoon dried rosemary, crushed
    4 bone-in center-cut pork loin chops (3/4 inch
        thick and 7 ounces *each*)

In a bowl, combine the first five ingredients; stir until sugar is dissolved. Pour 1-1/2 cups into a large resealable plastic bag; add the pork chops. Seal bag and turn to coat; refrigerate for 8 hours or overnight. Cover and refrigerate remaining marinade for basting.

If grilling, coat grill rack with nonstick cooking spray before starting the grill. Drain and discard marinade. Grill pork, covered, over medium heat or broil 4-6 in. from the heat for 4-5 minutes on each side or until a meat thermometer reads 160°, basting frequently with reserved marinade. **Yield:** 4 servings.

Nutritional Analysis: 1 pork chop equals 237 calories, 9 g fat (3 g saturated fat), 87 mg cholesterol, 65 mg sodium, 5 g carbohydrate, trace fiber, 31 g protein.
Diabetic Exchange: 4 lean meat.

Apricot-Pecan Stuffed Pork Tenderloin

(Pictured above)

Prep: 20 min. **Bake:** 40 min.

This unique blend of sweet apricot and thyme is a pleasant surprise. My sister gave the recipe to me 15 years ago, and it's been a favorite ever since.
—Mary Ann Dell, Phoenixville, Pennsylvania

    1 pork tenderloin (1 pound)
  3/4 cup dried apricots
  4-1/2 teaspoons chopped pecans
    3 teaspoons dried thyme, *divided*
    1 garlic clove, minced
  1/4 teaspoon salt
  1/8 teaspoon pepper
  1-1/2 teaspoons molasses
    1 teaspoon canola oil
  1/2 cup reduced-sodium chicken broth

Cut tenderloin horizontally from the long side to within 1/2 in. of opposite side. Open meat so it lies flat; cover with plastic wrap. Flatten to 1/2-in. thickness; remove plastic.

In a food processor, combine the apricots, pecans, 2 teaspoons thyme, garlic, salt and pepper; cover and process until finely chopped. Add molasses and oil; process until blended. Spread apricot mixture over meat to within 3/4 in. of edges. Roll up, starting with a long side; tie with kitchen string at 1-1/2-in. intervals.

Line a roasting pan with heavy-duty foil. Place meat on a rack in prepared pan. Pour broth over meat and sprinkle with remaining thyme. Bake at 400° for 40-45 minutes or until juices run clear and a meat thermometer reads 160°. Let stand for 5-10 minutes before slicing. **Yield:** 4 servings.

Nutritional Analysis: 4 ounces stuffed cooked pork equals 233 calories, 7 g fat (2 g saturated fat), 63 mg cholesterol, 274 mg sodium, 19 g carbohydrate, 3 g fiber, 24 g protein.
Diabetic Exchanges: 3 lean meat, 1 fruit, 1/2 fat.

Mexican Pork Tenderloins

(Pictured above)

Prep: 10 min. **Grill:** 25 min.

We spoon the black bean salsa that accompanies this dish over grilled tenderloin slices. You can save on last-minute prep time by making the salsa and the cumin-coriander pork rub ahead.
—Maria Chiarino, Concord, North Carolina

2 tablespoons ground cumin
1 tablespoon ground coriander
1 teaspoon *each* onion powder, garlic powder, dried oregano and pepper
1/2 teaspoon salt
1 teaspoon olive oil
2 pork tenderloins (1 pound *each*)
BLACK BEAN SALSA:
1 can (15 ounces) black beans, rinsed and drained
2 plum tomatoes, diced
1 can (11 ounces) Mexicorn, drained
2 tablespoons chopped red onion
1 jalapeno pepper, seeded and chopped
2 tablespoons olive oil
2 tablespoons minced fresh cilantro
1 tablespoon lime juice
1/2 teaspoon ground cumin
1/8 teaspoon salt
1/8 teaspoon pepper

Combine the seasonings. Rub oil and seasoning mixture over the meat; let stand for 10 minutes.

Coat grill rack with nonstick cooking spray before starting the grill. Grill meat, covered, over medium heat for 10-12 minutes on each side or until a meat thermometer reads 160°. Remove from the grill. Cover and let stand for 5 min-utes before slicing.

For salsa, in a bowl, combine the beans, tomatoes, corn, onion and pepper. Whisk together the oil, cilantro, lime juice, cumin, salt and pepper. Drizzle over the bean mixture; toss to coat. Serve with tenderloin. **Yield:** 8 servings.

Editor's Note: When cutting or seeding hot peppers, use rubber or plastic gloves to protect your hands. Avoid touching your face.

Nutritional Analysis: 3 ounces cooked pork with 1/2 cup salsa equals 257 calories, 8 g fat (2 g saturated fat), 63 mg cholesterol, 550 mg sodium, 18 g carbohydrate, 5 g fiber, 27 g protein.
Diabetic Exchanges: 3 lean meat, 1 starch, 1/2 fat.

Orange Sauce over Pork Chops

Low-carb

Prep/Total Time: 30 min.

Tender pork chops are served with a thick, glossy citrus sauce that's swiftly heated in the microwave. This looks very attractive and is a snap to make.
—Marie Hoyer, Lewistown, Montana

1 tablespoon cornstarch
3 tablespoons orange juice
1 can (15 ounces) mandarin oranges
1 tablespoon sliced green onion
1 tablespoon chopped green pepper
1 tablespoon all-purpose flour
1/4 teaspoon salt
1/8 teaspoon pepper
4 boneless pork loin chops (4 ounces *each*)
2 teaspoons canola oil

In a microwave-safe bowl, combine cornstarch and orange juice until smooth. Drain oranges, reserving juice; set oranges aside. Stir reserved juice into cornstarch mixture; add onion and green pepper. Microwave, uncovered, on high for 2-3 minutes or until thickened, stirring twice. Stir in oranges; set aside and keep warm.

In a large resealable plastic bag, combine the flour, salt and pepper. Add pork chops, one at a time, and shake to coat. In a large nonstick skillet, cook pork in oil over medium heat until a meat thermometer reads 160°. Serve with orange sauce. **Yield:** 4 servings.

Editor's Note: This recipe was tested in a 1,100-watt microwave.

Nutritional Analysis: 1 pork chop with 1/3 cup sauce equals 225 calories, 8 g fat (2 g saturated fat), 57 mg cholesterol, 199 mg sodium, 15 g carbohydrate, 1 g fiber, 23 g protein.
Diabetic Exchanges: 3 lean meat, 1 fruit.

🍎 Milder Red Onions

I LOVE the flavor of red onions, but sometimes it's too sharp. Soaking the onion slices in ice water for an hour before serving and changing the water three or four times mellows the onion's bite while maintaining its color and flavor.
—Vance Werner, Jr., Franklin, Wisconsin

Fish & Seafood Fare

Fabulous fish dinners and sensational seafood entrees can add appetizing variety to any cook's healthy menu planning. You'll quickly get hooked on these from-the-sea favorites swimming in fantastic flavor!

Pepper Shrimp Scampi (page 157)

Chicken and Shrimp Satay

(Pictured above)

Low-carb

Prep: 20 min. + marinating **Cook:** 10 min.

I lightened up a recipe that I found in a cookbook, and these grilled kabobs were the tasty result. The scrumptious dipping sauce is always a hit.
—*Hannah Barringer, Loudon, Tennessee*

- 3/4 **pound uncooked medium shrimp, peeled and deveined**
- 3/4 **pound chicken tenderloin, cut into 1-inch cubes**
- 4 **green onions, chopped**
- 2 **garlic cloves, minced**
- 1 **tablespoon butter**
- 1 **tablespoon minced fresh parsley**
- 1/2 **cup white wine** *or* **chicken broth**
- 1 **tablespoon lemon juice**
- 1 **tablespoon lime juice**

SAUCE:
- 1/4 **cup chopped onion**
- 1 **tablespoon butter**
- 2/3 **cup reduced-sodium chicken broth**
- 1/4 **cup reduced-fat chunky peanut butter**
- 2-1/4 **teaspoons brown sugar**
- 3/4 **teaspoon lemon juice**
- 3/4 **teaspoon lime juice**
- 1/4 **teaspoon salt**
- 1/4 **teaspoon** *each* **dried basil, thyme and rosemary, crushed**
- 1/8 **teaspoon cayenne pepper**

Thread shrimp and chicken onto twelve soaked bamboo or metal skewers; place in a large shallow dish. In a skillet, saute the green onions and garlic in butter. Stir in the parsley, wine or broth, lemon juice and lime juice; cool slightly. Pour over the skewers and turn to coat. Cover and refrigerate for 4 hours, turning every 30 minutes.

In a skillet, saute onion in butter. Add remaining ingredients. Cook and stir until blended. Remove from the heat.

Coat grill rack with nonstick cooking spray; prepare for indirect heat. Drain and discard marinade. Grill skewers, covered, over indirect medium heat for 7-8 minutes; turn often. Brush with 1/4 cup sauce the last minute of grilling. Serve with remaining sauce. **Yield:** 6 servings.

Nutritional Analysis: 2 kabobs with 2 tablespoons sauce equals 190 calories, 7 g fat (3 g saturated fat), 126 mg cholesterol, 339 mg sodium, 7 g carbohydrate, 1 g fiber, 25 g protein.
Diabetic Exchanges: 3 very lean meat, 1 fat, 1/2 starch.

Open-Faced Crab Salad Sandwiches

(Pictured below)

Prep/Total Time: 25 min.

Everyone loved the crab salad my mother-in-law contributed to a family gathering, so I reduced the fat in her recipe to create this version. It can be served hot or cold…or even as a spread for crackers.
—*Lanie Kappe, Santa Ana, California*

- 1/2 **cup reduced-fat mayonnaise**
- 1/8 **teaspoon salt**
- 1/8 **teaspoon pepper**
- 2 **packages (8 ounces** *each***) imitation crabmeat, chopped**
- 1 **cup (4 ounces) shredded mozzarella cheese**
- 1/4 **cup chopped sweet red pepper**
- 1/4 **cup chopped green onions**
- 1/4 **cup chopped celery**
- 1 **loaf (8 ounces) unsliced French bread, halved lengthwise**

In a large bowl, combine the mayonnaise, salt and pepper. Stir in the crab, cheese, red pepper, onions and celery. Spoon over bread halves. Place on a baking sheet; broil 5 in. from the heat for 7-8 minutes or until lightly browned. Slice into 3-in. pieces. **Yield:** 8 servings.

Nutritional Analysis: 1 piece equals 236 calories, 9 g fat (3 g saturated fat), 44 mg cholesterol, 420 mg sodium, 24 g carbohydrate, 1 g fiber, 13 g protein.
Diabetic Exchanges: 1-1/2 starch, 1-1/2 fat, 1 lean meat.

Pepper Shrimp Scampi
(Pictured below and on page 155)

Prep/Total Time: 30 min.

Assorted vegetables, pasta and shrimp create this eye-catching combination that always wins raves.
—Linda Lashley, Redgranite, Wisconsin

   6 ounces uncooked angel hair pasta
   1 small zucchini, quartered and sliced
   1 medium onion, chopped
   1 medium green pepper, chopped
   1 small sweet red pepper, chopped
   4 garlic cloves, minced
1-1/2 pounds uncooked medium shrimp, peeled and deveined
   1/4 cup reduced-fat butter, cubed
   2 teaspoons dried oregano
   1 teaspoon dried basil
   2 tablespoons grated Parmesan cheese

Cook pasta according to package directions. Meanwhile, in a large nonstick skillet coated with nonstick cooking spray, saute the zucchini, onion, peppers and garlic until tender.

Add the shrimp; cook and stir for 2-4 minutes or until shrimp turn pink. Stir in the butter, oregano and basil. Drain pasta; add to skillet and toss to coat. Sprinkle with Parmesan cheese. **Yield:** 6 servings.

Editor's Note: This recipe was tested with Land O' Lakes light stick butter.

Nutritional Analysis: 1-1/3 cups equals 258 calories, 6 g fat (3 g saturated fat), 183 mg cholesterol, 275 mg sodium, 27 g carbohydrate, 2 g fiber, 24 g protein.
Diabetic Exchanges: 3 very lean meat, 1-1/2 starch, 1 vegetable, 1 fat.

Stir-Fried Scallops and Asparagus
(Pictured above)

Prep/Total Time: 25 min.

Served over quick-cooking ramen noodles, this stir-fry is perfect for busy families on hurried weeknights. It comes together in about half an hour.
—Barbara Schindler, Napoleon, Ohio

   1 package (3 ounces) chicken ramen noodles
   1 pound fresh asparagus, trimmed and cut into 1-inch pieces
   1 garlic clove, minced
   1 tablespoon olive oil
   1 medium sweet red pepper, julienned
   3 green onions, thinly sliced
   1 pound sea scallops, halved horizontally
   1 tablespoon lime juice
   2 tablespoons reduced-sodium soy sauce
   1 teaspoon sesame oil
   1 teaspoon hot pepper sauce

Discard seasoning package from ramen noodles or save for another use. Cook ramen noodles according to package directions; keep warm.

Meanwhile, in a nonstick skillet or wok, cook and stir asparagus and garlic in oil for 2 minutes. Add red pepper; cook and stir 1 minute longer. Add green onions; cook and stir 2 minutes longer. Stir in scallops. Cook for 3 minutes or until scallops are firm and opaque.

Combine the lime juice, soy sauce, sesame oil and hot pepper sauce; stir into skillet. Serve over ramen noodles. **Yield:** 4 servings.

Nutritional Analysis: 1 cup scallop mixture and 1/4 cup noodles equals 269 calories, 9 g fat (3 g saturated fat), 37 mg cholesterol, 578 mg sodium, 22 g carbohydrate, 2 g fiber, 24 g protein.
Diabetic Exchanges: 3 very lean meat, 1 starch, 1 vegetable, 1 fat.

Mediterranean Shrimp 'n' Pasta

(Pictured at left)

Prep: 15 min. **Cook:** 20 min.

Sun-dried tomatoes and curry take center stage in this dish that's loaded with tender shrimp and pasta.
—*Shirley Kunde, Rhinelander, Wisconsin*

  1 cup boiling water
1/2 cup dry-pack sun-dried tomatoes, chopped
  6 ounces uncooked fettuccine
  1 can (8 ounces) tomato sauce
  2 tablespoons clam juice
  2 tablespoons unsweetened apple juice
  1 teaspoon curry powder
1/4 teaspoon pepper
  1 pound fresh asparagus, trimmed and cut
     into 1-inch pieces
  1 tablespoon olive oil
1/2 cup thinly sliced green onions
  2 garlic cloves, minced
  1 pound uncooked medium shrimp, peeled and
     deveined

In a small bowl, pour boiling water over sun-dried tomatoes; let stand for 2 minutes. Drain and set aside. Cook fettuccine according to package directions.

Meanwhile, in a small bowl, combine the tomato sauce, clam juice, apple juice, curry powder and pepper; set aside. In a large nonstick skillet coated with nonstick cooking spray, cook asparagus in oil for 2 minutes. Add green onions and garlic; cook and stir 2 minutes longer. Stir in shrimp. Cook and stir 3 minutes longer or until shrimp turn pink. Stir in tomato mixture and sun-dried tomatoes; heat through. Drain fettuccine and add to skillet; heat through. **Yield:** 4 servings.

Nutritional Analysis: 1-1/2 cups equals 368 calories, 6 g fat (1 g saturated fat), 173 mg cholesterol, 702 mg sodium, 46 g carbohydrate, 5 g fiber, 32 g protein.

Grilled Halibut With Mustard Dill Sauce

(Pictured at left)

Low-carb

Prep/Total Time: 20 min.

Moist fish steaks are draped with a thick and creamy sauce in this flavorful recipe.
—*Laura Perry, Exton, Pennsylvania*

1/3 cup fat-free plain yogurt
  2 tablespoons reduced-fat mayonnaise
  2 tablespoons snipped fresh dill *or* 2 teaspoons
     dill weed
  2 teaspoons Dijon mustard
  4 halibut steaks (6 ounces *each*)
1/4 teaspoon salt
1/8 teaspoon pepper

In a small bowl, combine the yogurt, mayonnaise, dill and mustard; cover and refrigerate.

Sprinkle halibut with salt and pepper. Coat grill rack with nonstick cooking spray before starting the grill. Grill halibut, covered, over medium heat for 4-6 minutes on each side or until fish flakes easily with a fork. Serve sauce with halibut. **Yield:** 4 servings.

Nutritional Analysis: 6 ounces halibut with 2 tablespoons sauce equals 224 calories, 7 g fat (1 g saturated fat), 57 mg cholesterol, 447 mg sodium, 3 g carbohydrate, trace fiber, 36 g protein.
Diabetic Exchanges: 5 lean meat, 1 fat.

Salmon and Asparagus in Phyllo

Prep: 30 min. **Bake:** 15 min.

Slice open these golden phyllo bundles from our Test Kitchen, and you'll find salmon fillets and tender asparagus in a creamy filling.

  4 cups water
12 asparagus spears, trimmed and halved
     widthwise
  4 ounces reduced-fat cream cheese
  2 tablespoons egg substitute
  1 tablespoon finely chopped onion
  1 teaspoon dried tarragon
1/4 teaspoon salt
1/4 teaspoon pepper
  8 sheets phyllo dough (14 inches x 9 inches)
  4 salmon fillets (4 ounces *each*)

In a large saucepan, bring water to a boil; add asparagus. Cook for 3 minutes or until crisp-tender. Drain and rinse under cold water; pat dry and set aside.

In a small bowl, combine the cream cheese, egg substitute, onion, tarragon, salt and pepper; set aside. Place one sheet of phyllo dough on a work surface with the short side at the bottom; spray with nonstick cooking spray. Repeat with one more sheet of phyllo. (Keep remaining phyllo covered with plastic wrap and a damp towel to prevent drying.)

Spread 2 rounded tablespoons of the cream cheese mixture over the bottom third of the rectangle to make a base for a salmon fillet. Top with six asparagus halves and one salmon fillet. Fold sides and bottom edge over fillet and roll up to enclose salmon; trim end of phyllo if necessary. Spray outer layers of phyllo with nonstick cooking spray.

Place seam side down on an ungreased baking sheet. Repeat with remaining ingredients. Bake at 400° for 15-20 minutes or until golden brown. **Yield:** 4 servings.

Nutritional Analysis: 1 serving equals 355 calories, 19 g fat (7 g saturated fat), 87 mg cholesterol, 445 mg sodium, 16 g carbohydrate, 1 g fiber, 30 g protein.
Diabetic Exchanges: 3 lean meat, 2-1/2 fat, 1 starch.

"Smoked" Salmon

TO BOOST the flavor of salmon, I often reach for a bottle of Liquid Smoke instead of the salt shaker. I just rub the Liquid Smoke onto the salmon fillets before cooking them. It's delicious!
—*Marie Pitcairn, Medford, Oregon*

Catfish with Spiced Fruit Salsa

(Pictured above)

Prep/Total Time: 30 min.

I frequently serve fish fillets because they're good for my family's health and easy to prepare. I incorporated the homemade salsa into this meal to help us meet our daily fruit quotas, and everyone loves it.
—Karen Martis, Merrillville, Indiana

- 4 catfish fillets (6 ounces *each*)
- 2 teaspoons canola oil
- 2 teaspoons ground coriander
- 1 teaspoon ground cumin
- 1/4 teaspoon ground cinnamon
- 1/4 teaspoon cayenne pepper
- 3/4 teaspoon salt
- 1/2 cup dried tropical fruit
- 1/3 cup unsweetened apple juice
- 1 tablespoon cider vinegar
- 1 tablespoon 100% apricot spreadable fruit
- 2 tablespoons minced fresh parsley

Rub both sides of fillets with oil. Combine the coriander, cumin, cinnamon and cayenne; set aside 1/2 teaspoon. Add salt to remaining spice mixture; rub over both sides of fillets.

In a saucepan, combine the tropical fruit, apple juice, vinegar and reserved spice mixture. Bring to a boil; stir in spreadable fruit. Remove from the heat; let stand for 5 minutes.

In a large nonstick skillet coated with nonstick cooking spray, cook fillets over medium-high heat for 3-4 minutes on each side or until fish flakes easily with a fork. Serve with fruit salsa; sprinkle with parsley. **Yield:** 4 servings.

Nutritional Analysis: 1 fillet with 2 tablespoons salsa equals 349 calories, 16 g fat (4 g saturated fat), 80 mg cholesterol, 561 mg sodium, 22 g carbohydrate, 2 g fiber, 27 g protein.
Diabetic Exchanges: 4 lean meat, 1 fruit, 1 fat, 1/2 starch.

Peking Shrimp

(Pictured below)

Prep/Total Time: 25 min.

In the summer, we spend as much time as possible at our vacation home in a beach town. I prepare lots of seafood because it's so fresh and readily available there. This entree is always a winner.
—Janet Edwards, Beaverton, Oregon

- 1 tablespoon cornstarch
- 1/4 cup water
- 1/4 cup corn syrup
- 2 tablespoons reduced-sodium soy sauce
- 2 tablespoons sherry *or* chicken broth
- 1 garlic clove, minced
- 1/4 teaspoon ground ginger
- 1 small green pepper, cut into 1-inch pieces
- 2 tablespoons canola oil
- 1 pound uncooked medium shrimp, peeled and deveined
- 1 medium tomato, cut into wedges
Hot cooked rice, optional

In a small bowl, combine cornstarch and water until smooth. Stir in the corn syrup, soy sauce, sherry or broth, garlic and ginger; set aside.

In a nonstick skillet or wok, stir-fry green pepper in hot oil for 3 minutes. Add shrimp; stir-fry 3 minutes longer or until shrimp turn pink. Stir cornstarch mixture and add to the pan. Bring to a boil; cook and stir for 2 minutes or until sauce is thickened. Add tomato; heat through. Serve with rice if desired. **Yield:** 4 servings.

Nutritional Analysis: 3/4 cup shrimp mixture (calculated without rice) equals 237 calories, 8 g fat (1 g saturated fat), 168 mg cholesterol, 532 mg sodium, 21 g carbohydrate, 1 g fiber, 19 g protein.
Diabetic Exchanges: 2 lean meat, 1-1/2 fat, 1 starch, 1 vegetable.

Teriyaki Salmon Burgers

(Pictured below)

Prep: 10 min. + chilling **Grill:** 10 min.

My teenage son absolutely loves these burgers.
We also like to top the patties with melted cheese.
—*Resia Ayres, Lexington, Kentucky*

1/4 cup unsweetened pineapple juice
  2 tablespoons brown sugar
  2 tablespoons reduced-sodium teriyaki sauce
1/4 teaspoon salt
1/4 teaspoon garlic pepper blend
  1 salmon fillet (1 pound), skin removed and cubed
1/2 cup soft bread crumbs
  6 teaspoons fat-free mayonnaise
  4 hamburger buns, split
  4 lettuce leaves
  4 tomato slices
  1 red onion slice, separated into rings

In a large resealable plastic bag, combine the first five ingredients; add salmon. Seal bag and turn to coat; refrigerate for 1 hour.

Drain and discard marinade. Place salmon in a food processor. Add bread crumbs; cover and process until blended. Shape into four patties; cover and refrigerate for 1 hour.

Coat grill rack with nonstick cooking spray before starting the grill. Grill patties, uncovered, over medium heat for 6-7 minutes. Turn and grill 3-5 minutes longer or until a meat thermometer reads 140°. Spread 1-1/2 teaspoons mayonnaise on each bun. Serve patties on buns with lettuce, tomato and onion. **Yield:** 4 servings.

Nutritional Analysis: 1 burger equals 383 calories, 15 g fat (3 g saturated fat), 68 mg cholesterol, 565 mg sodium, 33 g carbohydrate, 2 g fiber, 27 g protein.
Diabetic Exchanges: 3 lean meat, 2 starch, 1 fat.

Easy Crab Cakes

(Pictured above)

Prep/Total Time: 25 min.

Canned crabmeat makes these delicate patties simple
enough for busy weeknight dinners. For a change of
pace, try forming the crab mixture into four thick
patties instead of eight cakes.
—*Charlene Spelock, Apollo, Pennsylvania*

  2 cans (6 ounces *each*) crabmeat, drained, flaked and cartilage removed
  1 cup seasoned bread crumbs, *divided*
  1 egg, beaten
1/4 cup finely chopped green onions
1/4 cup finely chopped sweet red pepper
1/4 cup reduced-fat mayonnaise
  1 tablespoon lemon juice
1/2 teaspoon garlic powder
1/8 teaspoon cayenne pepper
  1 tablespoon butter

In a large bowl, combine the crab, 1/3 cup bread crumbs, egg, onions, red pepper, mayonnaise, lemon juice, garlic powder and cayenne.

Divide mixture into eight portions; shape into 2-in. balls. Roll in remaining bread crumbs. Flatten to 1/2-in. thickness. In a large nonstick skillet, cook crab cakes in butter for 3-4 minutes on each side or until golden brown. **Yield:** 4 servings.

Nutritional Analysis: 2 crab cakes equals 295 calories, 12 g fat (3 g saturated fat), 142 mg cholesterol, 879 mg sodium, 23 g carbohydrate, 1 g fiber, 23 g protein.
Diabetic Exchanges: 3 very lean meat, 1-1/2 starch, 1-1/2 fat.

Flounder Zucchini Bundles

(Pictured above)

Low-carb   Low-fat

Prep/Total Time: 30 min.

A hint of lemon accents this colorful meal-in-one. My husband isn't a fish eater, but he enjoys this recipe.
—*Isabelle Rooney, Summerville, South Carolina*

8 flounder fillets (3 ounces *each*)
1/4 teaspoon lemon-pepper seasoning
1 medium lemon, thinly sliced
1 medium zucchini, cut into 1/4-inch slices
12 cherry tomatoes, halved
1/4 teaspoon dill weed
1/4 teaspoon dried basil

For each bundle, place two fillets on a double thickness of heavy-duty foil (18 in. x 15 in.); sprinkle with lemon-pepper. Top with lemon slices, zucchini and tomatoes. Sprinkle with dill and basil.

Fold foil around fish and seal tightly. Place on a baking sheet. Bake at 425° for 15-20 minutes or until fish flakes easily with a fork. **Yield:** 4 servings.

Nutritional Analysis: 1 bundle equals 159 calories, 2 g fat (trace saturated fat), 80 mg cholesterol, 160 mg sodium, 5 g carbohydrate, 1 g fiber, 29 g protein.
Diabetic Exchanges: 4 very lean meat, 1 vegetable.

Seafood Pesto Pasta

Prep: 25 min. **Cook:** 15 min.

Pesto turns shrimp and scallops into superstars in this fresh-flavored entree. The recipe is from my dad.
—*Marnie Franze, Battle Lake, Minnesota*

1/4 cup plus 1 tablespoon olive oil, *divided*
1 cup loosely packed fresh basil leaves
1 cup loosely packed fresh oregano leaves
2 tablespoons minced fresh parsley
4 to 6 garlic cloves, *divided*
12 ounces uncooked linguine

2 green onions, chopped
1 tablespoon butter
1/2 pound uncooked medium shrimp, peeled and deveined
1/4 cup white wine *or* chicken broth
1 tablespoon lemon juice
1/4 teaspoon cayenne pepper
1/2 pound fresh sea scallops
1/2 cup grated Parmesan cheese

For pesto, place 1/4 cup oil, basil, oregano, parsley and one garlic clove in a blender or food processor. Cover and process until smooth; set aside. Mince the remaining garlic. Cook pasta according to package directions.

Meanwhile, in a nonstick skillet, saute onions and minced garlic in butter and remaining oil until tender. Add the shrimp, wine or broth, lemon juice and cayenne; saute for 2 minutes. Add scallops; saute for 2 minutes or until shrimp turn pink and scallops are firm and opaque. Drain pasta; toss with pesto and Parmesan. Top with seafood mixture. **Yield:** 8 servings.

Nutritional Analysis: 1 cup equals 306 calories, 14 g fat (3 g saturated fat), 61 mg cholesterol, 297 mg sodium, 28 g carbohydrate, 2 g fiber, 18 g protein.
Diabetic Exchanges: 2 lean meat, 1-1/2 starch, 1-1/2 fat.

Cod with Sweet Peppers

Low-carb   Low-fat

Prep/Total Time: 25 min.

This quick and delicious dish is a family favorite. I like to use three or four different colors of peppers.
—*Judy Grebetz, Racine, Wisconsin*

1 medium onion, halved and sliced
1 cup reduced-sodium chicken broth
1 tablespoon lemon juice
3 garlic cloves, minced
1-1/2 teaspoons dried oregano
1/2 teaspoon grated lemon peel
1/4 teaspoon salt
4 cod fillets (6 ounces *each*)
3/4 cup julienned green pepper
3/4 cup julienned sweet red pepper
2-1/2 teaspoons cornstarch
1 tablespoon cold water
1 medium lemon, halved and sliced

In a large nonstick skillet, combine the first seven ingredients. Bring to a boil. Reduce heat; cover and simmer for 6-8 minutes or until onion is tender.

Arrange fish and peppers over onion mixture. Cover and simmer for 6-9 minutes or until fish flakes easily with a fork and peppers are tender. Remove fish and vegetables and keep warm.

Combine cornstarch and water until smooth; gradually stir into pan juices. Bring to a boil; cook and stir for 2 minutes or until thickened. Spoon over fish and vegetables. Serve with lemon. **Yield:** 4 servings.

Nutritional Analysis: 1 fish fillet with 1/3 cup vegetable mixture and 1/4 cup sauce equals 168 calories, 1 g fat (trace saturated fat), 65 mg cholesterol, 398 mg sodium, 10 g carbohydrate, 2 g fiber, 29 g protein.
Diabetic Exchanges: 4 very lean meat, 1 vegetable.

Snapper with Spicy Pineapple Glaze

(Pictured above)

Prep/Total Time: 30 min.

Ginger and cayenne bring spice to this tangy treatment for red snapper fillets from our Test Kitchen. Sweet pineapple preserves round out the delectable combination of flavors.

1/2 cup pineapple preserves
2 tablespoons rice wine vinegar
2 teaspoons minced fresh gingerroot
2 garlic cloves, minced
3/4 teaspoon salt, *divided*
1/4 teaspoon cayenne pepper
4 fresh *or* frozen red snapper *or* orange roughy fillets (6 ounces *each*), thawed
3 teaspoons olive oil

For glaze, in a small bowl, combine the preserves, vinegar, ginger, garlic, 1/2 teaspoon salt and cayenne; set aside.

Place fillets on a broiler pan coated with nonstick cooking spray. Brush both sides of fillets with oil; sprinkle with remaining salt.

Broil 4-6 in. from the heat for 5 minutes. Brush with half of the glaze. Broil 5-7 minutes longer or until fish flakes easily with a fork. Brush with remaining glaze. **Yield:** 4 servings.

Nutritional Analysis: 1 fillet equals 304 calories, 6 g fat (1 g saturated fat), 63 mg cholesterol, 552 mg sodium, 27 g carbohydrate, trace fiber, 35 g protein.
Diabetic Exchanges: 5 very lean meat, 2 fruit.

Shrimp 'n' Veggie Pizza

(Pictured above)

Prep/Total Time: 30 min.

*Just half an hour is all it takes to make this colorful pizza.
It's a great way to use up leftover veggies.*
—*Terri Webber, Miami, Florida*

1/2 cup sliced onion
1/2 cup sliced fresh mushrooms
  3 asparagus spears, trimmed and cut into 1-inch
    pieces
  1 garlic clove, minced
  2 teaspoons olive oil
  4 ounces uncooked medium shrimp, peeled,
    deveined and halved lengthwise
  1 prebaked thin Italian bread shell crust (10
    ounces)
1/2 cup pizza sauce
  1 cup (4 ounces) shredded part-skim mozzarella
    cheese

In a nonstick skillet, saute vegetables and garlic in oil until
almost tender. Add shrimp; cook until shrimp turn pink.
Remove from heat. Place crust on baking sheet. Spread
with sauce. Top with shrimp mixture. Sprinkle with cheese.
Bake at 450° for 8-10 minutes or until cheese is melted.
Yield: 6 slices.

*Nutritional Analysis: 1 slice equals 215 calories, 7 g fat (2 g
saturated fat), 38 mg cholesterol, 426 mg sodium, 24 g carbohydrate, 1 g fiber, 13 g protein.*
Diabetic Exchanges: 1-1/2 starch, 1 lean meat, 1 fat.

Favorite Recipe Made Lighter

NOT ONLY do casseroles offer meal-in-one convenience, but they're practically guaranteed to satisfy that craving for comfort food we all experience. And Marie Roberts' Shrimp Rice Casserole is no exception.

"Served with a salad and wheat rolls, this dish makes a fine dinner," she shares from Lake Charles, Louisiana. "But I'm concerned about its nutritional values. I'd appreciate it if you could make it over for me."

As is often the case with casserole recipes, Marie's called for plenty of butter and cheese. Our staff reduced both of those ingredients and replaced the full-fat cheese with a lighter variety.

To slash the sodium, they eliminated the canned mushroom soup and created a simple sauce using fresh mushrooms, fat-free milk and a little flour. This decreased the total amount of sodium by 711 milligrams, while adding vitamins and minerals. And to boost the nutrients in Marie's casserole, they used brown rice instead of long grain rice for extra fiber.

Makeover Shrimp Rice Casserole offers all the creamy goodness of Marie's original—but it has only half the calories and sodium and 76% less fat.

Shrimp Rice Casserole

Prep: 30 min. **Bake:** 35 min.

- 1 large green pepper, chopped
- 1 medium onion, chopped
- 1/2 cup butter
- 1 pound uncooked medium shrimp, peeled and deveined
- 1/2 teaspoon salt
- 1/4 teaspoon cayenne pepper
- 3 cups cooked long grain rice

- 1 can (10-3/4 ounces) condensed cream of mushroom soup, undiluted
- 2 cups (8 ounces) shredded cheddar cheese, *divided*

In a large skillet, saute the green pepper and onion in butter until tender. Add the shrimp, salt and cayenne; cook and stir for 2-3 minutes or until shrimp turn pink. Add the rice, soup and 1 cup cheese; stir until combined.

Pour into a greased 1-1/2-qt. baking dish. Cover and bake at 325° for 30 minutes. Uncover; sprinkle with remaining cheese. Bake 5 minutes longer or until heated through and cheese is melted. **Yield:** 6 servings.

Nutritional Analysis: 1 cup equals 643 calories, 42 g fat (28 g saturated fat), 242 mg cholesterol, 1,332 mg sodium, 33 g carbohydrate, 2 g fiber, 33 g protein.

Makeover
Shrimp Rice Casserole

(Pictured below left)

Prep: 40 min. **Bake:** 30 min.

- 1 pound uncooked medium shrimp, peeled and deveined
- 2 tablespoons butter, *divided*
- 12 ounces fresh mushrooms, sliced
- 1 large green pepper, chopped
- 1 medium onion, chopped
- 3 tablespoons all-purpose flour
- 3/4 teaspoon salt
- 1/8 teaspoon cayenne pepper
- 1-1/3 cups fat-free milk
- 3 cups cooked brown rice
- 1 cup (4 ounces) shredded reduced-fat cheddar cheese, *divided*

In a large nonstick skillet, saute shrimp in 1 tablespoon butter for 2-3 minutes or until shrimp turn pink. Remove and set aside.

In the same skillet, saute mushrooms, green pepper and onion in remaining butter until tender. Stir in flour, salt and cayenne. Gradually add milk until blended. Bring to a boil; cook and stir for 2 minutes or until thickened. Add rice, 1/2 cup cheese and shrimp; stir until combined.

Pour into a 1-1/2-qt. baking dish coated with nonstick cooking spray. Cover and bake at 325° for 30-35 minutes or until heated through. Sprinkle with remaining cheese; cover and let stand for 5 minutes or until cheese is melted. **Yield:** 6 servings.

Nutritional Analysis: 1 cup equals 318 calories, 10 g fat (6 g saturated fat), 137 mg cholesterol, 621 mg sodium, 35 g carbohydrate, 4 g fiber, 24 g protein.
Diabetic Exchanges: 2 starch, 2 very lean meat, 1-1/2 fat, 1 vegetable.

Halibut with Crab Sauce

(Pictured at right)

Low-carb

Prep/Total Time: 30 min.

A thick and creamy crab sauce tops halibut fillets in this delightful dish. It's one of our favorite fish recipes.
—Shirley West, Lynnwood, Washington

    4 halibut fillets (6 ounces *each*)
1/4 teaspoon salt
1/4 teaspoon pepper
    2 teaspoons plus 2 tablespoons butter, *divided*
    3 tablespoons all-purpose flour
3/4 cup reduced-sodium chicken broth
1/3 cup fat-free milk
1/2 cup crabmeat, drained, flaked and cartilage removed
1/4 cup shredded Swiss cheese

Place each fillet in an individual broiler-proof serving dish. Sprinkle with salt and pepper. Melt 2 teaspoons butter; drizzle over fillets. Bake, uncovered, at 350° for 15-20 minutes or until fish flakes easily with a fork.

Meanwhile, in a small saucepan coated with nonstick cooking spray, melt remaining butter. Stir in flour until smooth; gradually stir in the broth and milk. Bring to a boil; cook and stir for 1-2 minutes or until thickened. Stir in crab. Remove from the heat; stir in cheese until melted. Pour over halibut. Broil 4-6 in. from the heat for 3-4 minutes or until lightly browned. **Yield:** 4 servings.

Nutritional Analysis: *1 fillet with 1/3 cup sauce equals 328 calories, 14 g fat (7 g saturated fat), 96 mg cholesterol, 517 mg sodium, 6 g carbohydrate, trace fiber, 43 g protein.*
Diabetic Exchanges: *6 very lean meat, 2 fat.*

Shrimp Stir-Fry

(Pictured at right)

Prep/Total Time: 30 min.

I love shrimp, and I'm always looking for new ways to fix it. This medley features peanuts and a hint of ginger.
—Josie Smith, Winamac, Indiana

    2 tablespoons cornstarch
3/4 cup cold water
    2 tablespoons reduced-sodium soy sauce
    1 teaspoon garlic powder
1/2 teaspoon ground ginger
    2 cups fresh broccoli florets
    2 tablespoons olive oil
    1 medium sweet red pepper, julienned
    3 green onions, chopped
    1 pound uncooked medium shrimp, peeled and deveined
    1 cup frozen Oriental vegetables, thawed
    3 garlic cloves, minced
1/4 cup chopped peanuts

In a small bowl, combine cornstarch and water until smooth. Stir in the soy sauce, garlic powder and ginger; set aside.

In a large nonstick skillet or wok, stir-fry broccoli in oil for 2 minutes. Add red pepper and onions; stir-fry for 2-3 minutes or until vegetables are crisp-tender. Add the shrimp, Oriental vegetables and garlic; cook 3 minutes longer.

Stir cornstarch mixture and stir into shrimp mixture. Add the peanuts. Bring to a boil; cook and stir for 2 minutes or until thickened. **Yield:** 4 servings.

Nutritional Analysis: *1 cup equals 273 calories, 13 g fat (2 g saturated fat), 129 mg cholesterol, 593 mg sodium, 18 g carbohydrate, 4 g fiber, 23 g protein.*
Diabetic Exchanges: *3 lean meat, 2 vegetable, 1 fat, 1/2 starch.*

Shrimp and Grits

Prep/Total Time: 30 min.

I serve a mixture of shrimp and vegetables alongside dressed-up grits for a deliciously sweet and spicy meal.
—Judith King, Madisonville, Tennessee

    2 cups water
    1 cup fat-free half-and-half
    4 teaspoons butter, *divided*
1/4 teaspoon salt
1/4 teaspoon pepper
3/4 cup quick-cooking grits
    1 medium onion, chopped
    3 celery ribs, chopped
    1 pound uncooked medium shrimp, peeled and deveined
1/4 cup ketchup
    1 tablespoon honey
    2 teaspoons lemon juice
1/2 to 1 teaspoon hot pepper sauce
    1 cup (4 ounces) shredded reduced-fat cheddar cheese

In a small saucepan, combine the water, half-and-half, 2 teaspoons butter, salt and pepper. Bring to a boil. Stir in grits. Reduce heat; simmer, uncovered, for 5-7 minutes or until grits are thickened.

Meanwhile, in a large skillet, saute the onion and celery in remaining butter until tender. Add the shrimp; cook and stir until shrimp turn pink. Combine the ketchup, honey, lemon juice and hot pepper sauce; stir into skillet. Stir cheese into grits. Serve with shrimp mixture. **Yield:** 4 servings.

Nutritional Analysis: *1/2 cup shrimp mixture with 3/4 cup grits equals 388 calories, 11 g fat (7 g saturated fat), 198 mg cholesterol, 823 mg sodium, 42 g carbohydrate, 3 g fiber, 30 g protein.*
Diabetic Exchanges: *3 starch, 3 very lean meat, 2 fat.*

Spaghetti with Creamy White Clam Sauce

Low-fat

Prep/Total Time: 20 min.

A handful of ingredients is all you need for this must-try main dish. I often make it when time is short.
—Linda Evancoe-Coble, Leola, Pennsylvania

  1 can (15 ounces) ready-to-serve reduced-fat New England clam chowder
  1 can (6-1/2 ounces) chopped clams, undrained
  1 tablespoon minced fresh parsley
  1/4 teaspoon garlic powder
  1/8 teaspoon salt
Dash white pepper
  8 ounces uncooked spaghetti

In a saucepan, combine the first six ingredients; bring to a boil. Reduce heat; cook and stir for 5 minutes or until slightly thickened. Meanwhile, cook spaghetti according to package directions; drain. Pour sauce over spaghetti. **Yield:** 4 servings.

Nutritional Analysis: *1 cup spaghetti with 1/2 cup sauce equals 342 calories, 3 g fat (1 g saturated fat), 35 mg cholesterol, 330 mg sodium, 57 g carbohydrate, 4 g fiber, 21 g protein.*
Diabetic Exchanges: *3-1/2 starch, 2 very lean meat.*

Grouper with Sweet Peppers

(Pictured above)

Low-carb

Prep: 15 min. + marinating **Cook:** 25 min.

This low-fat entree is the greatest. It's so colorful and looks as delicious as it tastes.
—Patricia Sweat, Saulsbury, Tennessee

1/4 cup reduced-sodium soy sauce
2 tablespoons lemon juice
2 pounds grouper *or* red snapper fillets
1 medium onion, cut into 6 wedges and separated
3 teaspoons olive oil, *divided*
1 medium green pepper, sliced into thin rings
1 medium sweet red pepper, sliced into thin rings
1 medium sweet yellow pepper, sliced into thin rings
1 can (14-1/2 ounces) diced tomatoes, drained

In a small bowl, combine soy sauce and lemon juice. Pour 1/4 cup marinade in a resealable plastic bag; add fish. Seal bag and turn to coat; refrigerate for 20 minutes. Cover and refrigerate remaining marinade.

Meanwhile, in a large nonstick skillet, cook onion in 1 teaspoon oil for 1 minute. Stir in peppers; cook and stir for about 5 minutes longer. Stir in tomatoes; cook 1-2 minutes longer or until tomatoes are heated through and vegetables are crisp-tender. Remove from the heat; keep warm.

Drain and discard marinade from fish. In a large nonstick skillet coated with nonstick cooking spray, cook fish in remaining oil for about 8 minutes on each side or until fish flakes easily with a fork. Arrange two-thirds of pepper mixture on a serving platter; top with fish. Top with remaining pepper mixture and drizzle with reserved marinade. Serve immediately. **Yield:** 6 servings.

Nutritional Analysis: *5 ounces cooked fish with 3/4 cup vegetables equals 202 calories, 4 g fat (1 g saturated fat), 56 mg cholesterol, 457 mg sodium, 10 g carbohydrate, 2 g fiber, 31 g protein.*
Diabetic Exchanges: *4 very lean meat, 2 vegetable, 1/2 fat.*

Stuffed Mountain Trout

Low-carb

Prep: 15 min. **Bake:** 25 min.

You can substitute any whole fish in this recipe, but I like it best when it's made with fresh-caught trout from our local mountain streams.
—Loretta Walters, Ogden, Utah

2 trout (10 to 11 ounces *each*)
4 tablespoons plus 1-1/2 teaspoons lemon juice, *divided*
3 teaspoons dill weed, *divided*
2 teaspoons lemon-pepper seasoning, *divided*
1 small onion, chopped
1 tablespoon butter
1/2 cup minced fresh parsley
2 cups soft bread crumbs

Place trout in a 13-in. x 9-in. x 2-in. baking dish coated with nonstick cooking spray. Sprinkle 3 tablespoons lemon juice, 1-1/2 teaspoons dill and 1-1/2 teaspoons lemon-pepper in the fish cavities and over outside of fish; set aside.

In a nonstick skillet, saute onion in butter until tender. Add the parsley and remaining dill and lemon-pepper. Stir in bread crumbs; heat through. Sprinkle with remaining lemon juice; stir gently until moistened. Stuff into fish cavities. Bake, uncovered, at 400° for 25-30 minutes or until fish flakes easily with a fork. **Yield:** 4 servings.

Nutritional Analysis: *1 serving equals 280 calories, 11 g fat (4 g saturated fat), 91 mg cholesterol, 442 mg sodium, 15 g carbohydrate, 1 g fiber, 30 g protein.*
Diabetic Exchanges: *4 lean meat, 1 starch.*

Nutritional Analysis: 1 fish fillet with 1/2 cup relish equals 148 calories, 1 g fat (trace saturated fat), 28 mg cholesterol, 238 mg sodium, 12 g carbohydrate, 1 g fiber, 22 g protein.
Diabetic Exchanges: 3 very lean meat, 1 vegetable, 1/2 fruit.

🍎 Homemade Bread Crumbs

I DRY leftover low-carb bread heels in the microwave and freeze them solid in a storage bag. Then I use a rolling pin to turn them into crumbs.
—*Connie Voog, Aitkin, Minnesota*

Sea Scallops and Mushrooms

Low-carb

Prep/Total Time: 15 min.

This is a foolproof yet elegant way to make sea scallops. I just cook them in the microwave.
—*Lynnae Neuberger, Marshfield, Wisconsin*

    1 pound fresh *or* frozen sea scallops, thawed
      and rinsed
   12 small fresh mushrooms, halved
    1 tablespoon white wine *or* chicken broth
1-1/2 teaspoons lemon juice
  1/2 teaspoon lemon-pepper seasoning
  1/4 teaspoon dried thyme
  1/8 teaspoon garlic powder
  1/8 teaspoon seasoned salt
    2 teaspoons butter, melted

Place scallops and mushrooms in a 9-in. glass pie plate or dish. Combine the wine or broth, lemon juice and seasonings; pour over scallop mixture. Cover and microwave at 50% power for 2 minutes; stir. Cover and microwave at 50% power for 4 to 4-1/2 minutes longer or until scallops turn opaque. Stir in melted butter. **Yield:** 3 servings.
   Editor's Note: This recipe was tested in a 1,100-watt microwave.

Nutritional Analysis: 4 ounces cooked scallops with 4 mushrooms equals 170 calories, 4 g fat (2 g saturated fat), 57 mg cholesterol, 407 mg sodium, 6 g carbohydrate, 1 g fiber, 27 g protein.
Diabetic Exchanges: 3 lean meat, 1 vegetable.

Fish with Cucumber-Orange Relish

Low-carb   Low-fat

Prep/Total Time: 25 min.

This quick-and-easy entree turned my family of fish haters into fish lovers. The tart relish is wonderful.
—*Amy Bauer, Griffith, Indiana*

    1 can (11 ounces) mandarin oranges, drained
    1 medium cucumber, seeded and chopped
    1 green onion, thinly sliced
  1/4 cup cider vinegar
    1 teaspoon minced fresh dill
  1/4 teaspoon salt
  1/4 teaspoon pepper
    4 orange roughy fillets (5 ounces *each*)

For relish, in a small bowl, combine the first five ingredients; set aside. Combine salt and pepper; sprinkle over fillets. Place

Honey-Orange Marinated Salmon

(Pictured below)

Low-carb

Prep: 10 min. + marinating **Bake:** 30 min.

My husband is a commercial fisherman, so we have fish often. This simple recipe is one of my favorites.
—*Sonesa Lundmark, Sitka, Alaska*

1/3 cup reduced-sodium soy sauce
1/4 cup orange juice
1/4 cup honey
  2 green onions, thinly sliced
  1 tablespoon olive oil
  1 tablespoon sherry *or* apple juice
  1 tablespoon minced fresh gingerroot
  1 salmon fillet (1 pound)

In a large resealable plastic bag, combine the first seven ingredients. Add salmon. Seal bag and turn to coat; refrigerate for 1 hour, turning several times.
   Line an 8-in. square baking dish with foil; coat the foil with nonstick cooking spray. Drain and discard marinade. Place salmon in prepared pan. Bake at 350° for 30-40 minutes or until fish flakes easily with a fork. **Yield:** 4 servings.

Nutritional Analysis: 4 ounces cooked salmon equals 238 calories, 13 g fat (3 g saturated fat), 67 mg cholesterol, 261 mg sodium, 5 g carbohydrate, trace fiber, 23 g protein.
Diabetic Exchanges: 3 lean meat, 1 fat, 1/2 starch.

Snapper with Vegetable Medley

(Pictured above)

Prep: 15 min. **Cook:** 55 min.

This recipe yields a deliciously complete and quick dinner with fish, herbed rice and stir-fried veggies. It only takes a few moments to prepare.
—Mary Ann Palestino, Brooklyn, New York

1-1/2 cups water
3/4 cup uncooked brown rice
1-1/2 teaspoons reduced-sodium beef bouillon granules
1-1/2 teaspoons dried parsley flakes
1-1/2 teaspoons dried minced onion
1/4 teaspoon garlic powder
1 medium red onion, thinly sliced
2 garlic cloves, minced
2 teaspoons canola oil
1/2 pound fresh snow peas
1-1/2 cups shredded carrots
1 tablespoon balsamic vinegar
4 red snapper fillets (5 ounces *each*)
2 teaspoons blackening seasoning

In a saucepan, combine the first six ingredients. Bring to a boil. Reduce heat; cover and simmer for 40-45 minutes or until rice is tender. Meanwhile, in a large nonstick skillet coated with nonstick cooking spray, cook red onion and garlic in oil over medium-high heat for 2 minutes. Add peas; cook for 2 minutes. Add carrots; cook 2 minutes longer or until vegetables are tender. Stir in vinegar. Remove and keep warm.

Sprinkle both sides of fillets with blackening seasoning. In the same skillet, cook fillets over medium-high heat for 4 minutes on each side or until fish flakes easily with a fork. Serve with rice and vegetables. **Yield:** 4 servings.

Nutritional Analysis: 1 fish fillet with 3/4 cup vegetable mixture and 1/2 cup rice equals 353 calories, 6 g fat (1 g saturated fat), 50 mg cholesterol, 305 mg sodium, 41 g carbohydrate, 5 g fiber, 34 g protein.
Diabetic Exchanges: 4 very lean meat, 2 starch, 2 vegetable, 1/2 fat.

Sassy Shrimp Stir-Fry

(Pictured below)

Prep/Total Time: 30 min.

Red pepper flakes, fresh ginger and garlic lend a spicy touch to this seafood stir-fry from our Test Kitchen staff. Pea pods, carrot and Chinese cabbage give the dish a fresh taste that's always welcome.

2 tablespoons cornstarch
1-1/2 cups reduced-sodium chicken broth
3 tablespoons reduced-sodium soy sauce
2 tablespoons rice wine vinegar
1 tablespoon honey
2 teaspoons sesame oil
1 teaspoon grated orange peel
1 teaspoon canola oil
1 pound uncooked medium shrimp, peeled and deveined
1-1/2 teaspoons minced fresh gingerroot
2 garlic cloves, minced
1/2 teaspoon crushed red pepper flakes
1/2 cup julienned carrot
2-1/2 cups chopped Chinese *or* napa cabbage
2 cups fresh pea pods
1/4 cup thinly sliced green onions
Hot cooked rice, optional

In a bowl, combine cornstarch and broth until smooth. Stir in the soy sauce, vinegar, honey, sesame oil and orange peel; set aside.

In a large nonstick skillet or wok, heat canola oil; stir-fry shrimp for 30 seconds. Add ginger, garlic and red pepper flakes; stir-fry 1-2 minutes longer or until shrimp turn pink. Remove and keep warm.

In the same pan, stir-fry the carrot for 1 minute. Stir broth mixture and stir into pan. Bring to a boil; cook and stir for 1-2 minutes or until thickened. Add the cabbage, peas, onions and shrimp mixture; heat through. Serve over rice if desired. **Yield:** 4 servings.

Nutritional Analysis: 1-1/4 cups stir-fry mixture (calculated without rice) equals 219 calories, 5 g fat (1 g saturated fat), 168 mg cholesterol, 896 mg sodium, 20 g carbohydrate, 4 g fiber, 24 g protein.
Diabetic Exchanges: 3 very lean meat, 1 starch, 1 vegetable, 1/2 fat.

Meatless Main Dishes

You won't find any meat in these main dishes ...but you won't miss it, either. This hearty vegetarian fare is so delightfully satisfying, even your most ardent meat-and-potatoes lovers will give it rave reviews.

Southwest Vegetarian Bake (page 173)

salsa over each tortilla. Cover and bake at 350° for 25 minutes. Uncover; sprinkle with cheese and cilantro. Bake 2-3 minutes longer or until cheese is melted. **Yield:** 8 servings.

Nutritional Analysis: 1 enchilada equals 271 calories, 6 g fat (2 g saturated fat), 10 mg cholesterol, 638 mg sodium, 43 g carbohydrate, 5 g fiber, 12 g protein.
Diabetic Exchanges: 2-1/2 starch, 1 lean meat, 1 vegetable.

Roasted Vegetable Lasagna

Meatless

Prep: 50 min. **Bake:** 45 min. + standing

This recipe is a favorite of my vegetarian friends. I lightened it by using egg substitute and reduced-fat cheese. I also added a few more vegetables.
—*Virginia Anthony, Blowing Rock, North Carolina*

  1 eggplant (1 pound), peeled and cut into 1/4-inch slices
1/2 pound fresh mushrooms, cut into 1/4-inch slices
  3 small zucchini, cut lengthwise into 1/4-inch slices
  2 sweet red peppers, cut lengthwise into 6 pieces
  3 tablespoons olive oil
  1 garlic clove, minced
  1 teaspoon salt
1/2 teaspoon pepper
  1 carton (15 ounces) reduced-fat ricotta cheese
1/4 cup grated Parmesan cheese
1/4 cup egg substitute
  1 jar (26 ounces) chunky meatless pasta sauce
 12 no-cook lasagna noodles
  2 cups (8 ounces) shredded part-skim mozzarella cheese, *divided*
  3 tablespoons minced fresh basil

Coat two 15-in. x 10-in. x 1-in. baking pans with nonstick cooking spray. Place eggplant and mushrooms on a prepared pan. Place the zucchini and red pepper on the second pan. Combine the oil and garlic; brush over both sides of vegetables. Sprinkle with salt and pepper. Bake, uncovered, at 400° for 15 minutes. Turn vegetables over. Bake 15 minutes longer. Remove eggplant and mushrooms. Bake zucchini and red pepper 5-10 minutes longer or until edges are browned.

In a bowl, combine the ricotta cheese, Parmesan cheese and egg substitute. Spread about 1/4 cup pasta sauce in a 13-in. x 9-in. x 2-in. baking dish coated with nonstick cooking spray. Layer with four lasagna noodles (noodles will overlap slightly), half of ricotta cheese mixture, half of vegetables, a third of pasta sauce and 2/3 cup mozzarella cheese. Sprinkle with half of basil. Repeat layers. Top with the remaining noodles and pasta sauce.

Cover and bake at 350° for 40 minutes. Uncover; sprinkle with remaining cheese. Bake 5-10 minutes longer or until edges are bubbly and cheese is melted. Let stand for 10 minutes before cutting. **Yield:** 9 servings.

Nutritional Analysis: 1 piece equals 361 calories, 15 g fat (6 g saturated fat), 31 mg cholesterol, 820 mg sodium, 40 g carbohydrate, 5 g fiber, 19 g protein.
Diabetic Exchanges: 2 lean meat, 2 starch, 2 vegetable, 1 fat.

Black Bean and Rice Enchiladas

(Pictured above)

Meatless

Prep: 40 min. **Bake:** 30 min.

I love Mexican food, but I'm always looking for ways to make it more healthy. I "renovated" a dish that I have enjoyed in restaurants to suit my taste and lifestyle.
—*Christie Ladd, Rockville, Maryland*

  1 green pepper, chopped
  1 medium onion, chopped
  3 garlic cloves, minced
  1 tablespoon olive oil
  1 can (15 ounces) black beans, rinsed and drained
  1 can (14-1/4 ounces) diced tomatoes with green chilies
1/4 cup picante sauce
  1 tablespoon chili powder
  1 teaspoon ground cumin
1/4 teaspoon crushed red pepper flakes
  2 cups cooked brown rice
  8 flour tortillas (7 inches), warmed
  1 cup salsa
  1 cup (4 ounces) reduced-fat shredded cheddar cheese
  3 tablespoons chopped fresh cilantro

In a large nonstick skillet, saute the green pepper, onion and garlic in oil until tender. Add the beans, tomatoes, picante sauce, chili powder, cumin and red pepper flakes; bring to a boil. Reduce heat; simmer, uncovered, until heated through and mixture thickens. Add rice; cook 5 minutes longer or until heated through.

Spoon a rounded 1/2 cup down the center of each tortilla. Fold sides over filling and roll up. Place in a 13-in. x 9-in. x 2-in. baking dish coated with nonstick cooking spray. Spoon

Pasta with Roasted Red Pepper Sauce

(Pictured below)

Low-carb *Meatless*

Prep/Total Time: 30 min.

This deep tomato-red sauce is sure to be a family favorite if you're looking for a low-carb, meatless pasta topping. Made with roasted red peppers and a hint of cayenne pepper, it will add a veggie kick to your dinner table.
—*Antoinette Ronzio, North Providence, Rhode Island*

> 1 can (14-1/2 ounces) Italian stewed tomatoes, undrained
> 1 jar (7 ounces) roasted red peppers, drained
> 1 teaspoon sugar
> 1/2 teaspoon ground cumin
> 1/4 teaspoon salt
> 1/4 teaspoon dried oregano
> 1/4 teaspoon cayenne pepper
> 1/4 teaspoon red wine vinegar
> 1 small onion, chopped
> 2 garlic cloves, minced
> 1 tablespoon olive oil
> Hot cooked pasta

In a blender, combine the first eight ingredients; cover and process until smooth. In a large nonstick skillet, saute onion and garlic in oil until tender.

Stir in the roasted red pepper mixture. Bring to a boil. Reduce heat; simmer, uncovered, for 10 minutes, stirring frequently. Serve pepper sauce over hot cooked pasta. **Yield:** 5 servings.

Nutritional Analysis: 1/2 cup sauce (calculated without pasta) equals 73 calories, 5 g fat (trace saturated fat), 0 cholesterol, 681 mg sodium, 8 g carbohydrate, 1 g fiber, 1 g protein.
Diabetic Exchanges: 1 vegetable, 1 fat.

🍎 Wash Away Sodium

RINSING canned beans is a great way to reduce sodium content…and it's easy to do. Just pour the canned beans into a strainer and rinse them under cool running water. You'll reduce the sodium by about 30 to 40%.

Southwest Vegetarian Bake

(Pictured on page 171)

Meatless

Prep: 40 min. **Bake:** 35 min. + standing

Creamy and comforting, this spicy meatless casserole hits the spot on chilly nights. But it's great any time I have a taste for Mexican food with all the fixings.
—*Patricia Gale, Monticello, Illinois*

> 3/4 cup uncooked brown rice
> 1-1/2 cups water
> 1 can (15 ounces) black beans, rinsed and drained
> 1 can (11 ounces) Mexicorn, drained
> 1 can (10 ounces) diced tomatoes and green chilies
> 1 cup salsa
> 1 cup (8 ounces) reduced-fat sour cream
> 1 cup (4 ounces) shredded reduced-fat cheddar cheese
> 1/4 teaspoon pepper
> 1/2 cup chopped red onion
> 1 can (2-1/4 ounces) sliced ripe olives, drained
> 1 cup (4 ounces) shredded reduced-fat Mexican cheese blend

In a large saucepan, bring rice and water to a boil. Reduce heat; cover and simmer for 35-40 minutes or until tender.

In a large bowl, combine the beans, Mexicorn, tomatoes, salsa, sour cream, cheddar cheese, pepper and rice. Transfer to a shallow 2-1/2-qt. baking dish coated with nonstick cooking spray. Sprinkle with onion and olives.

Bake, uncovered, at 350° for 30 minutes. Sprinkle with Mexican cheese. Bake 5-10 minutes longer or until heated through and cheese is melted. Let stand for 10 minutes before serving. **Yield:** 8 servings.

Nutritional Analysis: 1 cup equals 284 calories, 10 g fat (6 g saturated fat), 30 mg cholesterol, 899 mg sodium, 37 g carbohydrate, 7 g fiber, 16 g protein.
Diabetic Exchanges: 2 starch, 2 vegetable, 1 very lean meat, 1 fat.

Southwestern Veggie Wraps

(Pictured above)

Meatless

Prep: 15 min. **Cook:** 25 min.

I developed this recipe to use up my garden-grown zucchini, peppers and corn. It's fast and easy to fix.
—Rebekah White, Seaside, Oregon

  1 small onion, chopped
  1 garlic clove, minced
  1 tablespoon olive oil
  1 can (15 ounces) black beans, rinsed and drained
1-1/2 cups fresh *or* frozen corn, thawed
  1 medium sweet red pepper, chopped
  1 cup coarsely chopped zucchini
2/3 cup plus 2 tablespoons water, *divided*
  1 teaspoon chili powder
1/2 teaspoon salt
1/2 teaspoon dried oregano
1/2 teaspoon ground cumin
1/8 teaspoon pepper
  1 teaspoon cornstarch
  6 flour tortillas (10 inches), warmed
3/4 cup salsa
  6 tablespoons reduced-fat sour cream

In a large nonstick skillet, saute onion and garlic in oil until tender. Stir in the beans, corn, red pepper, zucchini, 2/3 cup water, chili powder, salt, oregano, cumin and pepper. Bring to a boil. Reduce heat; simmer, uncovered, for 10-15 minutes or until most of the liquid has evaporated.

Combine cornstarch and remaining water until smooth; stir into skillet. Bring to a boil; cook and stir for 1 minute or until thickened. Spoon about 2/3 cup down center of tortillas; top with salsa and sour cream. Roll up. **Yield:** 6 servings.

Nutritional Analysis: 1 wrap equals 371 calories, 8 g fat (2 g saturated fat), 5 mg cholesterol, 966 mg sodium, 59 g carbohydrate, 11 g fiber, 12 g protein.

Ratatouille Pasta

(Pictured below)

Meatless

Prep: 10 min. + standing **Cook:** 15 min.

This zesty veggie-packed entree has been a favorite for years, especially with my daughter who is vegetarian.
—Carol Dodds, Aurora, Ontario

  2 cups diced peeled eggplant
  2 cups sliced zucchini
1/2 teaspoon salt
1-1/3 cups uncooked spiral pasta
  1 cup sliced onion
  1 tablespoon olive oil
  1 can (14-1/2 ounces) diced tomatoes, undrained
  2 tablespoons tomato paste
  1 teaspoon dried oregano
1/2 teaspoon garlic powder
1/2 teaspoon dried basil
Dash pepper
  1 cup (4 ounces) shredded part-skim mozzarella cheese

Place eggplant and zucchini in a colander over a plate; sprinkle with salt and toss. Let stand for 30 minutes; rinse and drain well.

Cook pasta according to package directions. Meanwhile, in a large nonstick skillet, saute the eggplant, zucchini and onion in oil until tender. Add the tomatoes, tomato paste, oregano, garlic powder, basil and pepper. Bring to a boil. Reduce heat; cook, uncovered, over medium-low heat for 3 minutes, stirring occasionally.

Drain pasta; place on an ovenproof platter. Top with vegetable mixture. Sprinkle with mozzarella cheese. Broil 4-6 in. from the heat until cheese is melted. **Yield:** 3 servings.

Nutritional Analysis: 1 cup sauce with 2/3 cup pasta equals 344 calories, 12 g fat (5 g saturated fat), 22 mg cholesterol, 835 mg sodium, 45 g carbohydrate, 7 g fiber, 17 g protein.
Diabetic Exchanges: 3 vegetable, 2 starch, 1 lean meat, 1 fat.

Roasted Pepper Ravioli Bake

Meatless

Prep: 25 min. + standing **Bake:** 30 min.

I serve this casserole with a salad and Italian bread. The cheesy dish always gets compliments.
—*Carol Poindexter, Norridge, Illinois*

2 *each* medium green, sweet red and yellow
   peppers
1 package (25 ounces) frozen cheese ravioli
1 tablespoon olive oil
1 teaspoon sugar
1/4 teaspoon salt
2 cups meatless spaghetti sauce, *divided*
4 ounces sliced part-skim mozzarella cheese

Place peppers on a broiler pan. Broil 4 in. from the heat until skins blister, about 6-8 minutes. With tongs, rotate peppers a quarter turn. Broil and rotate until all sides are blistered and blackened. Immediately place peppers in a bowl; cover and let stand for 15-20 minutes.

Meanwhile, cook ravioli according to package directions; drain. Peel off and discard charred skin from peppers. Remove stems and seeds. Finely chop peppers; drain. In a large bowl, combine the peppers, oil, sugar and salt.

Spread 1-1/2 cups spaghetti sauce in a 13-in. x 9-in. x 2-in. baking dish coated with nonstick cooking spray. Layer with the ravioli, pepper mixture and cheese. Top with remaining spaghetti sauce. Cover and bake at 350° for 15 minutes. Uncover; bake 15-20 minutes longer or until heated through. **Yield:** 8 servings.

Nutritional Analysis: 1 serving equals 335 calories, 11 g fat (5 g saturated fat), 44 mg cholesterol, 415 mg sodium, 44 g carbohydrate, 5 g fiber, 16 g protein.
Diabetic Exchanges: 2-1/2 starch, 1-1/2 fat, 1 lean meat, 1 vegetable.

Spaghetti with Fresh Tomatoes

(Pictured above right)

Meatless

Prep/Total Time: 30 min.

With a savory combination of basil, tomatoes and mozzarella cheese, this pasta medley makes a wonderful meatless main course or side dish.
—*Sandy Jenkins, Avon Lake, Ohio*

1 package (16 ounces) spaghetti
2 pounds fresh tomatoes, seeded and chopped
12 ounces part-skim mozzarella cheese, cut
   into 1/4-inch cubes
1-1/4 cups julienned fresh basil
1 can (2-1/4 ounces) sliced ripe olives, drained
4 teaspoons balsamic vinegar
1/2 teaspoon salt
1/2 teaspoon coarsely ground pepper
3 garlic cloves, minced
2 tablespoons olive oil

Cook spaghetti according to package directions. Meanwhile, in a large serving bowl, combine the tomatoes, cheese,

basil, olives, vinegar, salt and pepper. Drain the spaghetti; add to the tomato mixture and toss to combine.

In a small nonstick skillet over medium heat, cook garlic in oil until tender. Pour over spaghetti mixture; toss to coat. **Yield:** 8 servings.

Nutritional Analysis: 1-2/3 cups equals 398 calories, 13 g fat (5 g saturated fat), 23 mg cholesterol, 457 mg sodium, 51 g carbohydrate, 3 g fiber, 20 g protein.

Broccoli Tofu Stir-Fry

Meatless

Prep/Total Time: 25 min.

A friend gave me this recipe when I was trying to eat more meatless meals. My family requests it often.
—*Denise Lee, Louisville, Kentucky*

1 package (12.3 ounces) reduced-fat extra-firm
   tofu, cubed
4 green onions, chopped
1 tablespoon minced fresh gingerroot
1 garlic clove, minced
1/4 teaspoon crushed red pepper flakes
4 teaspoons olive oil, *divided*
1 package (16 ounces) broccoli coleslaw mix
1/3 cup reduced-fat peanut butter
1/4 cup reduced-sodium teriyaki sauce

In a nonstick skillet or wok, stir-fry the tofu, onions, ginger, garlic and pepper flakes in 3 teaspoons oil until onions are tender. Remove and set aside. In the same pan, stir-fry the broccoli coleslaw mix in remaining oil for 4-5 minutes.

Combine the peanut butter and teriyaki sauce; stir into coleslaw mix. Return tofu mixture to the pan. Stir-fry for 1-2 minutes or until heated through. **Yield:** 4 servings.

Editor's Note: Broccoli coleslaw mix may be found in the produce section of most grocery stores.

Nutritional Analysis: 1 cup equals 276 calories, 15 g fat (3 g saturated fat), 0 cholesterol, 526 mg sodium, 23 g carbohydrate, 5 g fiber, 16 g protein.
Diabetic Exchanges: 2 lean meat, 1 starch, 1 vegetable, 1 fat.

Sweet Pepper Sandwiches

(Pictured above)

Meatless

Prep/Total Time: 25 min.

My husband and I love this easy vegetarian recipe. When we're in the mood for a change of pace, I sometimes add sauteed mushrooms to the rolls.
—Cara Neth, Fort Collins, Colorado

1 *each* small green, sweet red and yellow pepper, thinly sliced
1 small onion, thinly sliced
1 garlic clove, minced
1 tablespoon olive oil
1 tablespoon balsamic vinegar
2 ounces fresh mozzarella cheese
1/4 cup fat-free mayonnaise
1/2 teaspoon prepared horseradish
4 hard rolls, split and toasted
8 fresh basil leaves
1 plum tomato, thinly sliced

In a large nonstick skillet, saute peppers, onion and garlic in oil until crisp-tender. Drizzle with vinegar; toss to coat.

Cut mozzarella cheese into four slices. Combine the mayonnaise and horseradish; spread over cut sides of rolls. Spoon vegetable mixture onto bottom halves; top with cheese. Broil 4-6 in. from the heat for 2-4 minutes or until cheese is melted. Top with basil leaves and tomato. Replace roll tops. **Yield:** 4 servings.

Nutritional Analysis: 1 sandwich equals 278 calories, 10 g fat (3 g saturated fat), 13 mg cholesterol, 456 mg sodium, 39 g carbohydrate, 3 g fiber, 9 g protein.
Diabetic Exchanges: 2 starch, 1-1/2 fat, 1 vegetable.

Veggie Corn Cakes

(Pictured below)

Low-fat   Meatless

Prep/Total Time: 30 min.

These golden hot cakes are chock-full of corn and vegetables, plus a zippy hint of hot pepper sauce.
—Cindy Neville, Fountaintown, Indiana

1 cup all-purpose flour
1 cup cornmeal
Sugar substitute equivalent to 2 teaspoons sugar
2 teaspoons baking powder
1/2 teaspoon salt
1 egg
1-1/2 cups fat-free milk
1 cup frozen corn, thawed
1/4 cup chopped red onion
1/4 cup chopped green pepper
1/4 cup finely chopped roasted sweet red pepper
1/4 teaspoon hot pepper sauce
14 tablespoons salsa
7 tablespoons reduced-fat sour cream

In a large bowl, combine the first five ingredients. Combine the egg, milk, corn, onion, peppers and hot pepper sauce; stir into dry ingredients until well blended.

Heat a large nonstick griddle or skillet coated with nonstick cooking spray; drop batter by 1/4 cupfuls onto griddle. Fry until golden brown, about 3 minutes on each side. Serve with salsa and sour cream. **Yield:** 7 servings.

Editor's Note: This recipe was tested with Splenda No Calorie Sweetener.

Nutritional Analysis: 2 corn cakes with 2 tablespoons salsa and 1 tablespoon sour cream equals 225 calories, 3 g fat (1 g saturated fat), 37 mg cholesterol, 530 mg sodium, 41 g carbohydrate, 3 g fiber, 8 g protein.
Diabetic Exchange: 2-1/2 starch.

Tomato Spinach Pizza

(Pictured above)

Meatless

Prep: 1 hour **Bake:** 20 min.

When you want to get kids to eat spinach, try this classic. A bread machine cuts prep time.
—Sharlin Blamires, Coweta, Oklahoma

   1-1/4 cups water (70° to 80°)
   2 tablespoons olive oil
   3/4 teaspoon salt
   4 cups all-purpose flour
   1 tablespoon active dry yeast
TOPPINGS:
   1 tablespoon olive oil
   3 tablespoons grated Parmesan cheese
   1 tablespoon Italian seasoning
   3/4 teaspoon garlic salt
   1 package (10 ounces) frozen chopped spinach, thawed and squeezed dry
   3 plum tomatoes, thinly sliced
   2 cups (8 ounces) shredded part-skim mozzarella cheese

In bread machine pan, place the first five ingredients in order suggested by manufacturer. Select dough setting (check dough after 5 minutes of mixing; add 1 to 2 tablespoons of water or flour if needed).

When cycle is completed, turn dough onto a lightly floured surface. Roll into a 16-in. x 11-in. rectangle. Transfer to a 15-in. x 10-in. x 1-in. baking pan coated with nonstick cooking spray. Build up edges slightly. Prick dough thoroughly with a fork. Brush with oil; sprinkle with Parmesan cheese, Italian seasoning and garlic salt. Top with spinach, tomatoes and mozzarella cheese.

Bake at 375° for 17-22 minutes or until crust is golden brown and cheese is melted. Broil 4-6 in. from the heat for 2-3 minutes or until cheese is golden brown. **Yield:** 9 servings (18 slices).

Nutritional Analysis: *2 slices equals 330 calories, 10 g fat (4 g saturated fat), 16 mg cholesterol, 523 mg sodium, 46 g carbohydrate, 3 g fiber, 14 g protein.*
Diabetic Exchanges: *3 starch, 1 lean meat, 1 fat.*

Refried Bean Enchiladas

Meatless

Prep: 20 min. **Bake:** 20 min.

These yummy meatless enchiladas are easy to prepare and great when you're craving Mexican food.
—Carolyn Sykora, Bloomer, Wisconsin

   2 cups vegetarian refried beans
   1 cup (8 ounces) 1% cottage cheese
   1-1/2 cups (6 ounces) shredded reduced-fat cheddar cheese, *divided*
   1 tablespoon olive oil
   4-1/2 teaspoons all-purpose flour
   1 tablespoon chili powder
   1/2 teaspoon garlic powder
   1/4 teaspoon salt
   1-1/2 cups water
   1 teaspoon cider vinegar
   1/2 teaspoon dried minced onion
   12 flour tortillas (6 inches)

In a large bowl, combine the beans, cottage cheese and 1 cup cheddar cheese; set aside. For sauce, in a large nonstick skillet, whisk the oil, flour, chili powder, garlic powder and salt until smooth. Gradually stir in the water, vinegar and onion. Bring to a boil; cook and stir for 2 minutes or until thickened. Remove from the heat.

Dip both sides of each tortilla into sauce. Place about 1/2 cup bean mixture down the center of each tortilla. Roll up and place seam side down in a 13-in. x 9-in. x 2-in. baking dish coated with nonstick cooking spray. Pour remaining sauce over top; sprinkle with remaining cheese.

Cover and bake at 350° for 20-25 minutes or until heated through. **Yield:** 6 servings.

Nutritional Analysis: *2 enchiladas equals 384 calories, 11 g fat (5 g saturated fat), 22 mg cholesterol, 729 mg sodium, 48 g carbohydrate, 7 g fiber, 24 g protein.*
Diabetic Exchanges: *3 starch, 2 lean meat, 1 fat.*

🍎 Light Dessert for Mexican Meal

FOR a great low-fat dessert, I spray fat-free flour tortillas with butter-flavored spray and sprinkle them with cinnamon-sugar. Then I cut them into wedges and bake them until golden brown. I top the wedges with sauteed apple slices and whipped topping.
—Jeanne Sula, Winona, Minnesota

Gingered Sweet Potato Pancakes

Low-fat Meatless

Prep: 15 min. **Cook:** 20 min.

Ginger gives a surprisingly pleasant taste to these golden pancakes. We like them with applesauce or syrup.
—*Mildred Sherrer, Fort Worth, Texas*

  3 medium sweet potatoes, peeled and shredded
  1 medium potato, peeled and shredded
  2 eggs, lightly beaten
1/3 cup all-purpose flour
1/3 cup finely chopped onion
  1 tablespoon minced fresh gingerroot
3/4 teaspoon salt
1/2 teaspoon pepper
  3 teaspoons canola oil, *divided*

In a bowl, combine the first eight ingredients; toss to mix. In a nonstick skillet coated with nonstick cooking spray, heat 1 teaspoon oil over medium heat. Drop batter by 1/4 cupfuls into skillet; press lightly to flatten. Fry 3-4 minutes on each side or until golden brown. Repeat with remaining oil and batter. **Yield:** 12 servings.

Nutritional Analysis: 2 pancakes equals 93 calories, 2 g fat (trace saturated fat), 35 mg cholesterol, 164 mg sodium, 16 g carbohydrate, 2 g fiber, 3 g protein.
Diabetic Exchanges: 1 starch, 1/2 fat.

Tofu-Stuffed Pasta Shells

(Pictured above and on front cover)

Meatless

Prep: 25 min. **Bake:** 35 min.

Your gang won't even miss the meat in this pasta dish. I jazz up tofu with mozzarella cheese, spinach and fresh garlic for unbeatable flavor.
—*Jenni Dise, Phoenix, Arizona*

 15 uncooked jumbo pasta shells
1-1/2 cups firm silken tofu
  3 tablespoons grated Romano cheese, *divided*
  2 garlic cloves, peeled
  1 package (10 ounces) frozen chopped spinach, thawed and squeezed dry
  1 can (14-1/2 ounces) Italian diced tomatoes, drained
  1 can (8 ounces) tomato sauce
1/4 cup dry red wine *or* vegetable broth
1/2 cup shredded part-skim mozzarella cheese

Cook pasta shells according to package directions. Meanwhile, in a blender, combine the tofu, 2 tablespoons Romano cheese and garlic; cover and process until smooth. (Add 1 tablespoon of water if mixture is too thick.) Add spinach; process until blended. Drain shells; stuff with tofu mixture.

In a bowl, combine the tomatoes, tomato sauce and wine or broth. Spread about 1/2 cup sauce in an 11-in. x 7-in. x 2-in. baking dish coated with nonstick cooking spray. Arrange stuffed shells over sauce. Top with remaining sauce.

Cover and bake at 350° for 25 minutes. Uncover; sprinkle with mozzarella and remaining Romano cheese. Bake 8-10 minutes longer or until shells are heated through and cheese is melted. **Yield:** 5 servings.

Nutritional Analysis: 3 stuffed shells equals 262 calories, 5 g fat (2 g saturated fat), 10 mg cholesterol, 754 mg sodium, 39 g carbohydrate, 4 g fiber, 14 g protein.
Diabetic Exchanges: 3 vegetable, 1-1/2 starch, 1 lean meat.

Chickpea Sandwich Spread

Meatless

Prep/Total Time: 20 min.

I came up with this spread as an alternative to lunch meat. The pickle juice gives this hummus-like mixture added flavor without extra fat.
—*Trish Quinn, Cheyenne, Wyoming*

1/2 cup dill pickle relish
1/3 cup reduced-fat mayonnaise
1/4 cup dill pickle juice
  1 tablespoon honey Dijon mustard
  2 cans (19 ounces *each*) chickpeas *or* garbanzo beans, rinsed and drained, *divided*
1/3 cup finely chopped celery
1/3 cup shredded carrot
  7 whole wheat pita bread halves
  2 cups fresh torn spinach
  7 tomato slices, halved

In a blender or food processor, combine the pickle relish, mayonnaise, pickle juice and mustard. Add one can of chickpeas; cover and process until smooth. Gradually add remaining can of chickpeas; blend until smooth.

Transfer to a bowl; stir in celery and carrot. Line pita bread with spinach leaves and tomato slices. Place about 1/2 cup chickpea mixture in each pita half. **Yield:** 7 servings.

Nutritional Analysis: 2 filled pita halves equals 293 calories, 8 g fat (1 g saturated fat), 4 mg cholesterol, 601 mg sodium, 48 g carbohydrate, 9 g fiber, 10 g protein.
Diabetic Exchanges: 3 starch, 1 very lean meat.

Spinach Cheddar Squares

Low-carb *Meatless*

Prep: 15 min. **Bake:** 40 min. + standing

I really enjoy preparing healthy spinach entrees like this one, which gets many compliments.
—*Elaine Anderson, Aliquippa, Pennsylvania*

    1 tablespoon dry bread crumbs
  3/4 cup shredded reduced-fat cheddar cheese, *divided*
    1 package (10 ounces) frozen chopped spinach, thawed and squeezed dry
  1/4 cup finely chopped sweet red pepper
1-1/2 cups egg substitute
  3/4 cup fat-free milk
    2 tablespoons grated Parmesan cheese
  1/2 teaspoon dried minced onion
  1/2 teaspoon salt
  1/4 teaspoon garlic powder
  1/4 teaspoon pepper

Sprinkle bread crumbs evenly into an 8-in. square baking dish coated with nonstick cooking spray. Top with 1/2 cup cheese, spinach and red pepper. In a small bowl, combine the remaining ingredients; pour over the top.

Bake, uncovered, at 350° for 35 minutes. Sprinkle with remaining cheese. Bake 2-3 minutes longer or until a knife inserted near the center comes out clean. Let stand for 15 minutes before cutting. **Yield:** 4 servings.

Nutritional Analysis: 1 serving equals 219 calories, 10 g fat (6 g saturated fat), 31 mg cholesterol, 596 mg sodium, 9 g carbohydrate, 2 g fiber, 26 g protein.
Diabetic Exchanges: 3 lean meat, 1 vegetable, 1/2 starch.

Penne with Cannellini Beans

Low-fat *Meatless*

Prep/Total Time: 30 min.

You'll need only five ingredients for this meatless pasta dish. With spinach, beans and tomatoes, it's so filling that you'll never miss the meat.
—*Brenda Harrell, Joplin, Missouri*

  8 ounces uncooked penne *or* medium tube pasta
  2 cans (14-1/2 ounces *each*) Italian diced tomatoes
  1 can (15 ounces) cannellini *or* white kidney beans, rinsed and drained
  1 package (10 ounces) fresh baby spinach, chopped
1/2 cup shredded Romano cheese

Cook pasta according to package directions. Meanwhile, in a large saucepan, bring the tomatoes and beans to a boil. Reduce heat; simmer, uncovered, for 10 minutes. Add spinach; cook and stir for 2 minutes or until spinach is wilted. Drain pasta; top with tomato mixture. Sprinkle with cheese. **Yield:** 5 servings.

Nutritional Analysis: 1-1/2 cups equals 325 calories, 2 g fat (1 g saturated fat), 4 mg cholesterol, 1,056 mg sodium, 62 g carbohydrate, 7 g fiber, 15 g protein.

Mediterranean Fettuccine

(Pictured below)

Meatless

Prep/Total Time: 30 min.

This wonderful recipe is quick and easy to prepare. The pasta specialty makes an impressive main course or a satisfying side dish.
—*Elise Ray, Fairway, Kansas*

  1/2 cup vegetable broth
    8 sun-dried tomatoes (not packed in oil), halved
    6 ounces uncooked fettuccine
    1 medium sweet yellow pepper, thinly sliced
    1 medium sweet red pepper, thinly sliced
    1 cup chopped green onions
    2 garlic cloves, minced
    1 tablespoon olive oil
  10 Greek olives, pitted and coarsely chopped
  1/4 cup minced fresh basil
    1 tablespoon capers, drained
    1 teaspoon dried oregano
    1 package (4 ounces) crumbled feta cheese

In a small saucepan, bring broth to a boil. Remove from the heat; add tomatoes. Let stand for 5-7 minutes. Cut tomatoes into thin slices and return to broth; set aside.

Cook fettuccine according to package directions. Meanwhile, in a large nonstick skillet coated with nonstick cooking spray, saute the peppers, onions and garlic in oil for 3-4 minutes or until tender. Reduce heat. Stir in the olives, basil, capers, oregano and reserved tomato mixture; heat through.

Drain fettuccine; place in a large serving bowl. Add the feta cheese and pepper mixture; toss to coat. **Yield:** 4 servings.

Nutritional Analysis: 1-1/2 cups equals 331 calories, 12 g fat (4 g saturated fat), 15 mg cholesterol, 854 mg sodium, 44 g carbohydrate, 6 g fiber, 14 g protein.
Diabetic Exchanges: 2 starch, 2 vegetable, 1-1/2 fat, 1 lean meat.

Salsa Spaghetti Squash

(Pictured above)

Meatless

Prep/Total Time: 30 min.

This colorful combination is one example of the many flavorful uses for spaghetti squash.
—*Clara Coulston, Washington Court House, Ohio*

- **1 medium spaghetti squash**
- **1/2 cup chopped onion**
- **2 cups salsa**
- **1 can (15 ounces) black beans, rinsed and drained**
- **3 tablespoons minced fresh cilantro**
- **1 medium ripe avocado, peeled and cubed**

Cut squash in half lengthwise; discard seeds. Place squash cut side down on a microwave-safe plate. Microwave, uncovered, on high for 15-18 minutes or until tender. Meanwhile, in a nonstick skillet coated with nonstick cooking spray, cook onion until tender. Stir in the salsa, beans and cilantro; heat through. Gently stir in avocado; cook 1 minute longer.

When squash is cool enough to handle, use a fork to separate strands. Divide squash among four plates; top with salsa mixture. **Yield:** 4 servings.

Editor's Note: This recipe was tested in a 1,100-watt microwave.

Nutritional Analysis: 1-1/4 cups spaghetti squash with 1 cup salsa mixture equals 308 calories, 9 g fat (2 g saturated fat), 0 cholesterol, 822 mg sodium, 54 g carbohydrate, 20 g fiber, 16 g protein.

Black Bean Pasta

Low-fat   Meatless

Prep/Total Time: 30 min.

Here is one of my favorite light recipes. With zip from cumin and red pepper flakes, the spicy Southwestern dish is a hearty meal-in-one.
—*Stephanie Land, Sudbury, Ontario*

- **8 ounces uncooked spiral pasta**
- **1 cup finely chopped green pepper**
- **1 medium onion, chopped**
- **2 garlic cloves, minced**
- **1 teaspoon dried oregano**
- **1/2 teaspoon ground cumin**
- **1/2 teaspoon crushed red pepper flakes**
- **2 cups tomato sauce**
- **1 can (15 ounces) black beans, rinsed and drained**
- **1/2 cup shredded reduced-fat cheddar cheese**

Cook pasta according to package directions; drain. Meanwhile, in a large saucepan coated with nonstick cooking spray, combine the green pepper, onion, garlic, oregano, cumin and red pepper flakes. Cook over medium heat for 5 minutes or until vegetables are tender. Add tomato sauce and black beans; bring to a boil. Reduce heat; simmer, uncovered, for 5 minutes or until heated through. Stir in pasta. Sprinkle with cheese. **Yield:** 6 servings.

Nutritional Analysis: 1 cup equals 252 calories, 2 g fat (1 g saturated fat), 5 mg cholesterol, 567 mg sodium, 46 g carbohydrate, 6 g fiber, 13 g protein.
Diabetic Exchanges: 2-1/2 starch, 1 very lean meat, 1 vegetable.

Macaroni and Cheese

Meatless

Prep: 20 min. **Bake:** 35 min. + standing

When my husband had heart problems, I searched for recipes that replaced our full-fat standbys. Over the years, I've updated this recipe to accommodate new lower-in-fat products, and my family continues to enjoy it.
—*Cora Johnson Schloetzer, Topeka, Kansas*

- **3 cups uncooked elbow macaroni**
- **12 ounces reduced-fat process cheese (Velveeta), sliced**
- **1/2 cup finely chopped onion**
- **1/3 cup all-purpose flour**
- **2 teaspoons ground mustard**
- **1/8 teaspoon pepper**
- **1 can (12 ounces) fat-free evaporated milk**
- **1-1/4 cups fat-free milk**
- **1/2 cup dry bread crumbs**
- **2 tablespoons butter**

Cook macaroni according to package directions; drain. In a 13-in. x 9-in. x 2-in. baking dish coated with nonstick cooking spray, layer a third of the macaroni, half of the cheese and half of the onion. Repeat layers. Place remaining macaroni on top.

In a bowl, combine the flour, mustard, pepper, evaporated milk and fat-free milk; pour over layers. Combine bread crumbs and butter; sprinkle over top.

Cover and bake at 375° for 20 minutes. Uncover; bake 15 minutes longer or until bubbly. Let stand for 10 minutes before serving. **Yield:** 8 servings.

Nutritional Analysis: 3/4 cup equals 353 calories, 7 g fat (4 g saturated fat), 25 mg cholesterol, 161 mg sodium, 48 g carbohydrate, 2 g fiber, 22 g protein.

From the Bread Basket

Is your family getting enough grains?
It's easy to ingrain the goodness of wheat,
oats, rye and more into your meal plans
when you present an incredible assortment
of breads, rolls and muffins.

Aniseed Braids (page 190)

Cabbage Patch Bread

(Pictured above)

Low-sodium Meatless

Prep: 25 min. + rising **Bake:** 25 min.

I make my own bread, but I could never get my children to eat any of the whole-grain breads I considered more nutritious...until I came across this one. The name caught their attention, but the taste got their approval!
—Jeanne Bennett, Minden, Louisiana

1 package (1/4 ounce) active dry yeast
1/3 cup warm water (110° to 115°)
1 can (5 ounces) evaporated milk
1/4 cup canola oil
1 egg
3/4 cup coarsely chopped cabbage
1 medium carrot, cut into chunks
1/4 cup sliced celery
1/4 cup minced fresh parsley *or* 4 teaspoons dried
  parsley flakes
2 tablespoons honey
1 teaspoon salt
3 cups whole wheat flour
1-1/4 cups all-purpose flour

In a large mixing bowl, dissolve yeast in warm water. In a blender or food processor, combine the milk, oil, egg, cabbage, carrot, celery, parsley, honey and salt; cover and process until smooth. Add to yeast mixture. Stir in whole wheat flour and enough all-purpose flour to form a soft dough.

Turn onto a floured surface; knead until smooth and elastic, about 6-8 minutes. Place in a greased bowl, turning once to grease top. Cover and let rise in a warm place until doubled, about 1-1/2 hours.

Punch dough down. Turn onto a lightly floured surface; divide in half. Cover and let rest for 10 minutes. Shape into round loaves. Place on two greased baking sheets. Cover and let rise until doubled, about 1 hour.

Bake at 350° for 25-30 minutes or until golden brown.

Cover loosely with foil during the last 10 minutes if top browns too quickly. Remove from pans to wire racks to cool. **Yield:** 2 loaves (10 slices each).

Nutritional Analysis: 1 slice equals 138 calories, 4 g fat (1 g saturated fat), 13 mg cholesterol, 133 mg sodium, 22 g carbohydrate, 3 g fiber, 4 g protein.
Diabetic Exchanges: 1-1/2 starch, 1/2 fat.

Cinnamon Spiral Bread

Low-fat Meatless

Prep: 30 min. + rising **Bake:** 35 min. + cooling

Delicate cinnamon swirls make this classic sweet bread a treat any time of day. I like to use thick slices of this loaf for French toast.
—Sharon Moeller, Ceresco, Nebraska

5-1/4 to 5-1/2 cups all-purpose flour
2 cups quick-cooking oats
2/3 cup nonfat dry milk powder
1/4 cup packed brown sugar
1 tablespoon salt
1 package (1/4 ounce) active dry yeast
2-1/2 cups water
2 tablespoons butter
1 egg
1 cup raisins
1/2 cup sugar
2 teaspoons ground cinnamon

In a large mixing bowl, combine 2 cups flour, oats, milk powder, brown sugar, salt and yeast. In a saucepan, heat water and butter to 120°-130°. Add to dry ingredients; beat just until moistened. Add egg; beat until smooth. Stir in enough remaining flour to form a firm dough. Stir in raisins.

Turn onto a floured surface; knead until smooth and elastic, about 6-8 minutes. Place in a bowl coated with nonstick cooking spray, turning once to coat top. Cover and let rise in a warm place until doubled, about 1 hour.

Punch dough down. Turn onto a lightly floured surface; divide in half. Roll each portion into an 18-in. x 9-in. rectangle. Combine sugar and cinnamon. Set aside 2 tablespoons for topping. Sprinkle remaining cinnamon-sugar over rectangles to within 1/2 in. of edges. Roll up jelly-roll style, starting with a short side; pinch seam to seal.

Place seam side down in two 9-in. x 5-in. x 3-in. loaf pans coated with nonstick cooking spray. Cover and let rise until doubled, about 30 minutes.

Sprinkle with reserved cinnamon-sugar. Bake at 375° for 35-40 minutes or until golden brown. Cool for 10 minutes before removing from pans to wire racks. **Yield:** 2 loaves (16 slices each).

Nutritional Analysis: 1 slice equals 140 calories, 1 g fat (1 g saturated fat), 9 mg cholesterol, 241 mg sodium, 28 g carbohydrate, 1 g fiber, 4 g protein.
Diabetic Exchanges: 1-1/2 starch, 1/2 fruit.

Favorite Recipe Made Lighter

"I LOVE going to British teas—we have a popular tearoom here in Albuquerque—but I need to watch what I eat," says Carole Jasler of Albuquerque, New Mexico. "I'm sending my recipe for traditional British Scones, hoping you can lighten it."

After sampling Carole's scones, our home economists realized they had a big challenge on their hands. They wanted to keep the outstanding flavor and tender flaky texture of Carole's scones, but knew they had to cut back on the whipping cream and butter in a major way.

They began by replacing half the butter with canola oil. This reduced the cholesterol and saturated fat while adding moisture to the dough.

Substituting 1% buttermilk for the whipping cream trimmed things down even further and added enough acid to keep the scones tender. Similarly, cake flour replaced some of the all-purpose flour, which also helped the scones retain their appealing texture.

Adding a little brown sugar to the dough gave Makeover British Scones a lovely, golden appearance when they were baked.

The results? The makeover scones contain 54 fewer calories than the original and 70% less saturated fat—but they are still tender and tasty.

British Scones

Meatless

Prep/Total Time: 30 min.

- 2 cups all-purpose flour
- 1 tablespoon sugar
- 2 teaspoons baking powder
- 1/2 teaspoon salt
- 6 tablespoons cold butter
- 2 eggs, lightly beaten
- 1/2 cup plus 1 tablespoon heavy whipping cream, *divided*
- 1/2 teaspoon vanilla extract

In a large bowl, combine the flour, sugar, baking powder and salt. Cut in butter until mixture resembles coarse crumbs. Combine the eggs, 1/2 cup cream and vanilla; add to crumb mixture and stir until a soft dough forms. Turn onto a floured surface; gently knead 6-8 times.

Pat dough into a 6-in. circle. Cut into eight wedges. Separate wedges and place 1 in. apart on an ungreased baking sheet. Brush tops with remaining cream. Bake at 400° for 12-14 minutes or until lightly browned. Remove to a wire rack. Serve warm. **Yield:** 8 scones.

Nutritional Analysis: 1 scone equals 273 calories, 16 g fat (10 g saturated fat), 99 mg cholesterol, 379 mg sodium, 26 g carbohydrate, 1 g fiber, 5 g protein.

Makeover British Scones

(Pictured below)

Meatless

Prep/Total Time: 30 min.

- 1-1/4 cups all-purpose flour
- 1 cup cake flour
- 2 tablespoons brown sugar
- 1-1/2 teaspoons baking powder
- 1/2 teaspoon salt
- 1/4 teaspoon baking soda
- 3 tablespoons cold butter
- 1 egg, lightly beaten
- 1/3 cup 1% buttermilk
- 2 tablespoons canola oil
- 1/2 teaspoon vanilla extract
- 1 tablespoon 2% milk
- 1 teaspoon sugar

In a large bowl, combine the flours, brown sugar, baking powder, salt and baking soda. Cut in butter until mixture resembles coarse crumbs. Combine the egg, buttermilk, oil and vanilla; add to crumb mixture and stir until a soft dough forms. Turn onto a floured surface; gently knead 6-8 times.

Pat dough into a 6-in. circle. Cut into eight wedges. Separate wedges and place 1 in. apart on an ungreased baking sheet. Brush tops with milk; sprinkle with sugar. Bake at 400° for 12-14 minutes or until lightly browned. Remove to a wire rack. Serve warm. **Yield:** 8 scones.

Nutritional Analysis: 1 scone equals 219 calories, 9 g fat (3 g saturated fat), 39 mg cholesterol, 343 mg sodium, 30 g carbohydrate, 1 g fiber, 4 g protein.
Diabetic Exchanges: 2 starch, 1-1/2 fat.

Cinnamon Loaf

(Pictured above)

Meatless

Prep: 20 min. **Bake:** 45 min. + cooling

This sweet, cake-like bread is easy to make and great to serve at breakfast, with dinner or as a snack.
—Dorothy Bateman, Carver, Massachusetts

    1/4 cup butter, softened
      1 cup plus 2 tablespoons sugar, *divided*
      2 eggs
      1 teaspoon vanilla extract
      2 cups all-purpose flour
      1 teaspoon baking powder
    1/2 teaspoon baking soda
    1/2 teaspoon salt
      1 cup 1% buttermilk
      1 teaspoon ground cinnamon

In a large mixing bowl, beat butter until light and fluffy, about 1 minute. Gradually beat in 1 cup sugar. Add eggs, one at a time, beating well after each addition. Stir in vanilla. Combine the flour, baking powder, baking soda and salt. Add to creamed mixture alternately with buttermilk just until mixed.

Transfer half of the mixture to a 9-in. x 5-in. x 3-in. loaf pan coated with nonstick cooking spray. Combine cinnamon and remaining sugar. Sprinkle three-fourths of mixture over batter. Top with remaining batter and sprinkle with remaining cinnamon mixture. Bake at 350° for 45-50 minutes or until a toothpick inserted near the center comes out clean. Cool for 10 minutes before removing from pan to a wire rack to cool completely. **Yield:** 14 servings.

Nutritional Analysis: *1 slice equals 173 calories, 4 g fat (2 g saturated fat), 40 mg cholesterol, 225 mg sodium, 30 g carbohydrate, 1 g fiber, 3 g protein.*
Diabetic Exchanges: *2 starch, 1/2 fat.*

Herb Cheese Bread

Meatless

Prep: 15 min. **Bake:** 20 min.

A flavorful blend of herbs makes this loaf from our Test Kitchen ideal for most any menu.

    1/4 cup finely chopped green onions
      2 garlic cloves, minced
    1/3 cup reduced-fat margarine
    1/2 teaspoon ground cumin
    1/4 teaspoon dried oregano
    1/4 teaspoon dried thyme
    1/8 teaspoon *each* salt and crushed red pepper
         flakes
      1 loaf (1 pound) unsliced French bread, halved
         lengthwise
    3/4 cup shredded reduced-fat cheddar cheese

In a small nonstick skillet, saute onions and garlic in margarine for 1-2 minutes; add seasonings. Brush herb mixture over both cut sides of bread; sprinkle with cheese.

Wrap each piece loosely in a large piece of heavy-duty foil. Seal edges of foil. Bake at 400° for 20-25 minutes or until heated through or until cheese is melted. Cut each piece into six slices. **Yield:** 12 servings.

Editor's Note: This recipe was tested with Blue Bonnet light stick margarine.

Nutritional Analysis: *1 slice equals 147 calories, 5 g fat (2 g saturated fat), 5 mg cholesterol, 339 mg sodium, 20 g carbohydrate, 1 g fiber, 5 g protein.*
Diabetic Exchanges: *1-1/2 starch, 1 fat.*

Apricot Coffee Cake

Meatless

Prep: 15 min. **Bake:** 40 min. + cooling

Having friends over for coffee? Serve this scrumptious yet light coffee cake from our home economists.

      1 jar (10 ounces) 100% apricot spreadable fruit,
         divided
    3/4 cup chopped pecans
Sugar substitute equivalent to 1/3 cup sugar
      4 teaspoons ground cinnamon
CAKE:
  3-1/4 cups reduced-fat biscuit/baking mix
Sugar substitute equivalent to 3/4 cup sugar
    1/8 teaspoon ground cardamom
      2 eggs
      1 cup fat-free milk
    2/3 cup reduced-fat sour cream
      1 tablespoon butter, melted

Place 3 tablespoons spreadable fruit in a small microwave-safe bowl; cover and refrigerate. In another bowl, combine the pecans, sugar substitute, cinnamon and remaining spreadable fruit; set aside.

For cake, in a large bowl, combine biscuit mix, sugar substitute and cardamom. Combine eggs, milk, sour cream and butter; stir into dry ingredients just until moistened.

Spread a third of the batter into a 10-in. fluted tube pan coated with nonstick cooking spray. Spread with half of the pecan mixture. Repeat layers. Top with the remaining batter.

Bake at 350° for 40-45 minutes or until a toothpick comes out clean. Cool for 15 minutes; remove from pan to a wire rack. In a microwave, warm the reserved spreadable fruit; brush over warm cake. Cool completely. **Yield:** 16 servings.

Editor's Note: This recipe was tested with Splenda No Calorie Sweetener.

Nutritional Analysis: 1 piece equals 213 calories, 8 g fat (2 g saturated fat), 32 mg cholesterol, 313 mg sodium, 32 g carbohydrate, 1 g fiber, 4 g protein.
Diabetic Exchanges: 1-1/2 starch, 1 fruit, 1 fat.

Whole Wheat Banana Bread

Low-sodium Meatless

Prep: 15 min. **Bake:** 45 min. + cooling

A hint of orange livens up this moist and nutty banana bread. It's always a hit.
—Kathy Merrick, Hammond, Indiana

1 cup whole wheat flour
3/4 cup all-purpose flour
1/2 cup toasted wheat germ
1 teaspoon baking soda
1 teaspoon grated orange peel
1/4 teaspoon salt
4 medium navel oranges, peeled and sectioned (about 1-1/2 cups)
2 medium ripe bananas
1 cup sugar
2 eggs
1/4 cup canola oil
1 teaspoon vanilla extract
1/2 cup chopped pecans

In a large bowl, combine the first six ingredients. In a food processor or blender, process the oranges, bananas, sugar, eggs, oil and vanilla until smooth. Stir into dry ingredients just until moistened. Fold in pecans.

Pour into two 8-in. x 4-in. x 2-in. loaf pans coated with non-stick cooking spray. Bake at 350° for 45-50 minutes or until a toothpick inserted near the center comes out clean. Cool for 10 minutes before removing from pans to wire racks to cool completely. **Yield:** 2 loaves (10 slices each).

Nutritional Analysis: 1 slice equals 154 calories, 6 g fat (1 g saturated fat), 21 mg cholesterol, 99 mg sodium, 25 g carbohydrate, 2 g fiber, 3 g protein.
Diabetic Exchanges: 1-1/2 starch, 1 fat.

Fruit-Filled Windmill Rolls

(Pictured at right)

Low-sodium Meatless

Prep: 30 min. + rising **Bake:** 15 min.

Created by our Test Kitchen staff, these cute sweet rolls make lovely additions to brunch buffets.

3 to 3-1/2 cups all-purpose flour
1/3 cup plus 2 tablespoons sugar, *divided*
1 package (1/4 ounce) quick-rise yeast

1/2 teaspoon salt
1/2 cup fat-free milk
1/3 cup butter, softened
1/4 cup water
1 egg
1 egg white
1 tablespoon orange juice
1/2 teaspoon ground cinnamon
TOPPING:
1 egg white
1 tablespoon water
2 teaspoons sugar
1/2 cup *each* 100% apricot and cherry spreadable fruit

In a large mixing bowl, combine 2 cups flour, 1/3 cup sugar, yeast and salt. In a small saucepan, heat the milk, butter and water to 120°-130°. Add to dry ingredients; beat until moistened. Add egg and egg white; beat on medium speed for 2 minutes. Stir in enough remaining flour to form a soft dough. Turn onto a lightly floured surface. Cover and let rest for 10 minutes.

Roll into a 12-in. square. Brush orange juice over dough. Combine cinnamon and remaining sugar; sprinkle over dough. Cut into sixteen 3-in. squares.

To form windmills, diagonally cut dough from each corner to within 3/4 in. of the center. Fold every other point toward the center, overlapping pieces. Place 3 in. apart on baking sheets coated with nonstick cooking spray. Cover and let rise in a warm place until doubled, about 40 minutes.

Press center firmly to seal. Beat egg white and water; brush over windmills. Sprinkle with sugar. Bake at 350° for 13-17 minutes or until golden brown. Remove to wire rack to cool slightly. Spoon spreadable fruit into center of windmills. Serve warm. **Yield:** 16 rolls.

Nutritional Analysis: 1 roll equals 196 calories, 4 g fat (2 g saturated fat), 24 mg cholesterol, 128 mg sodium, 35 g carbohydrate, 1 g fiber, 4 g protein.
Diabetic Exchanges: 2 starch, 1/2 fruit, 1/2 fat.

Quilt-Topped Corn Bread

(Pictured above)

Meatless

Prep: 20 min. **Bake:** 30 min.

We like to serve slices of this corn bread alongside salsa and light sour cream.
—Robyn Oro, Raytown, Missouri

- **2 cans (4 ounces *each*) whole green chilies**
- **1 large sweet red pepper**
- **2 packages (8-1/2 ounces *each*) corn bread/muffin mix**
- **1 can (14-3/4 ounces) cream-style corn**
- **1 can (11 ounces) Mexicorn, drained**
- **1 cup (4 ounces) shredded reduced-fat cheddar cheese**
- **2/3 cup water**
- **1 egg, lightly beaten**
- **1/4 cup egg substitute**

Coat two 9-in. round baking pans with nonstick cooking spray. Slice green chilies in half lengthwise; pat dry. Place six chili halves skin side down in a starburst pattern in each pan. Cut red pepper into twelve 1/4-in. slices and two 1-in. circles. Place slices between chilies and circles in center of pans.

Place bread mix in a large bowl. Combine cream-style corn, Mexicorn, cheese, water, egg and egg substitute; stir into bread mix just until moistened. Carefully pour into prepared pans. Bake at 425° for 30-35 minutes or until a toothpick inserted near center comes out clean. Immediately invert onto serving plates. **Yield:** 16 servings.

Nutritional Analysis: 1 wedge equals 187 calories, 5 g fat (2 g saturated fat), 25 mg cholesterol, 503 mg sodium, 31 g carbohydrate, 1 g fiber, 6 g protein.
Diabetic Exchanges: 2 starch, 1/2 fat.

🍎 Prune Power

I'VE FOUND that pureed prunes can often be used as a substitute for the oil or butter in baked goods. The prunes keep baked goods moist and tender. —*Helen White, Tulsa, Oklahoma*

Bell Pepper Muffins

Low-fat   Meatless

Prep/Total Time: 30 min.

Featuring three types of peppers, these half-hour muffins are great with chicken at supper or as a snack.
—Karen Shipp, San Antonio, Texas

- **1/4 cup *each* chopped green pepper, sweet yellow pepper and sweet red pepper**
- **2 tablespoons butter**
- **2 cups all-purpose flour**
- **2 tablespoons sugar**
- **2-1/2 teaspoons baking powder**
- **1/2 teaspoon salt**
- **1/2 teaspoon dried basil**
- **1 egg**
- **1/4 cup egg substitute**
- **1 cup fat-free milk**

In a nonstick skillet, saute peppers in butter until tender; set aside. In a large bowl, combine the flour, sugar, baking powder, salt and basil. Combine the egg, egg substitute and milk; stir into dry ingredients just until moistened. Fold in the peppers. Coat muffin cups with nonstick cooking spray; fill two-thirds full with batter.

Bake at 400° for 15-18 minutes or until a toothpick comes out clean. Cool for 5 minutes before removing from pan to a wire rack. **Yield:** 1 dozen.

Nutritional Analysis: 1 muffin equals 119 calories, 3 g fat (1 g saturated fat), 23 mg cholesterol, 228 mg sodium, 20 g carbohydrate, 1 g fiber, 4 g protein.
Diabetic Exchanges: 1 starch, 1/2 fat.

Raisin Rye Muffins

Meatless

Prep/Total Time: 30 min.

These wholesome muffins sweetened with honey are egg-, wheat- and milk-free, so they are wonderful for people with food allergies.
—Edna Hoffman, Hebron, Indiana

- **1 cup rye flour**
- **2 teaspoons baking powder**
- **1/2 teaspoon ground cinnamon**
- **1/4 teaspoon salt**
- **1/2 cup water**
- **2 tablespoons honey**
- **2 tablespoons canola oil**
- **1/2 cup raisins**

In a large bowl, combine the flour, baking powder, cinnamon and salt. Combine the water, honey and oil; stir into dry ingredients just until moistened. Fold in raisins. Fill six muffin cups coated with nonstick cooking spray two-thirds full.

Bake at 400° for 15-20 minutes or until a toothpick comes out clean. Cool for 5 minutes before removing from pan to a wire rack. Serve warm. **Yield:** 6 muffins.

Nutritional Analysis: 1 muffin equals 160 calories, 5 g fat (trace saturated fat), 0 cholesterol, 234 mg sodium, 29 g carbohydrate, 3 g fiber, 2 g protein.
Diabetic Exchanges: 1 starch, 1 fruit, 1 fat.

Favorite Recipe Made Lighter

IN HER Dunkirk, New York kitchen, Kathy Strawser loves to bake Zucchini Apple Bread. "But since I've been diagnosed as diabetic," she shares, "I think my recipe calls for too much sugar."

Our makeover team couldn't wait to try Kathy's harvest-time recipe. And just as she described, the moist loaves offered wonderful flavor but were quite high in calories, sugar and fat.

The original recipe was abundant in nuts, so the quantity was decreased to save some calories. Next, our home economists replaced a bit of the oil with applesauce and eliminated a few of the eggs.

Flavored with cinnamon and nutmeg, Makeover Zucchini Apple Bread delivers plenty of down-home goodness. The recipe still yields three nut-filled loaves but contains nearly 60% less fat than the original recipe.

Best of all, the sugar was decreased by 28%, and that's sweet news to Kathy. "The makeover recipe received rave reviews," she says. "No one believed it was a light version."

Zucchini Apple Bread

Low-sodium Meatless

Prep: 30 min. **Bake:** 55 min. + cooling

    4 cups all-purpose flour
    3 teaspoons baking soda
1-1/2 teaspoons ground cinnamon
    1/2 teaspoon ground nutmeg
    1/4 teaspoon salt
    5 eggs
1-1/2 cups vegetable oil
    2 cups sugar
    1 cup packed brown sugar
    1 teaspoon vanilla extract
    2 cups shredded zucchini
1-1/2 cups chopped pecans
    1 cup grated peeled apples

In a large bowl, combine the flour, baking soda, cinnamon, nutmeg and salt. In a large mixing bowl, beat the eggs until frothy. Add the oil, sugars and vanilla; beat until blended. Stir into dry ingredients just until moistened. Fold in the zucchini, pecans and apples.

Transfer to three greased 8-in. x 4-in. x 2-in. loaf pans. Bake at 350° for 55-60 minutes or until a toothpick inserted near the center comes out clean. Cool for 10 minutes before removing from pans to wire racks. **Yield:** 3 loaves (12 slices each).

Nutritional Analysis: 1 slice equals 246 calories, 14 g fat (2 g saturated fat), 30 mg cholesterol, 133 mg sodium, 29 g carbohydrate, 1 g fiber, 3 g protein.

Makeover Zucchini Apple Bread

(Pictured above)

Low-sodium Meatless

Prep: 30 min. **Bake:** 55 min. + cooling

    4 cups all-purpose flour
    3 teaspoons baking soda
1-1/2 teaspoons ground cinnamon
    1/2 teaspoon ground nutmeg
    1/4 teaspoon salt
    2 eggs
    3/4 cup canola oil
1-1/2 cups unsweetened applesauce
    1 cup sugar
    1 cup packed brown sugar
    1 teaspoon vanilla extract
    2 cups shredded zucchini
    1 cup grated peeled apples
    1/2 cup chopped pecans

In a large bowl, combine the flour, baking soda, cinnamon, nutmeg and salt. In a large mixing bowl, beat the eggs until frothy. Add the oil, applesauce, sugars and vanilla; beat until blended. Stir into dry ingredients just until moistened. Fold in the zucchini, apples and pecans.

Transfer to three 8-in. x 4-in. x 2-in. loaf pans coated with nonstick cooking spray. Bake at 350° for 55-60 minutes or until a toothpick inserted near the center comes out clean. Cool for 10 minutes before removing from pans to wire racks. **Yield:** 3 loaves (12 slices each).

Nutritional Analysis: 1 slice equals 161 calories, 6 g fat (1 g saturated fat), 12 mg cholesterol, 128 mg sodium, 24 g carbohydrate, 1 g fiber, 2 g protein.
Diabetic Exchanges: 1-1/2 starch, 1 fat.

Peanut Butter 'n' Jelly Muffins

(Pictured above)

Meatless

Prep: 10 min. **Bake:** 15 min. + cooling

There's a delightful surprise hiding within these yummy muffins. Our Test Kitchen made them simple to prepare, so they bake up easily.

2 cups all-purpose flour
2 teaspoons baking powder
3/4 teaspoon baking soda
1/4 teaspoon salt
2 eggs
3/4 cup apple juice concentrate
1/2 cup reduced-fat chunky peanut butter
1/4 cup fat-free milk
3 tablespoons butter, melted
1/3 cup 100% strawberry spreadable fruit

In a large bowl, combine flour, baking powder, baking soda and salt. Combine eggs, concentrate, peanut butter, milk and butter; stir into dry ingredients just until moistened.

Coat 12 muffin cups with nonstick cooking spray. Spoon half of the batter into cups. Spoon about 1-1/4 teaspoons spreadable fruit into the center of each; top with remaining batter. Bake at 350° for 15-20 minutes or until a toothpick inserted into muffin comes out clean. Cool for 5 minutes before removing from pan to a wire rack to cool completely. **Yield:** 1 dozen.

Nutritional Analysis: *1 muffin equals 225 calories, 8 g fat (3 g saturated fat), 43 mg cholesterol, 315 mg sodium, 33 g carbohydrate, 1 g fiber, 6 g protein.*
Diabetic Exchanges: *2 starch, 1-1/2 fat.*

Four-Grain Bread

Low-fat   Meatless

Prep: 10 min. **Bake:** 3 to 4 hours

My grandchildren really like this hearty loaf's crunchy crust and chewy interior.
—*John Reed, Lees Summit, Missouri*

1-1/2 cups water (70° to 80°)
1/2 cup honey

1-1/2 teaspoons salt
2 cups bread flour
1 cup whole wheat flour
3/4 cup rye flour
3/4 cup cornmeal
2-1/4 teaspoons active dry yeast

In bread machine pan, place all ingredients in order suggested by manufacturer. Select basic bread setting.

Choose crust color and loaf size if available. Bake according to bread machine directions (check dough after 5 minutes of mixing; add 1 to 2 tablespoons of water or flour if needed). **Yield:** 1 loaf (2 pounds, 24 slices).

Nutritional Analysis: *1 slice equals 108 calories, trace fat (trace saturated fat), 0 cholesterol, 148 mg sodium, 24 g carbohydrate, 2 g fiber, 3 g protein.*
Diabetic Exchange: *1-1/2 starch.*

Savory Pita Strips

Meatless

Prep/Total Time: 15 min.

These crispy sticks are terrific with saucy pasta dishes as well as soup and chili. I sometimes replace the butter with butter-flavored granules.
—*Tanya Belt, Newcomerstown, Ohio*

2 tablespoons grated Parmesan cheese
1/2 teaspoon Italian seasoning
1/4 teaspoon garlic powder
1/4 teaspoon dried rosemary, crushed
4 pita breads (6 inches)
2 tablespoons butter, melted

In a small bowl, combine the Parmesan cheese, Italian seasoning, garlic powder and rosemary; set aside. Cut pita breads into 1-in. strips; split in half. Spritz crust side with butter-flavored nonstick cooking spray; place crust side up on a broiler pan coated with nonstick cooking spray.

Broil 3-4 in. from the heat for 1 minute. Turn; brush with

🍎 Yeast Bread Basics

IT'S EASY to "rise" to the challenge of using yeast dough. Just remember the following:

- Be sure to measure all ingredients accurately.
- Proper rising gives the bread an ideal texture. Yeast dough should rise in a warm (80° to 85°) draft-free area.
- Use aluminum pans with a dull rather than a shiny or dark finish. Dark finishes and glass baking dishes produce dark crusts.
- Arrange the oven racks so the bread bakes in the center of the oven.
- When baking more than one loaf, leave at least 1 in. of space between the pans for proper air circulation. Similarly, keep an inch between the pans and sides of the oven.

butter and sprinkle with Parmesan mixture. Broil 1-2 minutes longer or until golden brown and crisp. **Yield:** 8 servings.

Nutritional Analysis: 6 strips equals 114 calories, 4 g fat (2 g saturated fat), 9 mg cholesterol, 213 mg sodium, 17 g carbohydrate, 1 g fiber, 3 g protein.
Diabetic Exchanges: 1 starch, 1/2 fat.

Blueberry Muffins

Meatless

Prep: 15 min. **Bake:** 30 min.

These berry-packed muffins are so sweet and fruity, my husband and two young daughters just love them.
—Teresa Christensen, Osceola, Wisconsin

  3 tablespoons butter, softened
  1 cup sugar
  1 egg
  1/2 cup fat-free evaporated milk
  1/4 cup water
  2 cups all-purpose flour
  2 teaspoons baking powder
  1 teaspoon salt
1-1/2 cups fresh *or* frozen blueberries

In a large mixing bowl, beat butter and sugar until crumbly, about 2 minutes. Add egg; beat well. Combine milk and water. Combine the flour, baking powder and salt; add to creamed mixture alternately with milk mixture. Fold in blueberries.

Coat muffin cups with nonstick cooking spray or use paper liners; fill three-fourths full with batter. Bake at 350° for 27-30 minutes or until a toothpick comes out clean. Cool in pans for 5 minutes before removing to a wire rack. **Yield:** 1 dozen.

Editor's Note: If using frozen blueberries, do not thaw before adding to batter.

Nutritional Analysis: 1 muffin equals 191 calories, 4 g fat (2 g saturated fat), 26 mg cholesterol, 283 mg sodium, 36 g carbohydrate, 1 g fiber, 4 g protein.
Diabetic Exchanges: 2 starch, 1/2 fat.

Cran-Apple Tea Ring

(Pictured above right)

Meatless

Prep: 45 min. + rising **Bake:** 20 min. + cooling

Filled with cranberries, apples and walnuts, this tea ring is a lovely addition to brunch.
—Nellie Grimes, Jacksonville, Texas

  1 package (1/4 ounce) active dry yeast
1/4 cup warm water (110° to 115°)
1/2 cup warm fat-free milk (110° to 115°)
  1 egg
  2 tablespoons butter, softened
  1 tablespoon grated orange peel
  1 teaspoon salt
  3 tablespoons plus 1/2 cup sugar, *divided*
2-3/4 to 3-1/4 cups all-purpose flour

  1 cup thinly sliced peeled apples
  1 cup dried cranberries
1/2 cup chopped walnuts, toasted
1-1/2 teaspoons ground cinnamon
  1 egg white
  1 tablespoon water
1/2 cup confectioners' sugar
  1 tablespoon orange juice

In a mixing bowl, dissolve yeast in warm water. Add the next five ingredients, 3 tablespoons sugar and 1 cup flour; beat until smooth. Stir in enough remaining flour to form a soft dough. Knead until smooth and elastic, about 6-8 minutes. Place in a bowl coated with nonstick cooking spray; turn once to coat. Cover and let rise in a warm place for 1 hour.

In a bowl, toss the fruit, walnuts, cinnamon and remaining sugar; set aside. Punch dough down; turn onto a lightly floured surface. Roll into a 20-in. x 10-in. rectangle. Combine egg white and water; chill 3 tablespoons. Brush remaining mixture over dough. Spoon fruit mixture to within 1 in. of edges. Roll up tightly jelly-roll style, starting with a long side; seal ends.

Place seam side down in a 15-in. x 10-in. x 1-in. baking pan coated with nonstick cooking spray; pinch ends to form a ring. With scissors, cut from outside edge two-thirds of the way toward center of ring at 1-in. intervals. Separate strips slightly; twist so filling shows. Cover and let rise until doubled, about 40 minutes.

Brush with reserved egg white mixture. Bake at 375° for 20-25 minutes or until golden brown (cover with foil during the last 10 minutes). Remove to a wire rack to cool. Combine confectioners' sugar and orange juice; drizzle over ring. **Yield:** 16 servings.

Nutritional Analysis: 1 piece equals 200 calories, 4 g fat (1 g saturated fat), 17 mg cholesterol, 174 mg sodium, 37 g carbohydrate, 2 g fiber, 4 g protein.
Diabetic Exchanges: 2 starch, 1 fat, 1/2 fruit.

Aniseed Braids

(Pictured on page 181)

Low-fat   Low-sodium   Meatless

Prep: 50 min. + rising **Bake:** 30 min. + cooling

Perfect for seasonal dinners and holiday gift-giving, this recipe yields two gorgeous loaves.
—Marion Erickson, Rock Island, Illinois

7 to 7-1/2 cups all-purpose flour
6 tablespoons sugar
2 packages (1/4 ounce *each*) active dry yeast
2 tablespoons aniseed
1 teaspoon salt
2 cups fat-free milk
1/2 cup butter, cubed
1/4 cup water
2 eggs
2 tablespoons sesame seeds

In a large mixing bowl, combine 2 cups flour, sugar, yeast, aniseed and salt. In a small saucepan, heat the milk, butter and water to 120°-130°. Add to dry ingredients; beat just until moistened. Add 1 egg; beat until smooth. Stir in enough remaining flour to form a firm dough (dough will be sticky).

Turn onto a floured surface; knead until smooth and elastic, about 6-8 minutes. Place in a bowl coated with nonstick cooking spray, turning once to coat top. Cover and let rise in a warm place until doubled, about 45 minutes.

Punch dough down. Turn onto a lightly floured surface; divide in half. Divide each portion into thirds. Shape each into a 14-in. rope. Place three ropes on a baking sheet coated with nonstick cooking spray and braid; pinch ends to seal and tuck under. Repeat with remaining dough. Cover and let rise until doubled, about 30 minutes. Beat remaining egg; brush over braids. Sprinkle with seeds. Bake at 350° for 30-35 minutes or until golden brown. Remove from pans to wire racks to cool. **Yield:** 2 loaves (20 slices each).

Nutritional Analysis: 1 slice equals 119 calories, 3 g fat (2 g saturated fat), 17 mg cholesterol, 92 mg sodium, 20 g carbohydrate, 1 g fiber, 3 g protein.
Diabetic Exchanges: *1 starch, 1/2 fat.*

Cranberry Scones

Meatless

Prep: 20 min. **Bake:** 15 min.

Cornmeal adds a slight crunch to these breakfast or brunch treats. They're nice with a cup of tea or coffee.
—Kathy Zielicke, Moore Haven, Florida

2 cups all-purpose flour
3/4 cup dried cranberries
1/3 cup cornmeal
1/4 cup plus 1 tablespoon sugar, *divided*
2 teaspoons baking powder
2 teaspoons grated orange peel
1/2 teaspoon baking soda
1/4 teaspoon salt
1/4 teaspoon ground nutmeg
2 egg whites, lightly beaten
2/3 cup 1% buttermilk
1/4 cup canola oil

In a large bowl, combine the flour, cranberries, cornmeal, 1/4 cup sugar, baking powder, orange peel, baking soda, salt and nutmeg. In another bowl, combine the egg whites, buttermilk and oil. Add to dry ingredients and stir until a soft dough forms. On a floured surface, gently knead 6-8 times. Pat dough into an 8-1/2-in. circle.

Place on a baking sheet coated with nonstick cooking spray. Cut into 12 wedges; do not separate. Sprinkle with remaining sugar. Bake at 400° for 15-17 minutes or until golden brown. Remove to wire rack. Serve warm. **Yield:** 1 dozen.

Nutritional Analysis: 1 scone equals 183 calories, 5 g fat (trace saturated fat), 0 cholesterol, 216 mg sodium, 30 g carbohydrate, 1 g fiber, 4 g protein.
Diabetic Exchanges: *1 starch, 1 fruit, 1 fat.*

Rosemary Onion Focaccia

(Pictured on front cover)

Low-fat   Low-sodium   Meatless

Prep: 30 min. + rising **Bake:** 25 min.

This terrific focaccia loaf smells and tastes so good that it warms the soul.
—Linda Parker, Thunder Bay, Ontario

1-1/2 teaspoons active dry yeast
1-1/2 cups warm water (110° to 115°)
2 teaspoons honey
1/2 cup chopped onion
3 tablespoons olive oil, *divided*
1/2 teaspoon salt
1 tablespoon plus 2 teaspoons minced fresh rosemary, *divided*
3 to 4 cups all-purpose flour
1/2 teaspoon kosher salt

In a large mixing bowl, dissolve yeast in warm water. Stir in the honey; let stand for 5 minutes. Meanwhile, in a nonstick skillet, saute onion in 1 tablespoon oil until tender. Add to yeast mixture. Add the salt, 1 tablespoon rosemary, 1 cup flour and 1 tablespoon oil; beat until smooth. Stir in enough remaining flour to form a soft dough.

Turn onto a lightly floured surface; knead until smooth and elastic, about 6-8 minutes. Place in a large bowl coated with nonstick cooking spray, turning once to coat top. Cover and let rise in a warm place until doubled, about 40 minutes.

Turn dough onto a lightly floured surface; divide in half. Pat each portion into a 9-in. circle. Place on a baking sheet lightly coated with nonstick cooking spray. Cover and let rise until doubled, about 35 minutes.

Brush with remaining oil; sprinkle with kosher salt and remaining rosemary. Bake at 375° for 25-30 minutes or until lightly browned. Remove from pans to wire racks. **Yield:** 2 loaves (8 wedges each).

Nutritional Analysis: 1 wedge equals 114 calories, 3 g fat (trace saturated fat), 0 cholesterol, 133 mg sodium, 19 g carbohydrate, 1 g fiber, 3 g protein.
Diabetic Exchanges: *1 starch, 1/2 fat.*

Favorite Recipe Made Lighter

NOT ONLY did Rhonda Urich want *Light & Tasty* to cut fat from her Morning Glory Muffins, but she also hoped our staff could give them a nutritional boost.

"The muffins are hearty due to carrot, apple and raisins, but they're also high in oil," explains the Loveland, Colorado cook. "I'd like to see flaxseed or whole wheat flour added, making them a healthy snack."

Our Test Kitchen staff first replaced some of the oil called for in Rhonda's recipe with a combination of applesauce and ground flaxseed. Additional liquid is usually needed when replacing fat with flaxseed, so orange juice was added to the recipe.

Applesauce was used to further decrease the amount of oil called for. The applesauce and orange juice added sweetness, so the sugar was cut back as well.

In addition, half of the all-purpose flour was replaced with whole grain flour, and two of the whole eggs were substituted with egg whites.

The result? Muffins with nearly 50% less fat than the original recipe and 82 fewer calories. In addition, the amount of fiber in each muffin was doubled.

Morning Glory Muffins

Low-sodium *Meatless*

Prep: 25 min. **Bake:** 20 min.

       2 cups all-purpose flour
1-1/4 cups sugar
2-1/2 teaspoons baking powder
       2 teaspoons ground cinnamon
   1/2 teaspoon salt
       3 eggs
       1 cup vegetable oil
       2 teaspoons vanilla extract
       2 cups grated carrots
   1/2 cup chopped pecans
   1/2 cup flaked coconut

   1/2 cup raisins
       1 medium tart apple, peeled and shredded

In a large bowl, combine the first five ingredients. In another bowl, beat the eggs, oil and vanilla. Stir into dry ingredients just until moistened. Fold in the carrots, pecans, coconut, raisins and apple.

Fill greased or paper-lined muffin cups three-fourths full. Bake at 350° for 20-25 minutes or until a toothpick comes out clean. Cool for 5 minutes before removing from pans to wire racks. **Yield:** 1-1/2 dozen.

Nutritional Analysis: 1 muffin equals 285 calories, 17 g fat (2 g saturated fat), 35 mg cholesterol, 138 mg sodium, 32 g carbohydrate, 2 g fiber, 3 g protein.

Makeover Morning Glory Muffins

(Pictured above left)

Meatless

Prep: 25 min. **Bake:** 15 min.

       1 cup all-purpose flour
       1 cup whole wheat flour
   3/4 cup ground flaxseed
   3/4 cup sugar
2-3/4 teaspoons baking powder
       2 teaspoons ground cinnamon
   3/4 teaspoon salt
   1/4 teaspoon baking soda
       4 egg whites
       1 egg
   1/2 cup unsweetened applesauce
   1/3 cup orange juice
   1/4 cup canola oil
       2 teaspoons vanilla extract
       2 cups grated carrots
   1/2 cup chopped pecans
   1/2 cup flaked coconut
   1/2 cup raisins
       1 medium tart apple, peeled and shredded

In a large bowl, combine the first eight ingredients. In another bowl, beat egg whites, egg, applesauce, juice, oil and vanilla. Stir into dry ingredients just until moistened. Fold in carrots, nuts, coconut, raisins and apple.

Coat muffin cups with nonstick cooking spray or use foil liners; fill three-fourths full. Bake at 350° for 15-18 minutes or until a toothpick comes out clean. Cool for 5 minutes before removing from pans to wire racks. **Yield:** 1-1/2 dozen.

Nutritional Analysis: 1 muffin equals 203 calories, 9 g fat (2 g saturated fat), 12 mg cholesterol, 207 mg sodium, 29 g carbohydrate, 4 g fiber, 5 g protein.
Diabetic Exchanges: 2 starch, 2 fat.

Italian Pinwheel Rolls

(Pictured above)

Low-fat   Meatless

Prep: 35 min. + rising **Bake:** 25 min.

Parmesan cheese, garlic and oregano make these rolls hard to resist. My family gets the munchies when they smell these rolls baking.
—*Patricia FitzGerald, Candor, New York*

1 package (1/4 ounce) active dry yeast
1 cup warm water (110° to 115°)
1-1/2 teaspoons sugar
1-1/2 teaspoons butter, softened
1 teaspoon salt
2-1/4 to 2-1/2 cups bread flour
FILLING:
2 tablespoons butter, melted
1/4 cup grated Parmesan cheese
2 tablespoons minced fresh parsley
6 garlic cloves, minced
1 teaspoon dried oregano

In a large mixing bowl, dissolve yeast in warm water. Add the sugar, butter, salt and 1 cup flour; beat until smooth. Stir in enough remaining flour to form a soft dough.

Turn onto a floured surface; knead until smooth and elastic, about 6-8 minutes. Place in a bowl coated with non-stick cooking spray, turning once to coat top. Cover and let rise in a warm place until doubled, about 1 hour.

Punch dough down. Turn onto a lightly floured surface. Roll into a 12-in. x 10-in. rectangle. Brush with melted butter; sprinkle Parmesan cheese, parsley, garlic and oregano to within 1/2 in. of edges. Roll up jelly-roll style, starting with a long side; pinch seam to seal. Cut into 12 rolls.

Place rolls cut side up in a 13-in. x 9-in. x 2-in. baking pan coated with nonstick cooking spray. Cover and let rise until doubled, about 30 minutes. Bake at 350° for 25-30 minutes or until golden brown. Remove from pan to a wire rack. **Yield:** 1 dozen.

Nutritional Analysis: 1 roll equals 110 calories, 3 g fat (2 g saturated fat), 8 mg cholesterol, 253 mg sodium, 18 g carbohydrate, 1 g fiber, 4 g protein.
Diabetic Exchanges: 1 starch, 1/2 fat.

Teddy Bear Paws

Meatless

Prep: 50 min. + rising **Bake:** 10 min. + cooling

I wanted to lighten up bear claws for a holiday brunch. Using frozen cranberries left from Thanksgiving, I created this cute variation.
—*Hollyce Swan, Spokane, Washington*

1 cup finely chopped fresh *or* frozen cranberries
Sugar substitute equivalent to 3/4 cup sugar
1-1/2 teaspoons grated orange peel
2 packages (1/4 ounce *each*) active dry yeast
1/2 cup warm water (110° to 115°)
1/2 cup warm fat-free milk (110° to 115°)
1/2 cup sugar
2 eggs
1/4 cup butter, softened
1 teaspoon salt
3-1/2 to 4 cups all-purpose flour
1/4 cup slivered almonds, toasted
ICING:
2 tablespoons butter, softened
1 cup confectioners' sugar
1/8 teaspoon almond extract
1 to 2 tablespoons fat-free milk

In a large saucepan, bring the cranberries, sugar substitute and orange peel to a boil. Reduce heat to medium; cook and stir for 5 minutes or until thickened. Cool.

In a large mixing bowl, dissolve yeast in warm water. Add milk, sugar, eggs, butter, salt and 2 cups flour; beat until smooth. Stir in enough remaining flour to form a soft dough. Turn onto a lightly floured surface; knead until smooth and elastic, about 6-8 minutes. Place in a bowl coated with nonstick cooking spray, turning once to coat top. Cover and let rise in a warm place until doubled, about 1 hour.

Punch dough down. Turn onto a lightly floured surface; cover and let rest for 10 minutes. Roll into a 16-in. x 12-in. rectangle. Cut in half, forming two 16-in. x 6-in. strips. Spread cranberry filling down the center of each strip to within 1 in. of long edge. Fold lengthwise over filling and pinch seam to seal. Cut each strip into eight pieces. With a kitchen scissors, cut each piece two times from pinched seam to about 1 in. from folded side. Push an almond sliver into the end of each section for bear claws.

Place 2 in. apart on baking sheets coated with nonstick cooking spray. Curve folded side slightly to separate strips and allow filling to show. Cover and let rise in a warm place until doubled, about 30 minutes.

Bake at 375° for 10-14 minutes or until golden brown. Remove from pans to wire racks to cool. Combine icing ingredients; spread over rolls. **Yield:** 16 rolls.

Editor's Note: This recipe was tested with Splenda No Calorie Sweetener.

Nutritional Analysis: 1 roll equals 223 calories, 6 g fat (3 g saturated fat), 38 mg cholesterol, 204 mg sodium, 38 g carbohydrate, 1 g fiber, 5 g protein.
Diabetic Exchanges: 2-1/2 starch, 1 fat.

Try Something New: Flaxseed

WHETHER it is used as a tasty topping on muffins or stirred into comforting casseroles, flaxseed is a great choice when you are trying to eat light. Because of its health benefits, appealing flavor and versatility, it's becoming more popular with good cooks everywhere.

The Facts on Flaxseed

One of the oldest cultivated plants, flaxseed is a grain that is full of fiber and protein as well as polyunsaturated fat and essential omega-3 fatty acids. In addition, studies have found that it may protect against certain cancers and help manage autoimmune disorders.

Packaged in small bags, flaxseed (also known as linseed) can be found in the baking aisle or whole foods section of most grocery stores. Look for it near the oat flour or wheat germ.

Flaxseed is available in two varieties—yellow and brown. Brown flaxseed is more common, but the two varieties have the same nutritional value and can be used interchangeably.

You can purchase flaxseed whole or ground into meal. Whole flaxseed is about the size of a sesame seed but harder. It adds eye-appeal and crunch when used as a topping for breads and other baked goods.

Milled flaxseed can be kept in the refrigerator or freezer in an airtight container for up to 4 months. Whole flaxseed can be stored at room temperature for a year. Many cooks purchase flaxseed whole and grind it themselves. A clean coffee grinder can be used to grind whole flaxseed into a fine meal.

Nutritionally speaking, ground flaxseed is slightly better for you than whole flaxseed because the nutrients are more easily absorbed by the body. Ground flaxseed can be stirred into shakes, cereals and soups. Or try it as a topper on salads, yogurt or stir-fries.

Baking with Flaxseed

Because flaxseed is high in good fats, it can often be substituted at a three-to-one ratio for some of the oil or butter called for in a recipe. For example, use 3 tablespoons ground flaxseed for each tablespoon oil. When substituting flaxseed for a significant amount of fat, you may need to increase the liquid called for in the recipe because flaxseed tends to absorb liquid.

Flaxseed browns quickly in baked goods, so baking times and/or temperatures may need to be adjusted. You may need to experiment when baking with flaxseed, but the nutritional benefits are well worth it.

Cranberry Flax Muffins

(Pictured at left)

Meatless

Prep/Total Time: 25 min.

I modified this recipe from a heart-smart cookbook, and my husband loved it.
—Jennifer Wertz, Council Bluffs, Iowa

1-1/2 cups bran flakes cereal
3/4 cup all-purpose flour
3/4 cup whole wheat flour
1/2 cup ground flaxseed
1/4 cup packed brown sugar
2 teaspoons baking powder
1 teaspoon ground cinnamon
1/2 teaspoon baking soda
1/4 teaspoon salt
1 egg
2 egg whites
1 cup 1% buttermilk
1/2 cup honey
1/4 cup canola oil
1-1/2 cups dried cranberries
2 tablespoons whole flaxseed

In a large bowl, combine the first nine ingredients. Whisk the egg, egg whites, buttermilk, honey and oil; stir into dry ingredients just until moistened. Stir in cranberries.

Coat muffin cups with nonstick cooking spray or use paper liners; fill two-thirds full. Sprinkle with whole flaxseed. Bake at 375° for 10-15 minutes or until a toothpick comes out clean. Cool for 5 minutes before removing to wire racks. **Yield:** 1-1/2 dozen.

Nutritional Analysis: 1 muffin equals 183 calories, 5 g fat (1 g saturated fat), 13 mg cholesterol, 174 mg sodium, 32 g carbohydrate, 3 g fiber, 4 g protein.
Diabetic Exchanges: 2 starch, 1 fat.

Spinach Herb Twists

Low-carb Low-fat Meatless

Prep: 35 min. + rising **Bake:** 15 min.

These impressive low-carb twists are a delicious way to serve spinach. My mom baked them when we were kids.
—Amy Estes, Wichita, Kansas

5 cups packed torn fresh spinach
2 green onions, sliced
1 garlic clove, minced
5 tablespoons butter, *divided*
1/4 cup grated Parmesan cheese
1/2 teaspoon dried basil
1/2 teaspoon dried oregano
1 package (16 ounces) hot roll mix
1 cup warm water (120° to 130°)
1 egg

Place spinach in a steamer basket; place in a saucepan over 1 in. of water. Bring to a boil; cover and steam for 2-3 minutes or until limp. Drain well and set aside. In a small skillet, saute onions and garlic in 1 tablespoon butter until tender; transfer to a bowl. Stir in the Parmesan cheese, basil, oregano and spinach; set aside.

In a large bowl, stir roll mix, warm water, egg and 2 tablespoons butter until dough pulls away from sides of bowl. Turn onto a lightly floured surface; knead until smooth and elastic, about 5 minutes. Cover and let rest for 5 minutes.

Divide dough in half. Roll each portion into a 12-in. x 10-in. rectangle. Melt the remaining butter; brush over dough. Spread spinach mixture over dough to within 1/4 in. of edges. Fold each rectangle in half lengthwise; pinch seams to seal. Cut each rectangle into twelve 1-in.-wide strips.

Twist strips and place on baking sheets coated with nonstick cooking spray. Cover and let rise in a warm place until doubled, about 25 minutes. Bake at 375° for 12-16 minutes or until golden brown. Serve warm. Refrigerate leftovers. **Yield:** 2 dozen.

Nutritional Analysis: 1 twist equals 90 calories, 3 g fat (2 g saturated fat), 16 mg cholesterol, 156 mg sodium, 12 g carbohydrate, 1 g fiber, 2 g protein.
Diabetic Exchanges: 1 starch, 1/2 fat.

Caramel Apple Bread

Meatless

Prep: 30 min. **Bake:** 45 min. + cooling

With its sweet caramel-like topping, this bread is great for snacking. It never lasts long in our house.
—Valerie Long, Bethany, Oklahoma

1 cup fat-free plain yogurt
3/4 cup sugar
2 eggs
2 teaspoons vanilla extract
2 cups all-purpose flour
2 teaspoons baking powder
1/2 teaspoon baking soda
1/2 teaspoon salt
1-1/2 cups chopped peeled tart apples
3/4 cup chopped pecans

1/4 cup packed brown sugar
2 tablespoons butter
1 tablespoon fat-free milk

In a large mixing bowl, beat the yogurt, sugar, eggs and vanilla. Combine the flour, baking powder, baking soda and salt; add to yogurt mixture and beat until just combined. Fold in apples and pecans.

Pour into a 9-in. x 5-in. x 3-in. loaf pan coated with nonstick cooking spray. Bake at 350° for 45-55 minutes or until a toothpick inserted near the center comes out clean. Cool for 10 minutes before removing from pan to a wire rack.

In a small saucepan, bring the brown sugar, butter and milk to a boil, stirring constantly. Cover and cook for 1 minute. Cool slightly. Spread over cooled bread. Let stand for 15 minutes. **Yield:** 1 loaf (12 slices).

Nutritional Analysis: 1 slice equals 239 calories, 8 g fat (2 g saturated fat), 41 mg cholesterol, 232 mg sodium, 38 g carbohydrate, 2 g fiber, 5 g protein.

Irish Soda Bread

Low-fat Meatless

Prep: 10 min. **Bake:** 20 min. + cooling

Both my husband and I are diabetics. This quick bread uses a sugar substitute and is really tasty.
—Ruth Russell, Clyde, North Carolina

1-1/2 cups all-purpose flour
1/2 cup whole wheat flour
Sugar substitute equivalent to 2 tablespoons sugar
1 teaspoon baking soda
1/2 teaspoon salt
2 tablespoons cold butter
1 cup 1% buttermilk
1/2 cup dried currants

In a large bowl, combine the flours, sugar substitute, baking soda and salt; cut in butter. Stir in buttermilk just until moistened. Fold in currants. Knead on a floured surface 8-10 times. Shape into a 7-in. round loaf; place on a baking sheet coated with nonstick cooking spray.

Bake at 375° for 20-25 minutes or until a toothpick inserted near the center comes out clean. Remove from pan to a wire rack. **Yield:** 1 loaf (12 slices).

Editor's Note: This recipe was tested with Splenda No Calorie Sweetener.

Nutritional Analysis: 1 slice equals 120 calories, 2 g fat (1 g saturated fat), 6 mg cholesterol, 245 mg sodium, 21 g carbohydrate, 2 g fiber, 3 g protein.
Diabetic Exchange: 1-1/2 starch.

Dazzling Desserts

It used to be the words "rich," "creamy" and "yummy" were never spoken in the same sentence as "low fat," especially when the conversation turned to desserts. But now you can have your cake and eat it, too!

Classic Pumpkin Pie (page 218)

Raisins and Rice Pudding

Low-fat

Prep/Total Time: 20 min.

I use vanilla pudding mix and just four other ingredients to create this no-fuss stovetop treat. It's wonderful served warm, but we also like it after it has chilled a bit.
—Mary Brown, Havre, Montana

3-1/2 cups fat-free milk
   1 cup uncooked instant rice
   1 package (4.6 ounces) cook-and-serve vanilla pudding mix
   1 cup raisins
  1/2 teaspoon ground cinnamon

In a saucepan, bring milk and rice to a boil over medium heat. Whisk in pudding mix; cook and stir for 1 minute or until thickened. Remove from the heat; fold in raisins. Cover and let stand for 5 minutes.

   Spoon into individual dessert bowls. Sprinkle with cinnamon. Serve warm. **Yield:** 6 servings.

   Nutritional Analysis: 3/4 cup equals 258 calories, trace fat (trace saturated fat), 3 mg cholesterol, 218 mg sodium, 58 g carbohydrate, 2 g fiber, 7 g protein.
   Diabetic Exchanges: 1 starch, 1 fruit, 1 fat.

Cheesecake Phyllo Cups

(Pictured above)

Low-sodium   Low-carb

Prep/Total Time: 25 min.

I borrowed this recipe from a friend, whose husband is diabetic, and have been making the colorful cheesecake bites ever since. Topped with kiwifruit and mandarin oranges, they are just delicious.
—Lorraine Chevalier, Merrimac, Massachusetts

   4 ounces reduced-fat cream cheese
  1/2 cup reduced-fat sour cream
Sugar substitute equivalent to 2 tablespoons sugar
   1 teaspoon vanilla extract
   2 packages (2.1 ounces *each*) frozen miniature phyllo shells, thawed
   1 can (11 ounces) mandarin orange slices, drained
   1 kiwifruit, peeled, sliced and cut into quarters

In a bowl, whisk together the cream cheese, sour cream, sugar substitute and vanilla until smooth. Pipe or spoon the mixture into phyllo shells. Top each with a mandarin orange segment and kiwi piece. Refrigerate until serving. **Yield:** 2-1/2 dozen.

   Editor's Note: This recipe was tested with Splenda No Calorie Sweetener.

   Nutritional Analysis: 3 cups equals 137 calories, 7 g fat (3 g saturated fat), 15 mg cholesterol, 83 mg sodium, 13 g carbohydrate, trace fiber, 3 g protein.
   Diabetic Exchanges: 1 starch, 1 fat.

🍎 Kiwifruit Cuisine

ON THE SURFACE, kiwifruit is no beauty. But its fuzzy brown "wrapper" hides a taste treasure. Here's the inside scoop:

- Kiwifruit is a great snack eaten raw out of hand. Rinse it, gently rub the skin with a cloth to remove excess fuzz and bite right in. Or cut the fruit in half and spoon it out like a melon.
- For fuzz-free eating, cut off the kiwifruit's top and bottom ends and remove its skin with a vegetable peeler. Use an egg slicer to cut uniform pieces for recipes or garnish.
- Mix chopped kiwifruit into pancake or waffle batter, then top the stack with additional slices.
- Use kiwifruit as a winter substitute for tomatoes in sandwiches, salads or salsa.
- Eat sliced kiwifruit with reduced-fat cheese and crackers.
- Stir cut kiwifruit into pasta or chicken salads.
- Prepare pavlova, a popular dessert in Australia and New Zealand that consists of a meringue shell topped with fresh fruit, including kiwi.
- Containing the enzyme actinidin, kiwifruit is a natural tenderizer. Puree the fruit and rub on meat or poultry; refrigerate for 30 minutes before cooking.
- One serving—two medium kiwifruits—has just 90 calories.

Key Lime Cheesecake

(Pictured below)

Prep: 25 min. **Bake:** 40 min. + chilling

I modified this old family recipe so it uses healthier ingredients. The texture is so smooth and light. It's a favorite dessert that everyone enjoys.
—Darlene Kohler, Flower Mound, Texas

3/4 cup reduced-fat graham cracker crumbs (about 8 squares)
Sugar substitute equivalent to 2 tablespoons sugar
2 tablespoons butter, melted
FILLING:
2 packages (8 ounces *each*) reduced-fat cream cheese, cubed
1 package (8 ounces) fat-free cream cheese, cubed
Sugar substitute equivalent to 2/3 cup sugar
1/3 cup sugar
3 tablespoons all-purpose flour
3 eggs, lightly beaten
1 cup (8 ounces) reduced-fat sour cream
1/3 cup key lime *or* lime juice
2 teaspoons grated lime peel
2 teaspoons vanilla extract
2 drops green food coloring, optional

Wrap bottom of a 9-in. springform pan with a double layer of heavy-duty foil; coat pan with nonstick cooking spray. Combine the first three ingredients. Press onto the bottom of pan. Bake at 350° for 8-10 minutes or until set. Cool.

In a mixing bowl, beat cream cheese until smooth. Combine the sugar substitute, sugar and flour; gradually beat into cream cheese. Add eggs; beat on low speed just until combined. Beat in the sour cream, lime juice, peel, vanilla and food coloring if desired just until combined. Pour into crust.

Place springform pan in a large baking pan; add 1 in. of hot water to larger pan. Bake at 350° for 40-45 minutes or until center is just set. Remove springform pan from water bath. Cool on a wire rack for 10 minutes. Carefully run a knife around the edge of pan to loosen; cool 1 hour. Remove

foil from pan. Chill overnight. Remove sides of pan. Refrigerate leftovers. **Yield:** 14 servings.

Editor's Note: This recipe was tested with Splenda No Calorie Sweetener.

Nutritional Analysis: 1 piece equals 205 calories, 12 g fat (7 g saturated fat), 81 mg cholesterol, 293 mg sodium, 16 g carbohydrate, trace fiber, 9 g protein.
Diabetic Exchanges: 2 fat, 1 starch, 1 lean meat.

Easy Cherry Cobbler

(Pictured above)

Prep: 5 min. **Bake:** 30 min.

A warm and welcome ending to any meal, this simple cobbler tastes as soothing as it sounds.
—Sherry Craw, Mattoon, Illinois

1 can (20 ounces) reduced-sugar cherry pie filling
1/4 teaspoon almond extract
2 cups reduced-fat biscuit/baking mix
2 tablespoons plus 1 teaspoon sugar, *divided*
1/2 cup fat-free milk
2 tablespoons reduced-fat margarine, melted

In a large bowl, combine pie filling and extract; spread into a 9-in. deep-dish pie plate. Bake, uncovered, at 400° for 10 minutes.

Meanwhile, in a bowl, combine the baking mix and 2 tablespoons sugar. In another bowl, combine the milk and margarine. Stir milk mixture into dry ingredients until a soft dough forms. Drop dough by spoonfuls over warmed pie filling. Sprinkle with remaining sugar. Bake, uncovered, at 400° for 20-25 minutes until topping is golden brown. Serve warm. **Yield:** 8 servings.

Editor's Note: This recipe was tested with Parkay light stick margarine.

Nutritional Analysis: 1 serving equals 206 calories, 4 g fat (1 g saturated fat), trace cholesterol, 393 mg sodium, 40 g carbohydrate, 1 g fiber, 3 g protein.
Diabetic Exchanges: 1-1/2 starch, 1 fruit, 1/2 fat.

Chocolate Peanut Butter Cookies

(Pictured above)

Low-carb   Low-sodium

Prep/Total Time: 25 min.

This soft and chewy low-carb cookie recipe, developed by our Test Kitchen, calls for canola oil instead of butter to reduce the saturated fat. It's hard to eat just one!

> 1 cup chunky peanut butter
> 1/4 cup canola oil
> 3/4 cup packed brown sugar
> 1/2 cup sugar
> 2 eggs
> 1 tablespoon vanilla extract
> 1 cup all-purpose flour
> 1/3 cup baking cocoa
> 1 teaspoon baking soda
> 1/2 teaspoon salt
> 1/2 cup miniature chocolate chips

In a large mixing bowl, combine peanut butter and oil. Add brown sugar and sugar; mix well. Add eggs and vanilla; mix well. Combine the flour, cocoa, baking soda and salt. Add to peanut butter mixture; mix until blended (dough will be sticky). Stir in chocolate chips.

Drop by rounded teaspoonfuls 2 in. apart on ungreased baking sheets. Flatten slightly with a glass. Bake at 350° for 8-10 minutes or until set and tops are cracked. Cool for 2 minutes before removing to wire racks. **Yield:** 4 dozen.

Nutritional Analysis: *1 cookie equals 86 calories, 5 g fat (1 g saturated fat), 9 mg cholesterol, 81 mg sodium, 10 g carbohydrate, 1 g fiber, 2 g protein.*
Diabetic Exchanges: *1 starch, 1/2 fat.*

Lemon Cream Pie

(Pictured above)

Prep: 15 min. **Cook:** 15 min. + chilling

With its creamy lemon filling and cinnamon-spiced graham cracker crust, this lovely pie is always popular.
—*Maria Dygert, Auburn, New York*

> 1-1/4 cups reduced-fat cinnamon graham cracker crumbs (about 14 squares)
> 1/4 cup reduced-fat margarine, melted
> 1 tablespoon plus 3/4 cup sugar, *divided*
> 5 tablespoons cornstarch
> 1/8 teaspoon salt
> 1 cup water
> 2/3 cup 1% buttermilk
> 1/2 cup egg substitute
> 1/2 cup lemon juice
> 2 teaspoons grated lemon peel
> 2-1/2 cups reduced-fat whipped topping

In a small bowl, combine the graham cracker crumbs, margarine and 1 tablespoon sugar; mix well. Press onto the bottom and up the sides of a 9-in. pie plate coated with non-stick cooking spray. Bake at 350° for 8-10 minutes or until golden brown. Cool on a wire rack.

In a heavy saucepan, combine the cornstarch, salt and remaining sugar. Gradually stir in water and buttermilk until smooth. Bring to a boil; cook and stir for 2 minutes or until thickened. Remove from the heat. Stir a small amount of hot filling into egg substitute. Return all to pan, stirring constantly. Bring to a gentle boil; cook and stir for 2 minutes longer. Remove from the heat. Stir in lemon juice and peel. Pour into crust. Cover and refrigerate for at least 4 hours. Just before serving, spread whipped topping over filling. **Yield:** 8 servings.

Editor's Note: This recipe was tested with Blue Bonnet light stick margarine.

Nutritional Analysis: 1 piece equals 252 calories, 6 g fat (3 g saturated fat), 1 mg cholesterol, 227 mg sodium, 45 g carbohydrate, 1 g fiber, 3 g protein.
Diabetic Exchanges: 3 starch, 1 fat.

Orange Pear Crisp

Low-sodium

Prep: 15 min. **Bake:** 20 min.

Our home economists developed this heartwarming delight. It's a fun twist on a classic dessert.

4 medium ripe pears, peeled and sliced
1/4 cup all-purpose flour
Sugar substitute equivalent to 1/4 cup sugar
1/4 cup orange juice
2 teaspoons grated orange peel
TOPPING:
3 reduced-fat graham crackers (about 5 inches x 2-1/2 inches), crushed
Sugar substitute equivalent to 1/4 cup sugar
2 tablespoons all-purpose flour
1 teaspoon ground cinnamon
3 tablespoons reduced-fat butter, melted

In a large bowl, combine the pears, flour, sugar substitute, orange juice and orange peel. Spoon into an 8-in. square dish coated with nonstick cooking spray.

In a small bowl, combine the graham cracker crumbs, sugar substitute, flour and cinnamon; stir in butter. Sprinkle over pear mixture. Bake at 350° for 20-25 minutes or until topping is crisp and lightly browned. Serve warm. **Yield:** 6 servings.

Editor's Note: This recipe was tested with Splenda No Calorie Sweetener and Land O' Lakes light stick butter.

Nutritional Analysis: 2/3 cup equals 163 calories, 4 g fat (2 g saturated fat), 10 mg cholesterol, 85 mg sodium, 32 g carbohydrate, 3 g fiber, 2 g protein.
Diabetic Exchanges: 1 starch, 1 fruit, 1/2 fat.

Honey Apricot Biscotti

(Pictured below)

Low-carb Low-fat Low-sodium

Prep: 25 min. **Bake:** 45 min. + cooling

Dried apricots, brown sugar and a hint of anise make these delectable treats ideal for serving alongside hot cups of coffee or tea. I like to include the biscotti on the cookie trays I give to my family and friends.
—Suzanne Smyth, Mountain Home, Arkansas

3 egg whites
1/4 cup plus 2 tablespoons honey
1/2 teaspoon anise extract
2 cups all-purpose flour
2/3 cup packed brown sugar
3/4 teaspoon baking powder
1/4 teaspoon baking soda
Dash salt
2/3 cup finely chopped dried apricots

In a small bowl, whisk together the egg whites, honey and extract; set aside. In another bowl, combine the flour, brown sugar, baking powder, baking soda and salt. Make a well in the center; add egg white mixture. Stir until moistened. Fold in apricots.

Spray a baking sheet with nonstick cooking spray; dust with flour. Divide the biscotti dough in half. On the prepared baking sheet, shape each portion of dough into a 12-in. x 2-in. rectangle, leaving a 6-in. space in between the rectangles. Bake at 325° for 30 minutes or until golden brown. Cool for 5 minutes.

Transfer the rectangles to a cutting board; cut each diagonally with a serrated knife into 1/2-in. slices. Place the cut side of the slices down on baking sheets. Bake for 7 minutes; turn over and bake 7 minutes longer or until golden brown. Remove to wire racks to cool. Store in an airtight container. **Yield:** 3 dozen.

Nutritional Analysis: 1 cookie equals 61 calories, trace fat (trace saturated fat), 0 cholesterol, 28 mg sodium, 14 g carbohydrate, trace fiber, 1 g protein.
Diabetic Exchange: 1 starch.

Chunky Banana Chip Ice Cream

(Pictured above)

Low-sodium

Prep: 15 min. + chilling **Freeze:** 2-1/2 hours

If a banana split is on your no-no list, treat yourself to this lower-in-fat option dreamed up by our Test Kitchen staff. Each smooth and creamy scoop is generously sprinkled with semisweet chocolate chips.

 2 cups 2% milk
 1 can (14 ounces) fat-free sweetened condensed milk
 1 envelope whipped topping mix
 2 tablespoons sugar
 2 teaspoons lemon juice
 1 teaspoon vanilla extract
 3 medium firm bananas, cut into 1-inch pieces
 1/2 cup miniature semisweet chocolate chips

In a large mixing bowl, beat the first six ingredients on high speed for 3 minutes. Cover and refrigerate overnight.

Stir bananas into milk mixture. Fill cylinder of ice cream freezer; freeze according to the manufacturer's directions. Stir in chocolate chips. Allow to ripen in ice cream freezer or firm up in the refrigerator freezer for 2-4 hours before serving. **Yield:** 8 servings.

Nutritional Analysis: 1/2 cup equals 301 calories, 5 g fat (4 g saturated fat), 8 mg cholesterol, 84 mg sodium, 57 g carbohydrate, 2 g fiber, 7 g protein.

Caramel Banana Cake Roll

(Pictured above)

Prep: 35 min. **Bake:** 10 min. + cooling

Our home economists created this sunny cake roll that's bursting with fresh banana goodness and a light, creamy caramel filling. As special and impressive as it looks, the delightful dessert isn't difficult to put together.

 1 cup cake flour
 1/2 teaspoon baking soda
 1/2 teaspoon salt
 1/4 teaspoon baking powder
 2 eggs
 3/4 cup sugar, *divided*
 1/2 cup mashed ripe banana (about 1 medium)
 1 teaspoon vanilla extract
 1 teaspoon grated lemon peel
 3 egg whites
 1 tablespoon confectioners' sugar
FILLING:
 4 ounces reduced-fat cream cheese
 1/2 cup packed brown sugar
 1/2 teaspoon vanilla extract
 1 cup reduced-fat whipped topping
 1 tablespoon confectioners' sugar
 2 tablespoons fat-free caramel ice cream topping

Line a 15-in. x 10-in. x 1-in. baking pan coated with nonstick cooking spray with waxed paper and coat the paper with nonstick cooking spray; set aside.

Combine the flour, baking soda, salt and baking powder. In a large mixing bowl, beat the eggs for 5 minutes; add 1/2 cup sugar, banana, vanilla and lemon peel. In a small mixing bowl, beat the egg whites on medium speed until soft peaks form. Gradually beat in the remaining sugar, a tablespoon at a time, on high until stiff peaks form. Add the flour mixture to the banana mixture; mix gently until combined. Fold in the egg white mixture.

Spread into prepared pan. Bake at 375° for 10-12 minutes or until cake springs back when lightly touched. Cool for 5 minutes. Turn cake onto a kitchen towel dusted with confectioners' sugar. Gently peel off waxed paper. Roll up cake in towel jelly-roll style, starting with a short side. Cool completely on a wire rack.

For filling, in a mixing bowl, beat cream cheese and brown sugar until smooth and sugar is dissolved. Beat in vanilla; fold in whipped topping. Unroll cake; spread filling over cake to within 1/2 in. of edges. Roll up again; place seam side down on a serving platter. Cover and refrigerate for at least 1 hour before serving. Before serving, sprinkle with confectioners' sugar, then drizzle with ice cream topping. Refrigerate leftovers. **Yield:** 8 servings.

Nutritional Analysis: 1 slice equals 269 calories, 4 g fat (2 g saturated fat), 58 mg cholesterol, 342 mg sodium, 54 g carbohydrate, 1 g fiber, 6 g protein.

🍎 Nutrition in Bunches

BANANAS slip easily into a healthy diet. Here are some fun facts about that appealing fruit:

- An average banana contains 11% of the U.S. recommended daily allowance of potassium, 16% of dietary fiber and 20% of vitamin B6.
- According to the U.S. Food and Drug Administration, eating potassium-rich, low-sodium foods like bananas may reduce the risk of high blood pressure, stroke, cancer and heart disease.
- Bananas help sustain the body for fitness, replenishing vitamins and minerals used in exercise.
- Among over 500 varieties of bananas in the world, the Cavendish is the yellow crescent-shaped type most commonly found in supermarkets.
- Some variety of the banana was likely cultivated by prehistoric inhabitants of Southeast Asia, where the plant is believed to have originated.
- The banana was officially introduced to the American public at the 1876 Philadelphia Centennial Exhibition, where a single banana sold for a dime.
- Today, bananas are among the most popular fruits in the U.S., with a typical American eating over 28 pounds per year.
- Bananas are one of the few fruits that ripen best off the plant.
- To store bananas, keep them at room temperature so they continue to ripen. To slow ripening, refrigerate. Bananas can be kept—peeled or mashed—in the freezer in an airtight container with a bit of lemon juice to reduce browning.

Rhubarb Sauce

(Pictured below)

Low-carb   Low-fat   Low-sodium

Prep/Total Time: 20 min.

Five ingredients are all you need for this lip-smacking sauce that's ideal over reduced-fat vanilla ice cream. We even like this topping served warm over biscuits with a dash of cinnamon and a dollop of whipped cream.
—Evelyn Gebhardt, Kasilof, Alaska

3 cups sliced fresh *or* frozen rhubarb
Sugar substitute equivalent to 1/2 cup sugar
1/4 cup water
1/8 teaspoon ground nutmeg
1/4 teaspoon vanilla extract
Reduced-fat no-sugar-added vanilla ice cream

In a saucepan, combine the rhubarb, sugar substitute, water and nutmeg. Bring to a boil. Reduce heat; simmer, uncovered, for 6-8 minutes or until rhubarb is tender. Remove from the heat; stir in vanilla. Serve warm or cold over ice cream. **Yield:** 5 servings.

Editor's Note: This recipe was tested with Splenda No Calorie Sweetener.

Nutritional Analysis: 1/4 cup sauce (calculated without ice cream) equals 26 calories, trace fat (trace saturated fat), 0 cholesterol, 3 mg sodium, 6 g carbohydrate, 1 g fiber, 1 g protein.
***Diabetic Exchange:** 1/2 fruit.*

Honey Spice Snack Cake

(Pictured above)

Prep: 15 min. **Bake:** 15 min. + cooling

Our Test Kitchen staff relied on ground cloves, applesauce and honey to give this scrumptious spice cake plenty of down-home goodness. The light and airy treat is topped off with a sprinkling of confectioners' sugar.

    2 cups all-purpose flour
Sugar substitute equivalent to 3/4 cup sugar
  2-1/2 teaspoons baking powder
  1-1/2 teaspoons ground cinnamon
    1/2 teaspoon baking soda
    1/4 teaspoon ground nutmeg
    1/4 teaspoon ground cloves
    1/8 teaspoon salt
     2 eggs
    3/4 cup unsweetened applesauce
    1/4 cup canola oil
    1/4 cup honey
    1/4 cup finely chopped walnuts, toasted
    1/2 teaspoon confectioners' sugar

In a large bowl, combine the first eight ingredients. Whisk the eggs, applesauce, oil and honey. Stir into dry ingredients just until moistened. Fold in walnuts.

Pour into a 9-in. square baking pan coated with nonstick cooking spray. Bake at 350° for 15-20 minutes or until a toothpick inserted near the center comes out clean. Cool on a wire rack. Dust with confectioners' sugar. **Yield:** 12 servings.

Editor's Note: This recipe was tested with Splenda No Calorie Sweetener.

Nutritional Analysis: 1 piece equals 181 calories, 7 g fat (1 g saturated fat), 35 mg cholesterol, 172 mg sodium, 26 g carbohydrate, 1 g fiber, 4 g protein.
Diabetic Exchanges: 1-1/2 starch, 1 fat.

Blueberry Dessert

Low-sodium

Prep: 15 min. **Bake:** 20 min. + cooling

I was really pleased with the results when I lightened up this dessert recipe that's been in our family for years.
—Alta Rodgers, Pottstown, Pennsylvania

1-1/2 cups graham cracker crumbs (about 16 squares)
  1/2 cup sugar, *divided*
  1/4 cup reduced-fat butter, melted
    1 package (8 ounces) reduced-fat cream cheese
    2 eggs
    1 teaspoon vanilla extract
    1 can (21 ounces) blueberry pie filling
    1 cup reduced-fat whipped topping

In a small bowl, combine the graham cracker crumbs and 1/4 cup sugar; stir in butter. Press into the bottom of a 13-in. x 9-in. x 2-in. baking dish coated with nonstick cooking spray. Bake at 350° for 10-15 minutes or until golden brown.

In a large mixing bowl, beat cream cheese and remaining sugar until smooth; add the eggs and vanilla. Pour over crust. Bake at 350° for 10-12 minutes or until set. Cool on a wire rack. Spread with pie filling. Refrigerate until serving. Garnish with whipped topping. **Yield:** 15 servings.

Editor's Note: This recipe was tested with Land O' Lakes light stick butter.

Nutritional Analysis: 1 piece equals 169 calories, 6 g fat (3 g saturated fat), 42 mg cholesterol, 136 mg sodium, 25 g carbohydrate, 1 g fiber, 3 g protein.
Diabetic Exchanges: 1-1/2 starch, 1 fat.

Spiced Honey Pears

Low-fat   Low-sodium

Prep/Total Time: 15 min.

Take one bite of these spiced pears whipped up by our home economists, and you'll enjoy a burst of flavors that will warm you up on even the chilliest nights.

    6 medium ripe pears
    2 tablespoons honey
  1/4 to 1/2 teaspoon Chinese five-spice powder
  1/4 to 1/2 teaspoon ground cinnamon

Cut a 3/4-in. slice off the top of each pear, reserving tops. Core pears, leaving bottoms intact. Cut 1/8-in. slice from bottoms to level if necessary. Drizzle insides of each pear with 1 teaspoon of honey. Combine five-spice powder and cinnamon; sprinkle inside pears. Replace pear tops.

Arrange pears upright in a shallow 2-qt. microwave-safe dish. Microwave, uncovered, for 4-7 minutes or until pears are tender, turning every 2 minutes. Serve warm with juices spooned over pears. **Yield:** 6 servings.

Editor's Note: This recipe was tested in a 1,100-watt microwave.

Nutritional Analysis: 1 pear equals 119 calories, 1 g fat (trace saturated fat), 0 cholesterol, trace sodium, 31 g carbohydrate, 4 g fiber, 1 g protein.
Diabetic Exchange: 2 fruit.

Favorite Recipe Made Lighter

HEALTH-CONSCIOUS COOKS are always looking for ways to improve recipes, including those that already use better-for-you ingredients.

Pat Doctor, for example, is watching her cholesterol, so she has eliminated flaked coconut from her diet because she knows it's high in fat and saturated fat. That's why Pat's Coconut Cookies call for coconut extract instead of flaked coconut. And frosted cornflakes help give the treats a crunchy texture.

"I love coconut, and these drop cookies are really good," she writes from Cocoa, Florida. "But I'd like them even better with less sugar and fat. Would you please help me make over this recipe?"

Our Test Kitchen home economists were happy to oblige. They began by decreasing the amount of fat called for in the original recipe and using canola oil in place of some of the butter. (Canola oil has no cholesterol and much less saturated fat, making it a great substitute in many baked goods.)

To further reduce the cholesterol and saturated fat, one whole egg and three egg whites were used instead of three whole eggs.

Our home economists also used regular cornflakes in place of the frosted variety…and the amount of sugar was successfully reduced.

The trimmed-down treats that resulted have two-thirds the calories, half the fat and just a quarter of the saturated fat and cholesterol. Yet they have a sweet taste and bit of crunch, just like the original.

Makeover Coconut Cookies

(Pictured above)

Low-carb Low-fat Low-sodium

Prep/Total Time: 25 min.

1/4 cup butter, softened
1/4 cup canola oil
1/2 cup packed brown sugar
1/4 cup sugar
  3 egg whites
  1 egg
  3 teaspoons vanilla extract
  2 teaspoons coconut extract
1-3/4 cups all-purpose flour
  3 teaspoons baking powder
1/2 teaspoon salt
  4 cups cornflakes

In a large mixing bowl, combine the butter, oil and sugars. Beat in egg whites, egg and extracts. Combine the flour, baking powder and salt; gradually add to egg mixture. Stir in cereal.

Drop by tablespoonfuls 2 in. apart onto baking sheets coated with nonstick cooking spray. Bake at 375° for 10-12 minutes or until lightly browned. Remove to wire racks to cool. **Yield:** 3-1/2 dozen.

Nutritional Analysis: 1 cookie equals 69 calories, 3 g fat (1 g saturated fat), 8 mg cholesterol, 94 mg sodium, 10 g carbohydrate, trace fiber, 1 g protein.
Diabetic Exchanges: 1/2 starch, 1/2 fat.

Coconut Cookies

Low-carb Low-sodium

Prep/Total Time: 25 min.

1-1/2 cups butter, softened
1/2 cup sugar
1/2 cup packed brown sugar
  3 eggs
  3 teaspoons vanilla extract
  2 teaspoons coconut extract
1-3/4 cups all-purpose flour
  3 teaspoons baking powder
1/2 teaspoon salt
4-1/2 cups frosted cornflakes

In a large mixing bowl, cream butter and sugars. Beat in eggs and extracts. Combine the flour, baking powder and salt; gradually add to the creamed mixture. Stir in cereal.

Drop by tablespoonfuls 2 in. apart onto ungreased baking sheets. Bake at 375° for 10-12 minutes or until lightly browned. Remove to wire racks to cool. **Yield:** 4 dozen.

Nutritional Analysis: 1 cookie equals 104 calories, 6 g fat (4 g saturated fat), 29 mg cholesterol, 131 mg sodium, 11 g carbohydrate, trace fiber, 1 g protein.

Coconut Strawberry Phyllo Cones

(Pictured above)

Low-fat

Prep: 35 min. **Bake:** 5 min. + cooling

Cute enough to serve weekend guests, these charming desserts from our Test Kitchen come together with phyllo dough and a few kitchen staples.

- 4 **sheets phyllo dough (14 inches x 9 inches)**
- 1 **cup cold fat-free milk**
- 1 **package (3.4 ounces) instant coconut cream pudding mix**
- 1/2 **cup reduced-fat whipped topping, thawed**
- 6 **fresh strawberries,** *divided*

Cut four 12-in. x 6-in. pieces of foil. Fold each in half widthwise. Shape each square into a loosely rolled cone, overlapping the edges about 1-1/2 in.; set aside.

Place one sheet of phyllo dough on a work surface; spray with nonstick cooking spray. Repeat with one more sheet of phyllo. (Keep remaining phyllo covered with plastic wrap and a damp towel to prevent drying.) Cut in half lengthwise and widthwise. Carefully wrap one phyllo section around each foil cone; spray again with nonstick cooking spray.

Place on an ungreased baking sheet. Bake at 425° for 4-5 minutes or until lightly browned. Immediately remove phyllo from foil cones to a wire rack to cool completely. Repeat entire procedure with remaining phyllo dough.

In a small bowl, whisk milk and pudding mix for 2 minutes; fold in whipped topping. Spoon into a pastry bag fitted with a #199 star tip. Finely chop three strawberries and spoon into cones. Pipe pudding mixture into cones. Slice remaining strawberries to use as garnish. Serve immediately. **Yield:** 8 servings.

Nutritional Analysis: *1 serving equals 87 calories, 2 g fat (2 g saturated fat), 1 mg cholesterol, 164 mg sodium, 16 g carbohydrate, 1 g fiber, 2 g protein.*
Diabetic Exchange: *1 starch.*

Double Chocolate Pudding

(Pictured below)

Low-fat   Low-sodium

Prep/Total Time: 25 min.

Our home economists set out to create a rich chocolate sensation, and they certainly succeeded with this soft, creamy pudding. A little German chocolate and baking cocoa make it a low-fat but mouth-watering hit.

- 3/4 **cup sugar**
- 1/3 **cup baking cocoa**
- 1/4 **cup cornstarch**
- 1/8 **teaspoon salt**
- 3 **cups fat-free milk**
- 1 **can (5 ounces) evaporated milk**
- 1 **ounce German sweet chocolate, grated**
- 1 **teaspoon vanilla extract**
- 1/4 **cup whipped topping**

In a large heavy saucepan, combine the sugar, cocoa, cornstarch and salt. Gradually add the milks. Bring to a boil over medium heat; cook and stir for 2 minutes or until thickened. Remove from the heat.

Stir in grated chocolate and vanilla. Spoon into individual serving dishes. Serve warm or cold with whipped topping. **Yield:** 8 servings.

Nutritional Analysis: *1/2 cup equals 166 calories, 2 g fat (1 g saturated fat), 4 mg cholesterol, 72 mg sodium, 33 g carbohydrate, 1 g fiber, 5 g protein.*
Diabetic Exchanges: *1-1/2 starch, 1/2 fat-free milk.*

Lemon Cake

(Pictured above)

Prep: 20 min. **Bake:** 25 min. + cooling

With a refreshing lemon glaze, this fluffy cake is full of citrus flavor but not much fat or cholesterol.
—Bonita Giesbrecht, Glenn, California

- 1 package (18-1/4 ounces) white cake mix
- 1 package (3 ounces) lemon gelatin
- 1 cup plus 2 tablespoons water
- 4 egg whites
- 1/3 cup unsweetened applesauce
- 1 tablespoon canola oil
- 1 teaspoon lemon extract
- 4 drops yellow food coloring, optional

LEMON GLAZE:
- 1-1/2 cups confectioners' sugar
- 1/3 cup lemon juice

In a large mixing bowl, combine the dry cake mix, gelatin, water, egg whites, applesauce, oil, lemon extract and food coloring if desired. Beat on medium speed for 2 minutes. Pour into a 13-in. x 9-in. x 2-in. baking pan coated with nonstick cooking spray. Bake at 350° for 25-30 minutes or until edges are lightly browned and a toothpick inserted near the center comes out clean. Cool on a wire rack for 10 minutes.

Meanwhile, for glaze, in a bowl, combine the confectioners' sugar and lemon juice until smooth. Drizzle about a third of glaze over cake; carefully spread evenly. Repeat with remaining glaze. Cool completely. **Yield:** 15 servings.

Nutritional Analysis: 1 piece equals 225 calories, 5 g fat (1 g saturated fat), 0 cholesterol, 266 mg sodium, 43 g carbohydrate, trace fiber, 3 g protein.

Cranberry-Chocolate Oatmeal Bars

Low-sodium

Prep: 10 min. **Bake:** 20 min. + cooling

I love the combination of cranberries and chocolate, particularly in this yummy bar recipe.
—Ann Michelson, Dayton, Washington

- 2 cups quick-cooking oats
- 1/2 cup whole wheat flour

- 2 squares (1 ounce *each*) semisweet chocolate, grated
- 3/4 teaspoon baking soda
- 1/2 teaspoon ground cinnamon
- 1/4 teaspoon salt
- 1/4 teaspoon ground nutmeg
- 2 eggs
- 1 egg white
- Sugar substitute equivalent to 1/2 cup sugar
- 1/2 cup unsweetened applesauce
- 1/4 cup canola oil
- 2 teaspoons vanilla extract
- 3/4 cup dried cranberries

In a large bowl, combine first seven ingredients. Whisk eggs, egg white, sugar substitute, applesauce, oil and vanilla; stir into dry ingredients just until moistened. Stir in berries.

Spread into a 9-in. square baking pan coated with nonstick cooking spray. Bake at 350° for 17-20 minutes or until set. Cool on a wire rack. **Yield:** 16 servings.

Editor's Note: This recipe was tested with Splenda No Calorie Sweetener.

Nutritional Analysis: 1 bar equals 135 calories, 6 g fat (1 g saturated fat), 27 mg cholesterol, 108 mg sodium, 18 g carbohydrate, 2 g fiber, 3 g protein.
Diabetic Exchanges: 1 starch, 1 fat.

Apple Brown Betty

Low-fat

Prep: 15 min. **Bake:** 55 min.

A light spin on a down-home traditional treat, this recipe has all of the comforting taste of the original.
—Dale Hartman, Coventry, Rhode Island

- 6 cups sliced peeled Golden Delicious apples
- Sugar substitute equivalent to 1/3 cup sugar
- 1/4 teaspoon ground cinnamon
- 2 slices reduced-calorie whole wheat bread
- 2 tablespoons reduced-fat butter, melted
- 1/2 cup orange juice
- 1/3 cup fat-free whipped cream cheese
- 1/2 cup reduced-fat whipped topping

Place apple slices in a bowl. Combine sugar substitute and cinnamon; sprinkle over apples and toss to coat evenly. Place bread in a food processor; cover and process until fine crumbs form. In a small bowl, combine bread crumbs and butter until blended.

Place half of apple mixture in an 8-in. square baking dish coated with nonstick cooking spray. Top with about 1/3 cup crumb mixture and remaining apples. Pour orange juice over apples. Cover and bake at 350° for 30 minutes. Uncover; sprinkle with remaining crumbs. Bake 25-30 minutes longer or until apples are tender and topping is golden brown.

In a mixing bowl, beat cream cheese until smooth. Beat in half of the whipped topping. Fold in remaining whipped topping. Serve with Apple Brown Betty. **Yield:** 6 servings.

Editor's Note: This recipe was tested with Splenda No Calorie Sweetener and Land O' Lakes light stick butter.

Nutritional Analysis: 1 serving with a rounded tablespoon of topping equals 134 calories, 3 g fat (2 g saturated fat), 8 mg cholesterol, 142 mg sodium, 25 g carbohydrate, 2 g fiber, 3 g protein.
Diabetic Exchanges: 1 fruit, 1/2 starch, 1/2 fat.

the cake, a third of the lemon mixture and all of the strawberries. Repeat cake and lemon mixture layers. Top with all the blueberries. Repeat with remaining cake pieces and lemon mixture. Top with all the raspberries.

Spread remaining whipped topping over raspberries; sprinkle with almonds. Cover and refrigerate for at least 8 hours. **Yield:** 16 servings.

Nutritional Analysis: 2/3 cup equals 203 calories, 2 g fat (2 g saturated fat), 2 mg cholesterol, 181 mg sodium, 40 g carbohydrate, 1 g fiber, 5 g protein.
Diabetic Exchanges: 2 starch, 1/2 fruit, 1/2 fat.

Streuseled Zucchini Bundt Cake

(Pictured at left)

Low-fat

Prep: 25 min. **Bake:** 55 min. + cooling

After losing 40 pounds, I rely on healthy recipes to help keep the weight off. This cake is a favorite morning snack. It even won a blue ribbon at our county fair.
—Regina Stock, Topeka, Kansas

          3 cups all-purpose flour
        3/4 cup sugar
    1-1/2 teaspoons baking powder
          1 teaspoon baking soda
        1/2 teaspoon salt
          2 egg whites
          1 egg
    1-1/3 cups fat-free plain yogurt
        1/3 cup canola oil
          2 cups shredded zucchini, patted dry
          1 tablespoon plus 1 teaspoon vanilla extract, *divided*
          1 tablespoon dry bread crumbs
        1/3 cup packed brown sugar
        1/3 cup chopped walnuts
        1/3 cup raisins
          1 tablespoon ground cinnamon
        1/2 teaspoon ground allspice
        3/4 cup confectioners' sugar
          2 to 3 teaspoons fat-free milk

In a large mixing bowl, combine the first five ingredients. In another bowl, beat the egg whites, egg, yogurt and oil until blended. Stir in zucchini and 1 tablespoon vanilla. Add to dry ingredients; mix well.

Coat a 10-in. fluted tube pan with nonstick cooking spray; sprinkle with bread crumbs. Pour a third of the batter into the pan. Combine the brown sugar, walnuts, raisins, cinnamon and allspice; sprinkle half over batter. Top with another third of the batter. Sprinkle with remaining brown sugar mixture; top with remaining batter.

Bake at 350° for 55-65 minutes or until a toothpick inserted near the center comes out clean. Cool for 10 minutes before removing from pan to a wire rack to cool completely. Combine confectioners' sugar, milk and remaining vanilla; drizzle over cooled cake. **Yield:** 14 servings.

Nutritional Analysis: 1 piece equals 279 calories, 8 g fat (1 g saturated fat), 16 mg cholesterol, 233 mg sodium, 48 g carbohydrate, 2 g fiber, 6 g protein.

Three-Berry Lemon Trifle

(Pictured above)

Low-fat

Prep: 25 min. + chilling

This recipe was given to me by a friend. Using low-fat convenience items, I lightened it up with beautiful results.
—Ilene Doty, Eau Claire, Wisconsin

      1 can (14 ounces) fat-free sweetened condensed milk
      1 carton (8 ounces) fat-free reduced-sugar lemon yogurt
    1/3 cup lemon juice
      2 teaspoons grated lemon peel
      1 carton (8 ounces) reduced-fat whipped topping, thawed, *divided*
      1 prepared angel food cake (16 ounces), cut into 1-inch cubes
      1 cup sliced fresh strawberries
      1 cup fresh blueberries
      1 cup fresh raspberries
      2 tablespoons slivered almonds, toasted

In a large bowl, combine the sweetened condensed milk, yogurt, lemon juice and peel. Fold in 2 cups whipped topping.

In a 3-qt. trifle bowl or deep salad bowl, layer a third of

Fruit-Filled Quesadillas

(Pictured below)

Prep/Total Time: 15 min.

Dessert doesn't get much easier than this stovetop treat that's loaded with fresh apricots and berries. Served with a scoop of low-fat ice cream, it seems anything but light.
—Cathy Yates, Cicero, New York

  5 fresh apricots, halved
1/4 cup apricot nectar
  2 teaspoons sugar, *divided*
1/2 cup sliced fresh strawberries
1/2 teaspoon ground cinnamon
  2 flour tortillas (8 inches)
Butter-flavored nonstick cooking spray
  2 cups reduced-fat vanilla ice cream
1/4 cup fresh raspberries

In a nonstick skillet, cook and stir the apricots, nectar and 1 teaspoon sugar over low heat until apricots are tender, about 5 minutes. Stir in the strawberries; cover and remove from the heat. Combine cinnamon and remaining sugar; set aside.

In another nonstick skillet, cook one tortilla over low heat for 1-2 minutes on each side or until golden and crisp. Spritz one side with butter-flavored spray and sprinkle with half of the cinnamon-sugar. Repeat with remaining tortilla.

Place a tortilla sugared side down; spread with fruit mixture. Top with remaining tortilla, sugared side up; cut into four wedges. Serve each wedge with 1/2 cup of ice cream and 1 tablespoon of raspberries. **Yield:** 4 servings.

Nutritional Analysis: 1 serving equals 214 calories, 5 g fat (2 g saturated fat), 9 mg cholesterol, 182 mg sodium, 39 g carbohydrate, 2 g fiber, 6 g protein.
Diabetic Exchanges: 1-1/2 starch, 1 fruit, 1 fat.

Oaty Peanut Butter Cookies

(Pictured above)

Low-carb Low-sodium

Prep: 15 min. **Bake:** 10 min.

I call these "What I Had on Hand Cookies" because I used whatever ingredients were in my kitchen at the time.
—Sherry Craw, Mattoon, Illinois

1-1/2 cups reduced-fat margarine, softened
  1/2 cup reduced-fat peanut butter
  1/3 cup sugar
  1/3 cup packed brown sugar
    1 egg
    2 egg whites
    2 cups old-fashioned oats
1-1/2 cups all-purpose flour
1-1/2 teaspoons ground cinnamon
  3/4 teaspoon baking soda
    1 cup (6 ounces) semisweet chocolate chips
  3/4 cup English toffee bits *or* almond brickle chips

In a large mixing bowl, cream margarine, peanut butter and sugars. Beat in egg and egg whites. Combine the oats, flour, cinnamon and baking soda; gradually add to creamed mixture. Stir in chocolate chips and toffee bits.

Drop by tablespoonfuls 2 in. apart onto baking sheets coated with nonstick cooking spray; flatten slightly. Bake at 350° for 9-11 minutes or until golden brown. Cool for 2 minutes before removing from pans to wire racks. **Yield:** 5 dozen.

Editor's Note: This recipe was tested with Parkay Light stick margarine.

Nutritional Analysis: 1 cookie equals 82 calories, 4 g fat (1 g saturated fat), 9 mg cholesterol, 59 mg sodium, 11 g carbohydrate, 1 g fiber, 2 g protein.
Diabetic Exchange: 1 starch.

Chocolate Peanut Butter Haystacks

Low-carb Low-sodium

Prep: 5 min. + standing

No one can resist the combination of chocolate and peanut butter in these sweet snacks. They really satisfy any craving for crunchy foods, too.
—*Laurie Mounce, Houston, Texas*

1 milk chocolate candy bar (1.55 ounces), broken into pieces
1/4 cup reduced-fat peanut butter
1 cup Fiber One bran cereal

In a microwave-safe bowl, combine the candy bar and peanut butter. Microwave at 50% power for 1 minute; stir. Microwave at 50% power 10-15 seconds longer or until candy is melted; stir until smooth. Stir in cereal until evenly coated. Drop by rounded tablespoonfuls onto waxed paper. Let stand until set, about 20 minutes. **Yield:** 8 servings.

    Editor's Note: This recipe was tested in a 1,100-watt microwave.

    Nutritional Analysis: 1 piece equals 90 calories, 5 g fat (2 g saturated fat), 1 mg cholesterol, 92 mg sodium, 13 g carbohydrate, 4 g fiber, 3 g protein.
    Diabetic Exchanges: 1 starch, 1/2 fat.

Frosty Fruit Pie

(Pictured above)

Prep: 15 min. + freezing

Our Test Kitchen staff used a prepared graham cracker crust to keep this delightful pie simple. Layers of banana, frozen strawberry yogurt and whipped topping make it oh-so-delicious. Store one in the freezer for a quick dessert when unexpected guests drop in.

1 medium firm banana, sliced
2 tablespoons lemon juice
1 reduced-fat graham cracker crust (8 inches)
3 cups reduced-fat frozen strawberry yogurt, softened
1 can (8-1/4 ounces) reduced-sugar fruit cocktail, drained
1-1/2 cups reduced-fat whipped topping
1/2 cup fresh raspberries
1/4 cup coarsely chopped pecans, toasted

In a small bowl, combine banana slices and lemon juice; let stand for 5 minutes. Drain well. Arrange banana slices over bottom of crust. Spread with frozen yogurt. Top with fruit cocktail and whipped topping. Freeze until firm. Remove from the freezer 10 minutes before serving. Garnish with raspberries and pecans. **Yield:** 8 servings.

    Nutritional Analysis: 1 piece equals 260 calories, 8 g fat (3 g saturated fat), 4 mg cholesterol, 141 mg sodium, 41 g carbohydrate, 2 g fiber, 5 g protein.
    Diabetic Exchanges: 2 starch, 1 fruit, 1 fat.

Fluffy Lemon Pudding Cake

Prep: 20 min. **Bake:** 40 min.

This warm pudding cake is one that my mother-in-law made when her children were growing up. Today, it is a perennial favorite around our house.
—*Leslie Wyatt, Chilhowee, Missouri*

4-1/2 teaspoons butter, softened
1 cup sugar
1/3 cup lemon juice
1 egg yolk
3 tablespoons all-purpose flour
2 teaspoons grated lemon peel
1/4 teaspoon salt
1 cup fat-free milk
3 egg whites

In a large mixing bowl, beat butter and sugar until crumbly. Beat in the lemon juice, egg yolk, flour, lemon peel and salt; mix well. Gradually beat in milk. In another large mixing bowl, beat egg whites until stiff peaks form; gently fold into lemon mixture.

    Pour into an ungreased 1-qt. baking dish. Place the dish in a 13-in. x 9-in. x 2-in. baking dish. Pour boiling water into the larger baking dish to a depth of 1 in.

    Bake at 325° for 40-45 minutes or until a knife inserted near the center comes out clean and top is golden. Serve warm. **Yield:** 6 servings.

    Nutritional Analysis: 2/3 cup equals 205 calories, 4 g fat (2 g saturated fat), 44 mg cholesterol, 178 mg sodium, 40 g carbohydrate, trace fiber, 4 g protein.
    Diabetic Exchange: 2-1/2 starch.

Favorite Recipe Made Lighter

WHEN Carol Gallagher serves her Rhubarb Shortcake Dessert, it's always a hit. The taste-tempting treat is so high in fat, however, that she can't bring herself to prepare it with a clear conscience.

"This is a favorite of ours, but I don't make it often because I feel guilty serving it," she writes from Papua, New Guinea where she works as a missionary. "If it could be lightened up, it would make us all happy."

Created by our Test Kitchen staff, Makeover Rhubarb Shortcake Dessert has just half the total fat of the original, and nearly 60% less saturated fat. The cholesterol was also reduced by more than half. But this treat is still absolutely luscious.

Rhubarb Shortcake Dessert

Prep: 30 min. **Bake:** 1-1/4 hours + cooling

    2 cups all-purpose flour
    2 tablespoons sugar
    1 cup cold butter
FILLING:
    6 egg yolks
    2 cups sugar
    1/4 cup all-purpose flour
    1/4 teaspoon salt
    5 cups chopped fresh *or* frozen rhubarb,
      thawed
    1 cup half-and-half cream
    2 teaspoons grated orange peel
MERINGUE:
    6 egg whites
    2 teaspoons vanilla extract
Dash salt
    3/4 cup sugar
    2 tablespoons finely chopped walnuts

Combine flour and sugar; cut in butter until crumbly. Press into a greased 13-in. x 9-in. x 2-in. baking dish. Bake at 350° for 10-15 minutes or until lightly browned. Cool.

In a mixing bowl, beat egg yolks; add the sugar, flour and salt. Stir in the rhubarb, cream and orange peel; pour over crust. Bake at 350° for 50-60 minutes or until a knife inserted near the center comes out clean.

In a large mixing bowl, beat the egg whites, vanilla and salt on medium speed until soft peaks form. Gradually beat in the sugar, 1 tablespoon at a time, until stiff peaks form. Immediately spread over hot filling, sealing edges; sprinkle with nuts.

Bake 12-15 minutes longer or until lightly browned. Cool for at least 1 hour before serving. Refrigerate leftovers. **Yield:** 12 servings.

Editor's Note: If using frozen rhubarb, measure rhubarb while still frozen, then thaw completely. Drain in a colander, but do not press out liquid.

Nutritional Analysis: 1 piece equals 490 calories, 21 g fat (12 g saturated fat), 157 mg cholesterol, 260 mg sodium, 69 g carbohydrate, 2 g fiber, 7 g protein.

Makeover Rhubarb Shortcake Dessert

Prep: 30 min. **Bake:** 1 hour + cooling

1-1/2 cups all-purpose flour
    2 tablespoons sugar
    1/2 cup cold butter
FILLING:
    3 egg yolks
    1/4 cup reduced-sugar orange marmalade
1-1/4 cups sugar
    1/3 cup all-purpose flour
    1/4 teaspoon salt
    5 cups chopped fresh *or* frozen rhubarb,
      thawed
    1 cup 2% milk
    1 tablespoon grated orange peel
MERINGUE:
    6 egg whites
    2 teaspoons vanilla extract
    1/4 teaspoon cream of tartar
    3/4 cup sugar
    1 tablespoon finely chopped walnuts

Combine flour and sugar; cut in butter until crumbly. Press into a 13-in. x 9-in. x 2-in. baking dish coated with nonstick cooking spray. Bake at 350° for 10-15 minutes or until lightly browned. Cool.

In a mixing bowl, beat egg yolks and orange marmalade; add sugar, flour and salt. Stir in the rhubarb, milk and orange peel; pour over crust. Bake at 350° for 35-40 minutes or until a knife inserted near the center comes out clean.

In a large mixing bowl, beat the egg whites, vanilla and cream of tartar on medium speed until soft peaks form. Gradually beat in the sugar, 1 tablespoon at a time, until stiff peaks form. Immediately spread over hot filling, sealing edges; sprinkle with nuts.

Bake 12-15 minutes longer or until lightly browned. Cool for at least 1 hour before serving. Refrigerate leftovers. **Yield:** 12 servings.

Editor's Note: If using frozen rhubarb, measure rhubarb while still frozen, then thaw completely. Drain in a colander, but do not press out liquid.

Nutritional Analysis: 1 piece equals 332 calories, 10 g fat (5 g saturated fat), 75 mg cholesterol, 168 mg sodium, 56 g carbohydrate, 2 g fiber, 6 g protein.

Berry Crisp

(Pictured below)

Low-sodium

Prep: 15 min. **Bake:** 25 min.

I like to take this to potlucks and socials. If you're looking for a great dessert that isn't too sweet, this is it.
—Linda Naumann, Harrison, Arkansas

1/3 cup honey
1/4 cup canola oil
2 cups quick-cooking oats
1/2 cup whole wheat flour
1/2 cup chopped pecans
2 tablespoons cornstarch
1 can (12 ounces) frozen apple juice concentrate, thawed, *divided*
1 teaspoon lemon juice
3 cups halved fresh strawberries
2 cups fresh blueberries *or* blackberries
1 cup fresh raspberries

In a bowl, combine honey and oil until blended. Stir in the oats, flour and pecans until blended; set aside for topping. In a small bowl, combine cornstarch and 1/4 cup apple juice concentrate until smooth. In a saucepan, combine lemon juice and remaining apple juice concentrate. Gradually whisk in cornstarch mixture. Bring to a boil; cook and stir for 1-2 minutes or until thickened.

Combine the berries in an 11-in. x 7-in. x 2-in. baking dish coated with nonstick cooking spray. Top with apple juice mixture; sprinkle with oat mixture. Bake, uncovered, at 350° for 25-30 minutes or until bubbly and the top is golden brown. Serve warm. **Yield:** 12 servings.

Nutritional Analysis: *1 serving equals 256 calories, 10 g fat (1 g saturated fat), 0 cholesterol, 10 mg sodium, 41 g carbohydrate, 5 g fiber, 4 g protein.*
Diabetic Exchanges: *2 fat, 1-1/2 fruit, 1 starch.*

Crunchy Macaroons

(Pictured above)

Low-carb *Low-fat* *Low-sodium*

Prep: 15 min. **Bake:** 20 min.

These chewy little cookies have a yummy coconut and almond flavor. The home economists in our Test Kitchen whipped them up using only five ingredients.

1-1/2 cups crisp rice cereal
1-1/4 cups flaked coconut
2 egg whites
3 tablespoons sugar
1/8 teaspoon almond extract

In a small bowl, combine all ingredients. With damp fingers, shape into 1-1/2-in. mounds on parchment paper-lined baking sheets. Bake at 300° for 20-25 minutes or until edges are lightly browned. Remove from pans to wire racks to cool. **Yield:** 2 dozen.

Nutritional Analysis: *2 cookies equals 76 calories, 3 g fat (3 g saturated fat), 0 cholesterol, 66 mg sodium, 11 g carbohydrate, trace fiber, 1 g protein.*
Diabetic Exchanges: *1 fat, 1/2 starch.*

Fat-Free Cream Cheese Frosting

Low-fat

Prep/Total Time: 10 min.

To dress up a cake or other dessert without adding extra fat, try this smooth frosting.
—Jonathan Palmiter, Battle Creek, Michigan

1 package (8 ounces) fat-free cream cheese
1/2 cup pink grapefruit juice
1/2 cup cold fat-free milk
2 packages (3.4 ounces *each*) instant vanilla pudding mix
1 carton (8 ounces) frozen fat-free whipped topping, thawed

In a large mixing bowl, beat cream cheese until fluffy; gradually beat in the juice and milk. Add the pudding mix. Beat on medium speed for 2 minutes. Fold in whipped topping. Store in refrigerator. **Yield:** 4 cups.

Nutritional Analysis: 1/3 cup equals 119 calories, 0 fat (trace saturated fat), 2 mg cholesterol, 346 mg sodium, 24 g carbohydrate, trace fiber, 3 g protein.
Diabetic Exchange: 1-1/2 starch.

Frozen Fruit Molds

(Pictured below)

Low-fat Low-sodium

Prep: 25 min. + freezing

Our home economists filled muffin tins with fruits and juices, then set them in the freezer to create icy cups.

> 1 can (8 ounces) unsweetened pineapple tidbits
> 12 fresh mint leaves
> 1-1/2 cups sliced bananas, *divided*
> 1-1/2 cups halved seedless red grapes
> 2 medium grapefruit, peeled, sectioned and chopped
> 1/2 cup maraschino cherries, halved
> 1-1/2 cups unsweetened pineapple juice
> 1/3 cup lime juice

Drain pineapple, reserving juice. Place a mint leaf in each of 12 jumbo muffin cups; top each with a banana slice. Divide the pineapple, grapes, grapefruit, cherries and remaining bananas among muffin cups.

In a small bowl, combine the pineapple juice, lime juice and reserved juice. Pour 1/4 cup into each muffin cup. Cover and freeze for 3 hours or until firm. Remove from the freezer 30 minutes before serving. Invert onto a baking sheet. **Yield:** 12 servings.

Nutritional Analysis: 1 serving equals 86 calories, trace fat (trace saturated fat), 0 cholesterol, 1 mg sodium, 22 g carbohydrate, 1 g fiber, 1 g protein.
Diabetic Exchange: 1-1/2 fruit.

Frosty Lemonade Pie

(Pictured above)

Prep: 20 min. + freezing

This creamy pie gets its citrus flavor from lemonade soft drink mix and crushed lemon sandwich cookies. It's a wonderful dessert to store in the freezer for nights when you need a low-sugar treat in a hurry.
—Emma Overby, East Prairie, Missouri

> 1 package (8 ounces) fat-free cream cheese
> 1 tub sugar-free lemonade soft drink mix
> 1 cup cold fat-free milk
> 1 package (1 ounce) sugar-free instant vanilla pudding mix
> 1 carton (8 ounces) frozen fat-free whipped topping, thawed
> 10 sugar-free lemon sandwich cookies, crushed
> 1 reduced-fat graham cracker crust (8 inches)

In a small mixing bowl, beat cream cheese and soft drink mix until smooth. In a bowl, whisk milk and pudding mix for 1-1/2 minutes (mixture will be very thick). Beat into cream cheese mixture. Beat in a third of the whipped topping. Fold in remaining whipped topping.

Set aside 3 tablespoons cookie crumbs. Fold remaining crumbs into cream cheese mixture. Spoon into crust. Sprinkle with reserved crumbs. Cover and freeze for 4-5 hours or until firm. Remove from the freezer 15 minutes before serving. **Yield:** 8 servings.

Editor's Note: This recipe was tested with Crystal Light lemonade soft drink mix. One container (2.1 ounces) contains four tubs.

Nutritional Analysis: 1 piece equals 251 calories, 6 g fat (2 g saturated fat), 3 mg cholesterol, 457 mg sodium, 40 g carbohydrate, 1 g fiber, 7 g protein.
Diabetic Exchanges: 2-1/2 starch, 1 fat.

TOPPING:
   1/2 cup heavy whipping cream
   1/4 cup confectioners' sugar
    2 teaspoons baking cocoa
   1/4 cup slivered almonds, toasted
    6 fresh strawberries, cut into thick slices

Place egg whites in a large mixing bowl; let stand at room temperature for 30 minutes. Coat the bottom of three 9-in. baking pans with nonstick cooking spray; line with waxed paper. Spray the paper with nonstick cooking spray and dust with flour; set aside. Sift the flour, cocoa, baking soda and salt together three times.

Beat egg whites on medium speed until soft peaks form. Gradually beat in sugar, about 2 tablespoons at a time, on high until stiff glossy peaks form and sugar is dissolved. Combine coffee and extracts. Fold dry ingredients into egg mixture alternately with coffee mixture.

Spread into prepared pans. Bake at 375° for 10-15 minutes or until a toothpick inserted near the center comes out clean. Cool for 10 minutes before removing from pans to wire racks. Gently peel off waxed paper. Cool completely.

In a bowl, gently mash the strawberries; stir in almond extract. Fold in whipped topping. Place one cake layer on a serving platter; top with half of the filling. Repeat layers. Top with remaining cake layer.

In a small mixing bowl, beat cream until it begins to thicken. Combine confectioners' sugar and cocoa; add to cream. Beat until stiff peaks form. Frost top of cake. Garnish with almonds and strawberries. Chill for at least 1 hour before cutting. Refrigerate leftovers. **Yield:** 12 servings.

Nutritional Analysis: 1 piece equals 271 calories, 8 g fat (4 g saturated fat), 14 mg cholesterol, 254 mg sodium, 45 g carbohydrate, 2 g fiber, 6 g protein.

Strawberry-Almond Chocolate Torte

(Pictured above)

Prep: 50 min. **Bake:** 10 min. + cooling

This layer cake is wonderful when strawberries are in season. Sometimes I'll make it and invite family members over for a spur-of-the-moment dessert night.
—Diane Kensinger, Manheim, Pennsylvania

   10 egg whites
    1 cup all-purpose flour
   2/3 cup baking cocoa
    1 teaspoon baking soda
   1/2 teaspoon salt
1-1/2 cups sugar
   2/3 cup cold brewed coffee
    1 teaspoon vanilla extract
   1/2 teaspoon almond extract
FILLING:
    1 cup sliced fresh strawberries
   1/2 teaspoon almond extract
    1 carton (8 ounces) frozen reduced-fat whipped topping, thawed

Peach Delight

(Pictured at left)

Low-sodium

Prep: 25 min. **Bake:** 15 min. + chilling

Colorful peach slices, a nutty crust and refreshing lemon gelatin take center stage in this creamy dessert.
—Clara Hunt, Lexington, North Carolina

   1/4 cup butter, softened
   1/2 cup sugar
    1 cup all-purpose flour
   1/4 cup chopped walnuts
FILLING:
    1 package (8 ounces) reduced-fat cream cheese
   3/4 cup confectioners' sugar
    1 carton (8 ounces) frozen reduced-fat whipped topping, thawed, *divided*
    7 medium fresh peaches, thinly sliced
GLAZE:
    3 tablespoons cornstarch
    2 cups water
    1 package (.3 ounce) sugar-free lemon gelatin

In a small mixing bowl, beat butter and sugar on medium speed for 2 minutes. Gradually beat in flour (mixture will be crumbly). Mix in nuts. Press onto bottom of a 13-in. x

9-in. x 2-in. baking pan coated with nonstick cooking spray. Bake at 350° for 14-16 minutes or until lightly browned. Cool on a wire rack.

For filling, in a large mixing bowl, beat cream cheese and confectioners' sugar until smooth. Fold in half of the whipped topping. Carefully spread over crust. Top with peaches.

For glaze, in a small saucepan, combine cornstarch and water until smooth. Bring to a boil; cook and stir for 2 minutes or until thickened. Gradually stir in gelatin until dissolved. Cool to room temperature. Spoon over peaches. Cover and refrigerate until firm. Dollop with remaining whipped topping. **Yield:** 15 servings.

Nutritional Analysis: 1 square equals 225 calories, 9 g fat (6 g saturated fat), 19 mg cholesterol, 109 mg sodium, 32 g carbohydrate, 1 g fiber, 4 g protein.
Diabetic Exchanges: 2 starch, 1-1/2 fat.

Strawberry Dessert Sauce

(Pictured below)

Low-fat Low-sodium

Prep: 10 min. + chilling

This colorful berry topping is delightful spooned over angel food cake or low-fat frozen yogurt.
—Evelyn Kennell, Roanoke, Illinois

1 pint fresh strawberries *or* 2 cups frozen unsweetened strawberries, thawed
3 tablespoons sugar
1 tablespoon cornstarch
1/4 cup water
1 tablespoon lemon juice

Mash strawberries; set aside. In a saucepan, combine the sugar, cornstarch and water until smooth. Bring to a boil; cook

and stir for 2 minutes or until thickened. Stir in strawberries; remove from the heat. Stir in lemon juice. Transfer to a small bowl. Cover and refrigerate until chilled. **Yield:** 4 servings.

Nutritional Analysis: 1/4 cup equals 70 calories, trace fat (trace saturated fat), 0 cholesterol, 1 mg sodium, 17 g carbohydrate, 2 g fiber, 1 g protein.
Diabetic Exchange: 1 fruit.

Strawberry Banana Delight

(Pictured above)

Low-fat Low-sodium

Prep: 15 min. + chilling

With a classic pairing of fruit flavors, this whipped gelatin is light and refreshing after a meal.
—Mary Blackledge, North Platte, Nebraska

1 package (.3 ounce) sugar-free strawberry gelatin
1 cup boiling water
6 ice cubes
2 medium ripe bananas, cut into chunks
4 tablespoons whipped topping
4 fresh strawberries

In a small bowl, dissolve gelatin in boiling water; cool for 10 minutes. Add enough water to ice cubes to measure 1 cup. Place gelatin and ice mixture in a blender; cover and process for 1 minute or until ice cubes are dissolved. Add bananas; process 1-2 minutes longer or until blended.

Pour into four dessert dishes. Refrigerate for at least 30 minutes or until set. Garnish each with 1 tablespoon whipped topping and a strawberry. **Yield:** 4 servings.

Nutritional Analysis: 1 serving equals 78 calories, 1 g fat (1 g saturated fat), 0 cholesterol, 48 mg sodium, 16 g carbohydrate, 2 g fiber, 2 g protein.
Diabetic Exchange: 1 fruit.

Coconut-Cherry Cream Squares

(Pictured at left)

Low-sodium

Prep: 30 min. + chilling

You'll be wowed by these cherry-topped delights from our Test Kitchen. With a delectable coconut-custard filling, one square will satisfy your sweet tooth.

- 3/4 cup all-purpose flour
- 1/3 cup flaked coconut
- 3 tablespoons brown sugar
- 3 tablespoons cold reduced-fat butter

FILLING:

- 1/3 cup all-purpose flour
- 1/4 cup sugar
- Sugar substitute equivalent to 1/4 cup sugar
- 1/4 teaspoon salt
- 2-1/2 cups fat-free milk
- 2 eggs, lightly beaten
- 1/2 cup flaked coconut
- 2 teaspoons coconut extract
- 1 can (20 ounces) reduced-sugar cherry pie filling

In a small bowl, combine the flour, coconut and brown sugar; cut in butter until crumbly. Press into a 9-in. square baking pan coated with nonstick cooking spray.

Bake at 400° for 7-10 minutes or until lightly browned. Cool on a wire rack.

In a small saucepan, combine the flour, sugar, sugar substitute and salt. Stir in milk until smooth. Cook and stir over medium-high heat until thickened and bubbly. Reduce heat; cook and stir 2 minutes longer. Remove from the heat. Stir a small amount of hot filling into eggs; return all to the pan, stirring constantly. Bring to a gentle boil; cook and stir 2 minutes longer.

Remove from the heat. Gently stir in coconut and extract. Pour over crust. Refrigerate until set. Top with pie filling. Refrigerate for at least 2 hours before cutting. **Yield:** 16 servings.

Editor's Note: This recipe was tested with Splenda No Calorie Sweetener and Land O' Lakes stick light butter.

Nutritional Analysis: *1 square equals 142 calories, 4 g fat (3 g saturated fat), 31 mg cholesterol, 95 mg sodium, 24 g carbohydrate, 1 g fiber, 4 g protein.*
Diabetic Exchanges: *1-1/2 starch, 1/2 fat.*

Creamy Apple Crumb Pie

(Pictured at left)

Low-sodium

Prep: 20 min. **Bake:** 50 min. + cooling

I revised this classic recipe from a cookbook. I knew it was a keeper when my mother-in-law asked for a copy.
—Linda Pawelski, Milwaukee, Wisconsin

- 1 pastry for single-crust pie (9 inches)
- 6 cups cubed peeled tart apples (about 6 medium)
- 1/3 cup sugar
- 3 tablespoons cornstarch
- 1 teaspoon ground cinnamon
- 1/4 teaspoon ground allspice
- 1 cup (8 ounces) reduced-fat sour cream
- 1 teaspoon vanilla extract

TOPPING:

- 1/2 cup all-purpose flour
- 1/4 cup packed brown sugar
- 1/2 teaspoon ground cinnamon
- 2 tablespoons cold butter

Line a 9-in. deep-dish pie plate with pastry; flute edges. In a large bowl, combine the apples, sugar, cornstarch, cinnamon and allspice. Combine sour cream and vanilla; stir into apple mixture. Spoon into pastry shell.

For topping, combine the flour, brown sugar and cinnamon in a bowl; cut in butter until mixture resembles coarse crumbs. Sprinkle over filling.

Bake at 400° for 25 minutes. Reduce heat to 350°; bake 25-30 minutes longer or until filling is bubbly and topping is golden. Cool on a wire rack. Store in the refrigerator. **Yield:** 8 servings.

Nutritional Analysis: *1 piece equals 299 calories, 11 g fat (6 g saturated fat), 22 mg cholesterol, 126 mg sodium, 49 g carbohydrate, 2 g fiber, 4 g protein.*
Diabetic Exchanges: *2 starch, 2 fat, 1 fruit.*

Peanut Butter Cheesecake Cups

Prep: 15 min. + chilling

My husband has diabetes, so I've learned to be more creative with carbs. This recipe is wonderful.
—Mary Lewis, Sanford, Maine

- 3/4 cup graham cracker crumbs, *divided*
- 1 package (8 ounces) reduced-fat cream cheese
- 1/3 cup reduced-fat creamy peanut butter
- 1-1/2 teaspoons sugar
- 1 carton (8 ounces) frozen fat-free whipped topping, thawed
- 1 tablespoon salted peanuts, finely chopped

Sprinkle 4 teaspoons of graham cracker crumbs into eight individual serving dishes. In a large mixing bowl, beat the cream cheese, peanut butter and sugar until smooth. Reserve 8 teaspoons whipped topping for garnish; cover and refrigerate. Fold remaining whipped topping into peanut butter mixture; spoon over crumbs. Cover and refrigerate for at least 1 hour.

Sprinkle with remaining graham cracker crumbs. Top with reserved whipped topping and sprinkle with peanuts. **Yield:** 8 servings.

Nutritional Analysis: *1 serving equals 214 calories, 11 g fat (5 g saturated fat), 20 mg cholesterol, 247 mg sodium, 21 g carbohydrate, 1 g fiber, 7 g protein.*
Diabetic Exchanges: *2 fat, 1-1/2 starch.*

Pistachio Cranberry Biscotti

(Pictured above)

Low-sodium

Prep: 30 min. **Bake:** 35 min. + cooling

*These biscotti taste great with a cup of steaming coffee.
The lemon drizzle makes them seem indulgent.*
—*Marta Perez-Stable, Westlake, Ohio*

1-1/2 cups dried cranberries
   2 tablespoons orange juice
  1/3 cup butter, softened
  2/3 cup sugar
   2 eggs
   1 teaspoon vanilla extract
   2 cups all-purpose flour
   2 teaspoons baking powder
  1/2 teaspoon salt
   1 cup shelled pistachios
   4 teaspoons grated lemon peel
ICING:
   1 cup confectioners' sugar
   1 teaspoon grated lemon peel
   1 to 2 tablespoons fat-free milk

Place cranberries in a small bowl; sprinkle with orange juice. In a large mixing bowl, cream butter and sugar. Add eggs, one at a time, beating well after each addition. Beat in vanilla. Combine the flour, baking powder and salt; gradually add to creamed mixture. Stir in pistachios and lemon peel. Drain cranberries; stir into dough. On a lightly floured surface, divide dough into thirds.

On a baking sheet coated with nonstick cooking spray, shape each portion into a 12-in. x 2-in. rectangle. Bake at 350° for 20-25 minutes or until golden brown. Cool for 5 minutes. Transfer to a cutting board; with a serrated knife, cut each loaf into 20 slices. Place cut side down on baking sheets coated with nonstick cooking spray. Bake for 12-15 minutes or until firm, turning once. Remove to wire racks to cool.

For icing, combine confectioners' sugar and lemon peel in a small bowl; stir in enough milk to achieve desired drizzling consistency. Drizzle over biscotti. Store in an airtight container. **Yield:** 5 dozen.

Nutritional Analysis: 2 cookies equals 129 calories, 4 g fat (2 g saturated fat), 20 mg cholesterol, 109 mg sodium, 21 g carbohydrate, 1 g fiber, 2 g protein.
Diabetic Exchanges: 1-1/2 starch, 1/2 fat.

Blueberry Raspberry Gelatin

Low-carb Low-sodium

Prep: 20 min. + chilling

*With chopped pecans and plenty of fresh blueberries,
this pretty gelatin is a great treat anytime.*
—*Judy Scott, Fortuna, California*

   1 package (.3 ounce) sugar-free raspberry gelatin
   1 cup boiling water
  3/4 cup cold water
   1 cup fresh *or* frozen unsweetened blueberries, thawed
TOPPING:
   2 ounces reduced-fat cream cheese
  1/4 cup fat-free sour cream
Sugar substitute equivalent to 2 teaspoons sugar
  1/2 teaspoon vanilla extract
   2 tablespoons chopped pecans, toasted

In a small bowl, dissolve gelatin in boiling water. Stir in cold water. Cover and refrigerate until partially set. Fold in blueberries. Transfer to an 8-in. x 4-in. x 2-in. loaf pan coated with nonstick cooking spray. Cover and refrigerate for 1 hour or until set.

For topping, in a small mixing bowl, beat the cream cheese and sour cream until blended. Stir in the sugar substitute and vanilla. Unmold gelatin; cut into six slices. Top each slice with topping and pecans. **Yield:** 6 servings.

Editor's Note: This recipe was tested with Splenda No Calorie Sweetener.

Nutritional Analysis: 1 slice equals 72 calories, 4 g fat (2 g saturated fat), 8 mg cholesterol, 80 mg sodium, 6 g carbohydrate, 1 g fiber, 3 g protein.
Diabetic Exchanges: 1 fat, 1/2 starch.

Easy Vanilla Ice Cream

Low-fat

Prep: 10 min. + freezing

*Three ingredients and an ice cream freezer are all that's
needed for this creamy creation. My husband is diabetic,
and we both love ice cream, so we came up with this
recipe. We top scoops with fresh fruit, nuts or cereal.*
—*Judy Vahs, Marshall, Michigan*

   2 cups cold fat-free milk
   1 can (14 ounces) fat-free sweetened condensed milk
   1 package (1 ounce) sugar-free instant vanilla pudding mix

In a large bowl, whisk all ingredients until blended and thickened. Freeze in an ice cream freezer according to manufacturer's directions. Transfer to a freezer container; cover and freeze for 1 hour or until firm. **Yield:** 7 servings.

Nutritional Analysis: 1/2 cup equals 196 calories, trace fat (trace saturated fat), 5 mg cholesterol, 264 mg sodium, 41 g carbohydrate, trace fiber, 7 g protein.
Diabetic Exchange: 2-1/2 starch.

Favorite Recipe Made Lighter

MANY COOKS have a "signature recipe" that folks ask for time and again. For Janice Perdue, it's a tried-and-true dessert classic.

"My husband and brother-in-law often request Peanut Butter Layer Cake," says the Oroville, California baker. "But they've both had bypass surgery, so I'm reluctant to prepare it. Can you help?"

Janice's request presented a doubly good challenge for our home economists—they needed to slim down both the cake and the frosting.

Their Makeover Peanut Butter Layer Cake tallies 113 fewer calories than the original, but it's still a wonderful treat. "My husband and I are so happy with the revamped recipe," Janice writes.

Peanut Butter Layer Cake

Prep: 25 min. **Bake:** 25 min. + cooling

1/2 cup butter, softened
1-1/4 cups sugar
1/2 cup peanut butter chips, melted and cooled
2 eggs
1 teaspoon vanilla extract
2 cups all-purpose flour
1 teaspoon baking soda
1/2 teaspoon baking powder
1/4 teaspoon salt
1-1/2 cups milk
PEANUT BUTTER FROSTING:
1 cup peanut butter chips, melted and cooled
1 package (8 ounces) cream cheese, softened
1 teaspoon vanilla extract
1/8 teaspoon salt
3 cups confectioners' sugar
3 tablespoons milk

In a large mixing bowl, cream butter and sugar. Add melted chips; mix well. Add eggs, one at a time, beating well after each addition. Beat in vanilla. Combine the flour, baking soda, baking powder and salt; add to creamed mixture alternately with milk.

Pour into two greased and floured 9-in. round baking pans. Bake at 350° for 25-30 minutes or until a toothpick inserted near the center comes out clean. Cool for 10 minutes before removing from pans to wire racks to cool completely.

For frosting, in a small mixing bowl, beat the melted chips, cream cheese, vanilla and salt until light and fluffy. Beat in confectioners' sugar and milk. Spread frosting between layers and over top and sides of cake. Store in the refrigerator. **Yield:** 12 servings.

Nutritional Analysis: 1 piece equals 545 calories, 23 g fat (13 g saturated fat), 81 mg cholesterol, 409 mg sodium, 78 g carbohydrate, 2 g fiber, 10 g protein.

Makeover Peanut Butter Layer Cake

Prep: 25 min. **Bake:** 20 min. + cooling

1/4 cup butter, softened
1 cup sugar
1 egg
2 egg whites
1/2 cup peanut butter chips, melted and cooled
1/4 cup unsweetened applesauce
1 teaspoon vanilla extract
2 cups all-purpose flour
1 teaspoon baking soda
1/2 teaspoon baking powder
1/4 teaspoon salt
1-1/2 cups 1% buttermilk
PEANUT BUTTER FROSTING:
1 package (8 ounces) reduced-fat cream cheese
1/2 cup peanut butter chips, melted and cooled
1 teaspoon vanilla extract
1/8 teaspoon salt
3 cups confectioners' sugar
Unsalted peanuts, optional

Coat two 9-in. round baking pans with nonstick cooking spray and line with waxed paper. Coat the paper with nonstick cooking spray and dust with flour; set aside. In a large mixing bowl, beat butter and sugar until crumbly. Beat in the egg, egg whites, melted chips, applesauce and vanilla. Combine the flour, baking soda, baking powder and salt; add to peanut butter mixture alternately with buttermilk.

Pour into prepared pans. Bake at 350° for 20-25 minutes or until a toothpick inserted near the center comes out clean. Cool for 10 minutes before removing from pans to wire racks to cool completely.

For frosting, in a small mixing bowl, beat cream cheese, melted chips, vanilla and salt until light and fluffy. Beat in confectioners' sugar until smooth. Spread between layers and over top and sides of cake. Garnish with peanuts if desired. Store in the refrigerator. **Yield:** 12 servings.

Nutritional Analysis: 1 slice equals 432 calories, 13 g fat (7 g saturated fat), 43 mg cholesterol, 397 mg sodium, 72 g carbohydrate, 2 g fiber, 9 g protein.

Remove top sheet of plastic wrap; invert pastry into a 9-in. pie plate. Remove remaining plastic wrap. Trim and flute edges. Chill.

Roll pastry scraps to 1/8-in. thickness. Cut with a 1-in. leaf-shaped cookie cutter. Place on an ungreased baking sheet. Bake at 375° for 6-8 minutes or until edges are very lightly browned. Cool on a wire rack. In a large mixing bowl, beat the egg, egg white, sugars, salt and spices until smooth. Beat in pumpkin. Gradually beat in milk. Pour into pastry shell. Bake at 375° for 45-50 minutes or until a knife inserted near the center comes out clean. Cool on a wire rack. Garnish with leaf cutouts. Refrigerate leftovers. **Yield:** 8 servings.

Nutritional Analysis: *1 piece equals 249 calories, 8 g fat (2 g saturated fat), 32 mg cholesterol, 295 mg sodium, 40 g carbohydrate, 3 g fiber, 6 g protein.*
Diabetic Exchanges: *2-1/2 starch, 1 fat.*

Lime Kiwi Cloud

Low-fat

Prep: 20 min. + freezing **Cook:** 10 min + chilling

I enjoy serving this delicious dessert any time of the year. Prepared angel food cake, fruit and a few other items are all it takes to whip up the tangy treat.
—Bernice Janowski, Stevens Point, Wisconsin

12 cups cubed angel food cake (about 12 ounces)
2 cartons (6 ounces *each*) reduced-fat vanilla yogurt
1/4 cup lime juice
2 teaspoons grated lime peel
1 carton (8 ounces) frozen reduced-fat whipped topping, thawed
6 medium kiwifruit, peeled and sliced
1 package (24 ounces) frozen unsweetened whole strawberries
2 tablespoons sugar
1 tablespoon cornstarch

Arrange half the cake cubes in an ungreased 13-in. x 9-in. x 2-in. dish. In a large bowl, combine the yogurt, lime juice and peel; fold in whipped topping. Spread half the yogurt mixture over the cake, pressing down to make a smooth layer. Layer with kiwi slices. Top with the remaining cake and yogurt mixture. Cover and refrigerate for 2-3 hours or until set.

Meanwhile, thaw strawberries, reserving juice. In a small bowl, combine the sugar, cornstarch and reserved juice until smooth; set aside. Place strawberries in a saucepan; bring to a boil over medium heat, mashing strawberries. Stir in cornstarch mixture; cook and stir for 2 minutes or until thickened. Remove from the heat; cool. Cover and refrigerate until serving. Scoop cake into dessert dishes; drizzle with strawberry sauce. **Yield:** 12 servings.

Nutritional Analysis: *1 cup cake mixture with 1/4 cup sauce equals 196 calories, 3 g fat (2 g saturated fat), 1 mg cholesterol, 232 mg sodium, 39 g carbohydrate, 3 g fiber, 4 g protein.*
Diabetic Exchanges: *1-1/2 starch, 1 fruit, 1/2 fat.*

Classic Pumpkin Pie

(Pictured above and on page 195)

Prep: 20 min. **Bake:** 45 min. + cooling

You can savor every delectable bite of this traditional pie from our Test Kitchen home economists.

1 cup all-purpose flour
1 teaspoon sugar
1/4 teaspoon salt
3 tablespoons canola oil
1 tablespoon butter, melted
2 to 3 tablespoons cold water
FILLING:
1 egg
1 egg white
1/2 cup packed brown sugar
1/4 cup sugar
1/2 teaspoon salt
1/2 teaspoon ground cinnamon
1/8 teaspoon *each* ground allspice, nutmeg and cloves
1 can (15 ounces) solid-pack pumpkin
1 cup fat-free evaporated milk

In a small bowl, combine the flour, sugar and salt. Using a fork, stir in oil and butter until dough is crumbly. Gradually add enough water until dough holds together. Roll out between sheets of plastic wrap into an 11-in. circle. Freeze for 10 minutes.

Cran-Apple Turnovers

Low-sodium

Prep: 25 min. **Bake:** 20 min. + cooling

Our Test Kitchen staff filled these flaky phyllo-dough triangles with fruit for a low-sugar dessert or snack.

- 2/3 cup diced peeled tart apple
- 1/4 cup dried cranberries
- Sugar substitute equivalent to 4 teaspoons sugar
- 2 teaspoons 100% orange marmalade spreadable fruit
- 1-1/2 teaspoons all-purpose flour
- 1/4 teaspoon ground cinnamon
- 1/8 teaspoon salt
- 4 sheets phyllo dough (14-inch x 9-inch size)
- 2 tablespoons butter, melted
- 1/4 teaspoon confectioners' sugar

In a small bowl, combine the first seven ingredients; set aside. Place one sheet of phyllo dough on a work surface; lightly brush with butter (keep remaining phyllo dough covered with plastic wrap and a damp towel to keep from drying out). Fold dough in half widthwise, making a 9-in. x 7-in. rectangle; lightly brush with butter. Cut dough in half lengthwise, making two 9-in. x 3-1/2-in. strips.

Place 1 heaping tablespoon of fruit filling on lower corner of each strip. Fold dough over filling, forming a triangle. Continue folding, like a flag, to end of strip. Lightly brush with butter, making sure all edges are sealed. Repeat with remaining dough and filling to make six more turnovers.

Place turnovers on a baking sheet lightly coated with nonstick cooking spray. Bake at 375° for 16-20 minutes or until golden brown. Cool on a wire rack. Lightly dust with confectioners' sugar. **Yield:** 4 servings.

Editor's Note: This recipe was tested with Splenda No Calorie Sweetener.

Nutritional Analysis: 2 turnovers equals 127 calories, 6 g fat (4 g saturated fat), 15 mg cholesterol, 139 mg sodium, 18 g carbohydrate, 1 g fiber, 1 g protein.
Diabetic Exchanges: 1 fat, 1/2 starch, 1/2 fruit.

Cranberry Apple Tart

(Pictured at right)

Low-fat   Low-sodium

Prep: 30 min. + rising **Bake:** 15 min. + chilling

From our home economists, this light and luscious fruit tart is sweetened with sugar substitute.

- 1/2 teaspoon active dry yeast
- 1 tablespoon warm water (110° to 115°)
- 2 tablespoons beaten egg
- 2 tablespoons butter, softened
- 4-1/2 teaspoons sugar
- 1 teaspoon grated orange peel
- 3/4 cup plus 2 tablespoons all-purpose flour
- 1/4 teaspoon salt

FILLING:
- 1 package (12 ounces) fresh *or* frozen cranberries
- 1-1/2 cups chopped dried apples
- 1-1/2 cups unsweetened apple juice
- 1-1/4 cups sugar
- Sugar substitute equivalent to 1 cup sugar
- 1/2 cup water
- 1/4 teaspoon salt
- 1/4 cup cornstarch
- 1/3 cup cold water

In a small mixing bowl, dissolve the yeast in warm water. Beat in the egg, butter, sugar and orange peel. Combine flour and salt; beat into the yeast mixture on low speed just until the mixture holds together. Shape into a ball. Place in a small bowl coated with nonstick cooking spray, turning once to coat the top. Cover and let rise in a warm place for 1-1/4 hours (dough will not double, but will leave a slight indentation when pressed).

Coat an 11-in. fluted tart pan with removable bottom with nonstick cooking spray; set aside. Place dough on a piece of waxed paper. Lightly flour dough; roll into a 13-in. circle. Invert into prepared pan; gently remove paper. Gently press dough into pan. Line unpricked tart shell with a double thickness of heavy-duty foil. Bake at 375° for 8 minutes. Remove foil; bake 6 minutes longer or until golden brown. Cool on a wire rack.

In a saucepan, combine the first seven filling ingredients. Cook and stir until mixture comes to a boil and berries pop. Combine cornstarch and water until smooth; gradually stir into cranberry mixture. Cook 2 minutes longer or until thickened. Cool for 20 minutes. Pour into crust. Refrigerate for 3 hours before cutting. **Yield:** 14 servings.

Editor's Note: This recipe was tested with Splenda No Calorie Sweetener.

Nutritional Analysis: 1 piece equals 183 calories, 2 g fat (1 g saturated fat), 14 mg cholesterol, 113 mg sodium, 41 g carbohydrate, 2 g fiber, 1 g protein.
Diabetic Exchanges: 2 starch, 1 fruit.

Lemonade Ice Cream Sandwiches

Low-fat Low-sodium

Prep: 20 min. + freezing

*I came up with these freezer treats as a variation on an
ice cream pie recipe. With the individual portions, you
can take out just what you need every time.*
—*Jeanne McCorkle, Livermore, California*

1-1/2 cups reduced-fat vanilla ice cream, softened
1-3/4 teaspoons sugar-free lemonade soft drink mix
  2 tablespoons water
1/2 cup reduced-fat whipped topping
 16 graham cracker squares

Place the ice cream in a bowl. Dissolve lemonade mix in
water; stir into ice cream. Fold in whipped topping. Freeze
for 20 minutes or until mixture reaches desired consistency.

Spread about 3 tablespoonfuls onto eight graham cracker
squares; top with remaining crackers. Wrap individually in foil
or plastic wrap. Freeze for at least 1 hour. **Yield:** 8 servings.

Nutritional Analysis: *1 ice cream sandwich equals 106 calories, 3 g fat (1 g saturated fat), 3 mg cholesterol, 106 mg sodium,
17 g carbohydrate, trace fiber, 2 g protein.*
Diabetic Exchanges: *1 starch, 1/2 fat.*

Cinnamon Pumpkin Cake

(Pictured above)

Prep: 15 min. **Bake:** 65 min. + cooling

*A cake mix, canned pumpkin and applesauce make
this moist cake a breeze to prepare. With the thick glaze,
it's hard to believe that this dessert has little fat.*
—*Connie Adams, Monaville, West Virginia*

  1 package (18-1/4 ounces) yellow cake mix
  1 can (15 ounces) solid-pack pumpkin
2/3 cup sugar
  2 eggs
1/2 cup egg substitute
1/3 cup water
1/4 cup unsweetened applesauce
2-1/2 teaspoons ground cinnamon, *divided*
1/4 teaspoon ground nutmeg
1-1/2 cups confectioners' sugar
1/2 teaspoon vanilla extract
  1 to 2 tablespoons fat-free milk

In a large mixing bowl, combine the cake mix, pumpkin,
sugar, eggs, egg substitute, water, applesauce, 1 teaspoon
cinnamon and nutmeg. Pour into a 10-in. fluted tube pan
coated with nonstick cooking spray.

Bake at 350° for 65-75 minutes or until a toothpick inserted near the center comes out clean. Cool for 10 minutes before removing from pan to a wire rack to cool completely.

In a small bowl, combine the confectioners' sugar,
vanilla, remaining cinnamon and enough milk to achieve desired drizzling consistency. Drizzle over cake. **Yield:** 14
servings.

Nutritional Analysis: *1 piece equals 271 calories, 4 g fat (2 g
saturated fat), 30 mg cholesterol, 261 mg sodium, 55 g carbohydrate, 2 g fiber, 4 g protein.*

Yogurt Spice Cake

Prep: 15 min. **Bake:** 25 min. + cooling

*This yummy apple-spice cake with an easy frosting
is a guilt-free way to dress up a boxed mix.*
—*Jolene Hermoe, Raymond, South Dakota*

  1 package (18-1/4 ounces) spice cake mix
3/4 cup water
  2 cartons (6 ounces *each*) reduced-fat vanilla
    yogurt, *divided*
1/4 cup unsweetened applesauce
  2 eggs, lightly beaten
  1 carton (8 ounces) frozen reduced-fat whipped
    topping, thawed

In a large mixing bowl, combine the cake mix, water, one carton of yogurt, applesauce and eggs until blended. Pour into a
13-in. x 9-in. x 2-in. baking dish coated with nonstick cooking
spray. Bake at 350° for 25-30 minutes or until a toothpick inserted near the center comes out clean. Cool on a wire rack.

For frosting, fold whipped topping into remaining yogurt;
spread over cake. Store in the refrigerator. **Yield:** 15 servings.

Nutritional Analysis: *1 piece equals 216 calories, 7 g fat (3 g
saturated fat), 39 mg cholesterol, 287 mg sodium, 34 g carbohydrate, trace fiber, 4 g protein.*
Diabetic Exchanges: *2 starch, 1 fat.*

🍎 Yummy Yogurt

STRAIGHT from the container, reduced fat or nonfat vanilla yogurt makes a great fruit dip. Or, try the
yogurt as a dressing for fruit salads.
—*Susan Forkner, Salem, Oregon*

Gingersnap Pumpkin Cheesecake

(Pictured below)

Prep: 30 min. **Bake:** 50 min. + chilling

A perfect finale to Thanksgiving dinner, this luscious cheesecake has a light cookie crust.
—Marsha Richmond, Danielsville, Georgia

7 tablespoons gingersnap cookie crumbs
2 packages (8 ounces *each*) reduced-fat cream cheese
1 package (8 ounces) fat-free cream cheese
Sugar substitute equivalent to 2/3 cup sugar
2/3 cup sugar
1 cup (8 ounces) reduced-fat sour cream
1 cup canned pumpkin
1 tablespoon cornstarch
2 teaspoons ground cinnamon
2 teaspoons vanilla extract
1/4 teaspoon salt
1/4 teaspoon ground nutmeg
2 eggs, lightly beaten
2 egg whites, lightly beaten
12 tablespoons fat-free whipped topping

Sprinkle crumbs onto the bottom of a 9-in. springform pan coated with nonstick cooking spray; set aside. In a large mixing bowl, beat cream cheeses until smooth. Add sugar substitute and sugar; beat until smooth. Add sour cream, pumpkin, cornstarch, cinnamon, vanilla, salt and nutmeg; beat until blended. Add eggs and egg whites; beat on low speed just until combined. Pour into prepared pan.

Place on a double thickness of heavy-duty foil (about 16 in. square). Securely wrap foil around pan. Place in a larger baking pan. Add 1 in. of hot water to larger pan. Bake at 325° for 50-60 minutes or until center is almost set. Remove pan from water bath. Cool on a wire rack for 10 minutes. Carefully run a knife around edge of pan to loosen; cool 1 hour longer. Remove foil from pan. Refrigerate overnight.

Remove the sides of pan. Dollop individual servings with

1 tablespoon whipped topping. Refrigerate leftovers. **Yield:** 12 servings.

Editor's Note: This recipe was tested with Splenda No Calorie Sweetener.

Nutritional Analysis: 1 slice equals 246 calories, 11 g fat (7 g saturated fat), 70 mg cholesterol, 390 mg sodium, 25 g carbohydrate, 1 g fiber, 10 g protein.
Diabetic Exchanges: 2 starch, 2 fat.

Rich Pumpkin Custard

(Pictured above)

Low-fat

Prep: 20 min. **Bake:** 35 min.

While on a low-fat diet, I couldn't bear the thought of celebrating Thanksgiving without my favorite pumpkin pie. So I altered the ingredients to create this custard.
—Mary Alice Dick, Fort Wayne, Indiana

3 egg whites, lightly beaten
2/3 cup sugar
1 teaspoon ground cinnamon
1/2 teaspoon salt
1/2 teaspoon ground ginger
1/4 teaspoon ground nutmeg
Dash ground cloves
1 can (15 ounces) solid-pack pumpkin
1 teaspoon vanilla extract
1 can (12 ounces) fat-free evaporated milk

In a large mixing bowl, beat the egg whites, sugar, cinnamon, salt, ginger, nutmeg and cloves. Add pumpkin and vanilla; mix well. Gradually beat in milk. Pour into eight ungreased 6-oz. custard cups.

Place the cups in a 13-in. x 9-in. x 2-in. baking pan; add 1 in. of water to pan. Bake at 325° for 35-40 minutes or until a knife inserted near the center comes out clean. Serve warm or chill. **Yield:** 8 servings.

Nutritional Analysis: 1 serving equals 125 calories, trace fat (trace saturated fat), 2 mg cholesterol, 220 mg sodium, 26 g carbohydrate, 2 g fiber, 5 g protein.
Diabetic Exchange: 1-1/2 starch.

Place seam side down on a baking sheet coated with nonstick cooking spray. With a sharp knife, cut diagonal slits into top of strudel. Brush with reserved butter mixture. Sprinkle with remaining sugar. Bake at 350° for 35-40 minutes or until golden. **Yield:** 8 servings.

Nutritional Analysis: 1 piece equals 205 calories, 7 g fat (2 g saturated fat), 8 mg cholesterol, 121 mg sodium, 35 g carbohydrate, 2 g fiber, 3 g protein.
Diabetic Exchanges: 1-1/2 fat, 1 starch, 1 fruit.

Apple Strudel

(Pictured above)

Low-sodium

Prep: 35 min. **Bake:** 35 min.

My family always loves it when I make this wonderful dessert. Old-fashioned strudel was too fattening and time-consuming, but this revised classic is just as good. It's best served warm from the oven.
—Joanie Fuson, McCordsville, Indiana

1/3 cup raisins
2 tablespoons water
1/4 teaspoon almond extract
3 cups coarsely chopped peeled apples
1/3 cup plus 2 teaspoons sugar, *divided*
3 tablespoons all-purpose flour
1/4 teaspoon ground cinnamon
8 sheets phyllo dough (18 inches x 14 inches)
2 tablespoons butter, melted
2 tablespoons canola oil

In a microwave-safe bowl, combine the raisins, water and almond extract. Microwave, uncovered, on high for 1-1/2 minutes; let stand for 5 minutes. Drain. Add the apples, 1/3 cup sugar, flour and cinnamon; toss to coat. Set aside.

Place 1 sheet of phyllo dough on a work surface. Combine butter and oil; set aside 2 teaspoons. Lightly brush some of the remaining butter mixture over phyllo dough (keep remaining phyllo dough covered with plastic wrap and a damp towel to avoid drying out). Repeat with 7 more sheets of phyllo. Spread the apple mixture over phyllo to within 2 in. of one long side and both short sides and within 4 in. of other long side. Fold the short edges over filling. Roll up jelly-roll style, starting from the long side where the apple filling is 2 in. from edge.

Delicious Angel Food Dessert

(Pictured below)

Prep: 20 min. + chilling

This is one of my favorite desserts. I took it to a family reunion, and everyone raved about it.
—Jessie Bradley, Bella Vista, Arkansas

2 cans (20 ounces *each*) unsweetened crushed pineapple, drained
4 medium firm bananas, sliced
1 loaf (10-1/2 ounces) angel food cake, cut into 1-inch cubes
3 cups cold fat-free milk
2 packages (1 ounce *each*) sugar-free instant vanilla pudding mix
1 carton (8 ounces) frozen reduced-fat whipped topping, thawed
1/3 cup chopped pecans, toasted

Place the pineapple in a bowl; gently fold in bananas. Place cake cubes in a 13-in. x 9-in. x 2-in. dish. Spoon fruit over cake.

In a bowl, whisk milk and pudding mixes for 2 minutes. Let stand for 2 minutes or until soft-set. Spread over fruit. Carefully spread whipped topping over pudding. Sprinkle with pecans. Cover and refrigerate for at least 2 hours before serving. **Yield:** 15 servings.

Nutritional Analysis: 1 serving equals 210 calories, 4 g fat (2 g saturated fat), 1 mg cholesterol, 291 mg sodium, 40 g carbohydrate, 2 g fiber, 4 g protein.
Diabetic Exchanges: 1 starch, 1 fruit, 1/2 fat-free milk.

Cranberry Cream Cheese Pie

(Pictured above)

Prep: 40 min. + chilling

Fluffy and colorful, this pie has been a Christmas tradition at our home for 30 years. Even after a big meal, we all find room for this treat.
—Cathy Wood, Salida, Colorado

1 cup fresh *or* frozen cranberries, *divided*
1 package (.3 ounce) sugar-free raspberry gelatin
Sugar substitute equivalent to 1/3 cup plus 1 tablespoon sugar, *divided*
1-1/4 cups cranberry juice
1 package (8 ounces) reduced-fat cream cheese
1 tablespoon fat-free milk
1 teaspoon vanilla extract
1 pastry shell (9 inches), baked
8 tablespoons fat-free whipped topping

Place half of the cranberries in a food processor. Cover and process until ground; set aside. In a small bowl, combine the gelatin and 1/3 cup sugar substitute. In a small saucepan, bring cranberry juice to a boil. Pour over gelatin mixture; stir until dissolved. Stir in the ground cranberries and remaining whole cranberries. Cover and refrigerate until slightly thickened, about 40 minutes.

In a small mixing bowl, combine cream cheese and remaining sugar substitute. Beat in milk and vanilla. Spread into pastry shell.

Transfer gelatin mixture to a mixing bowl; beat for 4-5 minutes or until foamy. Spoon over cream cheese layer. Cover and refrigerate for at least 2 hours or until firm. Garnish each piece with 1 tablespoon whipped topping. **Yield:** 8 servings.

Editor's Note: This recipe was tested with Splenda No Calorie Sweetener.

Nutritional Analysis: 1 piece equals 232 calories, 13 g fat (7 g saturated fat), 25 mg cholesterol, 248 mg sodium, 23 g carbohydrate, 1 g fiber, 5 g protein.
Diabetic Exchanges: 2-1/2 fat, 1 starch, 1/2 fruit.

🍎 Choosing Cranberry Juice

ON ITS OWN, cranberry juice is quite tart. Many juice makers sweeten it with high fructose corn syrup. These products are typically labeled "cranberry juice cocktail."

It's best to choose a cranberry juice labeled "100% juice" instead. Those drinks are sweetened with other fruit juices, which—unlike corn syrup—provide vitamins and phytonutrients.

Velvety Orange Gelatin Pie

(Pictured below)

Prep: 20 min. + chilling

It's hard to resist this pretty pie. Best of all, I can throw it together and set it in the refrigerator a day early.
—Jean Shourds, Sault Sainte Marie, Michigan

1 package (.3 ounce) sugar-free orange gelatin
1/2 cup boiling water
1 can (14 ounces) fat-free sweetened condensed milk
1 cup (8 ounces) reduced-fat sour cream
3 tablespoons grated orange peel
1 carton (8 ounces) frozen reduced-fat whipped topping, thawed
1 extra-servings-size graham cracker crust (9 ounces)

In a large bowl, dissolve gelatin in boiling water. Stir in the milk, sour cream and orange peel. Fold in the whipped topping. Spoon into crust. Cover and refrigerate for at least 4 hours. **Yield:** 10 servings.

Nutritional Analysis: 1 piece equals 321 calories, 11 g fat (5 g saturated fat), 10 mg cholesterol, 224 mg sodium, 48 g carbohydrate, 1 g fiber, 6 g protein.

Caramelized Pear Strudel

(Pictured above)

Low-fat   Low-sodium

Prep: 35 min. + cooling **Bake:** 20 min. + cooling

This easy, stylish dessert is sure to please everyone. Best served warm, it's delicious with a scoop of light vanilla ice cream or reduced-fat whipped topping.
—Leah Beatty, Cobourg, Ontario

  1/2 cup sugar
    1 tablespoon cornstarch
    3 large pears, peeled and finely chopped
  1/2 cup fresh *or* frozen cranberries, thawed
    2 tablespoons butter
  1/2 cup dried cranberries
    1 teaspoon ground ginger
    1 teaspoon grated orange peel
  1/2 teaspoon ground cinnamon
    6 sheets phyllo dough (14 inches x 9 inches)
    1 teaspoon confectioners' sugar

In a large bowl, combine sugar and cornstarch. Add pears and cranberries; toss gently to coat. In a large nonstick skillet, melt butter over medium-high heat. Add pear mixture; cook and stir for 7-8 minutes or until cranberries pop. Stir in the dried cranberries, ginger, orange peel and cinnamon. Cool.

Line a baking sheet with foil and coat the foil with non-stick cooking spray; set aside. Place one sheet of phyllo dough on a work surface; coat with nonstick cooking spray. (Until ready to use, keep phyllo covered with plastic wrap and a damp towel to prevent drying out.) Layer with remaining phyllo, coating each sheet with nonstick cooking spray. Spread pear mixture over dough to within 1 in. of edges. Fold in sides. Roll up, starting at a long side. Place seam side down on prepared baking sheet.

Bake at 400° for 20-23 minutes or until golden brown. Remove from pan to a wire rack to cool. Dust with confectioners' sugar before serving. **Yield:** 10 servings.

Nutritional Analysis: 1 slice equals 139 calories, 3 g fat (1 g saturated fat), 6 mg cholesterol, 50 mg sodium, 30 g carbohydrate, 2 g fiber, 1 g protein.
Diabetic Exchanges: 1 starch, 1 fruit, 1/2 fat.

White Chocolate Mousse

Low-carb

Prep: 10 min. + chilling

No one will suspect that this thick, rich mousse has little fat. I sometimes top it off with chocolate chips.
—Greta Byers, Dodgeville, Wisconsin

    4 ounces reduced-fat cream cheese
1-1/2 cups cold fat-free milk
    1 package (1 ounce) sugar-free instant white chocolate pudding mix
  3/4 cup reduced-fat whipped topping
  1/2 cup fresh raspberries

In a small mixing bowl, beat cream cheese and milk until smooth. Gradually beat in pudding mix; fold in whipped topping. Spoon into five dessert dishes. Refrigerate for 1 hour or until set. Garnish with raspberries. **Yield:** 5 servings.

Nutritional Analysis: 1 serving equals 126 calories, 5 g fat (4 g saturated fat), 14 mg cholesterol, 275 mg sodium, 13 g carbohydrate, 1 g fiber, 6 g protein.
Diabetic Exchanges: 1 starch, 1 fat.

Peachy Cinnamon Rice Pudding

Low-fat   Low-sodium

Prep: 10 min. **Cook:** 25 min. + cooling

This wonderful variation on a classic treat has become a family favorite I prepare often.
—Shanna Webb, Provo, Utah

    1 cup water
  1/3 cup uncooked long grain rice
    1 tablespoon butter
  1/8 teaspoon salt
    1 can (15 ounces) reduced-sugar sliced peaches
    2 teaspoons cornstarch
  1/2 cup fat-free milk
  1/4 cup 100% peach *or* apricot spreadable fruit
  1/2 teaspoon ground cinnamon

In a saucepan, bring the water, rice, butter and salt to a boil. Reduce heat; cover and simmer for 15-20 minutes or until rice is tender (some of the liquid will not be absorbed).

Drain peaches, reserving 1/3 cup juice; set peaches aside. In a small bowl, combine the cornstarch, milk and reserved juice until smooth.

Gradually stir into rice mixture. Bring to a boil; cook and stir for 2 minutes or until thickened.

Remove from the heat; stir in spreadable fruit and cinnamon until fruit is melted. Cool to room temperature. Chop peaches; stir into rice mixture. Serve immediately. **Yield:** 4 servings.

Nutritional Analysis: 2/3 cup equals 195 calories, 3 g fat (2 g saturated fat), 8 mg cholesterol, 125 mg sodium, 41 g carbohydrate, 2 g fiber, 3 g protein.
Diabetic Exchanges: 2 fruit, 1 starch, 1/2 fat.

Favorite Recipe Made Lighter

JUST over a year ago, Kristi Wells lost a remarkable 70 pounds. "I've kept the weight off, thanks to exercise and eating right," she shares from Raleigh, North Carolina.

"My husband and I both love Chocolate Texas Sheet Cake. It's fattening, but he says that only bad-for-you foods taste good. Can you prove him wrong?"

No problem, Kristi! Our experts created Makeover Chocolate Texas Sheet Cake, a lighter version that you and your husband are sure to enjoy.

Chocolate Texas Sheet Cake

Prep: 25 min. **Bake:** 20 min. + cooling

    1 cup butter, cubed
    1 cup water
1/4 cup baking cocoa
    2 cups all-purpose flour
    2 cups sugar
    1 teaspoon baking soda
1/2 teaspoon salt
    2 eggs, lightly beaten
1/2 cup sour cream
FROSTING:
1/2 cup butter, softened
3-3/4 cups confectioners' sugar
1/4 cup baking cocoa
    1 teaspoon vanilla extract
5 to 6 tablespoons milk

In a large saucepan, bring the butter, water and cocoa to a boil. Remove from the heat. Combine the flour, sugar, baking soda and salt; stir into butter mixture. Combine the eggs and sour cream; stir into butter mixture until blended.

Pour into a greased 15-in. x 10-in. x 1-in. baking pan.

Bake at 350° for 18-25 minutes or until a toothpick inserted near the center comes out clean. Cool on a wire rack.

For frosting, in a large mixing bowl, cream the butter and confectioners' sugar. Add cocoa, vanilla and enough milk to achieve desired consistency. Spread over cake. **Yield:** 20 servings.

Nutritional Analysis: 1 piece equals 359 calories, 16 g fat (9 g saturated fat), 63 mg cholesterol, 273 mg sodium, 54 g carbohydrate, 1 g fiber, 3 g protein.

Makeover Chocolate Texas Sheet Cake

(Pictured at left)

Prep: 25 min. **Bake:** 20 min. + cooling

1/2 cup butter, cubed
    1 cup water
1/4 cup baking cocoa
    1 cup all-purpose flour
    1 cup cake flour
    1 cup sugar blend for baking
    1 teaspoon baking soda
1/2 teaspoon salt
    2 eggs, lightly beaten
1/2 cup reduced-fat sour cream
1/2 cup unsweetened applesauce
FROSTING:
1/2 cup reduced-fat butter, softened
    3 cups confectioners' sugar
1/4 cup baking cocoa
    1 teaspoon vanilla extract
    2 to 3 tablespoons fat-free milk

In a saucepan, bring the butter, water and cocoa to a boil. Remove from the heat. Combine the flours, sugar blend, baking soda and salt; stir into butter mixture. Combine the eggs, sour cream and applesauce; stir into butter mixture until blended.

Transfer to a 15-in. x 10-in. x 1-in. baking pan coated with nonstick cooking spray. Bake at 350° for 18-25 minutes or until a toothpick inserted near the center comes out clean. Cool on a wire rack.

For frosting, in a large mixing bowl, beat butter and confectioners' sugar. Add cocoa, vanilla and enough milk to achieve desired consistency. Spread over cake. **Yield:** 20 servings.

Editor's Note: This recipe was tested with Land O' Lakes light stick butter and Splenda Sugar Blend for Baking. Look for Splenda Sugar Blend in the baking aisle of your grocery store.

Nutritional Analysis: 1 piece equals 242 calories, 8 g fat (5 g saturated fat), 44 mg cholesterol, 208 mg sodium, 40 g carbohydrate, 1 g fiber, 3 g protein.

Strawberry Cheesecake Minis

(Pictured below)

Prep: 15 min. **Bake:** 15 min. + cooling

My daughter and I trimmed down a recipe from a cooking show, and these little cheesecakes were the result. No one suspects they're light.
—*Lori Lewis, St. Johns, Michigan*

    2 packages (8 ounces *each*) reduced-fat cream cheese
Sugar substitute equivalent to 1/2 cup sugar
    1/2 cup sugar
      1 teaspoon vanilla extract
      1 egg, lightly beaten
    1/4 cup egg substitute
   12 reduced-fat vanilla wafers
      1 can (12 ounces) strawberry filling

In a small mixing bowl, beat cream cheese until smooth. Gradually beat in sugar substitute and sugar. Beat in vanilla. Add egg and egg substitute; beat until blended.

Place each vanilla wafer flat side down in a foil-lined muffin cup. Fill with cream cheese mixture. Bake at 350° for 15-20 minutes or until puffed and set. Cool on a wire rack for 1 hour (centers will sink slightly). Spoon filling into the center of each cheesecake. Store in the refrigerator. **Yield:** 1 dozen.

    Editor's Note: This recipe was tested with Splenda No Calorie Sweetener and Solo strawberry filling.

    Nutritional Analysis: 1 cheesecake equals 217 calories, 9 g fat (5 g saturated fat), 44 mg cholesterol, 209 mg sodium, 29 g carbohydrate, 1 g fiber, 5 g protein.
    Diabetic Exchanges: 2 starch, 2 fat.

Wonton Sundaes

(Pictured above)

Low-carb *Low-fat* ***Low-sodium***

Prep: 25 min. **Bake:** 10 min. + cooling

Served as a dessert or sweet appetizer, these cute little bites always vanish in a flash. I created the recipe by combining two of my favorite treats.
—*Betty Jo Morris, Little Rock, Arkansas*

   24 wonton wrappers
Refrigerated butter-flavored spray
      1 tablespoon plus 1/4 cup sugar, *divided*
      1 teaspoon ground cinnamon
      1 package (8 ounces) reduced-fat cream cheese
      1 teaspoon vanilla extract
    1/4 cup semisweet chocolate chips
    1/4 cup chopped pecans
   24 maraschino cherries with stems

Place wonton wrappers on a work surface; spritz with butter-flavored spray. Combine 1 tablespoon sugar and cinnamon; sprinkle over wontons. Press into miniature muffin cups coated with nonstick cooking spray.

Bake at 350° for 4-5 minutes or until lightly browned. Immediately remove wonton cups to an ungreased baking sheet. Bake 2-3 minutes longer or until bottoms of cups are lightly browned. Remove to a wire rack to cool.

In a small mixing bowl, beat the cream cheese, vanilla and remaining sugar until smooth. Stir in chocolate chips and pecans. Spoon into wonton cups. Top each with a cherry. **Yield:** 2 dozen.

    Editor's Note: This recipe was tested with I Can't Believe It's Not Butter Spray.

    Nutritional Analysis: 1 sundae equals 83 calories, 3 g fat (1 g saturated fat), 6 mg cholesterol, 74 mg sodium, 12 g carbohydrate, trace fiber, 2 g protein.
    Diabetic Exchange: 1 starch.

Chewy Chocolate Cookies

Low-fat   Low-sodium

Prep: 15 min. **Bake:** 5 min. + cooling

With only a trace of fat, these nibbles from our Test Kitchen staff will satisfy any chocoholic.

1-1/2 cups all-purpose flour
1/2 cup sugar
1/2 cup baking cocoa
1/2 teaspoon baking soda
1/2 teaspoon salt
3 egg whites
1/2 cup corn syrup
1 cup confectioners' sugar
4 teaspoons fat-free milk

In a large bowl, combine the flour, sugar, cocoa, baking soda and salt. Combine the egg whites and corn syrup; stir into dry ingredients just until moistened. Drop by tablespoonfuls 2 in. apart onto baking sheets coated with nonstick cooking spray. Bake at 350° for 5-7 minutes or until set (do not overbake). Remove to wire racks to cool.

In a small bowl, combine the confectioners' sugar and milk until smooth. Drizzle over cookies. Store in an airtight container. **Yield:** About 2-1/2 dozen.

Nutritional Analysis: 1 cookie equals 72 calories, trace fat (trace saturated fat), trace cholesterol, 73 mg sodium, 17 g carbohydrate, 1 g fiber, 1 g protein.
Diabetic Exchange: 1 starch.

Lemon Delight Cake

(Pictured above right)

Prep: 35 min. **Bake:** 40 min. + cooling

A boxed mix makes this cake easy, but the creamy filling and topping make it unforgettable.
—Lydia Mason, Brainerd, Minnesota

1 package (18-1/4 ounces) lemon cake mix
1-1/3 cups water
3/4 cup egg substitute
1/3 cup unsweetened applesauce
3 tablespoons poppy seeds
FILLING:
1 package (8 ounces) reduced-fat cream cheese
1 can (15-3/4 ounces) lemon pie filling
1/2 cup confectioners' sugar
TOPPING:
1/3 cup packed brown sugar
1/4 cup chopped pecans
3 tablespoons all-purpose flour
4-1/2 teaspoons butter, melted
1/2 teaspoon ground cinnamon
1/8 teaspoon vanilla extract
GLAZE:
1/2 cup confectioners' sugar
4 teaspoons lemon juice

In a large mixing bowl, beat the first five ingredients on medium speed for 2 minutes. Coat a 13-in. x 9-in. x 2-in. baking pan with nonstick cooking spray and dust with flour; spread half of the batter into pan.

In a large mixing bowl, beat cream cheese until smooth. Gradually beat in pie filling. Beat in confectioners' sugar. Drop by teaspoonfuls over batter; spread gently. Top with remaining batter. Combine topping ingredients; sprinkle over batter.

Bake at 350° for 40-45 minutes or until a toothpick comes out clean. Cool on a wire rack. Combine glaze ingredients; drizzle over cake. Refrigerate leftovers. **Yield:** 18 servings.

Nutritional Analysis: 1 piece equals 314 calories, 9 g fat (4 g saturated fat), 44 mg cholesterol, 288 mg sodium, 54 g carbohydrate, 1 g fiber, 5 g protein.

Fruit Fluff

Low-fat   Low-sodium

Prep/Total Time: 10 min.

When you want a refreshing dessert or a yummy snack, this sweet treat is a delightful choice.
—Marilyn Baumgartner, Ossian, Indiana

2 cups (16 ounces) fat-free reduced-sugar vanilla yogurt
1 package (1 ounce) sugar-free instant white chocolate *or* vanilla pudding mix
1 carton (8 ounces) frozen reduced-fat whipped topping, thawed
1 can (20 ounces) unsweetened pineapple tidbits, drained
1 can (11 ounces) mandarin oranges, drained
1/2 cup halved seedless red grapes

In a large bowl, whisk the yogurt and pudding mix for 2 minutes or until thickened. Fold in whipped topping. Fold in the fruit. Refrigerate until serving. **Yield:** 12 servings.

Nutritional Analysis: 1/2 cup equals 95 calories, 2 g fat (2 g saturated fat), 1 mg cholesterol, 93 mg sodium, 17 g carbohydrate, 1 g fiber, 1 g protein.
Diabetic Exchanges: 1/2 starch, 1/2 fruit, 1/2 fat.

Bake at 375° for 47-52 minutes or until a toothpick inserted near the center comes out clean. Cool on a wire rack. Run a knife around edge of pan to loosen. Remove sides of pan. Refrigerate leftovers. **Yield:** 10 servings.

Nutritional Analysis: 1 piece equals 268 calories, 9 g fat (3 g saturated fat), 33 mg cholesterol, 285 mg sodium, 43 g carbohydrate, 1 g fiber, 5 g protein.
Diabetic Exchanges: 3 starch, 1-1/2 fat.

Apple-Topped Cake

(Pictured above)

Prep: 25 min. **Bake:** 50 min. + cooling

Complete with apples, nuts and cinnamon, this cake is ideal with cups of coffee. Baking it in a springform pan helps ensure incredible results.
—David Heppner, Brandon, Florida

 3 tablespoons butter, softened
 3/4 cup sugar
 1 egg
 1 egg white
 1 cup vanilla yogurt
 1/3 cup unsweetened applesauce
 2 tablespoons canola oil
 2 teaspoons vanilla extract
 2 cups all-purpose flour
 1 teaspoon baking powder
 1/2 teaspoon baking soda
 1/2 teaspoon salt
 1-1/2 cups chopped peeled apples
 2 tablespoons chopped walnuts
 1 tablespoon brown sugar
 1/2 teaspoon ground cinnamon
 1/8 teaspoon ground allspice

In a large mixing bowl, beat butter and sugar until crumbly, about 2 minutes. Add egg, egg white, yogurt, applesauce, oil and vanilla; beat until smooth. Combine dry ingredients; add to yogurt mixture, beating just until moistened.

Pour into a 9-in. springform pan coated with nonstick cooking spray. Sprinkle with apples and walnuts. Combine the brown sugar, cinnamon and allspice; sprinkle over top.

Chocolate Peanut Torte

(Pictured below and on front cover)

Prep: 35 min. **Bake:** 30 min. + cooling

The smooth peanut butter layers and fudgy topping of this rich and impressive dessert are always a hit with my family and friends.
—Crystal Christopher, Hustonville, Kentucky

1-3/4 cups all-purpose flour
 1 cup sugar
 3/4 cup baking cocoa
 1/3 cup sugar blend for baking
1-1/2 teaspoons baking powder
 1 teaspoon salt
 1/4 teaspoon baking soda
 1 cup fat-free milk
 1/2 cup egg substitute
 1/4 cup canola oil
 2 teaspoons vanilla extract
 1 cup boiling water
CREAMY PEANUT FILLING:
1-3/4 cups plus 2 tablespoons cold fat-free milk, *divided*
 1 package (1 ounce) sugar-free instant vanilla pudding mix
 3/4 cup reduced-fat creamy peanut butter
TOPPING:
 3 tablespoons butter
 1 square (1 ounce) unsweetened chocolate
 1/2 cup confectioners' sugar
 2 tablespoons fat-free milk

Coat two 9-in. round baking pans, each lined with waxed paper, with nonstick cooking spray. Dust with flour; set aside.

In a mixing bowl, combine first seven ingredients. Combine milk, egg substitute, oil and vanilla; add to flour mixture. Beat for 2 minutes. Stir in water. Pour into pans. Bake at 350° for 30-35 minutes or until a toothpick comes out clean. Cool for 10 minutes; remove to wire racks. Cool.

In a bowl, whisk 1-3/4 cups milk and pudding mix for 2 minutes. In a saucepan over low heat, stir peanut butter and remaining milk until smooth. Fold into pudding. Spread half over one cake layer; top with second layer and remaining filling. Chill for 1 hour.

For topping, melt butter and chocolate. Stir in sugar and milk. Cool until spreadable; spread over cake. **Yield:** 16 servings.

Editor's Note: This recipe was tested with Splenda Sugar Blend for Baking.

Nutritional Analysis: 1 piece equals 287 calories, 11 g fat (3 g saturated fat), 7 mg cholesterol, 407 mg sodium, 41 g carbohydrate, 2 g fiber, 8 g protein.
Diabetic Exchanges: 2-1/2 starch, 2 fat.

Banana Chocolate Cake

Prep: 15 min. **Bake:** 25 min. + cooling

This light-as-air chocolate cake from our Test Kitchen has lots of banana flavor. It's scrumptious as is, but you can also dress it up with nuts.

Sugar substitute equivalent to 3/4 cup sugar
1/3 cup packed brown sugar
1/3 cup butter, softened
2 eggs
2 teaspoons vanilla extract
2 medium ripe bananas, mashed
1/2 cup water
1-1/3 cups all-purpose flour
1/2 cup nonfat dry milk powder
3 tablespoons baking cocoa
1 teaspoon baking powder
1/2 teaspoon baking soda
1/2 teaspoon salt
3/4 teaspoon confectioners' sugar

In a large mixing bowl, beat the sugar substitute, brown sugar and butter on medium speed for 3 minutes. Add eggs and vanilla; mix well. Add bananas and water; mix well. Combine the flour, milk powder, cocoa, baking powder, baking soda and salt; add to sugar mixture, beating just until blended.

Pour into a 9-in. square baking pan coated with nonstick cooking spray. Bake at 375° for 23-28 minutes or until a toothpick inserted near the center comes out clean and edges of cake are just starting to pull away from sides of pan. Cool on a wire rack. Dust with confectioners' sugar. **Yield:** 12 servings.

Editor's Note: This recipe was tested with Splenda No Calorie Sweetener.

Nutritional Analysis: 1 piece equals 179 calories, 6 g fat (3 g saturated fat), 50 mg cholesterol, 276 mg sodium, 26 g carbohydrate, 1 g fiber, 5 g protein.
Diabetic Exchanges: 1-1/2 starch, 1 fat.

Caramel Crunch Cake

(Pictured above)

Prep: 15 min. **Bake:** 35 min. + cooling

I love how this cake comes together with a boxed mix, water and egg whites. The candy bars are a fun and decadent touch in a light cake.
—Heather Dollins, Poplar Bluff, Missouri

1 package (18-1/4 ounces) devil's food cake mix
1-1/3 cups water
5 egg whites
1 can (14 ounces) fat-free sweetened condensed milk
1/2 cup fat-free caramel ice cream topping
5 fun-size Butterfinger candy bars, crushed
1 carton (8 ounces) frozen fat-free whipped topping, thawed

In a large mixing bowl, beat the cake mix, water and egg whites until blended. Pour into a 13-in. x 9-in. x 2-in. baking pan coated with nonstick cooking spray. Bake at 350° for 35-40 minutes or until a toothpick inserted near the center comes out clean. Cool on a wire rack.

With a meat fork or wooden skewer, poke holes about 2 in. apart into cake. Slowly pour condensed milk and caramel topping over cake; sprinkle with two-thirds of the crushed candy bars. Spread with whipped topping; sprinkle with remaining candy bars. Refrigerate until serving. **Yield:** 18 servings.

Nutritional Analysis: 1 piece equals 250 calories, 4 g fat (2 g saturated fat), 2 mg cholesterol, 290 mg sodium, 47 g carbohydrate, 1 g fiber, 5 g protein.

Cranberry Cheesecake

(Pictured below)

Prep: 40 min. **Bake:** 65 min. + chilling

The cranberry topping on this cheesecake is so good that I serve it separately as a Thanksgiving side dish.
—Mary Simonson, Kelso, Washington

- 9 whole cinnamon graham crackers (about 5 inches x 2-1/2 inches), crushed
- 1 tablespoon plus 1 cup sugar, *divided*
- 1/4 cup butter, melted
- 2 packages (8 ounces *each*) reduced-fat cream cheese, cubed
- 1 package (8 ounces) fat-free cream cheese, cubed
- 3/4 cup fat-free sour cream
- 3 egg whites, lightly beaten
- 1 tablespoon lemon juice
- 2 teaspoons vanilla extract
- 1 teaspoon rum extract

TOPPING:
- 3/4 cup sugar
- 1/4 cup orange juice
- 2 tablespoons water
- 1-1/2 teaspoons grated orange peel
- 1/4 teaspoon minced fresh gingerroot
- 2 cups fresh *or* frozen cranberries
- 1/4 cup chopped pecans

Combine cracker crumbs, 1 tablespoon sugar and butter. Press onto the bottom and 1 in. up the sides of a 9-in. springform pan coated with nonstick cooking spray. Place on a baking sheet. Bake at 350° for 10 minutes. Cool on a wire rack.

In a bowl, beat cream cheeses, sour cream and remaining sugar until smooth. Add egg whites; beat on low until combined. Stir in juice and extracts. Pour into crust. Place pan on a double thickness of heavy-duty foil.

Wrap foil around pan. Place in a larger baking pan. Add 1 in. hot water to larger pan. Bake for 55-60 minutes or until center is just set. Remove pan from water bath. Cool on a wire rack for 10 minutes. Carefully run a knife around edge of pan to loosen; cool 1 hour longer. Remove foil. Chill overnight.

In a saucepan, combine the first five topping ingredients; bring to a boil. Add the cranberries. Cook over medium heat until cranberries pop, about 10 minutes. Stir in the pecans;

cool. Cover; chill for at least 1 hour.

Remove sides of springform pan. Spoon topping over cheesecake to within 1 in. of edges. Refrigerate leftovers. **Yield:** 16 servings.

Nutritional Analysis: 1 slice equals 269 calories, 11 g fat (6 g saturated fat), 31 mg cholesterol, 294 mg sodium, 35 g carbohydrate, 1 g fiber, 7 g protein.
Diabetic Exchanges: 2 starch, 2 fat.

Oatmeal Date Bars

(Pictured above)

Low-sodium

Prep: 25 min. **Bake:** 20 min. + cooling

In no time at all, you can treat your family to these bars. They'll never suspect that the yummy snacks have just a few grams of fat in each piece.
—Helen Cluts, Sioux Falls, South Dakota

- 1 cup chopped dates
- 1/2 cup water
- 1/4 cup sugar
- 1-1/2 cups quick-cooking oats
- 1 cup all-purpose flour
- 1 cup packed brown sugar
- 1/2 teaspoon baking soda
- 1/4 teaspoon salt
- 1/3 cup butter, melted
- 1 egg white

In a small saucepan, combine the dates, water and sugar. Cook and stir until mixture comes to a boil. Reduce heat; simmer, uncovered, for 5 minutes or until mixture is smooth and thickened, stirring constantly.

In a large bowl, combine the oats, flour, brown sugar, baking soda and salt. Stir in the butter and egg white until blended. Pat half of the mixture into an 8-in. square baking dish coated with nonstick cooking spray. Carefully spread with date mixture. Gently pat remaining oat mixture over date mixture. Bake at 350° for 20-25 minutes or until lightly browned. Cool on a wire rack. Cut into bars. **Yield:** 16 servings.

Nutritional Analysis: 1 bar equals 186 calories, 4 g fat (2 g saturated fat), 10 mg cholesterol, 124 mg sodium, 36 g carbohydrate, 2 g fiber, 2 g protein.
Diabetic Exchanges: 1-1/2 starch, 1 fat, 1/2 fruit.

Favorite Recipe Made Lighter

WRITES Andy Heavilin from Carmel, Indiana, "A friend of mine serves the greatest dessert I've ever tasted. I'm sure that it's loaded with fat and calories, though...can you lighten it up?"

Andy is right about two things: Frozen Mocha Cheesecake Loaf is a terrific dessert, and it's full of fat and calories—25 grams of fat and 423 calories per slice, to be exact.

Our Test Kitchen makeover team never met a frozen dessert they didn't like, so they happily rolled up their sleeves and got to work using fat-free and reduced-fat ingredients.

The end result is a guilt-free tooth-tingler. No one will ever suspect that Makeover Frozen Mocha Cheesecake Loaf has 60% less fat and 124 fewer calories than the original. In addition, 72% of the cholesterol was cut from the frosty treat that Andy sent.

Frozen Mocha Cheesecake Loaf

Prep: 30 min. + freezing

- 2 cups cream-filled chocolate sandwich cookie crumbs
- 3 tablespoons butter, melted
- 1 package (8 ounces) cream cheese, softened
- 1 can (14 ounces) sweetened condensed milk
- 1 tablespoon vanilla extract
- 2 cups heavy whipping cream, whipped
- 2 tablespoons instant coffee granules
- 1 tablespoon hot water
- 1/2 cup chocolate syrup

Line a 9-in. x 5-in. x 3-in. loaf pan with heavy-duty foil. In a small bowl, combine cookie crumbs and butter. Press firmly onto the bottom and 1-1/2 in. up the sides of prepared pan.

In a large mixing bowl, beat the cream cheese until light and fluffy. Add the milk and vanilla; mix well. Fold in the whipped cream. Spoon half of the mixture into another bowl and set aside. Dissolve the coffee granules in hot water; fold into remaining cream cheese mixture. Fold in the chocolate syrup.

Spoon half of the chocolate mixture over crust. Top with half of the reserved cream cheese mixture. Repeat layers (pan will be full). Freeze, uncovered, for 6 hours or until set. Cover and freeze until serving. Use foil to lift out of pan; cut into slices. **Yield:** 12 servings.

Nutritional Analysis: 1 slice equals 423 calories, 25 g fat (14 g saturated fat), 67 mg cholesterol, 268 mg sodium, 45 g carbohydrate, 2 g fiber, 6 g protein.

Makeover Frozen Mocha Cheesecake Loaf

(Pictured above)

Prep: 30 min. + freezing

- 1-1/2 cups reduced-fat cream-filled chocolate sandwich cookie crumbs
- 4-1/2 teaspoons butter, melted
- 1 package (8 ounces) reduced-fat cream cheese
- 1 can (14 ounces) fat-free sweetened condensed milk
- 1 tablespoon vanilla extract
- 4 cups reduced-fat whipped topping
- 7 teaspoons instant coffee granules
- 1 tablespoon hot water
- 1/2 cup chocolate syrup

Line a 9-in. x 5-in. x 3-in. loaf pan with heavy-duty foil. In a small bowl, combine cookie crumbs and butter. Press firmly onto the bottom and 1/2 in. up the sides of the prepared pan.

In a large mixing bowl, beat cream cheese until light and fluffy. Add milk and vanilla; mix well. Fold in whipped topping. Spoon half of the mixture into another bowl and set aside. Dissolve coffee granules in hot water; fold into remaining cream cheese mixture. Fold in chocolate syrup.

Spoon half of the chocolate mixture over crust. Top with half of the reserved cream cheese mixture. Repeat layers (pan will be full). Freeze, uncovered, for 6 hours or until set. Cover and freeze until serving. Use foil to lift out of pan; cut into slices. **Yield:** 12 servings.

Nutritional Analysis: 1 slice equals 299 calories, 10 g fat (7 g saturated fat), 19 mg cholesterol, 219 mg sodium, 45 g carbohydrate, 1 g fiber, 6 g protein.

Chocolate Caramel Cheesecake

(Pictured above)

Prep: 35 min. **Bake:** 30 min. + chilling

Layers of caramel and nuts complement this dessert's chocolate flavor, proving you can bake terrific cheesecakes that don't have a lot of fat.
—*Tamara Trouten, Fort Wayne, Indiana*

6 whole reduced-fat honey graham crackers, crushed
3 tablespoons butter, melted
25 caramels
1/4 cup fat-free evaporated milk
1/4 cup chopped pecans
2 packages (8 ounces *each*) reduced-fat cream cheese
1/3 cup sugar
2 eggs, lightly beaten
1/3 cup semisweet chocolate chips, melted and cooled

In a small bowl, combine graham cracker crumbs and butter. Press onto the bottom of a 9-in. springform pan coated with nonstick cooking spray. Place on a baking sheet. Bake at 350° for 5-10 minutes or until set. Cool on a wire rack.

In a small saucepan over low heat, stir caramels and milk until smooth. Pour over crust. Sprinkle with pecans. In a small mixing bowl, beat cream cheese and sugar until smooth. Add eggs; beat on low speed just until combined. Stir in melted chocolate. Pour over caramel layer. Place pan on baking sheet.

Bake at 350° for 30-35 minutes or until center is almost set. Cool on a wire rack for 10 minutes. Carefully run a knife around edge of pan to loosen; cool 1 hour longer. Chill for 4 hours or overnight. Remove sides of pan. Refrigerate leftovers. **Yield:** 12 servings.

Nutritional Analysis: 1 piece equals 284 calories, 17 g fat (10 g saturated fat), 71 mg cholesterol, 270 mg sodium, 29 g carbohydrate, 1 g fiber, 7 g protein.
Diabetic Exchanges: 3 fat, 2 starch.

Oatmeal Cake With Broiled Frosting

(Pictured below)

Prep: 30 min. **Bake:** 30 min.

The broiled coconut frosting makes this tender snack cake terrific. It's great for dessert after a special meal...or even as a morning treat.
—*Pat Van Cleve, Winston-Salem, North Carolina*

1 cup quick-cooking oats
1-1/2 cups boiling water
1 cup sugar
1 cup packed brown sugar
1/2 cup unsweetened applesauce
2 eggs, lightly beaten
1-1/2 cups all-purpose flour
2 teaspoons baking powder
2 teaspoons ground cinnamon
1 teaspoon salt
1/2 teaspoon baking soda
1/4 teaspoon ground nutmeg
FROSTING:
1 cup flaked coconut
1/2 cup packed brown sugar
1/2 cup chopped walnuts
1/4 cup fat-free half-and-half
2 tablespoons butter, melted
1/2 teaspoon vanilla extract

In a small bowl, combine the oats and water; let stand for 20 minutes. In a large bowl, combine the sugars, applesauce and eggs. Add the oat mixture; mix well. Combine the flour, baking powder, cinnamon, salt, baking soda and nut-

meg; add to the batter and mix well.

Pour into a 13-in. x 9-in. x 2-in. baking pan coated with nonstick cooking spray. Bake at 350° for 25-30 minutes or until a toothpick comes out clean.

Combine frosting ingredients; spread over hot cake. Broil 6 in. from the heat for 1-2 minutes or until lightly browned and bubbly. **Yield:** 15 servings.

Nutritional Analysis: 1 piece equals 288 calories, 7 g fat (3 g saturated fat), 32 mg cholesterol, 305 mg sodium, 53 g carbohydrate, 2 g fiber, 4 g protein.

Lemon Meringue Angel Cake

(Pictured above)

Low-fat Low-sodium

Prep: 40 min. + standing **Bake:** 35 min. + cooling

I've been told this is the best angel food cake around. It's perfect to serve to guests and very low in fat.
—Sharon Kurtz, Emmaus, Pennsylvania

12 egg whites
1-1/2 cups sugar, divided
1 cup cake flour
2 teaspoons cream of tartar
1-1/2 teaspoons vanilla extract
1/4 teaspoon salt
1 jar (10 ounces) lemon curd

MERINGUE TOPPING:
4 egg whites
3/4 teaspoon cream of tartar
1/2 cup sugar

Place egg whites in a large mixing bowl; let stand at room temperature for 30 minutes. Sift 1/2 cup sugar and flour together twice; set aside. Add cream of tartar, vanilla and salt to egg whites; beat on medium speed until soft peaks form. Gradually beat in remaining sugar, 2 tablespoons at a time, on high until stiff glossy peaks form and sugar is dissolved. Gradually fold in flour mixture, about 1/2 cup at a time.

Gently spoon batter into an ungreased 10-in. tube pan. Cut through batter with a knife to remove air pockets. Bake on lowest oven rack at 350° for 35-40 minutes or until golden brown and entire top appears dry. Immediately invert pan; cool completely, about 1 hour.

Run a knife around side and center tube of pan. Remove cake; split into two horizontal layers. Place cake bottom on an ovenproof plate. Spread with lemon curd; replace cake top.

For meringue, in a small mixing bowl, beat egg whites and cream of tartar on medium until soft peaks form. Gradually beat in sugar, 1 tablespoon at a time, on high until stiff glossy peaks form and sugar is dissolved. Spread over top and sides of cake. Bake at 350° for 15-18 minutes or until golden brown. Refrigerate leftovers. **Yield:** 14 servings.

Nutritional Analysis: 1 piece equals 238 calories, 1 g fat (1 g saturated fat), 15 mg cholesterol, 121 mg sodium, 51 g carbohydrate, trace fiber, 5 g protein.

Mint Meringues

(Pictured at right)

Low-carb Low-fat Low-sodium

Prep: 25 min. **Bake:** 40 min. + cooling

It just wouldn't be Christmas at our house without these crunchy cookies that everyone enjoys.
—Karla Retzer, Grantsburg, Wisconsin

> 2 egg whites
> 1/8 teaspoon salt
> 1/8 teaspoon cream of tartar
> 1/8 teaspoon peppermint extract
> 6 to 8 drops green food coloring, optional
> 1/2 cup sugar
> 1/3 cup miniature semisweet chocolate chips

In a small mixing bowl, beat egg whites, salt, cream of tartar, extract and food coloring if desired on medium speed until soft peaks form. Gradually add sugar, 1 tablespoon at a time, beating on high until stiff glossy peaks form and the sugar is dissolved, about 6 minutes. Gently fold in the chocolate chips.

Drop by rounded teaspoonfuls 2 in. apart onto parchment paper-lined baking sheets. Bake at 250° for 40-45 minutes or until firm to the touch. Turn oven off; leave meringues in oven for 1-1/2 hours. Remove to wire racks. Store in an airtight container. **Yield:** 32 cookies.

Nutritional Analysis: *1 cookie equals 22 calories, 1 g fat (trace saturated fat), 0 cholesterol, 13 mg sodium, 4 g carbohydrate, trace fiber, trace protein.*
Diabetic Exchange: *Free food.*

Chocolate-Dipped Phyllo Sticks

(Pictured at right)

Low-carb Low-sodium

Prep: 35 min. **Bake:** 5 min. per batch

For something a little special to bake for holidays, try these elegant sweets from our Test Kitchen.

> 4 sheets phyllo dough (14 inches x 9 inches)
> 2 tablespoons butter, melted
> 1 tablespoon sugar
> 1/4 teaspoon ground cinnamon
> 2 squares (1 ounce *each*) semisweet chocolate, finely chopped
> 1/2 teaspoon shortening
> 1/2 ounce white baking chocolate, melted

Place one sheet of phyllo dough on a work surface; brush with butter. Cover with a second sheet of phyllo; brush with butter. (Until ready to use, keep remaining phyllo covered with plastic wrap and a damp towel to prevent drying out.) Cut phyllo in half lengthwise. Cut each half into five 4-1/2-in. x 2-3/4-in. rectangles. Tightly roll each rectangle from one long side, forming a 4-1/2-in.-long stick.

Combine sugar and cinnamon. Coat sticks with nonstick cooking spray; sprinkle with cinnamon-sugar. Place on an ungreased baking sheet. Bake at 425° for 3-5 minutes or until lightly browned. Remove to a wire rack to cool. Repeat with remaining dough, butter and cinnamon-sugar.

Splendid Substitutes

SUGAR SUBSTITUTES, such as Splenda, are a great way to cut back on calories and carbohydrates in desserts and other dishes. For instance, 1/2 cup of granulated sugar contains 387 calories and 100 g carbohydrate. In comparison, 1/2 cup Splenda offers 48 calories and 12 g carbohydrate. That's a savings of 339 calories and 88 g carbohydrate!

In a microwave or small heavy saucepan, melt semisweet chocolate and shortening; stir until smooth. Dip top half of phyllo sticks in melted chocolate. Place on waxed paper; let stand until set. Drizzle with white chocolate. **Yield:** 20 sticks.

Nutritional Analysis: *2 sticks equals 75 calories, 5 g fat (3 g saturated fat), 6 mg cholesterol, 43 mg sodium, 8 g carbohydrate, 1 g fiber, 1 g protein.*
Diabetic Exchanges: *1 fat, 1/2 starch.*

Vanilla Peach Tarts

Prep: 30 min. + chilling

Peaches and pudding create a smooth filling for these mini tarts shared by our home economists.

> Sugar substitute equivalent to 1/3 cup sugar
> 2 tablespoons cornstarch
> 1/8 teaspoon ground nutmeg
> 1/8 teaspoon ground cinnamon
> 1/2 cup water
> 2-1/4 cups sliced peeled fresh *or* frozen peaches, thawed, *divided*
> 1-1/2 cups cold fat-free milk
> 1 package (1 ounce) sugar-free instant vanilla pudding mix
> 8 individual graham cracker tart shells

In a small saucepan, combine the sugar substitute, cornstarch, nutmeg and cinnamon; stir in water until smooth. Add 2 cups peaches. Bring to a boil over medium heat; cook and stir for 2 minutes or until thickened. Cool to room temperature.

In a blender, process 1/2 cup peach mixture until smooth. In a large bowl, whisk milk and pudding mix for 2 minutes or until slightly thickened. Let stand for 2 minutes or until soft-set. Stir in pureed peach mixture.

Spoon remaining peach mixture into tart shells; top with the pudding mixture. Refrigerate until set. Cut the remaining peaches into small pieces and arrange on top. **Yield:** 8 servings.

Editor's Note: This recipe was tested with Splenda No Calorie Sweetener.

Nutritional Analysis: *1 tart equals 174 calories, 6 g fat (1 g saturated fat), 1 mg cholesterol, 314 mg sodium, 28 g carbohydrate, 2 g fiber, 3 g protein.*
Diabetic Exchanges: *1-1/2 starch, 1/2 fruit, 1/2 fat.*

FROSTING:
    1/4 cup butter, softened
    5 cups confectioners' sugar
    1/2 teaspoon vanilla extract
    4 to 5 tablespoons fat-free milk
Food coloring, optional

In a large mixing bowl, cream butter and sugar. Beat in the baby food, egg, molasses and milk. Combine the flour, ginger, cinnamon, aniseed, baking soda, cloves and fennel seed; gradually add to creamed mixture. Cover and refrigerate for 2 hours or until easy to handle.

On a lightly floured surface, roll out dough to 3/16 in. thickness. Cut with a floured 2-in. cookie cutter. Place 1 in. apart on baking sheets coated with nonstick cooking spray. Bake at 375° for 8-10 minutes or until edges are firm. Remove to wire racks to cool.

For frosting, in a large mixing bowl, cream butter and confectioners' sugar. Beat in vanilla and enough milk to achieve spreading consistency. Add food coloring if desired. Decorate cookies. **Yield:** 6 dozen.

Nutritional Analysis: 1 cookie equals 87 calories, 1 g fat (1 g saturated fat), 6 mg cholesterol, 34 mg sodium, 18 g carbohydrate, trace fiber, 1 g protein.
Diabetic Exchange: *1 starch.*

Grandma's Wheat Germ Cookies

Low-carb Low-sodium

Prep: 20 min. **Bake:** 10 min.

I lightened up an oatmeal chocolate chip cookie by adding wheat germ, eliminating butter and using applesauce.
—Pam Voigt, Clear Lake, Minnesota

1-1/2 cups all-purpose flour
1-1/2 cups toasted wheat germ
    1 cup quick-cooking oats
    1 cup packed brown sugar
    2 teaspoons baking powder
    1 teaspoon salt
    1/2 cup unsweetened applesauce
    1/2 cup canola oil
    2 eggs, lightly beaten
    1 cup (6 ounces) miniature chocolate chips
    1/2 cup chopped walnuts *or* pecans

In a large mixing bowl, combine the first six ingredients. Combine the applesauce, oil and eggs. Add to the flour mixture; mix well. Stir in the chocolate chips and walnuts.

Drop by rounded teaspoonfuls 2 in. apart onto baking sheets coated with nonstick cooking spray. Flatten slightly with a glass bottom coated with nonstick cooking spray. Bake at 350° for 10-12 minutes or until edges are lightly browned and cookies are set. Cool for 1 minute before removing to wire racks. **Yield:** 4 dozen.

Nutritional Analysis: 1 cookie equals 102 calories, 5 g fat (1 g saturated fat), 9 mg cholesterol, 64 mg sodium, 13 g carbohydrate, 1 g fiber, 2 g protein.
Diabetic Exchanges: *1 starch, 1 fat.*

Spice Cutout Cookies

(Pictured above)

Low-fat Low-sodium

Prep: 1 hour + chilling **Bake:** 10 min. per batch + cooling

With a tasty twist on gingerbread and little fat, these whimsical treats make a fun addition to holiday cookie platters and dessert buffets alike.
—Lyn Chapman, Provo, Utah

1/4 cup butter, softened
3/4 cup sugar
1/4 cup prune baby food
    1 egg
3/4 cup molasses
    3 tablespoons fat-free milk
3-3/4 cups all-purpose flour
1-1/2 teaspoons ground ginger
1-1/2 teaspoons ground cinnamon
1-1/2 teaspoons aniseed, crushed
    1 teaspoon baking soda
    1 teaspoon ground cloves
    1 teaspoon fennel seed, crushed

Family-Style Suppers

In this chapter, you'll meet cooks
who share how they prepare good-for-you
fare for their families' tables. You'll
also find two dinners that don't
break your household budget.

Hearty Taco Casserole, Island Fruit Salad and Cinnamon Chips 'n' Dip (page 247)

A Meal for Just $1.49 a Plate!

Roasted Parmesan Potato Wedges

Meatless

Prep: 10 min. **Bake:** 45 min.

These potatoes have an irresistible cheese and herb coating.
—Linda Rock, Stratford, Wisconsin

4 potatoes (2 pounds)
2 teaspoons canola oil
1/2 cup grated Parmesan cheese
1 teaspoon dried basil
1 teaspoon seasoned salt
1/4 teaspoon onion powder
1/4 teaspoon garlic powder
1/4 teaspoon pepper

Cut each potato lengthwise in half. Cut each half into three wedges. In a large bowl, sprinkle potatoes with oil; toss to coat. Combine the remaining ingredients. Add to potatoes; toss to coat.

Arrange potatoes in a single layer on a 15-in. x 10-in. x 1-in. baking pan coated with nonstick cooking spray. Sprinkle with any remaining coating. Bake at 350° for 45-55 minutes or until golden brown and tender. **Yield:** 6 servings.

Nutritional Analysis: 4 wedges equals 179 calories, 4 g fat (1 g saturated fat), 5 mg cholesterol, 387 mg sodium, 31 g carbohydrate, 3 g fiber, 6 g protein.
Diabetic Exchanges: 2 starch, 1/2 fat.

Flavorful Meat Loaf

Low-carb

Prep: 15 min. **Bake:** 45 min. + standing

Since I can't have much salt, I've come up with a recipe for meat loaf that is really tasty without it.
—Lillian Wittler, Norfolk, Nebraska

2 egg whites
1/2 cup 1% milk
3 slices whole wheat bread, torn into pieces
1/4 cup finely chopped onion
1 teaspoon Worcestershire sauce
1/4 teaspoon onion powder
1/4 teaspoon garlic powder
1/4 teaspoon ground mustard
1/4 teaspoon rubbed sage
1/4 teaspoon pepper
1 pound lean ground beef
3 tablespoons ketchup

In a large bowl, beat egg whites. Add milk and bread; let stand for 5 minutes. Stir in the onion, Worcestershire sauce and seasonings. Crumble beef over mixture and mix well.

Shape into a loaf in an 11-in. x 7-in. x 2-in. baking pan coated with nonstick cooking spray. Bake, uncovered, at 350° for 35 minutes; drain. Spoon ketchup over loaf. Bake 10-20 minutes longer or until a meat thermometer reads 160°. Let stand for 10 minutes before slicing. **Yield:** 5 servings.

Nutritional Analysis: One serving equals 228 calories, 9 g fat (4 g saturated fat), 35 mg cholesterol, 307 mg sodium, 13 g carbohydrate, 1 g fiber, 23 g protein.
Diabetic Exchanges: 3 lean meat, 1 starch.

Greens with Creamy Herbed Salad Dressing

Low-carb   Low-fat   Meatless

Prep/Total Time: 10 min.

If you're looking for a way to spice up everyday greens, try this dressing. It also makes a delectable veggie dip.
—Janet Les, Chilliwack, British Columbia

1/2 cup fat-free mayonnaise
2 tablespoons plus 2 teaspoons fat-free milk
4 teaspoons white vinegar
1 teaspoon dried oregano
1/2 teaspoon dried basil
1/4 teaspoon sugar
1/4 teaspoon salt
1/4 teaspoon garlic powder
1/4 teaspoon pepper
5 cups mixed salad greens

In a bowl, whisk together the fat-free mayonnaise, milk and vinegar. Whisk in the oregano, basil, sugar, salt, garlic powder and pepper. Serve over greens. **Yield:** 5 servings.

Nutritional Analysis: 1 cup mixed salad greens with 2 tablespoons salad dressing equals 33 calories, 1 g fat (trace saturated fat), 3 mg cholesterol, 328 mg sodium, 6 g carbohydrate, 2 g fiber, 1 g protein.
Diabetic Exchange: 1 vegetable.

A Meal for Just $1.24 a Plate!

Orange-Mustard Grilled Chicken

Low-carb Low-fat

Prep: 10 min. + marinating **Grill:** 10 min.

We love grilling out…and this is one of our favorite recipes. The ginger, orange and mustard flavors make a tantalizing sauce for the moist chicken.
—Paula Marchesi, Lenhartsville, Pennsylvania

1/4 cup lemon-lime soda
1/4 cup orange juice
1/4 cup Dijon mustard
1/4 cup reduced-sodium soy sauce
3 tablespoons honey
2 tablespoons minced fresh gingerroot
6 boneless skinless chicken breast halves
   (4 ounces *each*)

In a small bowl, combine the first six ingredients; mix well. Pour 3/4 cup marinade into a large resealable plastic bag; add the chicken. Seal bag and turn to coat; refrigerate for 45 minutes. Cover and refrigerate remaining marinade for basting.

Coat grill rack with nonstick cooking spray before starting the grill. Drain and discard marinade from chicken. Grill, covered, over medium heat 5-6 minutes on each side or until juices run clear, basting occasionally with reserved marinade. **Yield:** 6 servings.

Nutritional Analysis: *1 chicken breast half equals 153 calories, 2 g fat (trace saturated fat), 66 mg cholesterol, 402 mg sodium, 6 g carbohydrate, trace fiber, 27 g protein.*
Diabetic Exchange: *3 lean meat.*

Classic Macaroni Salad

Low-fat Meatless

Prep/Total Time: 30 min.

This medley is a light take on an all-time favorite.
—Dorothy Bayes, Sardis, Ohio

2 cups uncooked elbow macaroni
1 cup fat-free mayonnaise
2 tablespoons sweet pickle relish
Sugar substitute equivalent to 2 teaspoons sugar
3/4 teaspoon ground mustard
1/4 teaspoon salt
1/8 teaspoon pepper
1/2 cup chopped celery
1/3 cup chopped carrot
1/4 cup chopped onion
1 hard-cooked egg, sliced
Dash paprika

Cook macaroni according to package directions; drain and rinse with cold water. Cool completely. For dressing, in a small bowl, combine the mayonnaise, pickle relish, sugar substitute, mustard, salt and pepper. In a large bowl, combine the macaroni, celery, carrot and onion. Add dressing and toss gently to coat. Refrigerate until serving. Garnish with egg and paprika. **Yield:** 8 servings.

Editor's Note: This recipe was tested with Splenda No Calorie Sweetener.

Nutritional Analysis: *3/4 cup equals 111 calories, 2 g fat (trace saturated fat), 30 mg cholesterol, 362 mg sodium, 20 g carbohydrate, 2 g fiber, 4 g protein.*
Diabetic Exchange: *1-1/2 starch.*

Stir-Fry Supper Is Sizzling

MODERATION is the key to a full life for Betsy and John Larimer. Since they decided to decrease serving sizes at the dinner table, they not only feel healthier, but they've dropped a few clothes sizes, too.

"In our house, we monitor the portions of everything we eat," Betsy writes from Somerset, Pennsylvania.

Shortly after they were married, Betsy gained what she likes to call "wedding weight," and John was diagnosed with rising blood pressure and an increasing cholesterol level. "When John's cholesterol skyrocketed, I knew it was time to start eating right," Betsy says. "We needed a new way of life, not a temporary diet or a quick fix.

"We read the book *Change One* from Reader's Digest and learned how to make weekly improvements to our eating habits and lifestyles. In just 3 months, I lost 12 pounds and John lost 17. At first, eating healthy wasn't easy, but as our weight dropped, we were motivated to stick with it."

To reduce calories, fat and sodium, the couple trimmed their supper portions in half. "We found that we didn't need the large quantities of food we normally ate," says Betsy. "I began asking our butcher to cut salmon and steak into smaller sizes, and at the deli counter, I ordered reduced-fat cheese and lean meats sliced thinly.

"We learned to eat slowly, taking time to enjoy our

food, and we soon recognized when we felt satisfied as opposed to feeling stuffed. Eventually, John and I could differentiate between being truly hungry and merely craving food as an emotional response.

"We limited our visits to restaurants, knowing that we could prepare healthy food ourselves," Betsy explains. "Salads became a regular staple. The fiber filled us up, helping to limit our portions at dinner. We also ate nutritious breakfasts, lunches and snacks.

"My husband and I continue to eat right, motivating each other along the way," she confirms. "Checking in on one another during the day is easy since I'm an administrative assistant at the same company where John works as an engineer. Eating healthy can be tough at times, but we know that the benefits are immeasurable."

By experimenting in the kitchen, Betsy found strategies to keep fat, calories and sodium at bay. "When possible, I use light ingredients," she notes. Such is the case with the menu she shares here.

Betsy begins with mouth-watering Beef Vegetable Stir-Fry. Loaded with fresh veggies, the simple stir-fry makes frequent appearances at her table. "You can replace the beef with chicken, fish or even tofu," she recommends.

The easy entree offers a succulent sauce that ideally complements Seasoned Brown Rice. "I serve the stir-fry over the rice for a tasty no-fuss meal," Betsy notes. "For maximum flavor, use your fingertips to crumble the dried basil directly into the cooked rice.

"We think the stir-fry and rice make a perfectly sized meal with leftovers for the next day. When we have guests, however, I also whip up a salad." Betsy's recipe for Mixed Greens with Tangy Dressing comes together in minutes.

"Prepared mustard makes the salad dressing zesty," she adds. "If you like, try replacing the olive oil with pickle juice for an even lighter version. This may sound like a unique substitution, but if you want to lose weight, it pays to do a little experimenting in the kitchen."

Beef Vegetable Stir-Fry

Prep/Total Time: 25 min.

4-1/2 teaspoons cornstarch
   4 tablespoons reduced-sodium soy sauce, *divided*
   1 pound beef sirloin steak, cut into 2-inch strips
   2 medium green peppers, cut into strips
   2 medium onions, halved and thinly sliced
   1 tablespoon canola oil
1/2 pound sliced fresh mushrooms

In a large bowl, combine cornstarch and 2 tablespoons soy sauce until smooth. Add beef; stir to coat. In a large skillet or wok, stir-fry the green peppers and onions in oil for 3 minutes; add beef. Cook and stir for 3 minutes. Add mushrooms. Cook and stir for 3-5 minutes or until vegetables are tender and meat is no longer pink. Stir in remaining soy sauce. **Yield:** 4 servings.

Nutritional Analysis: 1 cup equals 254 calories, 9 g fat (3 g saturated fat), 63 mg cholesterol, 658 mg sodium, 17 g carbohydrate, 3 g fiber, 26 g protein.
Diabetic Exchanges: 3 lean meat, 3 vegetable, 1/2 fat.

Seasoned Brown Rice

Low-fat   Meatless

Prep: 5 min. **Cook:** 35 min.

1-1/3 cups water
   2/3 cup long grain brown rice
      1 tablespoon reduced-sodium soy sauce
   1/2 teaspoon dried basil
   1/4 to 1/2 teaspoon ground ginger
   1/8 teaspoon cayenne pepper

In a small saucepan, bring water and rice to a boil. Reduce heat; cover and simmer for 35-45 minutes or until water is absorbed and rice is tender. Stir in the remaining ingredients. **Yield:** 4 servings.

Nutritional Analysis: 1/2 cup equals 118 calories, 1 g fat (trace saturated fat), 0 cholesterol, 157 mg sodium, 24 g carbohydrate, 2 g fiber, 3 g protein.
Diabetic Exchange: 1-1/2 starch.

Mixed Greens With Tangy Dressing

Low-carb   Meatless

Prep/Total Time: 15 min.

   3 cups mixed salad greens
   2 medium carrots, sliced
1/2 cup sliced fresh mushrooms
   1 can (2-1/4 ounces) sliced ripe olives, drained
1/4 cup frozen peas, thawed
   1 tablespoon olive oil
   1 tablespoon red wine vinegar
   2 teaspoons prepared mustard
   2 teaspoons honey
1-1/2 teaspoons minced fresh basil

In a large serving bowl, toss the salad greens with the carrots, mushrooms, olives and peas. In a small bowl, whisk the oil, vinegar, mustard, honey and basil. Drizzle over salad; toss to coat. **Yield:** 4 servings.

Nutritional Analysis: 1-1/4 cups equals 92 calories, 5 g fat (1 g saturated fat), 0 cholesterol, 257 mg sodium, 10 g carbohydrate, 3 g fiber, 2 g protein.
Diabetic Exchanges: 1 vegetable, 1 fat.

🍎 Be a Smart Shopper

CREATING a weekly meal plan is Betsy Larimer's first step to stocking her house with nutritious food. "Once I know what I'm going to cook for the week, I make a shopping list," she explains. "This helps me resist buying junk food, as I simply avoid anything that's not on my list.

"I also shop at farmers markets and other spots that sell fruits, vegetables and grains at low cost," Betsy says. "For instance, I visit an Amish food store that sells grains in bulk. This way, I can afford to keep items such as bulgur and oatmeal on hand."

Italian Dinner Made Easy

EXERCISE makes for family fun at the Keller household in Roanoke, Virginia. "We try to keep active as a family," writes Rachel Keller.

"Our favorite activity is riding our bikes together. My husband, Maynard, takes the lead, pulling our daughter in a bike trailer, our three boys follow and I'm the caboose," she explains. Rachel and Maynard have four children: John, Daniel, Joseph and Sarah.

"I love working out, especially bicycling and running. In fact, Maynard and I are members of both a cycling club and a runners' group," she notes. "I also perform strength training and flexibility exercises, and Maynard usually cycles to his job as a financial planner.

"I keep busy home-schooling our children and teaching piano lessons," shares Rachel. "I also do some freelance writing when I can, and I enjoy working in the kitchen. I hope to pass on my love of cooking to my kids."

The Keller kids should have no trouble mastering healthy culinary skills, since cooking light is Rachel's focus when she prepares meals.

"I have a family history of diabetes and heart problems, as well as high cholesterol and blood pressure," Rachel shares, "so I try to stay active and eat right.

"I reduce sugars and fats in recipes and often replace refined flours with whole wheat flour, oat flour or whole grains. I also add ground flaxseed to baked goods, homemade cereals and pancakes," she writes.

"When grocery shopping, I read food labels very carefully, looking at the fat and sugar contents. I especially check for hydrogenated or partially hydrogenated oils and corn syrup. I try to avoid adding items with these ingredients to my meals."

One meal that's bursting with good-for-you appeal is the menu Rachel offers here. The perfect dinner for busy weeknights, it features Easy Chicken Cacciatore as the main dish.

"We love this combination of chicken and tomatoes," Rachel assures. "I like to top it with a little grated Parmesan cheese or part-skim mozzarella."

For a family-pleasing side dish, Rachel relies on comforting Creamy Spinach. "My children started eating vegetables at an early age," Rachel explains. "This spinach recipe is one of their all-time favorites."

When it comes to making a tasty treat that's low in sugar, Rachel likes to bake Peach Oat Cookies.

"I modified the original recipe to create soft and chewy cookies that are good for you," she says. "There's not too much sugar in them but lots of oats and fruit."

Easy Chicken Cacciatore

Prep: 10 min. **Cook:** 25 min.

- 3 tablespoons all-purpose flour
- 1-1/2 teaspoons Italian seasoning
- 6 boneless skinless chicken breast halves (4 ounces *each*)
- 2 teaspoons olive oil, *divided*
- 1/2 cup chopped onion
- 1/2 pound sliced fresh mushrooms
- 1 cup sliced zucchini
- 2 cans (14-1/2 ounces *each*) Italian stewed tomatoes
- 1 can (6 ounces) tomato paste
- 1 teaspoon salt
- 8 ounces uncooked spaghetti

In a large resealable plastic bag, combine flour and Italian seasoning. Add chicken; seal and shake to coat. In a large nonstick skillet coated with nonstick cooking spray, cook chicken in 1 teaspoon oil for 4-5 minutes on each side or until browned. Remove chicken from skillet and keep warm.

In same skillet, cook onion in remaining oil for 2 minutes. Add mushrooms and zucchini; cook until onion is tender. Stir in the tomatoes, tomato paste and salt. Bring to a boil. Return chicken to skillet. Reduce heat; cover and simmer 10-14 minutes or until chicken juices run clear. Cook pasta according to package directions; drain. Serve chicken and tomato mixture over pasta. **Yield:** 6 servings.

Nutritional Analysis: 1 chicken breast half with 3/4 cup sauce and 1 cup spaghetti equals 366 calories, 5 g fat (1 g saturated fat), 63 mg cholesterol, 931 mg sodium, 49 g carbohydrate, 6 g fiber, 32 g protein.

Diabetic Exchanges: 3 very lean meat, 3 vegetable, 2 starch, 1/2 fat.

Creamy Spinach

Low-carb   *Meatless*

Prep/Total Time: 25 min.

- 2 packages (10 ounces *each*) frozen chopped spinach
- 1 large onion, chopped
- 1 tablespoon olive oil
- 1/4 cup all-purpose flour
- 3/4 teaspoon salt
- 1/4 teaspoon pepper
- 2 cups fat-free milk
- 1/2 cup shredded part-skim mozzarella cheese

Prepare spinach according to package directions; drain and set aside. Meanwhile, in a saucepan, cook onion in oil until tender. Stir in the flour, salt and pepper until blended. Gradually stir in milk. Bring to a boil over medium heat; cook and stir for 1-2 minutes or until thickened. Stir in reserved spinach. Add cheese; stir until melted. **Yield:** 6 servings.

Nutritional Analysis: 2/3 cup equals 124 calories, 4 g fat (1 g saturated fat), 7 mg cholesterol, 452 mg sodium, 14 g carbohydrate, 3 g fiber, 9 g protein.

Diabetic Exchanges: 1 starch, 1 vegetable, 1/2 fat.

Peach Oat Cookies

Low-fat   *Low-sodium*

Prep/Total Time: 30 min.

- 1/3 cup butter, softened
- 1/2 cup sugar
- 1/2 cup packed brown sugar
- 2 eggs
- 1-1/2 teaspoons vanilla extract
- 1/2 cup *each* all-purpose flour, whole wheat flour and oat flour
- 2 teaspoons baking powder
- 1 teaspoon salt
- 2-1/2 cups quick-cooking oats
- 1/2 cup oat bran
- 1-1/2 cups reduced-sugar sliced peaches, drained and chopped
- 1 cup raisins

In a large mixing bowl, cream butter and sugars. Add eggs, one at a time, beating well after each addition. Beat in vanilla. Combine the flours, baking powder and salt; gradually add to creamed mixture. Beat in oats and oat bran just until combined. Stir in peaches and raisins.

Drop by rounded tablespoonfuls onto baking sheets coated with nonstick cooking spray. Bake at 350° for 9-13 minutes or until edges are lightly browned. Remove to a wire rack to cool. **Yield:** 5 dozen.

Nutritional Analysis: 2 cookies equals 120 calories, 3 g fat (1 g saturated fat), 20 mg cholesterol, 133 mg sodium, 22 g carbohydrate, 2 g fiber, 3 g protein.

Diabetic Exchanges: 1-1/2 starch.

🍎 Cook Creatively

EXPERIMENTING in the kitchen is fun for Rachel Keller. "Although I have quite a collection of cookbooks, I do most of my cooking without recipes," she writes. "I make stir-fries often because they're easy, colorful, nutritious and tasty.

"With just a few ingredients, I can make a variety of stir-fries. I can serve a vegetarian stir-fry over brown rice or beef it up by adding chicken, pork or steak strips."

Rachel encourages others to get creative when preparing stir-fries. "Add orange or lemon juice for extra flavor," she suggests, "or toss in some water chestnuts or sunflower kernels for a little crunch."

Seafood Meal for Summer

ON THE ROAD AGAIN could be the motto for Linda McLyman and her husband, Daniel Leete. "We've owned our own consulting firm for 21 years," Linda writes from the couple's home in Syracuse, New York. "We work with businesses throughout the U.S., so we travel about 2 weeks out of every month."

"We also stay at a lot of hotels," Linda adds, "which makes it hard to keep our weight on track, especially as we get older. So cooking healthy is a priority when we are home."

Linda and Daniel try to prepare healthy foods while avoiding fad diets, and so far they've been successful. Here are eight great suggestions from Linda for adapting a healthier lifestyle and eating right:

1. **Beef up on veggies.** "I use half the amount of meat and double the amount of vegetables in everything I cook," explains Linda. "I often serve two vegetable side dishes, skipping the starches entirely."

2. **Cut back on salt.** Using a dash of salt here and there is okay for most people, but Linda keeps a few other secrets up her sleeve. "Homemade spice blends add a lot of flavor without the sodium," she suggests. "And fresh herbs are a great way to season foods."

3. **Trim down dessert.** "I use nonfat half-and-half cream in puddings, and I bake a lot of fruit desserts because they often require less sugar," says Linda.

4. **Vary cooking methods.** In addition to using her outdoor grill, Linda prepares healthy fare in her slow cook-

er. "Today's slow cookers work much better with light recipes than older models did," she attests.

5. **Consider canned convenience.** "When we're tired but still want a nutritious meal, we pull out some canned goods," notes Linda. "We top brown rice with canned red, black or white beans."

6. **Shop right.** "I always eat something before I go grocery shopping so I'm not tempted to buy items I hadn't planned on...and I don't shop when I'm tired," Linda writes. "Taking my husband with me makes the task a bit more fun."

7. **Freeze fresh produce.** Daniel likes to chop vegetables and store them in the freezer for quick additions to recipes. "Our freezer is always stocked with chopped onions and peppers," says Linda.

8. **Snack smartly.** "I don't purchase low-fat or low-carb snack foods because we're trying to develop healthy long-term eating habits," notes Linda. Instead, she fixes her own light snacks.

One of Linda's favorite creations is the five-ingredient Basil Tuna Steaks in the menu below. "Tuna is delicious and can be grilled in no time," she says.

"Daniel is a big eater who likes generous portions," she adds. "So I look for hearty dishes that satisfy, and Lemony Vegetable Barley Salad does just that."

For a refreshing finale, Linda dresses up prepared angel food cake with a handful of items; Creamy Mango Loaf Cake is the luscious result. "If your family doesn't like mango, replace it with a cup of any other diced fruit," she says. "It tops off meals deliciously."

Basil Tuna Steaks

Low-carb

Prep/Total Time: 20 min.

    6 tuna steaks (6 ounces *each*)
4-1/2 teaspoons olive oil
    3 tablespoons minced fresh basil
  3/4 teaspoon salt
  1/4 teaspoon pepper

Brush both sides of tuna steaks with oil. Sprinkle both sides with basil, salt and pepper. Coat grill rack with nonstick cooking spray before starting the grill. Grill tuna, covered, over medium heat for 6-8 minutes on each side or until fish flakes easily with a fork. **Yield:** 6 servings.

Nutritional Analysis: 1 tuna steak equals 214 calories, 5 g fat (1 g saturated fat), 77 mg cholesterol, 358 mg sodium, trace carbohydrate, trace fiber, 40 g protein.
Diabetic Exchanges: *5 very lean meat, 1 fat.*

Lemony Vegetable Barley Salad

Meatless

Prep: 30 min. **Cook:** 10 min. + chilling

    1 cup quick-cooking barley
1/2 cup cut fresh green beans
1/2 cup coarsely chopped carrot
1/2 cup coarsely chopped celery
1/2 cup finely chopped fresh broccoli
1/2 cup chopped fresh spinach
    1 small onion, chopped
    1 small tomato, seeded and chopped
1/3 cup chopped sweet yellow pepper
1/3 cup chopped fresh mushrooms
DRESSING:
1/4 cup lemon juice
    2 tablespoons minced fresh basil
    2 tablespoons olive oil
    1 tablespoon water
1-1/2 teaspoons poppy seeds
1/2 teaspoon garlic salt
1/2 teaspoon salt-free lemon-pepper seasoning
1/2 teaspoon coarsely ground pepper
1/4 teaspoon salt

Cook barley according to package directions; drain and cool completely. Place beans in a saucepan and cover with water; bring to a boil. Reduce heat; simmer, uncovered, for 8-10 minutes or until crisp-tender. Drain and cool completely.

In a large bowl, combine the carrot, celery, broccoli, spinach, onion, tomato, yellow pepper, mushrooms, barley and beans. In a small bowl, whisk the dressing ingredients. Pour over salad and toss to coat. Cover and refrigerate for at least 4 hours before serving. **Yield:** 6 servings.

Nutritional Analysis: 1 cup equals 178 calories, 6 g fat (1 g saturated fat), 0 cholesterol, 272 mg sodium, 29 g carbohydrate, 7 g fiber, 5 g protein.
Diabetic Exchanges: *1-1/2 starch, 1 vegetable, 1 fat.*

Creamy Mango Loaf Cake

Low-fat

Prep: 20 min. + chilling

1-1/4 cups cold fat-free half-and-half
    1 package (1 ounce) sugar-free instant vanilla pudding mix
    1 medium mango, peeled and diced
    1 loaf (10-1/2 ounces) angel food cake
    1 medium kiwifruit, peeled and sliced

In a large bowl, whisk half-and-half and pudding mix for 2 minutes. Let stand for 2 minutes or until soft-set. Fold in mango. Slice cake horizontally into three layers; spread pudding mixture between layers and over top of cake. Top with kiwi. Refrigerate for at least 4 hours before serving. **Yield:** 6 servings.

Nutritional Analysis: 1 slice equals 207 calories, 1 g fat (trace saturated fat), 0 cholesterol, 611 mg sodium, 45 g carbohydrate, 2 g fiber, 5 g protein.
Diabetic Exchanges: *1-1/2 starch, 1/2 fruit, 1/2 fat-free milk.*

Fun Dishes Are Kid-Pleasing

IT'S NO SURPRISE that Krista Frank is a master at creating nutritious dishes. After all, she's been eating healthy for years.

"When I was growing up, my mother cooked with little salt and fat and with lots of fresh produce," Krista writes from Rhododendron, Oregon. "So after I married Kevin, I began cooking that way, too. Now I'm teaching our boys, Jonathan and Michael, to make good food choices."

The stay-at-home mom has a variety of ways to put together deliciously light meals that even little ones enjoy…and she doesn't mind sharing her secrets!

1. Involve the kids. Krista allows her sons to add their own toppings to certain recipes, making meals fun. "It also teaches them how to personalize recipes," she notes. "It's important to learn to tweak recipes to fit individual tastes and health needs."

2. Experiment often. In the Frank house, everyone has to taste everything once. "We've all become braver over the years, and even the kids have come to like sampling healthy foods."

3. Give soy a try. Krista replaces plain milk with vanilla or chocolate soy milk when baking muffins, cakes or waffles. "It adds flavor as well as protein and vitamins," she explains.

4. **Skim the fat.** Wherever possible, Krista omits full-fat cheese from recipes. Instead, she substitutes low-fat mozzarella or Parmesan in smaller quantities than what's called for.

5. **Focus on fruit.** "Popsicles made from smoothies are a great way to get kids to eat more fruit," suggests Krista. "Try garnishing meals with fresh fruit."

A favorite in Krista's home is a combo of Southwestern specialties, featuring Hearty Taco Casserole.

"When I didn't have the time to prepare homemade tortillas one night, I used the dough to make the crust of this dish instead," she says. "Topped with taco fixings, it was an instant hit."

On the side, Krista serves refreshing Island Fruit Salad. With pina colada yogurt and toasted coconut, the fruit medley brings a hint of the tropics to the table.

The perfect finale is found in Krista's Cinnamon Chips 'n' Dip. "A friend shared this recipe," she recalls. "We lightened it and came up with this treat. We hope you agree that it's a great way to end meals."

Hearty Taco Casserole

Prep: 35 min. **Bake:** 30 min.

2/3 cup uncooked brown rice
1-1/3 cups plus 4 to 5 tablespoons water, *divided*
3/4 cup all-purpose flour
3/4 teaspoon baking powder
1/8 teaspoon salt
2 tablespoons cold butter
FILLING:
1/2 pound lean ground beef
1/2 cup chopped onion
1/2 cup chopped green pepper
2 garlic cloves, minced
1 cup water
1 envelope taco seasoning
2 eggs, lightly beaten
1/4 cup minced fresh cilantro
1 cup (4 ounces) shredded reduced-fat cheddar cheese
2 cups shredded lettuce
2 medium tomatoes, chopped
3/4 cup salsa
1/2 cup fat-free sour cream

In a small saucepan, bring rice and 1-1/3 cups water to a boil. Reduce heat; cover and simmer for 30-35 minutes or until rice is tender and water is absorbed.

Meanwhile, in a large bowl, combine flour, baking powder and salt; cut in butter until crumbly. Stir in enough remaining water to form a soft dough. On a floured surface, roll dough into a 12-in. x 8-in. rectangle. Press into a 13-in. x 9-in. x 2-in. baking dish coated with nonstick cooking spray. Bake at 400° for 13-15 minutes or until very lightly browned.

For filling, in a large nonstick skillet, cook the beef, onion, green pepper and garlic over medium heat until meat is no longer pink; drain. Add water, taco seasoning and cooked rice. Bring to a boil. Reduce heat; simmer, uncovered, for 2-3 minutes or until thickened. Remove from the heat. Stir in eggs and cilantro. Spread over crust.

Cover and bake for 15-17 minutes or until filling is set. Cut into squares. Top with cheese, lettuce and tomatoes. Serve with salsa and sour cream. **Yield:** 8 servings.

Nutritional Analysis: 1 serving equals 284 calories, 10 g fat (5 g saturated fat), 87 mg cholesterol, 764 mg sodium, 34 g carbohydrate, 3 g fiber, 16 g protein.
Diabetic Exchanges: 2 starch, 1 lean meat, 1 vegetable, 1 fat.

Island Fruit Salad

Low-fat   Low-sodium   Meatless

Prep/Total Time: 15 min.

2 medium ripe bananas, sliced
1 medium mango, peeled and cubed
4 kiwifruit, peeled and cubed
1 can (20 ounces) unsweetened pineapple tidbits, drained
1 carton (6 ounces) reduced-fat pina colada yogurt
1/2 cup flaked coconut, toasted

In a large serving bowl, combine the bananas, mango, kiwi, pineapple and yogurt; toss to coat. Sprinkle with coconut. Serve with a slotted spoon. **Yield:** 8 servings.

Nutritional Analysis: 1/2 cup equals 134 calories, 3 g fat (2 g saturated fat), 1 mg cholesterol, 37 mg sodium, 27 g carbohydrate, 4 g fiber, 3 g protein.
Diabetic Exchanges: 2 fruit, 1/2 fat.

Cinnamon Chips 'n' Dip

Prep/Total Time: 20 min.

4 flour tortillas (8 inches)
Refrigerated butter-flavored spray
1 tablespoon sugar
1 teaspoon ground cinnamon
4 ounces reduced-fat cream cheese
1 carton (6 ounces) vanilla yogurt
4-1/2 teaspoons sugar
1/2 teaspoon ground cinnamon

For chips, spritz tortillas with butter-flavored spray; cut each into eight wedges. Place on ungreased baking sheets. Combine sugar and cinnamon; sprinkle over tortillas. Bake at 350° for 7-9 minutes or just until crisp.

For dip, in a small mixing bowl, beat the cream cheese, yogurt, sugar and cinnamon until smooth. Serve with cinnamon chips. **Yield:** 8 servings.

Editor's Note: This recipe was tested with I Can't Believe It's Not Butter Spray.

Nutritional Analysis: 4 chips with 2 tablespoons dip equals 146 calories, 5 g fat (3 g saturated fat), 12 mg cholesterol, 198 mg sodium, 20 g carbohydrate, trace fiber, 5 g protein.
Diabetic Exchanges: 1 starch, 1 fat.

Menu Cuts Fat, Keeps Flavor

TAKE two teenagers and a busy husband, and what do you get? A challenge for a cook trying to slim down meals. Nancy Granaman of Burlington, Iowa also faced another hurdle—and it meant changing her family's eating habits for good.

"Five years ago, I learned that my body overproduces and harbors bad cholesterol or LDL," Nancy explains.

"I had a high metabolism, low blood sugar and was underweight, so I needed to cook meals with enough calories for myself and our boys, who were teenagers at the time. But I also needed to decrease fat, sugar and cholesterol."

Luckily, Nancy's husband, Brian, and sons Ryan and Riley were willing taste testers. "Through trial and error, I worked reduced-fat ingredients into our favorite recipes," says Nancy.

Though she didn't care for lots of meat-based menus, her family did. So Nancy fixed the lean meats her gang liked, making them a little less often. "I gradually added

a few meatless nights to our lineup," she writes.

To add flavor without fat, Nancy began cooking with spices, vinegars, marinades and light dressings. "Today, my family actually prefers to eat nutritious, low-fat foods," she says proudly.

In fact, her gang has enjoyed her meals so much that Nancy is taking time away from her job as a registered nurse to work on a low-fat cookbook.

The menu Nancy shares here features healthier versions of well-liked restaurant dishes. To start, she assembles an easy Italian Salad that's served alongside the main course.

"Chicken Marsala is usually high in fat and calories," Nancy confirms. "In this version, the flavor comes from the broth and wine, so even though I eliminated extra oil, the taste isn't lost."

As a mouth-watering finale, she whips up Tiramisu Parfaits. "These are a longtime favorite," Nancy comments. "They look pretty with a drizzle of chocolate on top. I hope you'll enjoy them as much as we do."

Chicken Marsala

Low-carb

Prep: 25 min. + marinating **Bake:** 25 min.

- 6 boneless skinless chicken breast halves (4 ounces *each*)
- 1 cup fat-free Italian salad dressing
- 1 tablespoon all-purpose flour
- 1 teaspoon Italian seasoning
- 1/2 teaspoon garlic powder
- 1/4 teaspoon paprika
- 1/4 teaspoon pepper
- 2 tablespoons olive oil, *divided*
- 1 tablespoon butter
- 1/2 cup reduced-sodium chicken broth
- 1/2 cup Marsala wine *or* 3 tablespoons unsweetened apple juice plus 5 tablespoons additional reduced-sodium chicken broth
- 1 pound sliced fresh mushrooms
- 1/2 cup minced fresh parsley

Flatten chicken to 1/2-in. thickness. Place in a large resealable plastic bag; add salad dressing. Seal bag and turn to coat; refrigerate for 8 hours or overnight. Drain and discard marinade. Combine the flour, Italian seasoning, garlic powder, paprika and pepper; sprinkle over both sides of chicken. In a large nonstick skillet coated with nonstick cooking spray, cook chicken in 1 tablespoon oil and butter for 2 minutes on each side or until browned. Transfer to a 13-in. x 9-in. x 2-in. baking dish coated with nonstick cooking spray.

Gradually add broth and wine or apple juice mixture to skillet, stirring to loosen browned bits. Bring to a boil; cook and stir for 2 minutes. Strain sauce; set aside. In the same skillet, cook mushrooms in remaining oil for 2 minutes; drain. Stir sauce into mushrooms; heat through. Pour over chicken; sprinkle with parsley. Bake, uncovered, at 350° for 25-30 minutes or until chicken juices run clear. **Yield:** 6 servings.

Nutritional Analysis: 1 chicken breast half with 1/3 cup mushroom mixture equals 247 calories, 9 g fat (3 g saturated fat), 68 mg cholesterol, 348 mg sodium, 9 g carbohydrate, 1 g fiber, 26 g protein.
Diabetic Exchanges: 3 very lean meat, 1-1/2 fat, 1/2 starch.

Italian Salad

Low-fat   Meatless

Prep/Total Time: 30 min.

- 3 slices Italian bread, cubed
- Butter-flavored nonstick cooking spray
- 1 teaspoon Italian seasoning
- 1/2 teaspoon garlic powder
- 2 bunches romaine, torn
- 2 cups grape tomatoes, halved
- 1 can (2-1/4 ounces) sliced ripe olives, drained
- 1/4 cup grated Parmesan cheese
- 1 small red onion, thinly sliced and separated into rings
- 6 pepperoncinis
- 1/2 cup fat-free Italian salad dressing

For croutons, spritz bread cubes with butter-flavored spray; place in a bowl. Sprinkle with Italian seasoning and garlic powder; toss to coat evenly. Transfer to a 15-in. x 10-in. x 1-in. baking pan coated with nonstick cooking spray. Bake at 450° for 8-10 minutes or until golden brown, stirring once or twice. Cool.

In a large bowl, combine romaine, tomatoes, olives, cheese, onion and pepperoncinis. Drizzle with dressing and toss to coat. Top with croutons. **Yield:** 6 servings.

Editor's Note: Look for pepperoncinis (pickled peppers) in the pickle and olive section of your grocery store.

Nutritional Analysis: 1-1/2 cups equals 120 calories, 3 g fat (1 g saturated fat), 3 mg cholesterol, 943 mg sodium, 18 g carbohydrate, 4 g fiber, 6 g protein.
Diabetic Exchanges: 2 vegetable, 1/2 starch, 1/2 fat.

Tiramisu Parfaits

Low-fat

Prep: 40 min. + chilling

- 4-1/2 teaspoons instant coffee granules
- 1/3 cup boiling water
- 2 cups cold fat-free milk
- 2 packages (1 ounce *each*) sugar-free instant vanilla pudding mix
- 4 ounces fat-free cream cheese
- 1 package (3 ounces) ladyfingers, split and cubed
- 2 cups fat-free whipped topping
- 2 tablespoons miniature chocolate chips
- 1 teaspoon baking cocoa

Dissolve coffee in boiling water; cool to room temperature. In a large bowl, whisk milk and pudding mixes for 2 minutes. In a large mixing bowl, beat cream cheese until smooth. Gradually fold in pudding.

Place ladyfinger cubes in a bowl; add coffee and toss to coat evenly. Let stand for 5 minutes. Divide half of the ladyfinger cubes among six parfait glasses or serving dishes. Top with half of the pudding mixture, 1 cup whipped topping and 1 tablespoon chocolate chips. Repeat layers. Cover and refrigerate for 8 hours or overnight. Just before serving, dust with cocoa. **Yield:** 6 servings.

Nutritional Analysis: 1 parfait equals 189 calories, 3 g fat (1 g saturated fat), 55 mg cholesterol, 573 mg sodium, 32 g carbohydrate, 1 g fiber, 7 g protein.
Diabetic Exchange: 2 starch.

Carolers Share Christmas Menu

MAKING SPIRITS BRIGHT is an annual Christmas tradition for Julie Williquette and her family. "Our gang keeps quite busy each November and December, singing for others at various holiday gatherings," explains the Hartselle, Alabama cook.

"The six of us wear handmade Charles Dickens-era costumes and sing Christmas carols a cappella at holiday open houses, private parties, churches and elsewhere," Julie shares. "This year we have performed in seven different states. People seem to enjoy our costumes as much as our singing."

Julie, her husband, Mike, and their children, Emily, Grace, Jonathan and Andrew, start practicing in November. "Even the rehearsals end up creating wonderful family memories," she says.

"When Christmas arrives and our holiday performances are finished for the year, the children actually miss all the fun we had singing together. That's why we celebrate

our final night of caroling with a special family dinner."

Whether you've spent the day caroling, skiing or simply walking through a winter wonderland, a combination of seasonal delights creates an ideal menu when stepping in from the cold. Here, Julie shares tried-and-true favorites her family enjoys after their final night of caroling.

As the main course, she serves five-ingredient Christmas Carol Ham. Prepared in the slow cooker, it's ready when the family arrives home.

"It's made with healthier-for-you turkey ham," Julie says. "We often eat the slices without additional glaze because they're so flavorful."

Julie's thirst-quenching Citrus Wassail is warm and comforting and always welcome after a night of performing. "With four fruit juices, it uses just a little sugar. I often serve it with cinnamon sticks."

Since *A Christmas Carol* is one of Mike's favorite movies, Julie named the meal's finale after one of the story's most beloved characters. "My Tiny Tim Trifle is made with sugar-free chocolate pudding and fat-free frozen whipped topping, so it's easy on the waistline," she writes. "A trifle is such a pretty dessert, and this brownie version is always well received.

"We hope you and your family enjoy these recipes during the holiday season," Julie concludes. "And in the words of Tiny Tim, 'God bless us, everyone!'"

Christmas Carol Ham

Low-carb

Prep: 10 min. **Cook:** 2 hours

2 pounds fully cooked turkey ham, cut into eight slices
1/2 cup packed brown sugar
1/4 cup unsweetened pineapple juice
1-1/2 teaspoons white vinegar
1/4 teaspoon ground mustard

Place ham slices in a 3-qt. slow cooker. In a small bowl, combine the brown sugar, pineapple juice, vinegar and mustard; pour over ham. Cover and cook on low for 2-4 hours or until heated through. **Yield:** 8 servings.

Nutritional Analysis: 4 ounces cooked ham equals 186 calories, 5 g fat (2 g saturated fat), 83 mg cholesterol, 1,237 mg sodium, 15 g carbohydrate, trace fiber, 21 g protein.
Diabetic Exchange: 3 lean meat, 1 starch.

Citrus Wassail

Low-fat   Low-sodium

Prep/Total Time: 25 min.

2 quarts unsweetened apple juice
2 cups unsweetened pineapple juice
2 cups orange juice
1/2 cup lemon juice
1/4 cup sugar
1 teaspoon ground cinnamon
1/2 teaspoon ground cloves

In a Dutch oven, combine all of the ingredients. Bring to a boil. Reduce heat; simmer, uncovered, for 10-15 minutes. Serve warm. **Yield:** 13 servings (about 3 quarts).

Nutritional Analysis: 1 cup equals 128 calories, trace fat (trace saturated fat), 0 cholesterol, 5 mg sodium, 32 g carbohydrate, trace fiber, trace protein.
Diabetic Exchange: 2 fruit.

Tiny Tim Trifle

Prep: 35 min. + chilling **Bake:** 20 min. + cooling

1/2 cup plus 2 tablespoons butter, softened
1-1/3 cups sugar
2 eggs, lightly beaten
4 egg whites
1/2 cup reduced-fat sour cream

1/3 cup fat-free evaporated milk
1 teaspoon vanilla extract
1/4 teaspoon peppermint extract, optional
1-1/3 cups all-purpose flour
2/3 cup baking cocoa
1 teaspoon baking powder
1/4 teaspoon salt
PUDDING:
3-1/2 cups cold fat-free milk
2 packages (1.4 ounces each) sugar-free instant chocolate pudding mix
1 carton (8 ounces) frozen fat-free whipped topping, thawed
1 candy cane, crushed

In a large mixing bowl, beat butter. Gradually add sugar; beat for 2 minutes. Add the eggs, egg whites, sour cream, milk, vanilla and peppermint extract if desired. Combine the flour, cocoa, baking powder and salt; add to butter mixture just until blended.

Pour into a 13-in. x 9-in. x 2-in. baking pan coated with nonstick cooking spray. Bake at 350° for 20-25 minutes or until a toothpick inserted near the center comes out clean. Cool on a wire rack.

For pudding, in a large bowl, whisk milk and pudding mixes for 2 minutes. Let stand for 2 minutes or until soft-set. Crumble the brownies; place half of the crumbs in a 3-qt. bowl or trifle dish. Top with half of the pudding and whipped topping. Repeat layers. Sprinkle with crushed candy cane. Cover and refrigerate for at least 1 hour before serving. **Yield:** 16 servings.

Nutritional Analysis: 3/4 cup equals 267 calories, 9 g fat (5 g saturated fat), 50 mg cholesterol, 352 mg sodium, 40 g carbohydrate, 1 g fiber, 7 g protein.
Diabetic Exchanges: 2-1/2 starch, 1-1/2 fat.

Trimmed-Down Dishes for Two

Turn to this chapter if you're cooking for just two and neither of you cares to eat leftovers. These lighter recipes yield smaller quantities without sacrificing flavor.

Apple-Spice Acorn Squash (page 259)

Beef Filets with Portobello Sauce

(Pictured above)

Low-carb

Prep/Total Time: 30 min.

These tasty mushroom-topped steaks seem special, but they are fast enough for everyday dinners.
—Christel Stein, Tampa, Florida

2 beef tenderloin steaks (4 ounces *each*)
1/2 cup dry red wine *or* reduced-sodium beef broth
1 teaspoon all-purpose flour
1/2 cup reduced-sodium beef broth
1 teaspoon *each* steak sauce, Worcestershire sauce and ketchup
1/2 teaspoon ground mustard
4 ounces fresh baby portobello mushrooms, sliced
1/4 teaspoon pepper
1/8 teaspoon salt
1 tablespoon minced fresh chives, optional

In a large nonstick skillet coated with nonstick cooking spray, brown steaks over medium-high heat. Remove from pan; keep warm.

Reduce heat to medium; stir in wine or broth, loosening up the browned bits from the pan. Cook for 2-3 minutes or until liquid is reduced by half. Combine flour and broth until smooth; whisk into the skillet. Add the steak sauce, Worcestershire sauce, ketchup and mustard. Bring to a boil.

Return steaks to skillet along with mushrooms. Cook for 4-5 minutes on each side or until meat reaches desired doneness (for medium-rare, a meat thermometer should read 145°; medium, 160°; well-done, 170°). Transfer to serving platter. Sprinkle with pepper, salt and chives if desired. **Yield:** 2 servings.

Nutritional Analysis: 1 steak with 1/3 cup sauce equals 255 calories, 8 g fat (3 g saturated fat), 72 mg cholesterol, 422 mg sodium, 7 g carbohydrate, 1 g fiber, 26 g protein.
Diabetic Exchanges: 3 lean meat, 1 starch.

Grilled Chicken Sandwiches

(Pictured below)

Prep/Total Time: 15 min.

Once you bite into this grilled sandwich assembled by our home economists, you'll be surprised to learn that it is a light recipe. Despite its scrumptious buttery taste, it is made without butter or oil. Try it with sliced deli turkey for variety.

4 slices marble rye bread
2 slices (3/4 ounce *each*) reduced-fat Swiss cheese
6 ounces thinly sliced deli smoked chicken breast
1/4 cup egg substitute
1 tablespoon fat-free mayonnaise
1 tablespoon Dijon *or* spicy brown mustard

Top two slices of bread with cheese and chicken; cover with remaining bread. In a bowl, whisk the egg substitute, mayonnaise and mustard; spread outside of sandwiches with egg mixture. In a large nonstick skillet coated with nonstick cooking spray, cook sandwiches on both sides until golden brown. **Yield:** 2 servings.

Nutritional Analysis: 1 sandwich equals 314 calories, 5 g fat (1 g saturated fat), 47 mg cholesterol, 1,420 mg sodium, 34 g carbohydrate, 4 g fiber, 31 g protein.
Diabetic Exchanges: 4 very lean meat, 2 starch, 1 fat.

Lemon Herb Chicken

Low-carb

Prep/Total Time: 30 min.

The home economists in our Test Kitchen created this mouth-watering main course. A tasty sauce nicely glazes the tender, moist chicken.

> 2 boneless skinless chicken breast halves
> (4 ounces *each*)
> 2 teaspoons olive oil
> 1/2 cup chicken broth
> 1 tablespoon minced fresh basil *or* 1 teaspoon dried basil
> 2 garlic cloves, minced
> 1 teaspoon lemon juice
> 1/2 teaspoon minced fresh rosemary *or* 1/8 teaspoon dried rosemary, crushed
> 1/4 teaspoon grated lemon peel
> Dash pepper
> 1 teaspoon cornstarch
> 2 tablespoons water

In a nonstick skillet, brown chicken in oil on both sides over medium heat. Add the broth, basil, garlic, lemon juice, rosemary, lemon peel and pepper. Bring to a boil. Reduce heat; cover and simmer for 10-15 minutes or until chicken is no longer pink. Remove chicken; keep warm.

Combine cornstarch and water until smooth; stir into pan juices. Bring to a boil; stir for 1-2 minutes or until slightly thickened. Serve over chicken. **Yield:** 2 servings.

Nutritional Analysis: 1 serving equals 179 calories, 6 g fat (1 g saturated fat), 66 mg cholesterol, 307 mg sodium, 3 g carbohydrate, trace fiber, 27 g protein.
Diabetic Exchange: 3 lean meat.

Grilled Chicken Salad

(Pictured above)

Prep/Total Time: 30 min.

Perfect for two, this pretty entree salad features strips of hearty grilled chicken. Tomato, dried cranberries, olives and walnuts add wonderful flavor to each forkful.
—Mary Campe, Lakewood, Colorado

> 2 boneless skinless chicken breast halves
> (6 ounces *each*)
> 3 cups torn mixed salad greens
> 1 small tomato, chopped
> 1/4 cup dried cranberries
> 1/4 cup shredded reduced-fat cheddar cheese
> 1/4 cup sliced ripe olives
> 2 green onions, chopped
> 2 tablespoons chopped walnuts
> 1/4 cup fat-free Italian salad dressing

Grill chicken, covered, over medium heat for 8-10 minutes on each side or until no longer pink. Divide salad greens between two serving plates; top with tomato, cranberries, cheese, olives, onions and walnuts. Slice chicken; arrange over salads. Serve with Italian dressing. **Yield:** 2 servings.

Nutritional Analysis: 1 serving equals 383 calories, 14 g fat (4 g saturated fat), 105 mg cholesterol, 776 mg sodium, 24 g carbohydrate, 5 g fiber, 42 g protein.
Diabetic Exchanges: 5 very lean meat, 1-1/2 starch, 1-1/2 fat, 1 vegetable.

Simple Peach Crisp

Prep/Total Time: 25 min.

This four-ingredient dessert easily comes together for a spur-of-the-moment sensation. Both of you will be sweet on this satisfying specialty that's made with spiced instant oatmeal and convenient canned peaches.
—Claire Gable, Camarillo, California

> 1 can (15-1/4 ounces) sliced peaches, drained
> 1 envelope (1.6 ounces) instant cinnamon and spice oatmeal
> 2 tablespoons all-purpose flour
> 2 tablespoons butter, melted

Cut peaches into 3/4-in. pieces; place into two 10-oz. custard cups. Combine the oatmeal, flour and butter; sprinkle over peaches. Place custard cups on a baking sheet. Bake at 425° for 12-15 minutes or until topping is golden brown. **Yield:** 2 servings.

Nutritional Analysis: 1 serving equals 246 calories, 12 g fat (7 g saturated fat), 31 mg cholesterol, 250 mg sodium, 32 g carbohydrate, 3 g fiber, 4 g protein.
Diabetic Exchanges: 2 fat, 1 starch, 1 fruit.

Corn and Shrimp Salad

(Pictured above)

Prep: 15 min. + chilling

This is one of our favorite ways to enjoy corn.
—Ruth Randolph, Orefield, Pennsylvania

- **1/2 pound cooked medium shrimp, peeled and deveined**
- **1-1/3 cups fresh *or* frozen corn**
- **1/2 cup chopped sweet red pepper**
- **1/2 cup chopped green onions**
- **1 tablespoon cider vinegar**
- **1 tablespoon canola oil**
- **1/2 teaspoon minced fresh basil**
- **1/2 teaspoon lemon juice**
- **1/4 teaspoon sugar**
- **1/4 teaspoon salt**
- **Dash cayenne pepper**

In a bowl, toss shrimp, corn, red pepper and onions. In a small bowl, combine vinegar, oil, basil, juice, sugar, salt and cayenne. Pour over shrimp mixture; toss to coat. Cover and refrigerate for 1 hour or until chilled. **Yield:** 2 servings.

Nutritional Analysis: 1 cup equals 300 calories, 10 g fat (1 g saturated fat), 172 mg cholesterol, 471 mg sodium, 29 g carbohydrate, 4 g fiber, 27 g protein.
Diabetic Exchanges: 3 very lean meat, 1-1/2 starch, 1 vegetable, 1 fat.

Microwave Broccoli and Rice

Low-sodium *Meatless*

Prep/Total Time: 15 min.

Broccoli and instant rice make this speedy dish perfect alongside most any entree, and using the microwave helps you ring the dinner bell in no time.
—Shirley Tockey, Cleveland, Oklahoma

- **1/2 cup water**
- **1/2 cup uncooked instant rice**
- **2 teaspoons butter, cut up**
- **3/4 teaspoon reduced-sodium chicken bouillon granules *or* 1 vegetable bouillon cube**
- **1/8 teaspoon pepper**
- **2 cups fresh broccoli florets**

In a 3-cup microwave-safe bowl, combine the water, rice, butter, bouillon and pepper. Top with broccoli florets. Cover and microwave on high for 2-1/2 to 3 minutes or until the broccoli is tender. Let stand for 5 minutes. Stir before serving. **Yield:** 2 servings.

Editor's Note: This recipe was tested in a 1,100-watt microwave.

Nutritional Analysis: 1 cup equals 143 calories, 5 g fat (2 g saturated fat), 10 mg cholesterol, 132 mg sodium, 22 g carbohydrate, 3 g fiber, 4 g protein.
Diabetic Exchanges: 1 starch, 1 vegetable, 1 fat.

Broiled Scallops

(Pictured above)

Low-carb

Prep/Total Time: 25 min.

These quick scallops are perfect for two. They look like they were prepared in a fancy restaurant.
—Susan Coryell, Huddleston, Virginia

    2 green onions, sliced
    1 garlic clove, minced
    2 teaspoons olive oil
   12 ounces sea scallops
    2 teaspoons minced fresh parsley
    1 teaspoon finely chopped fresh basil
  1/4 cup vermouth *or* chicken broth
  1/8 teaspoon salt
  1/8 teaspoon white pepper
  1/3 cup soft bread crumbs
    2 teaspoons butter

In a nonstick skillet, saute the onions and garlic in oil until tender. Add the scallops, parsley and basil; cook and stir over medium heat until scallops are firm and opaque. Add the vermouth or broth, salt and pepper; cook, uncovered, over medium-low heat for 1 minute. Divide mixture evenly between two ovenproof 1-1/2-cup dishes. Sprinkle with bread crumbs; dot with butter. Broil 4-6 in. from the heat until crumbs are golden. **Yield:** 2 servings.

  Nutritional Analysis: *1 serving equals 296 calories, 10 g fat (3 g saturated fat), 66 mg cholesterol, 506 mg sodium, 13 g carbohydrate, 1 g fiber, 30 g protein.*
  Diabetic Exchanges: *4 very lean meat, 2 fat, 1/2 starch.*

Saucy Beef with Broccoli

Prep/Total Time: 30 min.

When I'm looking for a fast entree, I turn to this beef and broccoli stir-fry. It features a tantalizing sauce made special with fresh ginger.
—Rosa Evans, Odessa, Missouri

    1 tablespoon cornstarch
  1/2 cup reduced-sodium beef broth
  1/4 cup sherry *or* additional beef broth
    2 tablespoons reduced-sodium soy sauce
    1 tablespoon brown sugar
    1 garlic clove, minced
    1 teaspoon minced fresh gingerroot
  1/2 pound lean boneless beef sirloin steak, cut into 1/4-inch strips
    2 teaspoons canola oil, *divided*
    2 cups fresh broccoli florets
    8 green onions, cut into 1-inch pieces

In a bowl, combine the first seven ingredients until blended; set aside. In a large nonstick skillet or wok, stir-fry beef in 1 teaspoon oil for 1-2 minutes or until no longer pink. Remove and keep warm.

In the same pan, stir-fry broccoli in remaining oil for 4-5 minutes or until crisp-tender. Add onions; stir-fry for 1-2 minutes. Return beef to the pan. Stir cornstarch mixture and add to the pan. Bring to a boil; cook and stir for 1-2 minutes or until thickened. Reduce heat to low; cover and cook for 5-6 minutes or until meat and vegetables are tender. **Yield:** 2 servings.

Nutritional Analysis: 1-1/4 cups equals 313 calories, 11 g fat (3 g saturated fat), 68 mg cholesterol, 816 mg sodium, 20 g carbohydrate, 4 g fiber, 29 g protein.
Diabetic Exchanges: 3 lean meat, 2 vegetable, 1 fat, 1/2 starch.

Parmesan Zucchini Spears

Low-carb   Low-fat   Meatless

Prep/Total Time: 15 min.

This fast-and-fresh side dish can fit into many menus. It comes together in just 15 minutes.
—Judy Harris, Brainerd, Minnesota

    3 small zucchini (1 pound)
    1 teaspoon olive oil
  1/2 teaspoon grated lemon peel
  1/8 teaspoon salt
  1/8 teaspoon pepper
    1 tablespoon grated Parmesan cheese

Cut zucchini lengthwise into quarters, then cut in half crosswise. In a large nonstick skillet, cook and stir zucchini in oil over medium heat for 4 minutes. Sprinkle with lemon peel, salt and pepper. Cook and stir 4-5 minutes longer or until zucchini is crisp-tender. Remove from the heat; sprinkle with Parmesan cheese. Serve immediately. **Yield:** 2 servings.

Nutritional Analysis: 1 serving equals 64 calories, 3 g fat (1 g saturated fat), 2 mg cholesterol, 201 mg sodium, 7 g carbohydrate, 3 g fiber, 4 g protein.
Diabetic Exchanges: 1 vegetable, 1/2 fat.

Cappuccino Mousse

(Pictured above)

Low-fat   Low-sodium

Prep: 15 min. + chilling

Created in our Test Kitchen, this rich mousse has a hint of coffee and a pleasantly creamy texture. Make it ahead for a delightful finale.

  1/2 teaspoon unflavored gelatin
  1/4 cup fat-free milk
1-1/2 teaspoons baking cocoa
  1/4 teaspoon instant coffee granules
  1/3 cup fat-free coffee-flavored yogurt
    2 tablespoons sugar
  1/2 cup reduced-fat whipped topping

In a small saucepan, sprinkle gelatin over milk; let stand for 1 minute. Heat over low heat, stirring until gelatin is completely dissolved. Add cocoa and coffee; stir until dissolved. Transfer to a small mixing bowl; refrigerate until mixture begins to thicken.

Beat until light and fluffy. Combine yogurt and sugar; beat into gelatin mixture. Fold in whipped topping. Divide between two dessert dishes. Refrigerate until firm. **Yield:** 2 servings.

Nutritional Analysis: 3/4 cup equals 125 calories, 2 g fat (2 g saturated fat), 1 mg cholesterol, 40 mg sodium, 22 g carbohydrate, trace fiber, 3 g protein.
Diabetic Exchange: 1-1/2 starch.

Shrimp with Mustard Sauce

(Pictured above)

Low-carb

Prep/Total Time: 20 min.

Seasoned with white wine, mustard and garlic, this shrimp dish makes any dinner special.
—*Donna Richardson, St. Charles, Illinois*

1/4 cup finely chopped onion
2 garlic cloves, minced
2 teaspoons olive oil
1/4 cup white wine *or* apple juice
2 tablespoons Dijon mustard
1/8 teaspoon pepper
3/4 pound uncooked medium shrimp, peeled and deveined
1 small tomato, seeded and diced

In a nonstick skillet, saute onion and garlic in oil until tender. Stir in the wine or apple juice, mustard and pepper. Bring to a boil. Reduce heat to medium-low. Add shrimp; cook and stir until shrimp turn pink, about 5 minutes. Stir in tomato; heat through. **Yield:** 2 servings.

Nutritional Analysis: *1 serving equals 193 calories, 6 g fat (1 g saturated fat), 202 mg cholesterol, 598 mg sodium, 5 g carbohydrate, 1 g fiber, 23 g protein.*
Diabetic Exchanges: *3 very lean meat, 1 vegetable, 1 fat.*

Mushroom and Spinach Saute

Low-carb Meatless

Prep/Total Time: 10 min.

Mushrooms and spinach combine with plenty of garlic in this super-fast side dish for two. It requires just six ingredients and takes a mere 10 minutes to whip up on the stovetop, so it's ideal for busy weeknights. I've found that the recipe is also easy to double or triple when you're having a dinner party.
—*Pauline Howard, Lago Vista, Texas*

2 cups sliced fresh mushrooms
2 garlic cloves, minced
2 teaspoons olive oil
1 package (6 ounces) fresh baby spinach
1/8 teaspoon salt
1/8 teaspoon pepper

In a nonstick skillet, saute the mushrooms and garlic in oil for 2 minutes or until tender. Add the spinach; cook and stir until wilted, about 1 minute. Season with salt and pepper. Serve immediately. **Yield:** 2 servings.

Nutritional Analysis: *3/4 cup equals 82 calories, 5 g fat (1 g saturated fat), 0 cholesterol, 216 mg sodium, 7 g carbohydrate, 3 g fiber, 4 g protein.*
Diabetic Exchanges: *1 vegetable, 1 fat.*

 Go for the Green

IN GENERAL, salad greens are an excellent source of vitamin A and a good source of vitamin C. Where you see green, you get more nutritional bang for your buck. Specifically, to get a bigger boost of vitamin A, buy greens that are medium to dark green (the darker the leaves, the more vitamin A).

Many greens, such as spinach, kale and collards, are also known for their mineral content, especially iron, calcium and magnesium—as well as the vitamins folate, riboflavin (B2) and vitamin K. The leaves of such greens are very rich in disease-fighting antioxidants—carotenoids and beta-carotene, vitamin E and, of course, vitamin C.

Apple-Spice Acorn Squash

(Pictured above and on page 252)

Low-sodium *Meatless*

Prep/Total Time: 30 min.

For this delightful side dish, I fill warmed squash with chopped apple, golden raisins and spices.
—Joann Fell, Fostoria, Ohio

  1 medium acorn squash
  1 medium tart apple, chopped
1/4 cup golden raisins
1/8 teaspoon ground cinnamon
1/8 teaspoon ground nutmeg
  2 teaspoons butter

Cut squash in half; discard seeds. Place squash cut side down in a microwave-safe baking dish. Add 1/2 in. of water. Microwave, uncovered, on high for 10-13 minutes or until almost tender; drain.

Combine the apple, raisins, cinnamon and nutmeg; spoon into squash cavities. Dot with butter. Microwave, uncovered, on high for 6-8 minutes or until squash and apples are tender. Let stand for 5 minutes before serving. **Yield:** 2 servings.

Editor's Note: This recipe was tested in a 1,100-watt microwave.

Nutritional Analysis: 1 filled squash half equals 207 calories, 4 g fat (2 g saturated fat), 10 mg cholesterol, 47 mg sodium, 45 g carbohydrate, 5 g fiber, 2 g protein.
Diabetic Exchanges: *1-1/2 starch, 1-1/2 fruit, 1 fat.*

Oven French Fries

(Pictured at left)

Meatless

Prep: 15 min. + chilling **Bake:** 30 min.

These fries are crisp and offer a flavor you'll both enjoy. They go well with a variety of main courses.
—Margaret Taylor, Salem, Missouri

- 1 tablespoon cornstarch
- 2 cups water
- 1 tablespoon reduced-sodium soy sauce
- 2 medium potatoes, peeled and cut into strips
- 2 teaspoons olive oil
- 1/8 teaspoon salt

In a large bowl, combine the cornstarch, water and soy sauce until smooth. Add potatoes; cover and refrigerate for 1 hour. Drain potatoes and pat dry on paper towels. Toss potatoes with oil and sprinkle with salt. Place on a baking sheet coated with nonstick cooking spray. Bake at 375° for 15 minutes. Turn; bake 15-20 minutes longer or until tender and golden brown. **Yield:** 2 servings.

Nutritional Analysis: 3/4 cup equals 167 calories, 5 g fat (1 g saturated fat), 0 cholesterol, 457 mg sodium, 29 g carbohydrate, 2 g fiber, 3 g protein.
Diabetic Exchanges: 2 starch, 1 fat.

Sweet 'n' Tangy Pork Chops

(Pictured above)

Low-carb

Prep/Total Time: 30 min.

A handful of ingredients is all that's needed to fix these tender and tasty chops.
—Jami Ouellette, Houston, Texas

- 2 bone-in center-cut pork loin chops (7 ounces *each*)
- 1/8 teaspoon salt
- Dash pepper
- 1/4 cup beer *or* beef broth
- 4-1/2 teaspoons ketchup
- 1 tablespoon brown sugar

Sprinkle pork chops with salt and pepper. In a large nonstick skillet coated with nonstick cooking spray, brown chops for 3 minutes on each side.

In a small bowl, combine the beer or broth, ketchup and brown sugar. Pour over pork; bring to a boil. Reduce heat; simmer, uncovered, for 10-15 minutes or until a meat thermometer reads 160°. Remove chops and keep warm. Simmer sauce until reduced to 1/2 cup, about 5 minutes. Serve with pork chops. **Yield:** 2 servings.

Nutritional Analysis: 1 pork chop with 3 tablespoons sauce equals 245 calories, 8 g fat (3 g saturated fat), 86 mg cholesterol, 347 mg sodium, 10 g carbohydrate, trace fiber, 30 g protein.
Diabetic Exchanges: 4 lean meat, 1/2 starch.

Turkey-Stuffed Portobellos

Low-carb

Prep: 20 min. **Bake:** 40 min.

If you like mushrooms, you'll love these savory versions stuffed with ground turkey.
—Cindy Adams, Cheyenne, Wyoming

- 2 tablespoons crushed saltines
- 2 tablespoons finely chopped onion
- 2 tablespoons shredded zucchini
- 2 tablespoons shredded carrot
- 2 tablespoons chopped fresh mushrooms
- 2 tablespoons spicy hot V8 juice
- 1 garlic clove, minced
- 1/2 teaspoon dried marjoram
- 1/8 teaspoon salt
- 1/8 teaspoon pepper
- 1/2 pound lean ground turkey
- 2 large portobello mushrooms

In a bowl, combine the first 10 ingredients. Crumble turkey over mixture and mix well. Remove and discard stems of portobello mushrooms. Fill mushrooms with turkey mixture.

Place in an 8-in. square baking dish coated with nonstick cooking spray. Cover and bake at 350° for 30 minutes. Uncover; bake 10-15 minutes longer or until mushrooms are tender and a thermometer inserted into stuffing reads 165°. **Yield:** 2 servings.

Nutritional Analysis: 1 stuffed mushroom equals 227 calories, 10 g fat (3 g saturated fat), 90 mg cholesterol, 360 mg sodium, 10 g carbohydrate, 2 g fiber, 23 g protein.
Diabetic Exchanges: 3 lean meat, 1 vegetable.

Fine Dining Pared Down

A special occasion calls for candles, fine china and a marvelous meal. But there's no need to add to your guests' waistlines at the same time. Pamper friends and family with these elegant but light menus.

Cajun Beef Tenderloin, Caesar Orzo with Asparagus and Berries in Champagne Jelly (page 270)

Dressed-Up Chicken Dinner

Chicken with Garlic Sauce

Low-carb

Prep: 15 min. **Cook:** 30 min.

"Wow" is always the unanimous response from guests after their first bite of this moist herb chicken topped with garlic sauce. I received this recipe from my brother, and we were surprised at how mild the sauce is.
—Paula Bolt, Eden Prairie, Minnesota

   3 tablespoons all-purpose flour, *divided*
1-1/2 teaspoons minced fresh rosemary *or* 1/2
     teaspoon dried rosemary, crushed
1-1/2 teaspoons rubbed sage
  3/4 teaspoon salt
  1/2 teaspoon pepper
   4 boneless skinless chicken breast halves
     (1-1/2 pounds)
   2 tablespoons olive oil, *divided*
 20 garlic cloves, halved lengthwise
  1/2 cup chopped onion
  1/4 teaspoon crushed red pepper flakes
  1/4 cup white wine *or* reduced-sodium chicken broth
1-1/4 cups reduced-sodium chicken broth
   1 tablespoon butter, melted
   3 tablespoons minced fresh parsley

In a large resealable plastic bag, combine 2 tablespoons flour, rosemary, sage, salt and pepper; add chicken. Seal bag and shake to coat. In a large nonstick skillet, brown chicken in 1 tablespoon oil over medium heat for 4 minutes on each side. Transfer to an 8-in. square baking dish coated with nonstick cooking spray. Bake, uncovered, at 325° for 15 minutes.

Meanwhile, in the same skillet, saute garlic, onion and red pepper flakes in remaining oil until onion is tender and garlic begins to brown, about 3 minutes. Stir in wine or broth; bring to a boil. Boil until wine is reduced by half, about 2-3 minutes.

Stir in chicken broth; bring to a boil. Boil until broth is reduced by half, about 7-8 minutes. Remove from the heat.

Combine butter and remaining flour; whisk into skillet. Return to heat. Bring to a boil; cook and stir for 1-2 minutes or until sauce thickens. Serve warm over chicken breasts. Sprinkle with parsley. **Yield:** 4 servings.

Nutritional Analysis: 1 chicken breast half with 5 tablespoons sauce equals 339 calories, 12 g fat (4 g saturated fat), 106 mg cholesterol, 774 mg sodium, 12 g carbohydrate, 1 g fiber, 42 g protein.
Diabetic Exchanges: 5 lean meat, 1 vegetable, 1/2 starch.

Mixed Greens and Apple Salad

Low-carb *Low-fat* **Low-sodium** *Meatless*

Prep/Total Time: 10 min.

A sweet-tart yogurt dressing perfectly complements this refreshing salad from our Test Kitchen staff.

5-1/3 cups mixed salad greens
   2 medium apples, cored and cut into 3/4-inch pieces
   2 tablespoons crumbled feta cheese
LEMON HONEY SALAD DRESSING:
   4 teaspoons lemon juice
2-1/2 teaspoons honey
  3/4 teaspoon fat-free reduced-sugar vanilla yogurt
   1 teaspoon canola oil
  1/4 teaspoon minced fresh garlic
Dash salt
Dash white pepper
Dash ground nutmeg

In a large salad bowl, combine the salad greens, apple and feta cheese. In a jar with a tight-fitting lid, combine the salad dressing ingredients; shake well. Drizzle over salad; toss to combine. **Yield:** 4 servings.

Nutritional Analysis: 1-1/4 cups equals 82 calories, 3 g fat (1 g saturated fat), 4 mg cholesterol, 107 mg sodium, 15 g carbohydrate, 3 g fiber, 2 g protein.
Diabetic Exchanges: 1 vegetable, 1/2 fruit, 1/2 fat.

Orange Marmalade Sweet Rolls

Low-fat *Meatless*

Prep: 15 min. + rising **Bake:** 15 min.

My husband has heart trouble, so he needs to watch what he eats. I like to treat him with these tender rolls.
—Lacey Griffin, Fredonia, Pennsylvania

   1 loaf (1 pound) frozen bread dough, thawed
 1/3 cup 100% orange marmalade spreadable fruit
   2 tablespoons raisins
 1/3 cup confectioners' sugar
 1/2 teaspoon grated orange peel
   2 teaspoons orange juice

On a floured surface, roll dough into a 12-in. x 8-in. rectangle; brush with marmalade. Sprinkle with raisins. Roll up jelly-roll style, starting with a long side; pinch dough to seal. Cut into 12 slices. Place cut side down in muffin cups coated with nonstick cooking spray. Cover and let rise until doubled, about 45 minutes.

Bake at 350° for 15-20 minutes or until golden brown. Immediately remove to serving plates. Combine the confectioners' sugar, orange peel and orange juice; drizzle over warm rolls. **Yield:** 1 dozen.

Nutritional Analysis: 1 roll equals 140 calories, 2 g fat (trace saturated fat), 0 cholesterol, 211 mg sodium, 28 g carbohydrate, 1 g fiber, 4 g protein.
Diabetic Exchange: 2 starch.

Fabulous Seafood Supper

Onion Tarragon Shrimp

Low-carb

Prep: 15 min. + standing **Cook:** 10 min.

I've been making this recipe for more than 10 years, and it is the sole reason that I grow my own tarragon.
—Linda Lacek, Winter Park, Florida

    2 medium onions, finely chopped
    4 garlic cloves, minced
    2 tablespoons olive oil
    2 tablespoons minced fresh tarragon *or* 2
      teaspoons dried tarragon
  1/2 teaspoon salt
  1/8 teaspoon pepper
1-1/2 pounds uncooked medium shrimp, peeled and
      deveined
    2 tablespoons lemon juice

In a large nonstick skillet, saute onions and garlic in oil until tender. Add the tarragon, salt and pepper; saute 1 minute longer. Transfer to a large bowl and let cool. Add shrimp and lemon juice to onion mixture; let stand for 30 minutes.

Place the shrimp on a foil-lined broiler pan; spoon the onion mixture over shrimp. Broil 3-4 in. from the heat for 3-4 minutes or until shrimp turn pink and topping is browned. **Yield:** 4 servings.

Nutritional Analysis: 3/4 cup equals 200 calories, 8 g fat (1 g saturated fat), 202 mg cholesterol, 528 mg sodium, 9 g carbohydrate, 2 g fiber, 23 g protein.
Diabetic Exchanges: 3 lean meat, 1 vegetable.

Artichokes and Green Beans

Meatless

Prep/Total Time: 30 min.

This fuss-free but elegant treatment for vegetables complements a variety of main courses. Whenever I make it, someone always asks for the recipe.
—Carole Boys, Wheaton, Illinois

1-1/4 pounds fresh green beans, trimmed
  1/2 cup soft bread crumbs
    2 tablespoons olive oil, *divided*
  2/3 cup finely chopped onion
    1 garlic clove, minced
    1 can (14 ounces) water-packed artichoke hearts,
      rinsed, drained and quartered
  1/4 teaspoon salt
  1/8 teaspoon pepper
  1/4 cup shredded Parmesan cheese

Place the beans in a steamer basket. Place in a saucepan over 1 in. of water; bring to a boil. Cover and steam for 6-8 minutes or until crisp-tender. Remove from the heat and set aside.

In a nonstick skillet, toast bread crumbs over medium heat in 1 tablespoon oil; set aside. In the same skillet, saute onion and garlic in remaining oil until tender. Add the artichokes, salt, pepper and reserved beans. Cook and stir over low heat until heated through. Before serving, sprinkle with cheese and toasted bread crumbs. **Yield:** 5 servings.

Nutritional Analysis: 3/4 cup equals 158 calories, 7 g fat (2 g saturated fat), 3 mg cholesterol, 701 mg sodium, 19 g carbohydrate, 6 g fiber, 7 g protein.
Diabetic Exchanges: 2 vegetable, 1-1/2 fat, 1/2 starch.

Raspberry Custard Tart

Low-sodium

Prep: 25 min. **Cook:** 15 min. + chilling

Our Test Kitchen home economists created this pretty dessert to help you impress guests at your next gathering. With a yummy raspberry layer and nutty homemade crust, it's hard to believe that a slice isn't an invitation to stray from healthy eating goals.

    3 tablespoons reduced-fat butter
  1/2 cup sugar
  3/4 cup all-purpose flour
  1/4 cup finely chopped pecans, toasted
FILLING:
  1/3 cup sugar
  1/4 cup all-purpose flour
2-1/4 cups fat-free milk
    1 egg yolk
  1/4 teaspoon almond extract
    1 jar (12 ounces) 100% seedless raspberry
      spreadable fruit
1-1/2 cups fresh raspberries

In a small mixing bowl, beat the butter and sugar for 2 minutes or until crumbly. Beat in the flour and pecans. Press onto the bottom and up the sides of a 9-in. fluted tart pan with a removable bottom coated with nonstick cooking spray. Bake at 425° for 8-10 minutes or until lightly browned. Cool on a wire rack.

In a small saucepan, combine sugar and flour. Stir in milk until smooth. Cook and stir over medium-high heat until thickened and bubbly. Reduce heat; cook and stir 2 minutes longer. Remove from the heat. Stir a small amount of hot filling into egg yolk; return all to pan, stirring constantly. Bring to a gentle boil; cook and stir 2 minutes longer. Remove from the heat. Gently stir in almond extract. Pour over crust. Refrigerate until set.

In a small bowl, whisk fruit spread until smooth; spread over filling. Garnish with raspberries. **Yield:** 12 servings.

Editor's Note: This recipe was tested with Land O' Lakes light stick butter.

Nutritional Analysis: 1 piece equals 210 calories, 4 g fat (1 g saturated fat), 24 mg cholesterol, 42 mg sodium, 41 g carbohydrate, 2 g fiber, 3 g protein.
Diabetic Exchanges: 1-1/2 starch, 1 fruit, 1/2 fat.

Fire Up a Flame-Broiled Feast

Nectarine Arugula Salad

Low-carb   Low-sodium   Meatless

Prep/Total Time: 20 min.

Here's a summer salad that brightens any supper. The homemade dressing has a hint of raspberry.
—Christine Laba, Arlington, Virginia

- 4 **cups fresh arugula *or* baby spinach**
- 4 **cups torn Bibb *or* Boston lettuce**
- 3 **medium nectarines, sliced**
- 2 **tablespoons pine nuts, toasted**
- 2 **tablespoons crumbled blue cheese**
- 2 **tablespoons raspberry vinegar**
- 2 **teaspoons sugar**
- 1 **teaspoon Dijon mustard**
- 1/8 **teaspoon salt**

Dash pepper
- 3 **tablespoons olive oil**

In a large salad bowl, combine the first five ingredients. In a small bowl, whisk the vinegar, sugar, mustard, salt and pepper until blended. Gradually whisk in oil until dressing thickens. Drizzle over salad; toss to coat. **Yield:** 8 servings.

Nutritional Analysis: 1 cup equals 101 calories, 7 g fat (1 g saturated fat), 2 mg cholesterol, 86 mg sodium, 9 g carbohydrate, 1 g fiber, 2 g protein.
Diabetic Exchanges: 1-1/2 fat, 1/2 starch.

Tropical Tenderloin Steaks

Low-carb

Prep: 10 min. + marinating **Grill:** 20 min.

Marinated in citrus juices, ginger and rum extract, these steaks deliver unbelievable taste.
—Mitzi Sentiff, Alexandria, Virginia

- 1 **cup reduced-sodium chicken broth**
- 3/4 **cup orange juice**
- 1/4 **cup ketchup**
- 1/4 **cup unsweetened pineapple juice**
- 3 **tablespoons packed brown sugar**
- 3 **tablespoons lime juice**
- 2 **garlic cloves, minced**
- 1 **tablespoon minced fresh gingerroot**
- 1/4 **teaspoon vanilla extract**
- 1/4 **teaspoon rum extract**
- 1/4 **teaspoon ground cloves**
- 1/4 **teaspoon dried thyme**
- 1/4 **teaspoon cayenne pepper**
- 1 **beef tenderloin (2 pounds), cut into 8 pieces**

In a small bowl, combine the first 13 ingredients; mix well. Pour 2 cups into a large resealable plastic bag; add the beef. Seal bag and turn to coat; refrigerate for 3 hours. Cover and refrigerate remaining marinade for basting.

If grilling the steaks, coat grill rack with nonstick cooking spray before starting the grill. Drain and discard marinade from steaks. Grill, covered, over medium heat or broil 4-6 in. from the heat for 8-10 minutes on each side or until meat reaches desired doneness, brushing occasionally with reserved marinade. **Yield:** 8 servings.

Nutritional Analysis: 3 ounces cooked beef equals 223 calories, 11 g fat (4 g saturated fat), 72 mg cholesterol, 142 mg sodium, 6 g carbohydrate, trace fiber, 23 g protein.
Diabetic Exchanges: 3 lean meat, 1/2 starch.

Couscous with Grilled Vegetables

Low-fat   Meatless

Prep: 15 min. **Cook:** 15 min. + cooling

This hearty side dish is almost a meal in itself. I grill garden-fresh vegetables, then add them to couscous.
—Kathy Herrala, Martinez, California

- 2 **small zucchini, quartered lengthwise**
- 1/2 **medium eggplant, sliced widthwise 1/2 inch thick**
- 1 **medium sweet red pepper, quartered**
- 1 **small onion, sliced 1/2 inch thick**
- 3/4 **teaspoon salt, *divided***
- 1/2 **teaspoon pepper, *divided***
- 2 **cups reduced-sodium chicken *or* vegetable broth**
- 1 **package (10 ounces) couscous**
- 1/2 **cup chopped green onions**
- 4-1/2 **teaspoons lemon juice**
- 2-1/4 **teaspoons minced fresh thyme *or* 1/2 teaspoon dried thyme**

Spritz vegetables with nonstick cooking spray; sprinkle with 1/4 teaspoon salt and 1/4 teaspoon pepper. Coat grill rack with nonstick cooking spray before preparing grill for indirect heat. Arrange vegetables on grill over indirect heat. Grill, covered, over medium indirect heat for 4-5 minutes on each side or until tender. Let stand until cool enough to handle.

In a saucepan, bring broth to a boil. Stir in couscous. Remove from the heat; cover and let stand for 5 minutes or until liquid is absorbed. Cut grilled vegetables into 1/2-in. pieces. Fluff couscous with a fork. Add vegetables, green onions, lemon juice, thyme and remaining salt and pepper; toss until combined. **Yield:** 8 servings.

Nutritional Analysis: 1 cup equals 163 calories, trace fat (trace saturated fat), 0 cholesterol, 384 mg sodium, 34 g carbohydrate, 4 g fiber, 7 g protein.
Diabetic Exchanges: 2 starch, 1 vegetable.

🍎 Slimmed-Down Salad

DON'T have the nuts or cheese for Nectarine Arugula Salad (recipe at top left)? Skip them, and you'll save close to 20 calories per serving.

Italian-Style Dishes

Artichoke Crostini

Low-fat Meatless

Prep/Total Time: 30 min.

This appetizer is wonderful when vine-ripened tomatoes are at their best. I often rely on these fresh-tasting slices for parties and other events.
—*Janne Rowe, Wichita, Kansas*

- 1 sourdough baguette (1 pound)
- 2 cups chopped seeded tomatoes
- 1 can (14 ounces) water-packed artichoke hearts, rinsed, drained and chopped
- 2 tablespoons minced fresh basil
- 2 tablespoons olive oil
- 1/2 teaspoon seasoned salt
- 1/8 teaspoon pepper

Cut the baguette into 32 slices. Place on an ungreased baking sheet; spritz bread with nonstick cooking spray. Bake at 325° for 7-10 minutes or until crisp. Cool on a wire rack. In a bowl, combine the tomatoes, artichokes, basil, oil, seasoned salt and pepper. Spoon onto bread slices. **Yield:** 16 servings.

Nutritional Analysis: *2 pieces equals 106 calories, 3 g fat (trace saturated fat), 0 cholesterol, 314 mg sodium, 17 g carbohydrate, 2 g fiber, 3 g protein.*
Diabetic Exchanges: *1 starch, 1/2 fat.*

Tuscan Pork Roast

Low-carb

Prep: 10 min. + marinating **Bake:** 1-1/2 hours + standing

Treated to a flavorful rub the night before, this herb-crusted roast doesn't need any prep work on the day of your get-together. I've had so many compliments on how moist the pork is.
—*Diane Toomey, Methuen, Massachusetts*

- 3 garlic cloves, minced
- 2 tablespoons olive oil
- 1 tablespoon fennel seed, crushed
- 1 tablespoon dried rosemary, crushed
- 1 teaspoon salt
- 1/4 teaspoon pepper
- 1 boneless pork loin roast (3 pounds)

In a small bowl, combine the first six ingredients; rub over pork roast. Cover and refrigerate overnight.

Place roast on a rack in a shallow roasting pan. Bake, uncovered, at 350° for 1-1/2 hours or until a meat thermometer reads 160°, basting occasionally with pan juices. Let stand for 10 minutes before slicing. **Yield:** 10 servings.

Nutritional Analysis: *4 ounces cooked pork equals 229 calories, 10 g fat (3 g saturated fat), 80 mg cholesterol, 282 mg sodium, 1 g carbohydrate, 1 g fiber, 31 g protein.*
Diabetic Exchange: *4 lean meat.*

Basil-Parmesan Angel Hair

Meatless

Prep/Total Time: 30 min.

I've given this crowd-pleasing recipe to many people, and they all love how quick and simple it is.
—*Barbara Dorsett, Oro Valley, Arizona*

- 1 package (16 ounces) angel hair pasta
- 2 tablespoons olive oil
- 1 can (12 ounces) fat-free evaporated milk
- 2/3 cup shredded Parmesan cheese
- 1/2 cup thinly sliced green onions
- 1/4 cup minced fresh basil
- 1 teaspoon grated lemon peel
- 1/2 teaspoon salt
- 1/2 teaspoon garlic powder
- 1/4 teaspoon pepper
- Additional fresh basil
- 12 lemon slices

Cook pasta according to package directions. Drain and return to the pan. Add oil; toss to coat. Add the milk, Parmesan cheese, onions, basil, lemon peel, salt, garlic powder and pepper. Cook and stir over medium heat until heated through. Sprinkle with additional basil. Serve with lemon. **Yield:** 12 servings.

Nutritional Analysis: *2/3 cup equals 203 calories, 5 g fat (1 g saturated fat), 5 mg cholesterol, 219 mg sodium, 32 g carbohydrate, 2 g fiber, 9 g protein.*
Diabetic Exchanges: *1-1/2 starch, 1 fat, 1/2 fat-free milk.*

🍎 Subtler Seasoning

I LIKE to season meats with dried rosemary, but some of my friends and family don't care for rosemary in needle-like pieces. So I place it in a clean coffee grinder and grind it into a powder. Then I sprinkle it on the meat. The house smells so good while it cooks, and everyone enjoys the meal.

—*Charley Gomes, Tucson, Arizona*

New Year's Dinner Feast

Cajun Beef Tenderloin

Low-carb

Prep: 15 min. **Grill:** 50 min. + standing

This spicy entree really warms up New Year's Eve. The dry rub keeps the tenderloin nice and moist.
—Sue Dannahower, Parker, Colorado

- 1 beef tenderloin (3 pounds)
- 4 teaspoons salt
- 1 tablespoon paprika
- 2-1/4 teaspoons onion powder
- 1-1/2 teaspoons garlic powder
- 1-1/2 teaspoons white pepper
- 1-1/2 teaspoons pepper
- 1 to 3 teaspoons cayenne pepper
- 1 teaspoon dried basil
- 1/2 teaspoon chili powder
- 1/8 teaspoon dried thyme
- 1/8 teaspoon ground mustard
- Dash ground cloves

Tie tenderloin at 2-in. intervals with kitchen string. Combine the seasonings; rub over beef.

If grilling, prepare grill for indirect heat. Coat grill rack with nonstick cooking spray before starting the grill.

Grill tenderloin, covered, over indirect medium heat for 50-60 minutes, turning occasionally, or until meat reaches desired doneness (for medium-rare, a meat thermometer should read 145°; medium, 160°; well-done, 170°). Let stand for 10 minutes before slicing.

To roast the tenderloin, bake on a rack in a shallow roasting pan at 425° for 45-60 minutes or until meat reaches desired doneness. **Yield:** 12 servings.

Nutritional Analysis: 3 ounces cooked beef equals 207 calories, 11 g fat (4 g saturated fat), 72 mg cholesterol, 841 mg sodium, 2 g carbohydrate, 1 g fiber, 23 g protein.
Diabetic Exchanges: 3 lean meat, 1 fat.

Caesar Orzo with Asparagus

Prep/Total Time: 25 min.

My teenage sons love this creamy side dish so much, they'll eat it regardless of which vegetables I use.
—Karen Hoyle, Excelsior, Minnesota

- 2 cans (14-1/2 ounces *each*) reduced-sodium chicken broth
- 2 cups water
- 2 cups uncooked orzo pasta
- 2 pounds fresh asparagus, trimmed and cut into 2-inch pieces
- 2/3 cup shredded Parmesan cheese
- 2/3 cup reduced-fat creamy Caesar salad dressing

In a large saucepan, bring broth and water to a boil. Add orzo; cook and stir for 3 minutes. Add asparagus. Cook, uncovered, over medium heat for 6-8 minutes or until orzo and asparagus are tender, stirring frequently; drain. Stir in Parmesan cheese and salad dressing. **Yield:** 12 servings.

Nutritional Analysis: 2/3 cup equals 210 calories, 4 g fat (1 g saturated fat), 4 mg cholesterol, 504 mg sodium, 33 g carbohydrate, 3 g fiber, 9 g protein.
Diabetic Exchanges: 2 starch, 1 vegetable, 1/2 fat.

Berries in Champagne Jelly

Low-fat   Low-sodium

Prep: 40 min. **Cook:** 10 min. + chilling

My sister shared the recipe for this elegant dish. It's a refreshing alternative to fruit salads and heavy desserts.
—Andrea Barnhoorn, Scottsville, New York

- 2 cups cold water
- 4 envelopes unflavored gelatin
- 1-1/2 cups sugar
- 2 bottles (750 milliliters *each*) champagne *or* sparkling grape juice
- 2 cups sparkling grape juice
- 3 cups fresh raspberries
- 3 cups fresh blueberries
- 2 cups fresh blackberries

Place water in a large saucepan; sprinkle with gelatin. Let stand for 2 minutes. Add sugar. Cook and stir over medium-low heat until sugar and gelatin are dissolved (do not boil). Remove from the heat.

Measure 4 cups of champagne or juice; set aside remaining champagne and chill for another use. Slowly stir the 4 cups champagne and 2 cups grape juice into the saucepan. Transfer to a 13-in. x 9-in. x 2-in. dish coated with nonstick cooking spray. Cover and refrigerate for 8 hours or overnight.

Using a potato masher, gently break up champagne jelly. Layer the jelly and berries in 12 dessert dishes. Cover and refrigerate for at least 2 hours before serving. **Yield:** 12 servings.

Nutritional Analysis: One serving equals 217 calories, 1 g fat (trace saturated fat), 0 cholesterol, 11 mg sodium, 53 g carbohydrate, 4 g fiber, 3 g protein.
Diabetic Exchanges: 1-1/2 starch, 1 fruit, 1 fat.

🍎 Toast to Your Health

CONCERNED about packing on extra pounds during the holiday season? Remember these tips:
- Snack on plenty of fruits and veggies.
- Drink lots of water, particularly right before a dinner party.
- Only indulge in select foods, such as special ones that come around just once a year.
- Exercise. Sure, it's a busy time of year, but working out will burn calories and boost your energy.

General Recipe Index

This handy index lists every recipe by food category, major ingredient and/or cooking method, so you can easily locate recipes to suit your needs.

Alphabetical Index

*This handy index lists every recipe in alphabetical order
so you can easily find your favorite dish.*

Rich Pumpkin Custard, 221
Roasted Garlic Mashed Potatoes, 88
Roasted Lemon Chicken, 118
Roasted Parmesan Potato
    Wedges, 238
Roasted Pepper Ravioli Bake, 175
Roasted Red Pepper Dip, 25
Roasted Vegetable Lasagna, 172
Rosemary Onion Focaccia, 190
Rosemary Rice, 84
Rosemary Turkey Breast, 135

S

Sage Polenta, 74
Salad Dressing with a Kick, 66
Salmon and Asparagus in
    Phyllo, 159
Salsa Spaghetti Squash, 180
Sassy Shrimp Stir-Fry, 170
Saucy Beef with Broccoli, 257
Sausage Kale Soup, 40
Savory Pita Strips, 188
Scalloped Tomatoes, 84
Sea Scallops and Mushrooms, 169
Seafood Pesto Pasta, 162
Seasoned Brown Rice, 241
Sesame Snow Peas, 88
Shrimp and Grits, 166
Shrimp 'n' Veggie Pizza, 164
Shrimp Rice Casserole, 165
Shrimp Stir-Fry, 166
Shrimp with Mustard Sauce, 258
Simple Peach Crisp, 254
Sloppy Joe Mac and Cheese, 123
Slow-Cooked Sirloin, 109
Slow-Cooked Sweet 'n' Sour Pork, 151
Smoked Salmon Dip, 23
Snapper with Spicy Pineapple
    Glaze, 163
Snapper with Vegetable Medley, 170
Southern Seafood Gumbo, 42
Southwest Vegetarian Bake, 173
Southwestern Chicken Salad, 63
Southwestern Veggie Wraps, 174
Spaghetti with Creamy White Clam
    Sauce, 168
Spaghetti with Fresh Tomatoes, 175
Spice Cutout Cookies, 236
Spiced Cranberry Ketchup, 86
Spiced Honey Pears, 202
Spiced Tangerine Ham, 143
Spicy Chicken, 140
Spicy Citrus Gelatin Mold, 50
Spicy Crunchy Veggies, 56
Spicy Curried Chicken, 128
Spicy Pork Tenderloin Salad, 46
Spinach and Garbanzo Skillet, 75

Spinach Bean Soup, 30
Spinach Beef Salad, 70
Spinach Calzones, 22
Spinach Casserole, 83
Spinach Cheddar Squares, 179
Spinach Herb Twists, 194
Spinach Lentil Soup, 36
Spinach-Stuffed Beef
    Tenderloin, 113
Spinach-Stuffed Chicken Breasts, 132
Spinach Vegetable Soup, 35
Stir-Fried Chicken and Rice
    Noodles, 137
Stir-Fried Scallops and
    Asparagus, 157
Stovetop Beef 'n' Shells, 114
Strawberry-Almond Chocolate
    Torte, 212
Strawberry Banana Delight, 213
Strawberry Cheesecake Minis, 226
Strawberry Dessert Sauce, 213
Streuseled Zucchini Bundt
    Cake, 206
Stuffed Cornish Hens, 134
Stuffed Mountain Trout, 168
Stuffed Potato Skins, 21
Summer Soup, 33
Summer Squash Casserole, 95
Summer Tea Sandwiches, 124
Sunshine Gelatin Salad, 69
Sweet 'n' Sour Cashew Pork, 147
Sweet 'n' Tangy Pork Chops, 260
Sweet Mustard, 73
Sweet Pepper Sandwiches, 176
Sweet Potato Pear Bake, 87
Sweet Thyme-Mustard Spread, 88
Swiss Chicken Supreme, 133
Swiss Steak, 110

T

Tangy Four-Bean Salad, 55
Tarragon Broccoli, 90
Tarragon-Lemon Turkey Breast, 139
Tarragon Tuna Salad, 47
Tasty Italian Chicken, 138
Teddy Bear Paws, 192
Teriyaki Pork Tenderloin, 152
Teriyaki Salmon Burgers, 161
Teriyaki Turkey Burritos, 128
Terrific Turkey Meat Loaf, 130
Tex-Mex Rice and Bean Snack, 20
Thai Beef Noodle Salad, 60
Thai-Style Chicken, 138
Three-Berry Lemon Trifle, 206
Three-Pepper Chutney, 78
Thrive-on-Five Soup, 32
Tiny Tim Trifle, 251

Tiramisu Parfaits, 249
Toasted Almond Granola, 103
Tofu-Stuffed Pasta Shells, 178
Tomato Feta Salad, 65
Tomato Spinach Pizza, 177
Triple Mashed Vegetables, 72
Tropical Tenderloin Steaks, 266
Tuna Pate, 25
Turkey Barbecue, 116
Turkey Biscuit Bake, 119
Turkey Breakfast Sausage, 102
Turkey Marsala, 120
Turkey Meatballs with Lemon
    Sauce, 136
Turkey Noodle Supper, 120
Turkey Pasta Soup, 34
Turkey Reubens, 121
Turkey Soft Tacos, 138
Turkey-Stuffed Portobellos, 260
Turkey Tenderloin Sandwiches, 118
Turkey Tetrazzini, 132
Turkey Tortilla Spirals, 27
Tuscan Pork Roast, 268

V

Vanilla Peach Tarts, 234
Vegetable Barley Bake, 85
Vegetable Bean Barley Soup, 32
Vegetable Quesadillas, 26
Vegetarian Taco Salad, 52
Veggie Corn Cakes, 176
Veggie Egg Scramble, 102
Velvety Orange Gelatin Pie, 223

W

Walnut Green Bean Salad, 67
Whipped Cauliflower, 82
White Bean Dip, 25
White Chocolate Mousse, 224
Whole Wheat Banana Bread, 185
Wild Rice Pepper Salad, 55
Wintertime Beef Soup, 43
Wonton Sundaes, 226

Y

Yellow Pepper Beef Stir-Fry, 112
Yogurt Spice Cake, 220

Z

Zippy Chicken Coleslaw, 59
Zucchini Apple Bread, 187

Reference Index

Use this index to locate the many healthy cooking hints located throughout the book.